D1116608

The Problem of
CHRISTIANITY

Library of Congress Catalog Card Number: 68-16716.

THE UNIVERSITY OF CHICAGO PRESS, CHICAGO 60637
THE UNIVERSITY OF CHICAGO PRESS, LTD., LONDON, W.C. 1

© *1918 by The MacMillan Company*

Introduction by John E. Smith © *1968 by The University of Chicago*

Published 1968

Printed in the United States of America

Contents

Introduction *by John E. Smith*

Royce's idealistic philosophy has often puzzled philosophers, historians, and students of American thought. The fact is that his systematic form of idealism stood in a peculiar and ambiguous relation to the philosophical currents of his time. His quest, on the one hand, for a systematic view of reality and for absolute standards both in thought and conduct set him at variance with the pluralism and open-endedness of the pragmatism represented first by Peirce and James and later by Dewey. On the other hand, the voluntaristic element in Royce's thought—the stress on the expression of the individual human will which he learned from Schopenhauer—kept his position in touch with the dominant belief that knowledge is intimately related to human purposes and must always be connected with action. The perplexing fact is that Royce emphasized the will and rejected the so-called pure intellect without seeming to come any closer to the pragmatic philosophy of his contemporaries. Perhaps the main reason for the difference of opinion is found in Royce's lack of sympathy with the functional approach. Royce, as an idealist, sought for internal connections between things; he was always dissatisfied with what James called "working" conceptions aimed at showing how distinct elements operate together without further insight into why this should be so.

Faced with such contrasts as those between perception and conception, between thought and action, between the one and the many, between science and philosophy on one side and ethics and religion on the other, Royce tried to relate these pairs through unifying concepts; he was not content to assert merely that "somehow" the contrasting elements are together. Mediators and harmonizing ideas played a large part in Royce's philosophy. His most comprehensive mediating conception is found in the idea of *loyalty*, a virtue which he understood in neither exclusively political nor military terms, but instead as devotion to a cause or goal. Loyalty he believed to be the foundation of every enterprise in which human beings are engaged — science, morality, religion, government, and business. For him, loyalty meant the willing, practical, and whole-hearted devotion to a cause or ideal whose realization, however fragmentary in human history, requires the cooperative effort of many distinct individuals each performing a specific set of tasks. Loyalty, in Royce's view, like the Pauline charity, abounds. It sustains the community of those who seek knowledge, since the pursuit of truth demands that every inquirer put aside his personal interests and predilections and devote himself to the discovery of an objective truth that is the creation of no man and no nation. Loyalty resolves the moral problem for the individual by showing him a goal and a set of duties through which both he and the goal can be realized. Loyalty, finally, furnishes a foundation for religion — the unifying theme of *The Problem of Christianity* — in the Beloved Community which alone can redeem mankind by breaking the tragic circle of individual self assertion and disloyalty.

Royce's concern for religious questions and especially for clarifying the relation between religion and philosophy was older than *The Problem of Christianity*. The reader of his Gifford Lectures, *The World and the Individual*, delivered at Aberdeen at the turn of the century, knows that Royce was ultimately attempting to define the connections between philosophy, science, and religion and that he particularly wanted to show the need to understand religious beliefs in terms of a general theory of the nature of things and the types of beings there are. Between 1900 and the appearance of *The Problem of Christianity* in 1913, Royce was developing, as a result of studies both in ethics and the literature of religion, his philosophy of loyalty; the final outcome was the application of the loyalty doctrine to Christianity and the interpretation of the Pauline conception of love in terms of loyalty to the Beloved Community.

The Problem of Christianity is more than a philosophy of religion addressing the "problem" of Christianity as it confronts the modern man; the book expresses as well the final version of Royce's metaphysical idealism in the theory of reality as a community of interpretation. There is no need here to attempt a resolution of the vexing question about the continuity of Royce's thought and the relation between the absolutism exposed in his earlier works and the metaphysics of interpretation and community.[1] It is sufficient to point out that between the earliest versions of Royce's idealism in which both the reality of time and the distinctness of individuals were, if not actually denied, certainly not clearly asserted, and the doctrine of the community of interpretation set forth in *The Problem of Christianity*, definite changes in his thought took place. For, as will become clear, the later Royce took time seriously and resolutely denied that a community can ever be other than a certain type of unity holding between distinct individuals. The crucial factor in Royce's development was his study of several papers written by his contemporary Charles S. Peirce, notably those dealing with the denial of an intuitive self-consciousness, the theory of signs, the concept of interpretation, and the idea of a community of knowers. These ideas proved indispensable to Royce not only in his proposed resolution of the problem of Christianity, but also in his formulation of that problem as one which must be faced if the Christian ideas are to have any relevance for the modern man. Royce freely acknowledged his debt to Peirce (see p. 39) and he was clearly aware of the extent to which his own use or Peircean ideas for metaphysical purposes went beyond the bounds of Peirce's logical analyses.

  The Problem of Christianity is at once a profound and a perplexing book. Its profundity stems from the original philosophical reinterpretation Royce gave to the ancient theological tradition and from the straightforward way in which he faced the difficult question: In what sense, if any, can the modern man be, *in creed*, a Christian? Royce knew that whatever position the modern man may adopt *vis a vis* Christianity, he cannot avoid ideas and doctrine; he cannot resolve the problem of Christianity by reducing it either to morality or to a form of inward piety. The perplexity is found largely in Royce's style. The fact is that while the general drift of the argument remains clear, *The Problem of Christianity* is a curious and often confusing mixture of historical description, exhortation, logical

---

[1] I have touched on the problem in *Royce's Social Infinite* (New York: Liberal Arts Press 1950). The topic has also been discussed by J. H. Cotton in his *Royce on the Human Self* (Cambridge, Mass.: Harvard University Press, 1954) and most recently by Peter Fuss in *The Moral Philosophy of Josiah Royce* Cambridge, Mass.: Harvard University Press, 1965).

analysis, and metaphysical interpretation. Part of the difficulty stems from Royce's having retained the style and tone of the original lectures[2] with the result that the book is filled with extended preliminary statements preparing the listener for what is going to be discussed, frequent summaries of ground already covered, and most confusing of all, reformulations which sometimes involve changes of both language and meaning. These restatements may give the reader a sense of looking at the same scene twice, except that the second look seems slightly out of focus. In the end, however, it is the main thrust of the argument that counts: What sense are we to make of the classical Christian ideas in the modern world of science, of philosophy, and of technology? Royce's treatment of this question still commands serious attention over half a century later.

The central issue to which Royce addressed himself is one that has confronted Christians with ever-increasing force since the middle of the last century. "In what sense can the modern man consistently be, in creed, a Christian?" In posing this question, Royce saw clearly that any responsible answer must take account both of what is essentially Christian and of the wealth of scientific knowledge, philosophical thought, and technological development which the "modern man" has inherited. In short, the theology of the past must be set in relation to the thought of the present. That Royce was facing the issue in its hardest form is seen in the emphasis he laid on the expression, "in creed."

Unlike many others who have tried to bring about some adjustment between the Christian outlook and the modern critical temper, Royce refused to simplify his problem in either of the two well-worn ways. First, he refused to reduce Christianity to purely moral dimensions or to a concern for "values" for the purpose of minimizing doctrine or of avoiding the question of its meaning and validity. Second, he was too well acquainted with the content of classical Christianity to be satisfied with the favorite distinction of the so-called liberal theology between the religion *of* Jesus and the religion *about* Jesus. According to that view, the former expresses Jesus' own simple and direct gospel of love and forgiveness cast in the vivid form of parables, while the latter is merely a tissue of theological "accretions" introduced by Paul and the early church

---

[2]The work was delivered in its entirety as lectures at Manchester College, Oxford, in 1913, on the Hibbert Foundation. In November and December of the preceding year, the first eight lectures were delivered at the Lowell Institute in Boston.

without the sanction of the Founder himself. The implication is that if we hold fast to the simple gospel (which supposedly does not offend the modern critical mind), and set aside theological interpretation "about" Jesus as a secondary construction, we can gain acceptance for Christianity without requiring our modern man to accept doctrines which he is already inclined to reject as invalid or irrelevant.

Royce's grounds for rejecting both these lines of thought are clear. In the first place, as the discussion of the earlier chapters makes clear, he understood the distinction between religion and morality[3] and he grasped the futility of trying to fit the whole of Christianity within the limits of ethics. As he put it, the Beatitudes of Jesus, far from being the simple code of morality they are popularly supposed to be, are actually an outline of the religious dimension of life, and they are bound up with theological ideas. With regard to the distinction between the religion of and about Jesus, Royce was equally clear; the line he adopted is basic not only for his interpretation of Christianity, but for his solution as well. While he took seriously enough the gospel of love preached by Jesus and expressed in the parables and sayings of the New Testament, Royce regarded that gospel as incomplete. It is incomplete because it required the further development of its meaning and implications which it received at the hands of Paul and the experience of the early Christian communities. Royce, as we shall see, was convinced of the reality of the Spirit which is defined in John's Gospel as "leading into all truth." Indeed he saw in Paul's attempt to interpret the meaning of the work of Christ, the presence of that same interpreting Spirit.

The religion of Jesus—the parables and sayings—cannot constitute the whole of Christianity since the full meaning of Christ must include not only his actual ministry, but also *his death and resurrection* that resulted in the founding of the Beloved Community. Only an interpreter who is in a position, as Paul was, to view the entire cycle of events is qualified to apprehend what the Christian doctrine of life essentially is. The religion taught by Jesus is essential, but it is incomplete; Christianity is ultimately the religion based on the total work of Christ and therefore requires a further interpreter who can grasp its meaning. Royce believed that Paul was that

---

[3]See also his dramatic confrontation between the religious and the moral outlooks in *The Sources of Religious Insight* (New York: Charles Scribner's Sons, 1914), pp. 170–210.

interpreter and that he was aided in his task both by the community in which he lived and the Spirit pervading its life.

We may question Royce's selection of the ideas that are supposed to be essential to Christianity, and we may even wonder whether he went too far in summing up the Christian creed in the article about the church, but we cannot find fault with his unwillingness to make his task easier by avoiding the doctrinal questions. It is not that he thought of Christianity only in terms of theological and metaphysical ideas, but rather that he understood the importance of these ideas for the resolution of the most intensely practical moral and religious problems. On several occasions Royce chided his colleague William James for relegating theological conceptions to secondary status in favor of the "varieties of religious experience." The two were, in fact, at odds on the point, and Royce was fond of saying, by way of comparing his position with that of James, that whereas James was interested in how religion can be useful, he, Royce, was troubled by the more difficult question as to whether it is true!

Before considering the three Christian ideas Royce selected—the church or Beloved Community, the moral burden of the individual, and atonement—one will do well to understand his way of approach. One may, according to Royce, adopt one of three distinct attitudes toward Christianity. One may assume the role of the apologist and appear as an expounder and defender of the faith, asserting its truth in direct, even dogmatic, fashion. At the other extreme, one may appear as the opponent or hostile critic, claiming that modern knowledge invalidates Christian faith and that its view of God and man is not relevant to the life of modern industrial society. Included in the second category would be those who, though not openly hostile, are or claim to be indifferent. The third stance—the one Royce adopts—is that of the interpreter who is responsive both to Christianity and to the force of the objections that can be brought against it. The interpreter is neither apologist or critic, because ultimately he is both. He is sufficiently in sympathy with the Christian outlook to want to see if it can be stated in a form that will be intelligible to the modern man, and he sees sufficient truth in the criticisms stemming from secular learning and knowledge (described somewhat grandly by Royce as "the education of the human race") to call for an answer from those who accept the religious point of view.

For a person who stands in this essentially dialectical position, Christianity becomes a "problem." Royce claims, not to solve that problem, but rather to "clarify" it by means of a two-fold analysis that starts with the meaning of the Christian ideas in man's moral and religious experience and ends with an interpretation of the whole of reality in terms of the infinite community of interpretation. The aim of the first part of the argument is to uncover the actual experience that represents, in James' language, the "cash value" of such concepts as grace, love, sin, and repentance, and thereby to show the bearings of the Christian ideas in moral and religious terms. The second and more properly philosophical part of *The Problem of Christianity* sets these same ideas in relation to a metaphysical theory of the nature of things for the purpose of assessing their validity. The entire enterprise reduces to the question of the status of community itself; the Christian doctrine of life will find its plausibility if the Beloved Community is a reality and if the loyalty and form of interpretation upon which it is based likewise prove to be something more than mere ideals or convenient fictions.

The full sweep of Royce's program focuses attention on a problem that is of special importance at present. The danger is that religious ideas will be developed solely in relation to the plane of human experience to the neglect of the cosmic environment. Speaking of the Christian view, he asks, "Does this doctrine express a truth, not only about man, but about the whole world and about God?" (p.231). The later lectures must be seen as Royce's answer to this question. He perceived, quite correctly, that a modern thinker, unlike the theologians of the past who could assume that man and the earth were in the center of things, cannot afford to neglect the problem of relating religious insight to the world of nature and indeed to everything that is. For among other things in modern life, we have been forced to see ourselves as one type of being among others in an environment that is but a small part of vast galaxies spread throughout space. Man's relation to, as well as his difference from, what is beyond him must be kept in view; Royce was sensitive to the point and consequently was not satisfied with the interpretation of religion through human experience alone.

THE THREE CHRISTIAN IDEAS

As he repeatedly emphasized, Royce arrived at the three basic ideas of Christianity (pp. 68-70) by reflecting on the preaching of Jesus concerning the Kingdom of Heaven and the salvation of the individual through membership in that spiritual community. But as was previously noted, Royce did not believe that Jesus — at least in the documents available to us — had completely clarified his central ideas, or even that he could have done so from the vantage point of his earthly ministry. "Historically speaking," says Royce,

Christianity has never appeared simply as the religion taught by the Master. It has always been an interpretation of the Master and of his religion in the light of some doctrine concerning his mission, and also concerning God, man, and man's salvation, — a doctrine which, even in its simplest expressions, has always gone beyond what the Master himself is traditionally reported to have taught while he lived (p. 66).

Royce understood that the further interpretation to which he refers concerning Jesus and his mission came from Paul and the early church. Paul's interpretation far from being a merely "theological" addition to an otherwise simple gospel, must be seen as containing the substance of the Christian faith. It seems clear that Royce was correct in his contention, although Paul's interpretation itself continues to demand an interpretation in contemporary terms; we cannot be satisfied with a mere repetition of the traditional language.

The first of the ideas — the church or Beloved Community — expresses a doctrine that was as close to Royce's own philosophical and religious interest as it is essential to Christianity. He had long argued for the importance of the social principle in understanding the world. This is evident not only in the philosophy of loyalty which counsels the individual to look beyond himself to his relations to others in order to gain insight into his goal in life, but also in the theory of the human self and its striving to know itself and reach fulfillment. On this issue Royce set his view over against that of William James. To Royce it seemed that James concentrated exclusively on the individual and his first person experience, leaving out the fact that we are primarily social animals and that each one of us is enmeshed in a web of social relationships, responsibilities, and legacies long before we have achieved a clear idea of ourselves as unique individuals with unique constitutions and destinies. Royce was determined to redress the balance and he did so in a most dramatic way. He declared that the continuing substance of Christianity is to be found, not in the Founder as an isolated individual, but rather in the spiritual community established by and through the life and death of the Founder. This was a bold step, far more so than it would be at the present time; in the interim we have learned to take seriously the fact that we must start where Christianity started, namely, in the community of believers, and work back to Jesus through the documents that grew out of the experience of the earliest Christian communities. Royce's interpretation called forth the criticism of his contemporaries in the form of this question: Do you not displace the Founder and minimize his role in order to foster what is essentially a philosophical theory of the community dressed out as a doctrine of the church? This question will occupy our next section; at this point it is sufficient to call attention to the controversial nature of Royce's first essential idea.

Like Aristotle and Hegel, Royce believed that a community of individuals represents a distinct type of being which is neither an external collection of atomic members, nor a super-individual supposed to retain its being quite apart from the individuals who constitute its members. A community is neither an individual nor a universal; it is a new and distinctive level of being. Royce sought to define community in terms that do justice both to the many individuals involved and to the unifying factors that bind them together. He insisted, however, that we adjust our concepts and not attempt to understand what a community is with a theory of reality that is confined to only two types of being, particular facts and universal forms or structures. A community is a certain type of logically ordered togetherness of individual persons; it is neither a particular fact to be perceived nor the object denoted by any universal concept. The further analysis of community will be given later; here the concern is chiefly with the religious and moral significance of the idea.

Royce's conception of the Beloved Community[4] is derived from Paul's development of the conception of love which was first expressed by Jesus in the commandments. Jesus, according to Royce. understood love neither as a passive surrender of the individual nor as a form of moral altruism but instead as a positive and heroic virtue which both expresses the heart or center of the person and directs his conduct in particular situations. Jesus spoke of love as having two principal objects of concern, God and the neighbor.

[4]Royce believed in the existence of many communities in addition to the religious community. I have tried to sort out and identify them in an article, "Royce on Religion," in *The Journal of Religion*, 30 (1950): 261-66.

Love to God is the purity of heart which is the substance of religion, and love to the neighbor defines the relation between man and man which is the substance of morality. Royce's claim is that Jesus left us with the principle and virtue of love directed to two *individuals*—God and the neighbor—but that he did not deal with the problem of how we are to understand our neighbor or how we are to determine exactly what particular deeds will manifest our love for him. A further development of the meaning of love was needed; Royce's contention is that the needed development was supplied by Paul who first understood the saving power of the Christian community. To the objects of love, Paul added a third reality, "the Christian community itself" (p. 93) which is the living unity of the many members who are devoted to God, to each other, and to the goal for which their community exists. Paul is said to have interpreted Christian love as *loyalty*[5] and, in so doing, he took a decisive step in the direction of answering the question, "What shall I do for my brother?" by conceiving of each neighbor as a member of the same community to which all the others belong. What does such an idea contribute? If love is to issue in deeds and thus pass beyond a mere inspiration or feeling, these deeds must be guided by knowledge rather than by the proverbial "good intentions." It is therefore imperative that each individual gain knowledge both of his neighbor and of himself. Such insight, if gained at all, can come only through a community of persons able to penetrate the barriers of suspicion, misunderstanding, and anxiety that separate individuals from each other and make them strangers.

Royce's point is that Jesus had indeed first apprehended the meaning and power of love and that he had also understood our love for the neighbor as motivated by the fact that God sees him as a member of the Kingdom. Jesus, however, could not identify the Kingdom with the early church. It remained for Paul to transform this love into love for the neighbor *as a member of the Beloved Community.* The question that naturally arises is: What is the extent of this community and have we, as Christians, an obligation to love only those who belong to it? Royce's answer is that the Beloved Community is universal, that it is a community to which all "by the grace of God" belong or will belong. "The ideal Christian community," he

[5]"Christian love, as Paul conceives it, takes on the form of loyalty. This is Paul's simple but vast transformation of Christian love." (p. 95)

wrote, "is *to be* the community of all mankind" (p. 195).[6] There are, then, in principle, no restrictions with regard to identifying my neighbor.

The religious or redeeming function of the Beloved Community becomes clear only when understood in conjunction with the other two-ideas Royce emphasized. To speak of the community as a saving community leads us to ask what it is that man has to be saved from, and how salvation is to be accomplished. These questions lead logically to the second idea, the idea of sin or, in Royce's language, the moral burden of the individual. Clarification of this idea, as we shall see, leads on in turn to the third idea — atonement — and ultimately back to the community. The atoning deed of the Founder establishes the Beloved Community thus making real in the world a form of loyalty capable of overcoming the tragic fact of the moral burden which the individual *himself* cannot overcome.

Royce's interpretation of the moral burden[7] is one of the most original and penetrating parts of his philosophy of religion. The fact is somewhat ironic, since critics like George Santayana were under the impression that Royce had turned his back on classical Christianity and was offering his readers merely an "idealistic" substitute that was presumably both more comfortable and more palatable than traditional formulations. On the contrary, Royce understood better than any of his contemporaries, both philosophers and theologians, that the Christian doctrine of life includes a doctrine of man's natural defect or flaw which is at the root of the human predicament and poses the religious problem of salvation. As Reinhold Niebuhr once pointed out, if one wants to adjust Christianity or make it more attractive to the modern man, emphasizing the doctrine of sin is surely not the way to do it. For that doctrine is bound to give offense to those who think of man and the develop-

---

[6]Since Royce might be misunderstood on this point, it is important to note some other passages dealing with the problem. On p. 125 the Beloved Community and the "universal community" are identified; on p. 98, Paul is said to have envisaged "the universal community."

[7]It is interesting to note that Royce was sensitive to the problem posed by the connotations and associations attached to traditional language when one is trying to reinterpret past ideas by returning to the experience behind them. Accordingly, he referred to the "moral burden" of the individual rather than to "original sin" and to the Beloved Community" rather than to the "church." With regard to voluntary or willful misdeeds, however, he tended to use the term "sin" without further qualification. Royce was not entirely consistent in his usage, but it is clear that he saw the need for new terminology if his enterprise of reinterpretation was to succeed.

ment of human history in perfectionistic and progressivistic terms. A culture rooted in the indomitable will to construct, to control both nature and man cannot admit the possibility of ultimate obstacles to the triumph of human ingenuity. The spokesmen for such a culture will be outraged by the idea that there is some fundamental defect of the human will that more strenuous effort cannot remove. Royce understood all this, but he was too well acquainted with Christianity to believe that anyone can simply ignore the problem of human corruption and still claim to be taking Christianity seriously. Even more, Royce did not yield to the temptation to "soften" the doctrine by defining the human defect as due to fate or fortune, thus exempting us from responsibility, nor did he locate the evil in ignorance or in some form of temporary imperfection which, through effort, human beings might remove.

Royce believed that his task was to furnish a reinterpretation of the idea of sin in terms of the moral burden that would do justice to the Pauline theology and yet serve to make the idea intelligible in terms of contemporary experience and understanding.[8]

It should be clear that Royce was resolutely opposed to the retention of religious doctrines on merely dogmatic grounds; if acceptance of the Christian doctrine of life is to be a live option for the modern man, it is essential that Christian teaching about man should find some measure of verification in contemporary experience. Royce pressed the point rather far, claiming on occasions that even if Christianity had not set forth the ideas of atonement and the moral burden, the analysis and interpretation of our own experience would require us to introduce them. No one can ask for a less dogmatic approach than that!

Royce posed the problem of man's moral burden in a new way. He felt that controversy had obscured the religious meaning of the idea and that theological protagonists had lost sight of the factors in man's experience upon which the doctrine of sin was based. Royce wanted especially to avoid sterile and inconclusive arguments based largely on impressionistic generalizations about human conduct, its baseness or nobility. The humanistic defenders of human nature say that men often exhibit fine and noble qualities and that this fact refutes the "slander" against man expressed in the doctrine of total depravity or corruption so dear to the Calvinistic tradition in

---

[8]See esp. pp. 105-6.

America. The dogmatic theologians, on the other hand, point to the not inconsiderable record of man's inhumanity, cruelty, and capacity for injustice as the ground for reasserting the traditional doctrine of man's corruption, often implying at the same time that the humanist rejection of the doctrine is further evidence of its truth! Royce avoids this fruitless debate by pointing out that the issue turns not on generalizations about our conduct itself, but upon our consciousness of its nature and quality. "Paul's main thesis about our moral burden," Royce writes, "relates not to our conduct, but to our consciousness about our conduct" (p. 110). Royce has in mind Paul's statement in the seventh chapter of *Romans*,[9] "Howbeit, I had not known sin, but for the law." This expression of Paul's consciousness concerning his own conduct forms the basis of Royce's ingenious reinterpretation of the moral burden in terms of his theory of the social self, the community, and the origin of man's self-awareness and conscience through his ability to compare himself with other men and with the law or social will to which he is supposed to conform.

There is no need to follow the details of Royce's argument; the reader, however, must attend carefully if he is not to be confused, for in the discussion of the moral burden Royce restated his thesis several times and with the usual subtle differences.[10] His attempt, moreover, to find the basis for the idea of original sin through an analysis of man's historical experience without explicit reference to Christianity may cause further confusion. The main drift of the argument, nevertheless, remains clear; several of its main points should be underlined. The argument rests ultimately on Royce's philosophical thesis, resulting from studies in social psychology and his reading of Peirce's arguments against an intuitive self-consciousness,[11] that we come to know ourselves, our interests and purposes only through social intercourse. According to Royce, we do not first know ourselves through a clear and infallible intuition, and then proceed to understand others by a series of analogies. On the

[9]It is important to notice that Royce refused to begin with the opening chapter of *Romans* which stresses the inexorable divine will through which man is condemned to his vile conduct for his disobedience and rejection of God. In Royce's view, setting the problem initially in theological terms tends to obscure the experiential account of sin recorded in the seventh chapter.

[10]The best statement is in the summary, pp. 126-27.

[11]See the list of relevant papers in the note on pp. 275-76.

contrary, our relations with other selves are primary and only slowly do we arrive at knowledge of our own individuality through extended processes of comparison and interpretation. His contention is that man, as a being capable of sustaining many complex forms of community, is trained through these communities to a high grade of self-consciousness that leads in turn to self-assertion. Highly integrated social structures breed highly self-conscious individuals; social training teaches a man to say, "not thy will, but *mine* be done." The law in the individual comes in conflict with the social will. Instead of harmony, there is tension, conflict, and misunderstanding. "High cultivation," Royce claims, "breeds spiritual enemies" (p. 113). To sustain itself against the divisive thrust of the *individualism*[12] which the community itself breeds, the community must assert the authority of its own will. The consequent restraint heightens the individual's awareness of himself, leading him to look upon his fellows not as brothers, but as enemies. The individual is forced to submit to the law which expresses the social will, but inwardly he rebels. For in the process of social cultivation, his conscience develops and he is prompted to turn against the law that restrains him because he sees it as no more than an external authority. The tension remains; the individual may have a *respect* for the law, but he has no *love* for it, and he remains within himself with a divided consciousness. Royce saw in this process the basis in experience for what was expressed by Paul in essentially religious terms, "O wretched man that I am!"

This state moreover is, as Royce says, "no mishap of my private fortune" (p. 116), but belongs to the structure of human life as we know it. Royce never tried to avoid or to mitigate the fact that Paul saw man's tragic predicament as one from which the "natural man" cannot escape when he is confined to his own resources. The curse infects all "flesh" and cannot be overcome on the basis of that same flesh. And Royce knew that by "flesh" Paul meant the "natural man" so that the struggle he described between "flesh" and "spirit" is not a body-mind or matter-mind dualism but the tension between the

[12]At times Royce's language is apt to give the impression that he regarded the fact of individuality itself as the source of corruption in man, as when, for example, he speaks of the need to be redeemed from being a "mere" individual. But these expressions are misleading. First by "individualism" he meant, not the fact of being an individual, but the form of self-assertion that stands opposed to community; Royce had a high regard for the individual, but he rejected individualism. Second, his contrast between Christianity and Buddhism (pp. 189-93.) makes it clear that he was not interpreting the Christian idea of sin to mean being individual or being finite.

broken situation of the natural man who is trained in self-assertion or rebellion through social intercourse, and the vision of the one form of community that breaks through the tragic circle.[13]

The ultimate resolution of the human predicament through the form of love that pervades the Beloved Community — how that Community is established and in what manner the redeeming function is accomplished — cannot be made clear without aid from the third idea, the idea of atonement. Royce set the stage for his discussion of atonement by extending the idea of sin to cover overt or willful acts which a man knows run counter to what he himself believes to be right. In this way Royce introduced the problem of guilt, or as it has been somewhat misleadingly called, "the sense of sin." The question now concerns the response a man is to make to the fact that he has wronged his neighbor, failed to do what he should have done, or did the deed which he ought not to have done. What is a man to think and feel and do in the face of that fact? In characteristic fashion, Royce sets out to answer the question by adopting the view which he thinks the modern man would be likely to take. He cites Matthew Arnold's essay, "St. Paul and Protestantism," which is based on the return to the religion of Jesus that played so large a part in the development of modern liberal Christianity. Arnold's advice, which reflects a typical humanist reaction both to Paul and to Puritanism, is simple: we are to stop brooding about sin and get rid of it. Or, more exactly, we are to think about sin only as long as is necessary to enhance our effort to be free of it and the guilt that goes with it. Arnold's proposal was to return to the sayings of Jesus about repentance as a prelude to "falling in love" with the person of Jesus and overcoming sin through loving union with the spirit of Christ. Quite apart from the fact that Royce could not accept either Arnold's interpretation or his solution, it is important to notice that it led him back to the sayings of Jesus for the purpose of expressing his own interpretation of the issue at hand. Royce's view is that Jesus judged every act of the person from the standpoint of his attitude or his "heart"; whatever act fails to spring from a whole-hearted devotion to God and the cause of the Kingdom of Heaven, is sin. The emphasis falls on the separation or

[13]The "flesh"–"spirit" contrast in Paul has often been misunderstood. Royce knew that Paul understood the natural man when he spoke of "being in the flesh." Compare, for example, Calvin's *Commentary on Romans, Rom.* 7:5 (London, 1834), p. 277: "to be in the flesh" means "our being endowed with the alone gifts of nature."

The Problem of
CHRISTIANITY

by

Josiah Royce

with a new introduction by

John E. Smith

The University of Chicago Press   *Chicago & London*

alienation from God and the Kingdom which results from the failure to follow the divine commandment that embraces both the love of God and the love of man.

The question arises—still keeping to the doctrine expressed by Jesus in the New Testament record—whether there is any escape to be found in the preaching of Jesus from the destruction which is sin. In Royce's view—which I believe to be a substantially correct reading of the Gospel record—the escape preached by Jesus is "by the road of repentance." Repentance, as in the classic Parable of the Prodigal Son, is a turning of the heart and the mind, a turning back to the Father and the principle of love announced in the central Commandment. One might suppose, Royce argues, that the problem is now solved; the sinner "comes to himself," repents, and like the lost sheep is returned to the fold where he is once again embraced by the divine love. But as Royce correctly notes, this account omits something crucial. Jesus spoke of forgiving sins and of our need to forgive the sins of others as we look for the remission of our own sins. Jesus, in addition, appears as the one who has the power to forgive sins, a power which, as is clear from the record, was regarded by his contemporaries as a very mysterious power indeed. Repentance, then, is not the only factor involved; it is necessary, but equally necessary is that power which we do not originate: the power to forgive. Who or what is to provide that power?

Royce's answer depends on his belief that the Christian community made itself responsible for interpreting both what Jesus said and embodied. That community started with the conviction that *somehow* Jesus saved men from sin; the problem was to understand what this meant. Royce takes the doctrine of atonement as the answer; reflection on the work of Christ gradually led to the belief that Jesus had performed a deed which, when properly understood, meant the overcoming of the moral burden. Interpretations of the "somehow" might vary, as indeed they did, but one conviction ran throughout all of them: the moral burden from which the individual is saved is one that cannot be thrown off without the assistance of Christ. Should that assistance not be forthcoming, the individual faces the penalty of unforgiven sin which is, in traditional language, the endless second death.

As interpreter committed to seeing both sides of an issue, Royce was vividly aware of how strange such a doctrine sounds when addressed to a twentieth century man. Surely it is no more than ancient mythology; moreover, it is profoundly unjust and an insult to a free, moral agent. How can such an agent be subject to penalties imposed by a will that seems to be the expression of an arbitrary despot? To meet these difficulties, Royce resorted to the sort of argument he had used on other occasions, most notably in his famous argument for the existence of God from the possibility of error.[14] The method is to develop the implications of an objection brought against a given thesis or conclusion in an attempt to show that the objection implies (or involves)[15] what it is supposed to nullify. Just as Royce in the earlier work tried to show that the possibility of an error implies the reality of truth, here he asks whether the genuine moral agent, if he is consistent, is not ultimately forced to impose upon himself something very much like the condemnation which the biblical conception suggests. To be a moral agent, Royce argued, is to have an ideal and to be capable of judging ones actions in accordance with it. Now suppose a moral agent were to ask himself this question: Is there some deed such that if I were to do it of my own free will, I could never afterward forgive myself? For Royce, to ask this question is to approach, not from the theological standpoint but from the standpoint of the moral agent, the problem that Christianity faces in its doctrine of sin and punishment. The problem is the problem of disloyalty to the ideal, and the response which the moral agent himself must make to that possibility. How would that agent consistently judge himself? Royce's answer is that the person must condemn himself to what he called "the hell of the irrevocable." The deed for which we cannot forgive ourselves is a finished fact; it is irrevocable. Some new consciousness about it may be gained, but in itself the deed remains forever what it was. Royce's claim is that the moral individual must, at one and the same time, acknowledge the deed as his own and confess that he can neither change the fact of his disloyalty nor ever forgive himself for what he has done. He may repent and seek to do better in the future, but the fact of the disloyalty remains. He thus finds himself in the same position to which he had previously objected;

---

[14]See *The Religious Aspect of Philosophy* (Boston: Houghton, Mifflin, 1885), Chapter 11.

[15]Not all uses of this form of argument are equally strong, from a logical point of view. Royce's analysis of error represents a stronger case than the one referred to in the text. The reason is that we have a better chance of being correct in our understanding of what an error in knowledge means than we have in determining what a consistent moral agent would say about his conduct.

the main difference is that he has imposed the "hell of the irrevocable" upon himself and has not been condemned by an arbitrary
divine power. The self-imposed penalty is intelligible to a moral
agent whereas the arbitrary one is not.

In the foregoing analysis, Royce hoped to bring the idea of
atonement into an intelligible relation with experiences which all
share. He overestimated the scope of his account, and he failed to
see that anyone viewing the matter in the way he describes is likely
to have been influenced by the Christian outlook in the first place.
Despite these limitations, the idea of the "hell of the irrevocable"
paves the way for the doctrine of atonement and the problem of
finding a new meaning for the deed which cannot be undone.[16]
With atonement the circle of theological ideas closes as the atoning
deed establishes the Beloved Community — the locus of redeeming
loyalty.

Christians have always believed that Christ performed a deed
which "somehow" resolves the problem posed by the moral burden.
The chief difficulty has been to explain the "somehow," and the
many theories of atonement in Christian thought are the result of as
many attempts to remove the difficulty. Royce had his own interpretation of the issue; we can grasp his view most readily by
contrasting it with the two opposed doctrines of atonement traditionally known as the moral and the penal theories. Given the fact
of the deed for which a man cannot forgive himself, the question is:
Can anyone, anything "undo" the deed, in the sense of leading the
doer to see it in new perspective so that he becomes reconciled both
to himself and to the ideal from which his misdeed has alienated
him? Atonement, says Royce, "transforms the meaning of that very
past which it cannot undo" (pp. 180-81). How is this result to be accomplished? According to the penal theory, Christ stands as advo-
cate and surrogate before God, laying down his life in a sacrifice
which alone can be adequate *satisfaction* for human sin. The stress
here falls on an "objective" transaction that takes place in accordance
with the divine demand, quite apart from the faith, the repentance,
the love of any creature other than Christ. Royce rejected this interpretation on the ground that the pacification of an angry God in no
way enables the sinner to become reconciled to himself; the theological transaction understood in the legal terms of debt and ransom

[16]See the discussion of atonement in *Royce's Social Infinite*, pp. 150–58.

does not show the individual how he can accept himself, though he remains the doer of the treasonable deed. The proponents of the moral interpretation of the atonement have noted this difficulty and consequently place their emphasis elsewhere. They argue that the reconciliation comes about when the sinner contemplates the loving sacrifice of Christ and responds in love, gratitude, and repentance. If the penal theory bases everything on an objective transaction to which the sinner is only externally related, the moral theory locates the change solely in the sinner's heart, so that we are apt to lose sight of Christ's actual deed and its consequences.

In rejecting both approaches, Royce was proposing a new alternative which he regarded as consistent with the Pauline theology and verifiable in the experience of the sinner. The willful sinner who has done the irrevocable deed has, above all else, alienated himself from the Kindom; he has broken the bond of community through disloyalty. The question is, Can the community be re-established so as to include the sinner, reconciling him to himself and to the community at the same time? Royce's answer is yes—the suffering servant is able to establish the Beloved Community on, so to speak, the far side of the treasonable act and to bring a new form of life out of the tragedy. The past is not undone, but it now has a new meaning, for from the misdeed of the sinner comes—as a result of the atoning deed—a new form of community which the act of treason itself has helped to make possible. Royce's interpretation will be recognized at once as a form of the ancient *felix culpa* under-standing of atonement. The community of love is a new creation and its very existence makes the world better than it would have been had the treasonable act never taken place (p. 185). Royce saw in this interpretation a way of doing justice to both aspects of atone-ment; it allows for an objective transformation in reality—the actual founding of the Beloved Community—as well as a change in the consciousness of the sinner, who is again included in that commu-nity despite his act of disloyalty.

Before following Royce in the second part of his enterprise—the attempt to connect the Christian ideas with a theory of the general nature of things through the theory of interpretation and the doctrine of signs—it is necessary to face a certain charge that was leveled against him in his own time and which continues to be of interest at present. The issue concerns the relation between the community and its Founder. Royce was charged by W. E. Hocking,

among others, with neglecting the Founder in favor of the community and with failing to take the historical individuality of both
seriously enough.[17] While I have no desire to defend Royce come
what may, I did not see that the criticism is well founded. The
crucial fact is that despite Royce's zeal in assigning priority to the
community as the locus of the Spirit and as the special means of
grace, he repeatedly asserted that Jesus was unique in founding or
creating the Beloved Community, the only means whereby the
tragic circle of social cultivation and individual self-will can be
broken. True, Royce emphasized the transcendence of Christian
love over the historical churches and argued, in terms not so different
from those of the modern ecumenical spirit, that the church referred
to in the Creed is not identical with any one historical denomination.
But it is not clear why either of these contentions should imply that
he denied the historical character of the Founder or of the community established in his name. The fact is that Royce saw the need
for a break in the tragic circle he described: Jesus *first* loved and
envisaged the community he was to create, and it is difficult to
understand how the priority implied is to be understood in other
than historical terms. There is, moreover, no suggestion in Royce's
analysis that a "natural" development takes place within the
communities breeding self-will which leads gradually to the new
level of love and loyalty to be found in the Beloved Community.
Jesus brings into being a new form of loyalty not to be understood
in terms of the social process that leads to the moral burden. The
discussion of the founding of the Beloved Community makes that
clear enough. Referring to the actual beginning of the church,
Royce Says,

The individual who initiates this process will then plausibly appear to an
onlooker, such as Paul was when he was converted, to be at once an individual and the spirit . . . of a community. But his origin will be inexplicable
in terms of the processes which he himself originates. His power will come
from another level than our own. . . . The Master was an individual man.
To Paul's mind, his mission was divine. He both knew and loved his
community before it existed on earth. . . . On earth he called into this

---

[17]I have discussed the charge in *Royce's Social Infinite*, pp. 118-23 and I would still
maintain what I wrote there.

community its first members. He suffered and died that it might have life.
. . . *He is now identical with the spirit of this community.*[18]

Despite Royce's repeated claim that he had no special interpretation to offer concerning the traditional theological doctrine known as
the "Person of Christ," it is clear that he was trying to pass beyond
the sterile disputes that took place on the American scene between
the defenders of orthodoxy who dogmatically asserted the divinity
of Christ and the proponents of the liberal view who sought to
interpret Jesus in human, moral, and religious terms. Royce, more
fully aware of the dialectical nature of the issue than the disputants
on either side, tried to find a new way of expressing the classical
Christian belief that Jesus was indeed a man, but also the one who
fills the office of the Christ and therefore has a more than human
significance. Royce's way of dealing with the problem was to begin
where all must begin, namely, with the fact of the Beloved Community; without that reality there would have been no record of Jesus
at all. Royce wants to say that without Jesus who first loved and had
the power to create the community, it would never have come into
being. On the other hand, without the community created by the
deed of the suffering servant, there would have been no development
of Jesus' teaching and no clear discovery of his special office as the
Christ. Moreover, without the community there would be no
special locus of grace and the divine spirit. Although Royce only
hinted at the point, it is clear from what he says that he had the
Trinitarian conception in the back of his mind. His view, expressed
in the traditional language of that conception, amounts to saying
that the community is founded by the loving sacrifice of the Second
Person who returns to dwell in it as the Spirit which is the Third
Person. (See esp. p. 403.)

THE LOGIC AND METAPHYSICS OF COMMUNITY

Royce had long maintained that the intellectual appraisal of religious

[18]Pp. 130-31. Other relevant passages are: pp. 124, 130, 133, 140, 180. The impression that Royce minimized the importance of the Founder comes largely from his unguarded use of language; there are numerous passages in which the Founder appears
to be secondary to the community he has brought into existence. My point, however,
in citing the above passages is to combat the charge that Royce regarded the Beloved
Community as a "purely human" community, or that he thought of Jesus as a "mere
man," or that he failed to take seriously the *historical* reality of either Jesus or the
community.

insight had to be accomplished, if at all, through philosophical analysis and interpretation. He well understood the connections that have existed between philosophy and Christian thought, and he rejected the position of those who, like Harnack, seek to drive a wedge between the Christian ideas and the philosophical traditions on the ground that philosophy dispells religious belief and substitutes mere abstractions. Royce's aim was to show that the central idea of Christianity — the idea of a redeeming power present in the Beloved Community — has a claim upon both our understanding and our creative will, since we can show that community is a genuine type of reality and that the loyalty which sustains it is able to overcome the divisive force of individual self will. In addition, Royce argued that everything that exists must be understood to be real only insofar as the cosmic community of interpretation is real both as a process and as an outcome in the form of a goal which has been realized. Royce, in short, was arguing that ultimately the resolution of the problem of Christianity can be accomplished only on the basis of an essentially idealistic metaphysics. A full scale examination of that claim is beyond the scope of this Introduction; I shall, however, return to the point at the end in a brief discussion of the bearing of modern idealism on the validity of Christian faith.

The most illuminating part of *The Problem of Christianity* from a strictly philosophical point of view is Royce's adaptation of Peirce's logical studies of signs and interpretation for defining the nature of community. The development is a fine example of applied logic and of the fruitful results that may come from the use of formally exact concepts to express the structure of otherwise elusive objects and experiences. By a community, Royce understood a well-ordered togetherness of distinct individuals unified by certain ideas, events, and goals that are acknowledged by each member as related in an essential way to himself. A community is not a casual group, nor is it a crowd or a mob. Community is distinguished from these collections because of its relation to a time order and to the process of history; without a remembered past and a hoped-for future, there is no common life or substance to relate the individuals to each other. As a result of studying the developing social psychology of his time, Royce was impressed by the idea that cultural products — art, religion, language, myth — cannot be understood as the invention of any individual or even of any finite collection of individuals existing together without some form of unifying power to weld them into an intelligent unity. The point is being rediscovered at present by those who argue that descriptions of the behaviour of nations and other groups cannot be translated into statements about singular individuals or sets of individuals. If we ignore temporal passage and take a "cross section"[19] of the social order, all we find are the particular doings of particular individuals and the coexistence of different individuals, but no communities. A community requires a sufficient portion of time to acquire a memory and to project its goal or cause. As essentially involved in history, a community cannot be "compressed" into a moment. There is, therefore, a lower bound or time limit necessary for the existence of community; if we view the social order as it exists below that limit, no community is evident. The point is exactly analogous to the contention of Whitehead that there is no nature "at an instant" because time enters into the being of everything; there is likewise no community at an instant, although the time scale for one is vastly different from that of the other.

In addition to time, community requires many distinct individuals. Royce went out of his way to insist on the point by indicating the features that serve to hold individuals apart—immediate experiences, deeds, intentions. He even looked with suspicion on James' conception of the interpenetration of selves issuing from his struggle with the problem posed by the "compounding of consciousness."[20] Royce did not want a blending or melting together of individuals in the sense of the mystical transcendence of distinctness. On the contrary, it is essential for the existence of community that the members retain their individual identity because their involvement must be freely acknowledged and it must express itself in practical tasks which the individual alone can perform. From a logical point of view, community is dependent on the reality of relations and, as we shall see, on the capacity of certain mediating ideas to bring about mutual understanding between distinct selves. The selves are real and the items relating them to each other are

---

[19]Like the problem of determining the duration of the "present," the temporal "thickness" of such a segment cannot be exactly determined. It is fortunately not necessary that it should be; Royce's point turns on the contrast between a period of time long enough for the development of language, customs, traditions, etc., and what we find in a social order if we ask for its coexistences at any moment in the historical process.

[20]See p. 242.

equally real; community is a genuine form of the coming together of a one and a many.

More important for the theory of the community than either the reality of time or the distinctness of individuals, is Royce's conception of the nature of the human person.[21] He had developed a rather unusual theory of the self, and it was perfectly suited to the philosophy of community. The central point consists in the claim that the individual self is not an object of perception nor is it a datum for any present experience; the self is what Royce called an interpretation. At any moment no more than a portion of the self is present because the whole self stretches out in time so that the present self is always in the position of having to remember its past and anticipate its future. In Royce's language, the present self interprets the past self to the future self; *the* self is the unity of the three. The self develops in time, but its growth is no mere unfolding of an essence "given" at the outset; a person has a creative will and therefore some measure of freedom in extending himself and in choosing a life plan and the objects of loyalty to which he will be committed. Our capacity for ideally extending ourselves makes community possible; two otherwise distinct selves may come to view themselves as having, for example, the same fact of past life as part of themselves. These past facts may be "natural" facts as in the case of ancestors, country of birth, etc., or cultural facts having to do with the history and evaluation of past events and traditions such as the sacred history of a religious tradition. Two distinct selves who are willing to acknowledge or to interpret the same past fact as belonging to themselves are said by Royce to constitute a *community of memory* with respect to that past fact. Similarly, with regard to future events or hoped-for goals; the willingness on the part of two individuals to include the same hoped-for future within their individual selves constitutes them as a community of hope with regard to the common fact. The underlying structure is that of a triadic relation consisting of three distinct terms, the two individual selves and the common fact to which each is related in the same way. Community is never, in Royce's view, a dyadic relation, which is to say that two individuals are never related immediately but only in virtue of a "third" or mediating element which unites them in a specific way.

[21]See my "The Contemporary Significance of Royce's Theory of the Self," in *Revue Internationale de Philosophie*, 79–80 (1967), pp. 77–89.

If we apply this analysis to the Beloved Community we can identify the mediating element in the form of the memory of the
ministry, the teachings, the death and resurrection of Christ, and
in the anticipation of the coming universal community of all mankind which is the goal or cause for which the Beloved Community
exists. The early church preserved the record of its memorable
events and projected in what we now know to be essentially symbolic
and mythological terms, the hoped-for future as the end of the world
and the triumph of the community of the faithful who enjoy fellowship with God. The many members are identified through their
willingness to extend or interpret themselves to include this
Christian memory and hope. Through loyalty and practical devotion they are all linked with the cause which defines the community,
and they are at the same time linked with each other; each member
knows that every other member acknowledges as part of his own
self the same sacred past and future which he acknowledges. The
individual members, though remaining distinct, live in a unity that
becomes actual through their self-consciousness and their devotion.[22]

Thus far we have considered no more than the bare structure of
community and its basis in the triadic relations that arise when the
members accept the common or mediating elements as belonging to
their own being. We must now direct attention to the logical or
intellectual process involved when the individual members *interpret*
themselves and are constituted as a community. Royce called his
communities, communities of *interpretation*, and in so doing he was
pointing to a type of understanding which is essential to community
and which he regarded as unique in the sense that it has a logical
structure of its own and is not reducible to other intellectual
processes. (See esp. pp. 275-81.)

Royce's studies in modern philosophy, notably in Kant's analysis
of human knowledge, led him to consider whether any purely dyadic

---

[22]Since Royce's argument depends so heavily on his interpretation of Pauline
theology, especially with regard to the Christian community, the reader will do well
to pay attention to the opinions of contemporary exegetes about the idea of the
church in the New Testament. One of the most important studies in recent years,
Images of the Church in the New Testament by Paul S. Minear (Philadelphia: West-
minister Press, 1960) contains material, particularly in chapters 5 and 6, which offers
striking confirmation of the soundness of much that Royce claimed about Paul's
understanding of the community. Royce approached the community idea in terms of
the logic of relations; it is interesting to compare his approach with Minear's penetrating analysis of Paul's language, especially what Minear calls the "prepositions of
mutuality" — with, through, for, etc.

structure will be adequate for expressing all the intellectual processes of which human beings are capable. Kant had distinguished the *perceptual* from the *conceptual* "faculties" and sought to relate them to each other through the transcendental imagination in the belief that actual knowledge is some form of unity or synthesis of the two. For a variety of reasons many later philosophers did not find the Kantian way of synthesizing the two elements acceptable, or even entirely intelligible. One result was that the problem was abandoned and the objects of perception — particular data realized through the senses — and the objects of conception — abstract universals of various types — were left in purely external relations to each other. William James sought to connect the two, or to set them in "working" relation to each other, in his doctrine of the stream of experience. Royce was dissatisfied with those who abandoned the problem, but also with James' proposed solution. The reasons for his attitude were two-fold; first, he believed that there are processes of thought which we cannot understand in terms of perceiving and conceiving taken as two entirely distinct activities; second, he regarded the ontology underlying the perception-conception distinction as too limited. The richness of the world cannot be adequately expressed in terms of the singular data of perception plus the abstract universals of conception. There are, Royce argued, two beings in the world neither of which can be identified with the appropriate objects of perception or conception. These beings are individual selves and communities; Royce challenges us to include either in a theory of reality which allows only for sensible particulars and abstract universals. The person who is my neighbor is not identical with any of my percepts nor with any abstract universal or set of universals which I can conceive. Similarly, with respect to communities, the living unity of many distinct members is not something that can be the distinct object of any perception or of any abstract conception. The question is, Is there any form of understanding which is appropriate for knowing selves and communities? Royce found his answer in the theory of interpretation set forth originally by Peirce.

Royce posed three questions: What is an interpretation? Who can interpret? What functions does interpretation perform? "Interpretation," he writes, "differs from other mental processes and types of knowledge in the objects to which it is properly applied, in the relation in which it stands to these objects, and in the ends which it serves." (p. 275) In order to bring out the differences between interpretation and other processes, Royce began with the percept-concept distinction and couched his argument in the then familiar terms of "cash" and "bank notes." For every percept there must correspond a cash value in the form of things, changes, etc., which, when actually encountered, are in fact what the percepts mean. Concepts—a general character, type, quality—on the other hand, are analogous to bank notes in the sense that when they are valid and verifiable they can be "cashed" in the form of the perceptual objects to which they refer and of which they are descriptions.[23] Royce proposed, as illustrations, some situations which he believed could not be understood in terms of exchanging concepts for percepts in the form of a one to one correspondence. His initial illustration is the traveller who crosses a border and confronts the problem of currency exchange. (pp. 282-84) The cash of one country is not legal tender in another, nor can bank notes from one side of the border be converted into the case of the other side, without the introduction of a special process which differs from exchanging concepts for percepts. With this half-literal, half-symbolic example, Royce was trying to show that the process of interpreting the values of one domain in terms of the values of another involves a new and distinctive operation of thought. The new process is triadic in character because some third system of value must be introduced to which both systems in question are related in the same way. We can translate, for example, United States dollars into British pounds only because there is a system of exchange values not identical with the values established within either country. We can relate the values of the two currencies to each other by first relating each to the same third standard. Royce's point is that the logical process involved is not the same as the exchange of concepts for their corresponding percepts.

Royce saw an important analogy between the situation of the traveller and our position when we attempt to gain knowledge of each other and, ultimately, knowledge of ourselves. In order to understand another person, I must draw on my own experience, my own percepts, my own insights, memories, hopes, etc. I am not,

[23]Royce was dealing with but one of James' proposals for expressing the relation between percepts and concepts. James' writing is ambiguous on the point, but it is clear that he has at least two different theories. In one, concepts are regarded as merely surrogates for percepts, the percepts being representative of reality, i.e., all the "cash" there is. In this case, the concept has no special or unique cognitive office; it is a means or map which has its entire being in its function of leading us to the percepts to which it refers. This is the view which Royce selects for attention. On James' other view, concepts are assigned a distinct cognitive function.

however, in a position to verify directly the extent to which my own first person experience is a reliable guide to the discovery of what is true about my neighbor. What I take to be an expression of my neighbor's affection for me is in fact a subtle rebuff; what I take to be a sign of his hostility is no more than a momentary weariness or distraction brought about by his thinking of an unpleasant duty he has yet to perform. We can easily multiply examples of such situations; they all serve to point up the need for interpretation. I must understand as far as possible the state of my friend's mind, his plans, his experience, his character. I do not accomplish my aim merely by perceiving my friend, nor by describing him in terms of abstract characters. When I venture beyond my own experience and enter another's domain, I find that I am not verifying concepts but am engaged largely in a dialogue in which I must try to interpret signs in the effort to discover the intentions and plans behind them and expressed through them.

Although the currency exchange example does illustrate the triadic logical structure Royce regarded as definitive of interpretation, it does not bring out as clearly as might be desired the meaning of interpretation as a process of reading signs. Royce was less careful than he should have been in setting forth this central concept of his theory. He generalized too freely in treating examples of triadic processes and confused comparison and interpretation without realizing that he had done so. Since Peirce introduced the idea of "thirds" or mediating ideas through an analysis of the process of comparison, and Royce also made much of the same process, a brief consideration of what comparison involves is in order. If we show a person two geometrical figures, a circle and an ellipse, and ask him to compare the figures, we are asking him to introduce a third idea, not identical with the idea of either figure — the idea of some *respect* or other in which the two figures differ or are the same. He cannot compare them unless he considers some features — shape, size, location, color etc., — such that he can first examine one figure *in that respect* and then the other figure *in the same respect* in order to arrive at a judgment relating the two figures to each other in the respect chosen. A common sense answer to our question would be that the circle is "round" and the ellipse "is shaped like an egg"; this is a correct but rather vague comparison. A more precise statement would involve referring to the relative sizes of the axes in the two figures: when the two are equal, the figure is round; and every ellipse differs from a circle in that its axes are of unequal length.

The process of comparison is distinctive in that it requires the one who performs comparisons to introduce relevant respects or third terms to which each of the compared terms must stand related if a comparative judgment is to result. The thinker, therefore, must assume a creative role; not all respects are relevant or fruitful and very few are as obvious as surface features like shape and size. The process of comparison becomes more complex and more difficult as the items to be compared become more complex and varied. Comparing geometrical figures is a far simpler and more exact affair than the comparison of two artistic styles, two religious forms, two literary masterpieces, two persons.

One may wonder at this point what comparison has to do with the theory of community and interpretation. The answer is two-fold; first, comparison is essential for gaining self knowledge, and second, comparison is an example of "the same fundamental cognitive process" (p. 344) as interpretation and furnishes further evidence of the unifying power of "thirds" or mediating ideas. Royce had long maintained the view that our knowledge of ourselves is not intuitive and is not a matter of merely retiring into our interior for the purpose of reading off what we find. Instead, we come to know ourselves through a process of interpretation that has comparison at its root. The process involves a community of persons and is thoroughly social in character. Who we are, what capabilities we have, what goals we seek can be discovered only by comparing ourselves with other selves and with our own selves at different times. Our knowledge of others, moreover, is gained in the same way. With regard to the relation between comparison and interpretation, it is clear that Royce virtually identified the two. I regard the identification as a confusion and a fundamental one at that. Both processes, it is true, are genuinely triadic in character; each involves three terms that are related in some determinate way. But comparison, as Royce was well aware, has no essential connection with a time order as does interpretation, nor does comparison necessarily have to do with signs in the sense of minds or quasi-minds.[24] Interpretation in the proper sense requires an asymmetrical ordering of terms — present, past, future — and it has to do with signs that are themselves expressions of intellectual purport and intention. It is

[24]See my paper, "Community and Reality," in *Perspectives on Peirce*, ed. R. J. Bernstein (New Haven: Yale University Press, 1965).

true that in setting forth the conception of reality itself as a community of interpretation, Royce claimed that the entire furniture of the universe is a set of signs, but in his development of the theory of interpretation as the foundation of community, the emphasis falls on signs in the more restricted sense of "an object that fulfills the functions of a mind."[25] It is in this sense that interpretation figures in the philosophy of community, especially with respect to the Beloved Community and the problem of Christianity. Let us now consider the interpretation of signs in the restricted sense and show how it structures the ongoing life of the community.

Royce's example is a situation in which we are confronted with a text in a language not our own; the text needs to be translated. We offer, let us say, an English translation of an Egyptian text such that our translation purports to say in the English language what was said by the writer of the text in the Egyptian tongue. The translator is a mediator who must know two languages in order to perform his task. He must, that is to say, interpret one language in terms of another. He addresses his translation to a future reader with the understanding that the English translation says exactly what the original text said. The original text was a set of signs expressing perhaps some ancient mind or minds; the translator can read these signs and he offers a new set of signs which purport to be equivalent in meaning to the original set. The new set also consists of signs and therefore in turn needs to be read or interpreted by someone who understands the appropriate language. The translator or interpreter mediates between minds in the sense that he interprets the past mind to some future mind thereby creating a community of understanding. "Thus," says Royce,

an interpretation is a relation which not only involves three terms, but brings them into a determinate order. One of the three terms is the interpreter;[26] a second term is the object — the person or the meaning or the text — which is interpreted; the third is the person to whom the interpretation is addressed (p. 287).

The process is never ending since the result of every interpretation

---

[25]P. 345; cf. "A sign may be called the expression of a mind . . ." *(Ibid).*

[26]It is important to notice that by "interpreter" Royce sometimes meant the one who makes the interpretation and sometimes the idea or signs through which the interpretation is made. The same ambiguity is found in Peirce's account. See *Royce's Social Infinite,* pp. 87–88.

is expressed in signs which require a future interpreter. Royce extended the process to include selves; his view is that we stand to each other as sets of signs which need to be read. We speak, gesture, act, write, struggle, love, in the many social situations in which we exist; if we are to know each other and thus transcend the boundaries that separate each of us from the other, we shall need the help of interpretation. Interpretation is a mediator; whenever one self is interpreted to another we have a community of selves brought together by the mediating idea, thought, act, or other sign which some future interpreter can read. Royce was fond of pointing to the self-limiting character of other intellectual processes when compared with interpretation. Perceiving things and conceiving them in accordance with their qualities or types, are terminating processes; they come to an end in the object seen and described. Interpretation is a never ending process because its results are always new signs; it is thus fitted to be the unifying power of a community of persons enduring through time and undergoing change and development.

In a passage cited earlier,[27] Royce claimed that interpretation differs from other mental processes in three respects: the types of objects to which it is applied, the relations in which it stands to these objects, and the ends which it serves. We are now in a position to clarify that claim. In the first place, interpretation is appropriate for the knowledge of selves and communities, for each is a living unity of understanding and loyalty and neither can be known as if it were a datum of perception or an abstract universal. Both the individual person and the communities to which he belongs have an intelligent life of continual dialogue in which their past is interpreted to their future at some present time. The life of each depends on the continuation of this process. Second, in referring to the relation of interpretation to its objects, Royce was thinking of the fact that the objects of interpretation are signs whose significance consists precisely in their being read; every reading of a sign must bring forth new signs which in turn call for interpretation. His emphasis on the triadic nature of the relationship was intended to point out that interpretation is a creative act, since the meaning of most signs is far from clear and frequently many trials must be made before the proper interpretation is reached, and that every interpretation is a linkage of distinct individuals who are thereby brought into a

[27]See p. 275.

community. Third, and most important for its social consequences, the aim of interpretation is always to bring into existence some form of mutuality, of understanding, of love, and loyalty. Interpretation seeks to overcome divisions and create community. In one of his last works, *War and Insurance*, Royce contrasted dyadically related persons with those triadically related, in an effort to illustrate the vital function of mediation. Conflicts in society come through opposed interests that are not mediated. Thus plaintiff and defendant, buyer and seller, insured and beneficiary, employer and employee are what Royce called "dangerous pairs" because they stand opposed in their interests; the success of one could mean the ruin of the other. The problem is to transform these pairs into triads or communities of understanding through a mediating function. On its intellectual side, the function is that of interpretation; the interests of each must be interpreted to the other if conflict is to be avoided. Interpretation, therefore, always has a moral dimension because it is rooted in the will to interpret and has the aim of creating community where none existed before.

We cannot here follow Royce in his attempt to extend the doctrine of the community of interpretation to the whole of reality. It is sufficient to point out that Royce derived from Peirce's analyses of scientific knowledge and his idea that the work of science is carried on by a *community* of investigators, his own theory that the world of common objects and of stable knowledge is a result of many and repeated acts of interpretation. He agreed with Peirce's view that reality is what is disclosed to the community of knowers when its goal is reached, but he added a moral and religious dimension to the theory of knowledge. There is not only the intellect to be satisfied, but the loyal will as well. Knowledge is a thoroughly social affair. Both the isolated individual and the isolated judgment are fallible; error is avoided only through a community of individuals and of judgments. The world and its many members constitute a vast community of interpretation in the sense that nature furnishes us at every moment with signs of its own past which, when read by those qualified to interpret them, constitute the body of knowledge to be addressed to future minds. Human communities likewise record and interpret their own life and that of their members in the form of signs addressed to members of the future. Royce's ultimate aim was to establish the point that the Beloved Community, conceived as the community commanding the loyalty of all mankind, is well founded because reality itself depends on such a community. Community, moreover, wherever it exists, makes itself felt; it brings harmony out of strife, understanding out of ignorance and confusion, renewed loyalty out of infidelity and treason. The modern man, according to Royce, has reason to take Christianity seriously as the religion of loyalty because, whatever be the state of the historical churches and communions, Christianity has made possible that redeeming community without which the twin evils of individualism and collectivism cannot be overcome.

IDEALISM AND CHRISTIANITY

If we consider the bearing of Royce's discussion of the problem of Christianity on the present religious situation, some striking facts present themselves. To begin with, Royce saw clearly the inevitability of change in all aspects of life, but particularly religion, and the need for the reinterpretation (not the mere repetition) of past ideas in the light of new experience and knowledge. Hence his own struggle to restate Christianity in a way that would do justice to ancient ideas and to modern knowledge at the same time. A living religion may draw inspiration from the past, but if it tries to live there, it will die. This point is nicely brought out in his discussion of what is "historical" and what is "essential" to Christianity (p. 363). Royce anticipated current discussions about "demythologizing" Christianity in that he understood the extent to which the essential Christian message first found expression through thought forms and beliefs many of which are forever tied to a bygone age. The early Christians, for example, thought in terms of a cosmology, physiology, and even psychology that are now largely outmoded. Moreover, they held beliefs, like that of the coming end of the world, which proved to be false. The problem is to extract from this mixture what is perennial and essential to the Christian faith so that it can be restated in contemporary terms and freed from the onerous baggage of fancy and myth.

Royce also saw what is now painfully evident to every student of religion, namely, that religion in its institutional form no longer has the support of the collective social will which it once had. We no longer take religion for granted; it has to prove itself. Not only have science and technology changed the form of our life in myriad ways, but new enterprises of the human will—intellectual, political, social, and mercantile—have arisen to enlist the loyalty and the energy that in earlier days might have been devoted to the religious cause. Royce perceived that in America the devotion that once was given to the church now finds itself expressed in serious social and political causes. This insight led him to suggest that Christianity must pay more attention in the future to the power of its ideas than to the form of its institutions. He had in mind principally the idea of loyalty and its appeal to the conscientious individual. He was convinced that interpreting Christianity as the religion of loyalty would save it from seeking to preserve itself in several ways which he found dubious. Christianity, Royce argued, should not try to sustain itself in the modern world either through pietism, mysticism, moralism, or dogmatism. It cannot go underground in a personal form of pietism because it values time and history highly and must remain dedicated to the performance of important social tasks in the world. It cannot identify itself with mysticism — although, as Royce pointed out, there are mystical tendencies in Christianity — because mysticism erases the individual and cannot sustain community (p. 216). It cannot transform itself wholly into morality because it embraces an interpretation of the world and God and has a concern for what a man is to be and not only for what he is to do. Finally, it cannot hope to preserve itself through dogmatism. The modern critical mind is no longer overawed by authority, and rightly so; moreover, the modern man demands of every doctrine of life that it prove itself through discussion in a public forum. Reasserting Christianity in a dogmatic way and in traditional language that is no longer meaningful in terms of contemporary experience, can avail nothing. Royce believed that the modern man does not have to accept any of these possibilities if he sees Christianity as the religion of loyalty. He must ask himself whether the central idea of Christianity, the idea of the Beloved Community and its redeeming function in overcoming the moral burden of the individual, does not present itself to him as the most intelligible solution to the religious problem. The appeal in the end is to his understanding, but also to his creative will. As Royce puts it, the Beloved Community is already founded, but still in every period of history it has to be created through the loyal spirit.

Previously I indicated that I would return at the end of this discussion to a brief consideration of the bearing of modern idealism on the validity of the Christian faith. Royce believed that his idealism provided a defensable metaphysical basis for Christianity;

a full scale appraisal of his claim is beyond our scope. In lieu of that more ambitious project, some comments on Christianity and idealism are in order. I am fully aware that at the present time there are many who are convinced that Christianity was hindered rather than helped by its association with an idealist philosophy. Even Tillich, whose own thought was so largely shaped by the German idealists of the last century, held this view and urged that Christianity should be interpreted on a more realistic basis. In response to the charge that idealism has been a liability to Christianity, one must admit that there is some truth in it. Modern idealism has often been too intellectualistic, ignoring the full depth of personality while stressing knowledge and defining reality exclusively in terms of what it would be like for a knower who possessed a perfect knowledge. Royce saw this problem, even though he contributed to it himself, and tried to redress the balance by introducing the will and man's purpose. Idealism, moreover, sometimes failed to appreciate the power of evil in the world, defining it too simply as a result of ignorance or finitude which a more fully developed reason could dispell. Royce did not make this mistake. As *The Problem of Christianity* shows, he understood well enough the problem posed by our misconduct and consequent guilt, and his discussions of atonement, the problem of evil, and the religious function of sorrow, testify to his realistic grasp of the negative in existence.[28]

If it is true that Christianity is no closer to any one philosophical perspective than to any other, and therefore that its validity does not depend on the success or failure of any particular philosophy, the problem of Christianity's relation to idealism does not arise. Nor does that problem arise if, as has been maintained by many philosophers and theologians alike, metaphysics is no longer possible. Neither of these views, however, is without difficulties. If Christianity were equally distant from every philosophical position, then philosophy would be irrelevant. That this is not the case is readily shown. There are, for example, forms of materialism, of atomism, and of empiricism which, if true, would entail either the meaninglessness or the falsity of central Christian convictions. There must therefore

---

[28]See "The Problem of Job," in *Studies of Good and Evil* (New York: D. Appleton & Co., 1898); "The Religious Mission of Sorrow," in *The Sources of Religious Insight* (New York: Charles Scribner's Sons, 1914).

be some relevant connection between Christianity and these positions. Moreover, the attempts to avoid philosophy made by the purely biblical theologians have not succeeded, because the Bible is not self-interpreting, and deriving a body of doctrine from it forces us to use secular knowledge of which philosophy is a part. With regard to the death of metaphysics, that is only a passing phase on the philosophical scene; those philosophers who stand in the analytic tradition which is supposed to have eliminated metaphysics, now cautiously reintroduce the term to denote a certain type of analysis concerned largely with the idea of the individual and what is now called the philosophy of mind. The fact is that all thinkers make assumptions that are essentially metaphysical in the sense that they imply decisions concerning what there is. These assumptions are no less metaphysical for being implicit; some philosophers still prefer to make them explicit so that they can be critically discussed in relation to other alternatives. The only hope for philosophy in the future lies in this direction.

If the question of the relation between Christianity and an idealist metaphysics can at least be discussed, one essential claim can be made: Christianity must defend at least two realities if it is to make any claim at all to truth — individual selves and communities of selves — and the tradition of modern idealism has offered a better developed and more defensible theory of both realities than any other philosophy has done. As Royce saw years ago, Christianity is committed to defending the reality of Spirit understood not in some purely psychological, emotional, or sentimental way, but in the sense of *living, intelligent, organic unities* combining a many in a one in terms that allow for their development in time and history. Spirit in this sense is necessary for expressing the nature of God, of individual persons, and of the church. Unless we can understand how Spirit can be a contemporaneous reality, there is no possibility of understanding how Christianity can be relevant to the present condition of man. The type of idealism found in the tradition of Hegel, of Peirce, of Royce, and, in certain respects, of Hartshorne, is the only one which has attempted to do justice to the problem. *The Problem of Christianity* focuses this issue and the reappearance of Royce's argument after so long a time is bound to lead to a renewal of the discussion.

JOHN E. SMITH

Yale University

Author's Preface

The present book is the result of studies whose first outcome appeared, in 1908, in my "Philosophy of Loyalty." Since then, two volumes of my collected philosophical essays have dealt, in part, with the same problems as those which "The Philosophy of Loyalty" discussed. Of these two latter volumes, one is entitled "William James and other Essays on the Philosophy of Life"; and contains, amongst other theses, the assertion that the "spirit of loyalty" is able to supply us not only with a "philosophy of life," but with a religion which is "free from superstition" and which is in harmony with a genuinely rational view of the world. In 1912 were published, by the Scribners in New York, the "Bross Lectures," which I had delivered, in the autumn of 1911, at Lake Forest University, Illinois, on "The Sources of Religious Insight." One of these "Bross Lectures" was entitled "The Religion of Loyalty"; and the volume in question contained the promise that, in a future discussion, I would, if possible, attempt to "apply the principles" there laid down to the special case of Christianity. The present work redeems that promise according to the best of my ability.

I

The task of these two volumes is defined in the opening lecture of the first volume. The main results are carefully summed up in Lectures XV and XVI, at the close of the second volume. This book can be understood without any previous reading of my "Philosophy of Loyalty," and without any acquaintance with my "Bross Lectures." Yet in case my reader finds himself totally at variance with

the interpretation of Christianity here expounded, he should not
finally condemn my book without taking the trouble to compare its
principal theses with those which my various preliminary studies
of "loyalty," and of the religion of loyalty, contain.

In brief, since 1908, my "philosophy of loyalty" has been growing.
Its successive expressions, as I believe, form a consistent body of
ethical as well as of religious opinion and teaching, verifiable, in its
main outlines, in terms of human experience, and capable of furnishing a foundation for a defensible form of metaphysical idealism.
But the depth and vitality of the ideal of loyalty have become better
known to me as I have gone on with my work. Each of my efforts
to express what I have found in the course of my study of what
loyalty means has contained, as I believe, some new results. My
efforts to grasp and to expound the "religion of loyalty" have at
length led me, in this book, to views concerning the essence of
Christianity such that, if they have any truth, they need to be carefully considered. For they are, in certain essential respects, novel
views; and they concern the central life-problems of all of us.

II

What these relatively novel opinions are, the reader may, if he
chooses, discover for himself. If he is minded to undertake the task,
he will be aided by beginning with the "Introduction," which immediately follows this preface. This introduction contains an outline
of the lectures, — an outline which was used, by my audience, when
the text of this discussion was read at Manchester College, Oxford,
between January 13 and March 6, 1913.

But a further brief and preliminary indication is here in order to
prepare the reader a little better for what is to follow.

This book is not the work of an historian, nor yet of a technical
theologian. It is the outcome of my own philosophical study of
certain problems belonging to ethics, to religious experience, and
to general philosophy. In spirit I believe my present book to be in
essential harmony with the bases of the philosophical idealism set
forth in various earlier volumes of my own, and especially in the
work entitled "The World and the Individual" (published in 1899-
1901). On the other hand, the present work contains no mere repetition of my former expressions of opinion. There is much in it
which I did not expect to say when I began the task here accomplished. As to certain metaphysical opinions which are stated, in

outline, in the second volume of this book, I now owe much more to our great and unduly neglected American logician, Mr. Charles Peirce, than I do to the common tradition of recent idealism, and certainly very much more than I ever have owed, at any point of my own philosophical development, to the doctrines which, with technical accuracy, can be justly attributed to Hegel. It is time, I think, that the long customary, but unjust and loose usage of the adjective "Hegelian" should be dropped. The genuinely Hegelian views were the ones stated by Hegel himself, and by his early followers. My own interpretation of Christianity, in these volumes, despite certain agreements with the classical Hegelian theses, differs from that of Hegel, and of the classical Hegelian school, in important ways which I can, with a clear conscience, all the more vigorously emphasize, just because I have, all my life, endeavored to treat Hegel both with careful historical justice and with genuine appreciation. In fact the present is a distinctly new interpretation of the "Problem of Christianity."

One of the most thoughtful and one of the fairest of the reviewers of my "Spirit of Modern Philosophy" said of my former position, as stated, in 1892, in the book thus named, that I then came nearer to being a follower of Schopenhauer than a disciple of Hegel. As far as it went this statement gave a just impression of how I then stood. I have never, since then, been more of an Hegelian than at that time I was. I am now less so than ever before.

III

One favorite and facile way of disposing of a student of idealistic philosophy who writes about religion is to say that he has first formed a system of "abstract conceptions," whose interest, if they have any interest, is purely technical, and whose relation to the concrete religious concerns of mankind is wholly external and formal; and that he has then tried to steal popular favor by misusing traditional religious phraseology, and by identifying his "sterile intellectualism," and these his barren technicalities, with the religious beliefs and experiences of mankind, through taking a vicious advantage of ambiguous words.

I can only ask any one who approaches this book to read Volume I [Part I] before he undertakes to judge the metaphysical discussions which form the bulk of Volume II [Part II]; and also to weigh the relations between my metaphysical and my religious phraseology

in the light of the summary contained in Lectures XV and XVI of
the second volume.

If after such a reading of my actual opinions, as set down in this
book, he still insists that I have endeavored artificially to force a set
of foreign and preconceived metaphysical "abstractions" upon the
genuine religious life of my brethren, I cannot supply him with
fairness of estimate, but ought to remain indifferent to his manner
of speech.

As a fact, this book is the outcome of experience, and, in its somewhat extended practical sections, it is written (if I may borrow a
phrase from the Polish master of romance, Sienkiewicz), "for the
strengthening of hearts." That some portions of the discussion are
technically metaphysical is a result of the deliberate plan of the
whole work; and technical assertions demand, as a matter of course,
technical criticisms. The novelty of some of my metaphysical theses
in my second volume, and the lack of space for their adequate statement in this book, have made their exposition, as I here have time to
give it, both incomplete, and justly subject to many objections, some
of which I have anticipated in my text. But, in any case, I have not
been merely telling anybody's old story over again.

Since I have been writing from the life, I of course owe a great
deal to the inspiration that I long ago obtained from William James's
"Varieties of Religious Experience." I even venture to hope that
(while I have of course laid stress upon no interests which I could
recognize as due to merely private concerns of my own) I might
still be addressing at least some few readers who are able to understand, and perhaps sometimes to echo, a cry of genuine feeling when
they hear it. For, after all, it is more important that we should together recognize in religion our own common personal needs and
life-interests than that we should agree about our formulas. So I
have indeed tried, in this book, to speak as one wanderer speaks to
another who is his friend, when the way is long and obscure.

Yet in one very important respect the religious experience upon
which, in this book, I most depend, differs very profoundly from
that whose "varieties" James described. He deliberately confined
himself to the religious experience of individuals. My main topic
is a form of social religious experience, namely, that form which
in ideal, the Apostle Paul viewed as the experience of the Church
This social form of experience is that upon which loyalty depends.
James supposed that the religious experience of a church must needs

be "conventional," and consequently must be lacking in depth and in sincerity.

This, to my mind, was a profound and a momentous error in the whole religious philosophy of our greatest American master in the study of the psychology of religious experience. All experience must be *at least* individual experience; but unless it is *also* social experience, and unless the whole religious community which is in question unites to share it, this experience is but as sounding brass, and as a tinkling cymbal. This truth is what Paul saw. This is the rock upon which the true and ideal church is built. This is the essence of Christianity.

If indeed I myself must cry "out of the depths" before the light can come to me, it must be my Community that, in the end, saves me. To assert this and to live this doctrine constitute the very core of Christian experience, and of the "Religion of Loyalty." In discussing "the varieties of religious experience," which here concern us, I have everywhere kept this thesis in mind.

IV

The assertion just made summarizes the single thought to whose discussion, illustration, defence, and philosophy this book is devoted. This assertion is the one which, in my "Philosophy of Loyalty," I was trying, so far as I then could, to expound and to apply. We are saved, if at all, by devotion to the Community, in the sense of that term which these two volumes attempt to explain and to defend. This is what I mean by loyalty. Because the word "loyalty" ends in *ty*, and because what a "Community" is, is at present so ill understood by most philosophers, my former discussions of this topic have been accused of basing all the duties of life upon an artificial abstraction. When I now say that by loyalty I mean the *practically devoted love of an individual for a community*, I shall still leave unenlightened those who stop short at the purely verbal fact that the word "community" also ends in *ty*. But let such readers wait until they have at least read Lectures I, III, and VII of my first volume. Then they may know what is at issue.

This book, if it is nothing else, is at least one more effort to tell what loyalty is. I also want to put loyalty — this love of the individual for the community — where it actually belongs, not only at the heart of the virtues, not only at the summit of the mountains which the human spirit must climb if man is really to be saved, but also (where it equally belongs) at the turning-point of human history,—at the point when the Christian ideal was first defined,—and when the Church Universal,—that still invisible Community of all the faithful, that homeland of the human spirit, "which eager hearts expect," was first introduced as a vision, as a hope, as a conscious longing to mankind. I want to show what loyalty is, and that all this is true of the loyal spirit.

Some of my main theses, in this book, are the following: First, Christianity is, in its essence, the most typical, and, so far in human history, the most highly developed religion of loyalty. Secondly, loyalty itself is a perfectly concrete form and interest of the spiritual life of mankind. Thirdly, this very fact about the meaning and the value of universal loyalty is one which the Apostle Paul learned in and from the social and religious life of the early Christian communities, and then enriched and transformed through his own work as missionary and teacher. Still another of my theses is this: Whatever may hereafter be the fortunes of Christian institutions, or of Christian traditions, the religion of loyalty, the doctrine of the salvation of the otherwise hopelessly lost individual through devotion to the life of the genuinely real and Universal Community, must survive, and must direct the future both of religion and of mankind, if man is to be saved at all. As to what the word "salvation" means, and as to why I use it, the reader can discover, if he chooses, from the text of these lectures.

V

The doctrines of the Community, of Loyalty, of the "lost state of the natural individual," and of Atonement as the function in which the life of the community culminates, appear, in the volumes of this book, in two forms, whose clear distinction and close connection ought next to be emphasized in this preface. First, these doctrines, and the ideas in terms of which they are expressed, are verifiable results of the higher social religious experience of mankind. Were there no Christianity, were there no Christians in the world, all these ideas would be needed to express the meaning of true loyalty, the saving value of the right relation of any human individual to the community of which he is a member, and the true sense of life. These doctrines, then, need no dogmas of any historical church to define them, and no theology, and no technical metaphysical theory, to furnish a foundation for them. In the second place, however, these Christian ideas are based upon deep metaphysical truths whose significance is more than human.

Historically speaking, the Christian church first discovered the Christian ideas. The founder of Christianity, so far as we know what his teachings were, seems not to have defined them adequately. They first came to a relatively full statement through the religious life of the Pauline Churches; and the Pauline epistles contain their first, although still not quite complete, formulation. Paul himself was certainly not the founder of Christianity. But the Pauline communities first were conscious of the essence of Christianity.

Consequently those are right who have held, what the "modernists" of the Roman Church were for a time asserting, — before officialism turned its back, in characteristic fashion, upon the really new and deeply valuable light which these modernists were, for the time, bringing to their own communion. Those, I say, are right who have held that the Church, rather than the person of the founder, ought to be viewed as the central idea of Christianity.

On the other hand, neither the "modernists" of recent controversy, nor any other of the apologists for the traditions of the historical Christian church, have yet seen the meaning of the "religion of loyalty" as the Apostle Paul, in certain of his greatest moments and words, saw and expressed that meaning. The apostle's language, regarding this matter, is as imperishable as it is well warranted by human experience, and as it is also separable from the accidents of later dogmatic formulation, and inexhaustible in the metaphysical problems which it brings to our attention.

Hence the most significant task for a modern revision of our estimate of what is vital in Christianity depends upon the recognition of certain aspects of Christian social experience and of human destiny, aspects to whose exposition and defence, first in empirical terms, and then in the light of a reëxamination of certain fundamental metaphysical ideas, these two volumes are devoted.

The "Christian ideas" of the Church, of the lost state of man, of grace, and of atonement, are here discussed, first separately, and then in their natural union. In this examination, Pauline Christianity receives a prominence which I believe to be justified by the considerations which are emphasized in my text. After an extended discussion, in the second volume, of the "metaphysics of the Christian ideas," I return, at the conclusion of the whole research, to the relation of Christianity to our modern social experience, and to the problems of today.

The outcome of this method of dealing with "The Problem of Christianity" involves, I believe, not indeed a "solution," but a great simplification of the problems of Christology, of dogma in general, and of the relations between the true interests of philosophy upon the one side, and religion upon the other. The reader will somewhat dimly see the nature of the simplification in question when he reads Lecture I. In Lecture III, on the "Realm of Grace," he will begin to anticipate with greater clearness the characteristic outlines of my version of the "religion of loyalty." But not until Lectures XV and XVI will the outcome of the closely connected story to which, despite many episodes, the whole book is devoted, be ready for the reader's final judgment.

VI

It is necessary still to forestall one fairly obvious criticism. Both "orthodox" and "liberal" Christianity, as they usually state their otherwise conflicting opinions, very commonly agree in making their different attempted solutions of the "Problem of Christianity" depend upon the views which they respectively defend regarding the person of the founder of the faith. In Lecture VIII of the first volume, and in Lecture XVI of the second volume, I have summarized the little that I have to say about the person of the founder.

I cannot find in the ordinary "liberal" solution of the problem of the personality of Jesus, as Harnack, as Weigel, and as most "advanced liberal" discussion of our topic state that solution, anything satisfactory.

My principal reason for this dissatisfaction, when urged against the usual "liberal" view of the significance of the person of Jesus, is a novel, but, if I am right, a momentous reason. If Christianity is, in its inmost essence, the "religion of loyalty," the religion of that which in this book I have called "The Beloved Community," and if Pauline Christianity contained the essence of the only doctrine by which mankind, through devotion to the community, through loyalty, are to be saved,—then Buddhism is right in holding that the very form of the individual self is a necessary source of woe and of wrong. In that case, no individual human self can be saved except through ceasing to be a *mere* individual.

But if this be so, Harnack's view and the usual "liberal" view, to the effect that there was an ideally perfect human individual, whose example, or whose personal influence, involves a solution of the problem of human life, and is saving, — this whole view is an opinion essentially opposed to the deepest facts of human nature, and to the very essence of the "religion of loyalty." Not through imitating nor yet through loving any mere individual human being can we be saved, but only through loyalty to the "Beloved Community."

Equally, however, must I decline to follow any of the various forms of traditionally orthodox dogma or theory regarding the person of Christ. Legends, doubtful historical hypotheses, and dogmas leave us, in this field, in well-known, and, to my mind, simply hopeless perplexities.

Hence this book has no positive thesis to maintain regarding the person of the founder of Christianity. I am not competent to settle any of the numerous historical doubts as to the founder's person, and as to the details of his life. The thesis of this book is that the essence of Christianity, as the Apostle Paul stated that essence, depends upon regarding the being which the early Christian Church believed itself to represent, and the being which I call, in this book, the "Beloved Community," as the true source, through loyalty, of the salvation of man. This doctrine I hold to be both empirically verifiable within the limits of our experience, and metaphysically defensible as an expression of the life and the spiritual significance of the whole universe.

A distinguished authority upon Christology, who has kindly listened to some of my lectures, and who has kindly honored me with his criticism, points out to me, however, the final objection which I can here mention.

"You imagine," he says, "that early Christianity depended, for the significance of its faith, upon the fact that a certain body of men, constituting the Pauline churches, were loyal to the spiritual unity, to the ideal charity, which, as they believed, the saving work of Christ had freely given to them, and to their community. But you speak of this early Christian community as if it were its own creator, — as if it grew up spontaneously, as if its form of saving and universal loyalty arose without any cause. Can you make religious history intelligible in this way? Who created the church? Who inspired the new loyalty? Was not the founder the cause of his church? How could the church have existed without its founder? Must not the founder have possessed, as an individual, a spiritual power equivalent to that which he exerted? Must it not then have been Jesus himself, and not the Community,—not the church,—which is the central source of Christianity? Otherwise does not your theory hang in the air? But if the founder really created this community and its loyalty, does not the whole meaning of the Christian religion once more centre in the founder, in his life, and in his person?"

I can here only reply to my kindly critic that this book (as Lecture III carefully points out) has *no* hypothesis whatever to offer as to how the Christian community originated. Personally I shall never hope, in my present existence, to know anything whatever about that origin, beyond the barest commonplaces. The historical evidence at hand is insufficient to tell us how the church originated. The legends do not solve the problem. I have a right to decline, and I actually decline to express an opinion as to any details about the person and life of the founder. For such an opinion the historical evidences are lacking, although it seems to me natural to suppose that the sayings and the parables which tradition attributed to the founder were the work of some single author, concerning whose life we probably possess some actually correct reports.

On the other hand, regarding the essence of the Christianity of the Pauline churches and concerning the actual life of those churches, we possess, in the Pauline epistles, information which is priceless, which reveals to us the religion of loyalty in its classic and universal form, and which involves the Christian ideas expounded, in my own poor way, in what here follows.

The transformation, not of historical, but of Christological, of ethical, and of religious ideas which would follow upon an adequate recognition of these simple considerations amply justifies the effort of one who undertakes, as I do, *not* to add to or to take away from early Christian history, and not to solve the problems of that history, but simply to expound the essence of the Christian doctrine of life, and the relation of the Christian ideas to the real world.

VII

This preface must close with a few words of acknowledgment and of explanation.

In 1911 the "President and Fellows of Harvard University"—a body which is also known as "The Corporation"—appointed me, for three years, holder of the endowment known as "The Cabot Fellowship," with the understanding that I should devote some of my time to study and research. In the beginning of 1912, when my work was, for a brief period, interrupted, the Harvard Corporation put me under an additional obligation, by granting me an extraordinary leave of absence. Since then, I have been allowed the opportunity not only to write these lectures, but to accept an offer made in the summer of 1912 by the Trustees of the "Hibbert Foundation" to deliver this entire course on "The Problem of Christianity" at Manchester College, Oxford; while the added generosity of President Lowell, who also acted, in this matter, as Trustee of the Lowell Institute in Boston, has enabled me to deliver the first part of the course (the discussions contained in Volume I of this book) as public lectures before the Lowell Institute in November and December of 1912. At Manchester College, on the "Hibbert Foundation," the lectures have been read between January 13 and March, 1913, and have thus continued throughout the whole of one Oxford term.

Seldom, then, has a student of philosophy been so much indebted to official and to personal kindliness for the chance to perform such a task. I have heartily to thank the persons and authorities just mentioned, and to insist that, under such conditions, the faults of my book must be regarded as wholly my own, and judged sternly.

Prominent among the authors who have influenced my discussion of the idea of Atonement is the late Dr. R. C. Moberly, whose book on "Atonement and Personality" also had a deep effect upon my treatment of the idea of the Church. To Professor Sanday's "Christologies, Ancient and Modern" I owe a great debt. Dinsmore's "Atonement in Literature and Art" came into my hands only after my own discussion of Atonement had assumed definitive shape.

Among the friendly critics who have aided me in preparing my text, I ought to mention Professor E. C. Moore, Professor James Jackson Putnam, and Professor George H. Palmer of Harvard University. Professor Lawrence P. Jacks of Manchester College, Oxford, has helped me, from the beginning of my task, in ways which I cannot here acknowledge in any adequate fashion. I have also to acknowledge the assistance of Principal J. Estlin Carpenter, of Professor Charles M. Bakewell of Yale University, and of Dr. and Mrs. R. C. Cabot of Boston. Dr. J. Loewenberg has helped me not only with stimulating and sometimes decisively effective criticism of my lectures as they grew, but with other much-needed aid in preparing this book. Time would quite fail me to tell of the numerous other friends, both at home and in Oxford, who have accompanied, encouraged, and assisted my efforts.

JOSIAH ROYCE
Cambridge, Massachusetts,
April 13, 1913.

Author's Introduction

When these lectures were delivered at Manchester College, Oxford, the hearers were supplied with the following outline under the general title: "Plan of Lectures on the Problem of Christianity." This plan is here repeated with its headings as they appeared on this printed programme.

PRELIMINARY NOTE

These lectures are divided into two parts: Part I (Lectures I—VIII), on "The Christian Doctrine of Life"; Part II (Lectures IX—XVI), on "The Real World and the Christian Ideas."

Part I is a study of the human and empirical aspect of some of the leading and essential ideas of Christianity. Part II deals with the technically metaphysical problems to which these ideas give rise. Parts I and II are contrasted in their methods, the first part discussing religious experience, the second part dealing with its metaphysical foundations. The two parts, however, are closely connected in their purpose; and at the close, in Lectures XV and XVI, the relations between the metaphysical and the empirical aspects of the whole undertaking are reviewed.

The "Christian Ideas" which the lecturer proposes to treat as "leading and essential" are: (1) The Idea of the "Community" (historically represented by the Church); (2) The Idea of the "Lost State of the Natural Man"; (3) The Idea of "Atonement," together with the somewhat more general Idea of "Saving Grace."

Each of these ideas is, for the purposes of these lectures, to be generalized as well as interpreted. The "Community" exists, in human history, in countless different forms and grades, of which the visible and historical Christian Church is one instance. The ideal community in which, according to Christian doctrine, the Divine Spirit finds its expression, presents a problem which cannot be adequately treated without considering whether the whole universe is or is not, in some sense, both a community, and a divine being. The "lost state of the natural man" is a doctrine dependent upon the views about the nature of human individuality which are most characteristic of the Christian spirit.

Christianity has always been a religion, not only of Love, but of Loyalty. By loyalty is meant the thoroughgoing and loving devotion of an individual to a community. The "morally detached" individual, who has not found the community to which to be loyal, or who, having first found that community, has lost his relation to it through an act of deliberate disloyalty, is (according to such a religion) wholly unable, through any further individual deed of his own, to win or to regain the true goal of life. The ideas of "grace" and of "atonement" have to do with the question regarding the way in which the individual, whom no deed of his own (according to this religious view) can save or restore, can, nevertheless, be saved through a deed "*not* his own"—a deed which the community or which a servant of the community in whom its Spirit "fully dwells," may accomplish on behalf of the lost individual. In this fashion it is possible to indicate how our three Christian ideas may be and should be generalized for the purpose of the present lectures.

These three Christian ideas—that of the Community, of the Lost Individual, and of Atonement—have a close relation to a doctrine of life, which, when duly generalized, can be at least in part studied as a purely human "Philosophy of Loyalty," and can be estimated in empirical terms, apart from any use of technical dogmas, and apart from any metaphysical opinion. The "Community" is the object to which loyalty is due. The "Lost State" is the state of those who have never found, or who, once finding, have then lost their loyalty. "Atonement" and "Divine Grace" may be considered as if they were expressions of the purely human process whereby the community seeks and saves, through its suffering servants and its Spirit, that which is lost.

Nevertheless, no purely empirical study of the Christian doctrine of life can, by itself, suffice to answer our main questions. It is indeed necessary to consider the basis in human nature which the religion of loyalty possesses, and to portray the relation of this religion to the social experience of mankind; and to this task the first part of these lectures is confined. But such a preliminary study sends us beyond itself.

For each of the Christian ideas demands a further interpretation in terms of a theory of the real world. Religion can be experienced and lived apart from metaphysics; but (if we adapt Anselm's well-known use of a Scriptural word) we may say that whoever has learned what it is to "do the will" of the loyal spirit has a right to endeavor to "know the doctrine" which shall teach whether, and in what sense, the Spirit, the Community, and the process of salvation are genuine realities, transcending any of their human embodiments.

The task of the second part of these lectures is therefore to consider the neglected philosophical problem of the sense in which the community and its Spirit are realities. For this purpose a some-what new form of Idealism, and, in particular, a new chapter in the theory of knowledge must be studied.

TOPICS OF THE INDIVIDUAL LECTURES
Part I *The Christian Doctrine of Life*

Lecture I *The Problem and the Method*
The "Problem of Christianity" stated. The creed of the "modern man." The modern man and the "education of the human race." The methods to be employed in this study. Question: "In what sense, if in any, does the Divine Spirit dwell in the Church?" First glimpses of the course of the inquiry.

Lecture II *The Idea of the Universal Community*
Tragic fortunes of great ideals especially exemplified by the history of the ideal of the Church. The conflict of spirit and letter. The basis of loyalty in human nature. The ideal of loyalty in its non-Christian forms. The Pauline development and transformation of the original doctrine of Christian love through the doctrine of charity in its relation to the Christian community.

Lecture III *The Moral Burden of the Individual*
Social aspects of the doctrine which is stated in the seventh chapter of the Epistle to the Romans. "The Law" as a factor in the develop-

ment of Self-consciousness. The natural and social cultivation of the conscience as a training in self-will. Modern illustrations of the process which was first observed by the Apostle. Individualism and collectivism. The community of hate and the community of love. The burden of the individual and the escape through the spirit of loyalty. The "new creature."

Lecture IV *The Realm of Grace*

A further view of Christianity, as a Religion of Loyalty. Loyalty in its natural origin and in its genuinely spiritual forms. The doctrine of the "two levels" of human nature. The problem of the origin of the "beloved community" and of the beginnings of a "life in the spirit." Relations of Christian loyalty to the origins of Christian dogma. The Spirit *in* the Community, and the personal Spirit *of* the Community. The Founder and the problem of the "two natures." The "two natures" and the "two levels." Illustration from the Fourth Gospel.

Lecture V *Time and Guilt*

Matthew Arnold on Puritanism and on "getting rid of sin." Conflicts between the modern spirit and the doctrine of the "endless penalty" of sin. Reconsideration of these conflicts. The rational theory of the nature of "mortal sin." The relation of our acts to the whole time-process. Every deed is irrevocable. Consequence in case of the deliberately disloyal deed. Repentance no adequate remedy for guilt. Inability of the traitor to atone for his own treason. The rational doctrine of "endless penalty" not a morbid, or a cheerless, or an arbitrary doctrine. Decisiveness of character and rigidity of self-judgment. "I was my own destroyer and will be my own here-after," is not an expression of weak brooding, but of rational self-estimate.

Lecture VI *Atonement*

The idea of Atonement reviewed with reference to the "problem of the traitor." Typical and symbolic value of this problem. Conscience and personal freedom. The traitor's own self-estimate is decisive as to what can atone for his guilt, provided only that he is completely awakened to an insight into the irrevocable facts. Inadequacy both of the "penal-satisfaction" theories and of the so-called "moral" theories of Atonement. Need of an objective Atonement. Neither by arousing repentance nor by awakening thankfulness can Atonement be accomplished. Statement of an objective theory of Atonement through the deed of a suffering servant of the community. Human instances. Universality and verifiability of atoning deeds. In them the life of the community culminates.

Lecture VII   *The Christian Doctrine of Life*
Contrast between Buddhism and Christianity. Synthesis of the Christian ideas. Resulting estimate of human life and rule for the service and conduct of the Community. The Christian Will.

Lecture VIII   *The Modern Mind and the Christian Ideas*
Human conditions of the survival of Christianity as a faith "upon earth." The social prospects of the near and remote future. The power of the Christian Ideas. Relations of the foregoing study to traditional Christianity.

Part II   *The Real World and the Christian Ideas*

Lecture IX   *The Community and the Time-Process*
The neglected article in Christian theology, and the problem of the metaphysics of the community. Social "pluralism," and "the compounding of consciousness." The doctrine of the community not mystical. The time-process as essential to the existence of the community. Communities of "hope" and of "memory."

Lecture X   *The Body and the Members*
The Pauline use of the resurrection as a means of clarifying the consciousness of the community. Modern analogies; communities of coöperation; conditions upon which loyalty depends. The community as an interpretation.

Lecture XI   *Perception, Conception, and Interpretation*
The theory of knowledge has been dominated in the past by the contrast between Perception and Conception. Need of the recognition of a third cognitive process. Charles Peirce's doctrine of Interpretation as a third and a triadic cognitive process, essentially social in its type. Criticism of Bergson's view of the ideal of knowledge. Interpretation, and the Metaphysics of the time-process.

Lecture XII *The Will to Interpret*
Interpretation in its relation to Charles Peirce's triadic type of
"Comparison." Comparison and interpretation under individual and
social conditions. Definition of a "Community of Interpretation."
Ideal value of such a community. Its form as the principal form
which the "life of the spirit" assumes. Examples, and generalization
of the ideals involved.

Lecture XIII *The World of Interpretation*
Outline of a form of idealism determined by the use of Peirce's
definition of the cognitive process of interpretation. Relation to
Bergson and to Plato. The world as a "Community of Interpretation." The One and the Many in such a world. The relation of
interpretation to Time. Thesis: "The universe contains its own
interpreter." The world of interpretation as not "static." Resulting
general doctrine as to the nature and the unity of the "Spirit of
the Community."

Lecture XIV *The Doctrine of Signs*
Definition of Peirce's term "Sign." The Signs as a third and triadic
category, corresponding to the cognitive process of interpretation.
The Doctrine of Signs in its relation to "Radical Empiricism," and
to Pragmatism. The primacy of the social consciousness. Loyalty as
the loving aspect of the "will to interpret." The metaphysics of the
saving process. The irrevocable and the temporal.

Lecture XV *The Historical and the Essential*
The relation of this form of idealism to traditional Christianity.
Pauline Christianity and our doctrine of interpretation. Final
statement of our "Problem of Christianity."

Lecture XVI *Summary and Conclusion*
Teleology and Induction. The larger teleological aspects of the
natural world. The Church and the sects; the Church and the
world; the future possibilities for religious development. Practical
results of the inquiry.

Part I

The Christian Doctrine
of Life

I

The
Problem
and the Method

I propose, in the course of these lectures, to expound and to defend certain theses regarding the vital and essential characteristics of the Christian religion. In the present lecture, which must be wholly confined to the work of preparing the way for the later discussion, I shall first briefly explain my title, and shall state what I mean by "The Problem of Christianity." Then I shall name certain aspects of this problem which will determine the whole course of our inquiry; and I shall indicate the nature of the method which I intend to follow. Since our topic is so wealthy and so complex, I must begin by means of very general and summary statements, and must leave to later lectures any effort to deal with the details of the matters that I shall try to treat.

Before all else, let me say one word as to the general spirit in which I venture into this so familiar, yet so mysterious and momentous, department of the philosophy of religion.

I

The present day is one marked by a new awakening of interest in religious experience, and in its bearing upon life. This interest finds expression both in general literature and in philosophical discussion. I myself have to approach all such topics with the interests and the habits, not only of a student of philosophy, but of one already committed to a certain type of philosophical opinions. This fact sets inevitable limits to the sort of contribution that I can make to the inquiry which my title names. Yet the novelty of the present situation of human thought, and the dramatic interest of certain crises through which opinion has recently been passing, give to even the least constructive of philosophical students numerous opportunities to experience, in the world of religious inquiry, what men were never permitted to experience before. The philosophical thought of our day is affected by new motives; and the religious life of the world is deepened by the presence of efforts which are due to the novel and far-reaching social and moral problems of our time. All these varied influences react upon one another. The student of philosophy may well feel himself moved, by recent discussions, to formulate opinions which the novelty of the life of other men may haply color, even when the one who formulates them has no power, derived from his own inner resources, to invent.

At all events, any sincere seeker for truth may hope that, however remote from his own powers it may be either to speak with tongues or to prophesy, he may gain new edification from his brethren, and may, in his turn, help others to share in the gifts of the spirit, and to be renewed and informed by some power which is not ourselves, and which seems, in this happy moment, to be coming into a close touch with the deeper thought and the better aspiration of our time.

With such a "trembling hope," — with such a hope to gain some advantage from the philosophical as well as from the religious movement of our times, — I myself have for a good while endeavored to reconsider some of the ancient and modern problems of the philosophy of religion. These lectures will embody the results of a few of these efforts towards reconsideration. Since I know that so many other inquirers are engaged in analogous tasks, and since I feel sure that unity of opinion regarding the office and the meaning of religion can only be approached through a variety of efforts, I am sure that my own venture is no mere outcome of lonely presumption.

II

The man who considers the interests of religion may choose any one of three attitudes toward Christianity. The first is the familiar attitude of the expounder and defender of some form of the Christian faith,—the position of the apologist and of the Christian teacher. Even this one mode of dealing with the tradition of Christianity is capable of an almost endless wealth of variations. The defender of the faith may adhere to this or to that branch of the Christian church. Or perhaps he may regard tradition from the point of view which is often called that of modern Liberal Christianity. Or— whatever his own creed may be—he may lay the principal stress upon some practical task, such as that of a pastor or of a missionary. In yet another spirit, he may emphasize technical theological questions. Finally, he may make the history of the church or of the religion his main interest. Through all such variations, as they appear in the words and the hearing of religious inquirers and teachers, there may run a tendency that unifies, and so characterizes them all,—the positive tendency, namely, to defend, to propagate, and, in one way or another, to render efficacious the Christian view of God, of the world, and of human destiny.

Secondly, however, the inquirer who deals with religious problems may take the position of the opponent or of the critic of Christianity, or may simply regard Christianity with a relative, although deliberately thoughtful, indifference. Such an opponent, or such an external critical observer of the Christian world, may be a representative of some other faith, as certain of the recent Oriental critics of Christian doctrine have been; or, in other cases, he may emphasize some aspect of the supposed conflict between the spirit and the results of modern science, on the one hand, and the tradition or the faith of Christendom on the other. At a very recent time in the history of European discussion, such attitudes of critical hostility or of thoughtful indifference towards Christianity were prominent factors in discussion, and occupied a favored place in the public mind. Such was the case, for instance, in the last century, during the early phases of the controversies regarding evolution, especially in the years between 1860 and 1880. As a philosophical student I myself was trained under the influence of such a general trend of public opinion. These attitudes of critical indifference or of philosophical hostility towards traditional faith, are still prominent in our world of religious discussion; but side by side with them there have recently become prominent tendencies belonging to a third group, — tendencies which seem to me to be, in their treatment of Christianity, neither predominantly apologetic nor predominantly hostile, nor yet at all indifferent. This third group of tendencies has suggested to me the title of these lectures. I wish briefly to characterize this group of ways of dealing with Christianity, and to indicate its contrast with the other groups.

III

The modern student of the problems of religion in general, or of Christianity in particular, may see good reason for agreeing with the apologists, — with the defenders of the faith, — in attributing to Christianity, viewed simply as a product of human evolution, a central importance in history, in the religious experience of our race, and in the endlessly renewed, yet very ancient, endeavor of mankind to bring to pass, or to move towards, the salvation of man. To such a student it may have become clear: — first, that whatever the truth of religion may be, the office, the task, the need of religion are the most important of the needs, the tasks, the offices of humanity; and, secondly, that both by reason of its past history and by reason of its present and persistent relation to the religious experience and to the needs of men, Christianity stands before us as the most effective expression of religious longing which the human race, travailing in pain until now, has, in its corporate capacity, as yet, been able to bring before its imagination as a vision, or has endeavored to translate, by the labor of love, into the terms of its own real life.

In view of these opinions, such a student of religion may tend to disagree with that spirit of critical indifference or of hostility towards Christianity which has characterized, and still characterizes, one of the two groups of religious inquirers whom I have just mentioned. With the apologists, then, and against the hostile or the thoughtfully indifferent critics of Christianity, such a student may stand, as one to whom the philosophy of religion, if there is to be a philosophy of religion at all, must include in its task the office of a positive and of a deeply sympathetic interpretation of the spirit of Christianity, and must be just to the fact that the Christian religion is, thus far at least, man's most impressive vision of salvation, and his principal glimpse of the home-land of the spirit.

Yet such a student may still see, for reasons which I need not at the outset of our quest fully state, how numerous are the questions yet to be answered, the reasonable doubts yet to be removed, the philosophical issues yet to be met, the historical problems yet to be solved, the tragedies of practical and of religious life yet to be overcome, the divisions of human faith yet to be reunited, before it can become quite clear to us, if it ever is to become clear, just what ones amongst the apologists are indeed defending the true Christian faith, and wherein the truth of that faith, if it be true, consists, and what the essence of Christianity is, and in what form, if in any form, Christianity is destined to win over to itself, if it is ever to win, that troubled human world which it has illumined, but whereto it has thus far brought, not peace, but a sword.

For such a student, who is neither predominantly an apologist, nor, in the main, any hostile or indifferent critic, the topic to be chiefly considered in his own reflections concerning the Christian religion would be explicitly "The Problem of Christianity."

That is, such a student would approach this religion regarding it, at least provisionally, not as the one true faith to be taught, and not as an outworn tradition to be treated with an enlightened indifference, but as a central, as an intensely interesting, life-problem of humanity, to be appreciated, to be interpreted, to be thoughtfully reviewed, with the seriousness and with the striving for reasonableness and for thoroughness which we owe to every life-problem wherewith human destiny is inseparably interwoven.

Such is the mode of approach to the study of Christianity which these lectures will adopt. This mode of approach is in no wise new, but it is the one which, at the present moment, in my opinion, the thoughtful public of our day both most desires and most deeply needs. And despite all that has been already done, and well done, in the direction of the sympathetic philosophical interpretation of Christianity, there is still ample work yet to do to make this third mode of approach to our topic more effective for the clarifying of men's insight and for the strengthening of the great common religious interests.

IV

If you ask in what way our problem of Christianity can be, at this stage, provisionally formulated, I may give you, in reply, a first glimpse both of the topics that we are to discuss, and of the general method to be used in their discussion, by employing for the moment a deliberately inadequate expression.

What I am minded to consider in these lectures includes some part of an answer to the question: "In what sense, if in any, can the modern man consistently be, in creed, a Christian?" This form of statement indicates what is at issue, but calls in a most obvious way for a more exact definition of our plan. Yet the very vagueness of the outlook which these words suggest will help us to advance almost at once to a more definite view of our task.

"In what sense can the modern man consistently be, in creed, a Christian?" You see, in any case, that we are to speak of some sort of creed, and of the consistency with which somebody may or may not hold that creed. In other words, our own "problem of Christianity," in these lectures, is to be one that, at least in part, has to do with the reasonable consistency of certain possible religious opinions. That is, we are to study our topic as students of philosophy view their issues. Our problem is, in itself considered, and apart from the limitations of our own mode of inquiry, a life-problem, an intensely practical, a passionately interesting, issue, the problem and the issue of a religion. But we are to approach this problem reflectively, and are to take account of interests that are not only those of religion, but also those of thought.

Herein lies one chosen limitation of our enterprise, in that we are not undertaking to contribute directly to religion itself, but only to an understanding of some of the problems which religious creeds suggest. In so far, then, vague as this first statement of our problem is, the word "creed," and the reference to the creed of the "modern man," serve to specify in some measure the range of our investigation. As a fact, I shall summarily study in these lectures certain aspects of the traditional creed of the Christian Church.

On the other hand, the term "modern man," as just used in my provisional statement of our problem, has a meaning whose deeper relation to our task we shall hardly be able to appreciate justly until the very close of this series of studies. "Can the modern man consistently hold a Christian creed?" But who, you will ask, is this modern man?

Superficially regarded, the conception of the "modern man" is one of the most arbitrary of the convenient fictions of current discussion. What views or types of views are, or ought to be, characteristic of the "modern man" hardly any of us will wholly agree in defining.

And if there is any typical "modern man," he would seem, at first sight, to be a creature of a day. Tomorrow some other sort of modern man must take his place. And of the modern man of a future century we now cannot even know the race,—much less, it would seem, the religious creed. What creed about religion, Christian or non-Christian, now befits the creature of a day whom our own young century calls the modern man,—why need we inquire? So you might comment upon the statement of our problem which I have just put into words.

Yet even at this stage of the discussion, if you consider for a moment the meaning that underlies the so frequent use of the phrase "modern man" in current discussion, and that inspires our familiar interest in the supposed views of the fictitious being called the "modern man," you will see that even this provisional mode of formulating the problem of Christianity may, after all, guide us to a study of matters which are not fictitious and which have a bearing on permanent religious concerns.

For by the "modern man" most of us mean a being whose views are supposed to be in some sense not only the historical result, but a significant summary, of what the ages have taught mankind. The term "modern man" condenses into a word the hypothesis, the postulate, that the human race has been subject to some more or less coherent process of education. The modern man is supposed to teach what this "education of the human race" has taught to him. The ages have their lesson. The modern man knows something of this lesson.

Such, I say, is the hypothesis, or postulate, which makes the phrase "modern man" so attractive. This hypothesis, this postulate, may be true or false. But at all events its meaning is deep and is connected with a certain more or less definite view of human nature and of the course of time,—a view which has played its own part in the history of religion, and which, in particular, has well-known relations to Christian belief.

We all remember that the apostle Paul conceived human history as including a process of education. As "modern man" of his own time, the apostle conceived himself to have become able to read the lesson of this process. But such a postulate, whether true or false, whether asserted in Paul's time or in our own, whether Christian in its formulation or not, includes a doctrine that will later occupy a large place in our inquiry,—the doctrine that the human race, taken as a whole, has some genuine and significant spiritual unity, so that its life is no mere flow and strife of opinions, but includes a growth in genuine insight.

Our customary speech about the modern man implies that, in the light of this common insight gradually attained by the whole race, our creeds should be tested and, if need be, revised. The "modern man," defined in terms of such an hypothesis, is conceived as the present minister of this treasury of wisdom which the ages have stored and which our progress is still increasing. But, from such a point of view, to ask whether the modern man can consistently be in creed a Christian, is the same as to ask how Christianity, considered as a body of religious beliefs, is related to the whole lesson of religious history, and how far this supposed education of the human race has been, and remains, in spirit, in meaning, in its true interpretation, a Christian education.

Only at the close of our entire discussion shall we be able to see the real scope of this last question, and its deeper relations to the problem of Christianity. It is not at all my intent to assume at this stage that the postulate just stated is true, namely, the postulate that the human race has been subject to some genuine process of education, that the ages have taught man some more or less connected lesson, and that the modern man can read this lesson. This first provisional formulation of our problem of Christianity in terms of the relation of Christianity to the creed of the modern man, is intended to direct attention at once to two aspects of our undertaking.

First, Christianity, as I have already pointed out, is, historically speaking, one great result of the effort of mankind to find the way of salvation, and is apparently thus far the most impressive and, in this sense, the greatest result of this very effort. Our problem of Christianity involves some attempt to find out what this great religion most essentially is and means, what its most permanent and indispensable features are. Secondly, our problem of Christianity is the problem of estimating these most permanent and indispensable features of Christianity in the light of what we can learn of the lesson that the religious history of the race, viewed, if possible, as a connected whole, has taught men.

So then, to state our problem of Christianity as a problem about whether the modern man can consistently be, in creed, a Christian, is to use language that seems to refer to the issues of the passing moment, but that at once leads back from the problem of the moment to the problem of the ages, from the modern man to humanity viewed as a whole. More carefully restated, then, our problem of Christianity is this: When we consider what are the most essential features of Christianity, is the acceptance of a creed that embodies these features consistent with the lessons that, so far as we can yet learn, the growth of human wisdom and the course of the ages have taught man regarding religious truth?

Our problem of Christianity is intended to be as now appears, a synthesis of certain philosophical and of certain historical problems. The Christian religion furnishes the topic. This religion is an outcome of a long history and it includes a doctrine about life and about the world. We are to estimate this doctrine, partly in the light of its history, partly in the light of a philosophical study of the meaning and lesson of this history.

V

The first statement of our problem brings next to our minds what is, I suppose, the most familiar issue which any one has to meet who undertakes to define the word "Christianity" in a manner suited to the spirit of recent discussion. This issue requires here a brief preliminary statement.

Christianity has two principal and contrasting characteristics. It is, in the first place, according to its own most ancient and familiar tradition, the religion which was taught and was first lived out, by an individual person, — by a man who dwelt among men, who counselled a mode of living, who aroused and expressed a certain spirit, and who taught that in this spirit, and in this life, the way of salvation is to be found for all men. This first characteristic of Christianity suggests to all of us a view regarding our problem which has been very greatly emphasized in recent discussions of religion, and which consists in asserting that, however deep the problem of Christianity may be, it is, in its essence, an impressively simple problem.

Let us consider for a moment the grounds of this assertion. They are well known. As a religion of a person, appealing to persons regarding the goal and the path of their own lives, Christianity in so far appears as an art of living, as a counsel for the attainment of the ends of human existence. Whatever may be your opinions or your doubts about God and the world and the mysteries of our nature and our destiny, it would in so far seem plausible that, as a modern man, you could reasonably estimate both the Master and his reported solution of the practical problem of human living, and that you could thus decide whether or no you can be in creed a Christian, without considering any very recondite matter. Your decision, "I am in creed a Christian," if, as a modern man, you made such a decision, might mean, from this point of view, simply this: "I find that the example and the personal inspiration of Jesus are for me of supreme value; and my experience shows me that the Christian plan of life promises to me, and to those of like mind with me, the highest spiritual success."

When thus defined, Christianity would mean the teaching, the personal example, and the spirit of the Master. If one's personal experience taught one that this teaching, this example, and this spirit are, from one's own point of view, the solution for the problem of human life, one both could be, and would be, in this sense of the word, in creed a Christian. So at least the assertion just repeated teaches. And if this assertion is true, our problem is essentially a simple problem.

So far I have merely stated a well-known opinion. But whoever thus attempts to simplify the problem of Christianity, can do so only by either ignoring or else minimizing the significance of the second of the two characteristics of the Christian religion, whose existence I have just mentioned. Historically speaking, Christianity has never appeared simply as the religion taught by the Master. It has always been an interpretation of the Master and of his religion in the light of some doctrine concerning his mission, and also concerning God, man, and man's salvation,—a doctrine which, even in its simplest expressions, has always gone beyond what the Master himself is traditionally reported to have taught while he lived.

Whatever the reason why the Master and the interpretation of his person and of his teaching have come to be thus contrasted, it is necessary at once to call attention to the historical fact that such an interpretation of the Master, of his person, and of his mission, always has existed ever since there was any Christian religion at all.

The question is here not one dependent upon our decision as to the trustworthiness or the authenticity of any one tradition. For Christian tradition, in all its forms, has always more or less clearly and extensively distinguished between its own account of the Master, of his sayings, of his deeds, of his personal character, and its own interpretation of his mission, of his dignity, and of the divine purpose that his life accomplished. The Master himself and the interpretation of his mission have thus been from the first contrasted. And they have been contrasted by the very tradition to which we owe the report of both of them. This fact stands in the way of all such attempts to simplify our problem as is the attempt which I have just outlined.

To mention one of the very earliest forms of this contrast between religion as taught by the Master and its later expression. Tradition tells us about sayings in which the Master set forth his teaching. It also tells us of his fortunes,—of his suffering and death. Now, however it was that his teachings were related to the causes that brought about his sufferings and death, any account of these his fortunes inevitably contains some indication of the reasons why, according to tradition, "it was needful that Christ should suffer." But these reasons, as tradition states them, have always included some account of the Master's office and of his mission,—an account which has gone beyond what, during his life, tradition views as having become explicit and manifest to his disciples. While the Master lived, these and these (so the reports run) were his teachings. In these and these deeds he manifested his person and spirit. But only after he had suffered and died, and—as was early reported—had risen again, did there become manifest, according to tradition, what, during his earthly life, could not become plain even to those who were nearest to him.

Thus, I repeat, tradition reports the matter, and thus it contrasts, from the very beginnings of Christian history, the Master to whom this teaching is attributed and the interpretation of his nature and mission, which, according to the same tradition, only his sufferings, his death, his reported resurrection, and the coming of his spirit into a new unity with his disciples, could begin to make manifest. Thus the Master and the interpretation early began to be distinguished. Thus they remain distinguished throughout Christian history.

And thus, for the fictitious being whom I called the "modern man" — for him also, in case he chooses to consider the problem of Christianity at all, it must sooner or later become manifest, I think, that he cannot decide whether or no he is in creed a Christian, without reflecting upon his attitude, both towards the Master and towards the interpretations which history has given to the mission of the Master. To ignore, or even to minimize, the importance of these interpretations, to suppose that Christianity can be viewed simply, or even mainly, as the religion taught during the founder's life by the Master himself, is, I think, to miss the meaning of history to a degree unworthy of the highly developed historical sense which should characterize the "modern man."

The "modern man" may have to decide, in the end, that he is, in creed, no Christian at all, simply because he may have to reject some or all of the interpretations which tradition has asserted to be true of the mission and of the divine relations of the Master. But the modern man will be unable, in my opinion, to be just to his own historical sense and to the genuine history of Christianity, unless he sees that the Christian religion always has been and, historically speaking, must be, not simply a religion taught by any man to any company of disciples, but always also a religion whose sense has consisted, at least in part, in the interpretation which later generations gave to the mission and the nature of the founder. The interpretation may involve a false doctrine of life. If so, and if the modern man thinks so, the modern man cannot consistently be and remain a Christian. But I do not believe that the modern man, when he considers the lesson of the history of Christianity, can long remain content with the view that Christianity is, in its principally effective features, historically reducible to the simple statement of what, according to tradition, the Master taught to those who, while he was alive, heard his words.

VI

Historically speaking, Christianity has, then, these two sharply contrasted aspects. I have said that the issue presented by this contrast is the most familiar one which, at the moment, any one who approaches the problem of Christianity has to meet. You may still ask: But what is this issue? I answer: It is the issue presented by the question: Of these two contrasting aspects of Christianity, which is, not only historically inevitable, but also the deeper, the more essential, the more permanently important aspect?

Now to such a question the history of Christianity, necessary as it is in preparing the way for a decision, cannot alone furnish the final answer. And at this point we are already able to give a reason for asserting that not only history, but the intrinsic nature of the interests which are involved, will require us, in our later lectures, to lay our main stress upon that aspect of Christianity which, in the order of time, came into existence later than the Master's own reported teaching. Let me state this reason at once, dogmatically and quite inadequately, but enough to indicate the course that we are to pursue.

The religion of the Master, as he is said to have taught it, involves many counsels, addressed to the individual man, regarding the art of life and regarding the way of entering what the Master called the Kingdom of Heaven. But these counsels, this preaching of the Kingdom of Heaven, — they appeared, in tradition, as stated in brief outlines and often as expressed in parables. It appears that, at least for the multitudes who listened, often for the disciples themselves, the parables needed interpretation, and that the sayings must be understood in the light of an insight which, at the time when these words were first uttered, was seldom or never in the possession even of those who were nearest to the Master.

This further insight, according to the same tradition, was something that, as was held, would come whenever the Master's spirit was still more fully revealed to his disciples. Often when they heard their Teacher speaking most plainly, the disciples, as we are told, did not yet quite understand what he meant. And now, as a fact, the reported sayings and parables of the founder possess, side by side with their so well-known directness and simplicity, certain equally well known but highly problematic traits which, in all the ages that have since elapsed have led to repeated questions as to what the Master meant by some of the most central doctrines that he taught. For instance, precisely what he taught about the office and work of love, and about self-sacrifice, and about casting off all care for the morrow — such things have often seemed mysterious.

And precisely these more problematic features of the original teachings of the Master are the ones to which the later Christian community gave interpretations that it believed to be due to the guidance of the Master's spirit, and that it therefore inevitably connected with its doctrine regarding his own person and his mission. Since these later interpretations have to do with matters that the original sayings and parables, so far as reported, leave more or less problematic, so as to challenge further inquiry; and since all these more problematic matters are indeed of central importance for the whole estimate of the Christian doctrine of life, we may indeed have to recognize that the primitive Christianity of the sayings of the Master was both enriched and deepened by the interpretation which the Christian community gave to his person, to his work, and to his whole religion. I believe this to be the case.

Our later discussion will set forth some of the further reasons for this opinion. These lectures will not be concerned with the history of dogma; and all our discussions concerning the truth of Christianity will be guided by an interest rather in the essentials of religion than in any of the refinements of theology. But it will be one of my theses that the essential ideas of Christianity include doctrines which indeed supplement, but which at the same time in spirit fulfil, the view of life and of salvation which the original teaching of the Master regarding the Kingdom of Heaven, as that teaching is reported by tradition, made known to those who heard him.

It will help our enterprise if, at this point, I simply state what, in my opinion, are the Christian ideas which both the history of Christianity, and the intrinsic importance of the religious concerns involved, will make it most needful for us to consider, for the sake of a fair comprehension of the problem of Christianity. These central Christian ideas, as I shall here name them and shall later discuss them, are three. They are all of them ideas that came to the mind of the Christian world in the course of later efforts to explain the true meaning of the original teaching regarding the Kingdom of Heaven. The Christian community regarded them as due to the guidance of the founder's spirit; but was also aware that, when they first came to light, they involved new features, which the reported sayings and parables of the Master had not yet made so explicit as they afterwards became. The Spirit which, as the early church came to believe, was in due time to guide the faithful to all truth, was held to be the interpreter who revealed these new things. Our own main interest is here not in the theological aspect of the development which led to these ideas. What concerns us is that these ideas actually appeared in the Christian community as an interpretation of what the founder had meant, while, as we shall later more clearly see, they came to constitute vital and essential portions of the religious message which Christianity had for mankind.

VII

We may be aided in our selection of these three central ideas by mentioning the fact that certain features of the founder's reported teaching of the Kingdom of Heaven have generally seemed, to later ages, to stand in need of an interpretation which the founder's recorded words did not wholly furnish. The three ideas here in question were first developed in the mind of the Christian community in the midst of the early efforts to reach this further interpretation of what the founder had meant by the words that were attributed to him by tradition.

The Master's teachings are, for the most part, directed, in his reported sayings, to individual men,—either to some one individual viewed as a typical man ("Thou shalt love thy neighbor as thyself"), or to companies of individuals viewed as of such nature that the same counsel applies equally to any or to all of these individuals alike ("Blessed are the meek;" "Be ye perfect as your Father in heaven is perfect"). Meanwhile, the Master freely speaks of what he calls the Kingdom of Heaven. And the Kingdom of Heaven appears, on its very face, to be some sort of social order, some sort of collective life, some kind of community. Yet the reported sayings do not, when taken by themselves, make perfectly explicit what that social order, what that community, is to which the name Kingdom of Heaven is intended to apply. Tradition represents the earliest interpretation of the term by the Disciples of Christ themselves, while he was yet speaking to them, as, in their own minds, more or less doubtful. Was the Master's kingdom to be of this world, or of some other? Was it to be a more or less visible political social order? Was it to be wholly a matter of the inner spiritual lives of many outwardly separate individuals ("The Kingdom of Heaven is within you").

Plainly, whatever the doctrine of the Kingdom really meant, its first expression was such as to call for a further development, and for a richer interpretation than any one of the parables of the Kingdom, as originally reported, gave to it. The doctrine of the Kingdom was at once simple, direct, personal, and deep, mysterious, prophetic of something yet to be disclosed. And herewith we at once remind ourselves how the Christian community, living, as it believed, in and through the spirit of the Master, was early led to develop the doctrine of the Kingdom into the doctrine of the Christian Church.

When, however, we consider, not the historical accidents and not the external show, but rather the deeper spirit of this doctrine about the Christian Church, we are led to look beyond, or beneath, all the special dogmas and forms in which the opinion and the practice of the historical Christian Church has found in various ages a manifold and often a very imperfect expression. And we are also led to state, as the inner and deeper sense of the whole process of the history of the Church, the first of the three ideas of Christianity,— which will hereafter guide our study.

And we may here state this first Christian idea in our own words thus, namely, as the doctrine that "The salvation of the individual man is determined by some sort of membership in a certain spiritual community,—a religious community and, in its inmost nature, a divine community, in whose life the Christian virtues are to reach their highest expression and the spirit of the Master is to obtain its earthly fulfilment." In other words: There is a certain universal and divine spiritual community. Membership in that community is necessary to the salvation of man.

I propose, in our later lectures, to consider, not the history and not, in any detail, the dogmas of the Christian Church, but the meaning, the foundation, the truth of this first of our three Christian ideas, —the idea of the divinely significant spiritual community of the faithful,—the idea that such a community exists, and is needed, and is an indispensable means of salvation for the individual man, and is the fitting realm wherein alone the Kingdom of Heaven which the Master preached can find its expression, and wherein alone the Christian virtues can be effectively practised. We are to ask, What is the foundation of this idea? What does it mean? In essence, is it a true idea? In what sense does it retain its meaning and its value today, and for the modern man, and (in so far as we can foresee) in what way is it destined to guide the future? This inquiry will constitute an essential part of our study of the Problem of Christianity.

The mention of this first of the three Christian ideas leads me at once to the mention of two other ideas. These two stand in the closest correlation with this first idea and with each other, and share with the first a character to which, as we shall later see, the mystery, the elementally human significance, and the beauty of the problem of Christianity are all of them due. Both of these ideas grew up because, in the preaching of the Kingdom of Heaven, the Master appealed to the individual man, but left certain aspects of this appeal mysterious, so that the question, What is the nature and the worth of the individual man? was left a matter of serious heart searching.

The second of our three ideas seems at first sharply contrasted with the gentle and hopeful spirit of some of the Master's best-known and most-loved statements. We shall later see, however, the deeper connection of this second idea with what the Master taught about the individual man. It is the grave, yes, the tragic idea that can be stated, in the form of a doctrine, thus: "The individual human being is by nature subject to some overwhelming moral burden from which, if unaided, he cannot escape." This burden is at once a natural inheritance and a burden of personal guilt. Both because of what has technically been called original sin, and because of the sins that he himself has committed, the individual is doomed to a spiritual ruin from which only a divine intervention can save him. The individual, as Paul first stated the case, is, apart from divine grace, "dead in trespasses and sins." His salvation, if it occurs at all, must involve a quickening,—a raising of the dead.

Thus tragic, thus strangely opposed in seeming to the more comforting and hopeful of the parables of the founder, thus also very sharply contrasted with some of our now most favorite modern doctrines concerning the moral dignity of human nature, and concerning the course of the natural evolution of man from lower to higher spiritual stages,—thus paradoxical is the second of the three Christian ideas that, in our latter discussion, we shall emphasize. The first of the three central ideas involves, as we just saw, the assertion that the way of salvation lies in the union of the individual with a certain universal spiritual community. The second of these ideas, the idea of the moral burden of the individual, includes the doctrine that of himself, and apart from the spiritual community which the divine plan provides for his relief, the individual is powerless to escape from his innate and acquired character, the character of a lost soul, or, in Paul's phrase, of a dead man, who is by inheritance tainted, and is also by his own deeds involved in hopeless guilt. You may well ask: Can the modern man make anything of such an idea? This question, as we shall see, is a very significant part of our problem of Christianity.

The third leading idea of Christianity which we shall have to consider is the one that many modern minds regard as the strangest, as the most hopelessly problematic, of the three. It is also the one whose relation to the original teachings of the Master seems most problematic. It is the idea expressed by the assertion: The only escape for the individual, the only union with the divine spiritual community which he can obtain, is provided by the divine plan for the redemption of mankind. And this plan is one which includes an Atonement for the sins and for the guilt of mankind. This atonement, and this alone, makes possible the entrance of the individual into a saving union with the divine spiritual community, and reveals the full meaning of what the Master meant by the Kingdom of Heaven. Without atonement, no salvation. And the divine plan has in fact provided and accomplished the atoning work.

VIII

The idea of the spiritual community in union with which man is to win salvation, the idea of the hopeless and guilty burden of the individual when unaided by divine grace, the idea of the atonement, —these are, for our purposes, the three central ideas of Christianity. Of these ideas the second, and still more the third, seems, at first sight, especially foreign to the modern mind, as most of us conceive that mind; and all three appear to be due to interpretations of the mind of the Master which came into existence only after his earthly period of teaching had ceased. The discussion of the meaning and the truth of each of these three ideas is to constitute our proposed contribution to the Problem of Christianity. The justification of our enterprise lies in the fact that, familiar as these three ideas are, they are still almost wholly misunderstood, both by the apologists who view them in the light of traditional dogmas, and by the critics who assail the letter of dogmas, but who fail to grasp the spirit.

We have in outline stated how we define this Problem of Christianity. We have enumerated three ideas which we are to regard as the essential ideas of Christianity. We have indicated the method that we are to follow in discussing these ideas and in grasping and in attempting to clarify our problem. Our method is to consist in an union of an effort to read the lesson of history with an effort to estimate, upon a reasonable basis, the philosophy of the Christian religion. Already, even in our opening statement, we have endeavored to illustrate this union of historical summary with philosophical reflection.

II

The Idea
of the
Universal Community

In accordance with the plan set forth at the close of our first lecture, we begin our study of the Problem of Christianity by a discussion of the Christian idea of the Church, and of its universal mission.

I

The Kingdom of Heaven, as characterized in the Sermon on the Mount and in the parables, is something that promises to the individual man salvation, and that also possesses, in some sense which the Master left for the future to make clearer, a social meaning. To the individual the doctrine says, "The Kingdom of Heaven is within you." But when in the end the Kingdom shall come, the will of God, as we learn, is to be done on earth as it is in heaven. And therewith the kingdoms of this world—the social order as it now is and as it naturally is—will pass away. Then there will come to pass the union of the blessed with their Father, and also, as appears, with

75

one another, in the heavenly realm which the Father has prepared for them.

This final union of all who love is not described at length in the recorded words of the Master. A religious imagery familiar to those who heard the parables that deal with the end of the world was freely used; and this imagery gives us to understand that the consummation of all things will unite in a heavenly community those who are saved. But the organization, the administration, the ranks and dignities, of the Kingdom of Heaven the Master does not describe.

When the Christian Church began, in the Apostolic Age, to take visible form, the idea of the mission of the Church expressed the meaning which the Christian community came to attach to the social implications of the founder's doctrine. What was merely hinted in the parables now became explicit. The Kingdom of Heaven was to be realized in and through and for the Church, — in the fellowship of the faithful who constituted the Church as it was on earth; through the divine Spirit that was believed to guide the life of the Church; and for the future experience of the Church, whenever the end should come, and whenever the purpose of God should finally be manifested and accomplished.

Such, in brief, was the teaching of the early Christian community. Unquestionably this teaching added something new to the original doctrine of the Kingdom. But this addition, as we shall later see, was more characteristic of the new religion than was any portion of the sayings that tradition attributed to the Master, and was as inseparable from the essence of primitive Christianity as the belief of the disciples themselves was inseparable from their very earliest interpretations of the person and the mission of their leader.

It is useless, I think, for the most eager defender and expounder of primitive Christianity in its purity to ignore the fact that, whatever else the Christian religion involves, some sort of faith or doctrine regarding the office and the meaning of the Church was an essential part of the earliest Christianity that existed after the founder had passed from earth.

Since our problem of Christianity involves the study of the most vital Christian ideas, how can we better begin our task than by asking what this idea of the Church really means, and what value and truth it possesses? Not only is such a beginning indeed advisable, but, at first sight, it seems especially adapted to enable us to use the manifold and abundant aids which, as we might suppose, the aspirations of all Christian ages would furnish for our guidance.

For, as you may naturally ask, is not the history of Christianity, viewed in at least one very significant way, simply the history of the Christian Church? Is not the idea of the Church, then, not only essential and potent, but one of the most familiar of the religious ideas of Christendom? Must not the consciousness of all really awakened Christian communities whose creeds are recorded stand ready to help the inquirer who wants to interpret this idea? May we not then begin this part of our enterprise with high hope, sure that, as we attempt to grasp and to estimate this first of our three essential Christian ideas, we shall have the ages of Christian development as our helpers? So, I repeat, you may very naturally ask. But the answer to this question is not such as quite fulfils the hope just suggested.

II

As a fact, the idea and the doctrine of the Christian Church constitute indeed a vital and permanent part of Christianity; and a study of this idea is a necessary, and may properly be the first, part of our inquiry into the Problem of Christianity.

But we must not begin this inquiry without a due sense of its difficulty. We must remember at the very outset the fact that all the Christian ages, up to the present one, unite, not to present to us any finished interpretation of the idea of the Church, but rather to prove that this idea is as fluent in its expression as it is universal in its aim; and is as baffling, by reason of the conflicts of its interpreters, as it is precious in the longings that constitute its very heart.

If this idea comforts the faithful, it is also a stern idea; for it demands of those who accept it the resolute will to face and to contend against the greatest of spiritual obstacles, namely, the combined waywardness of the religious caprices of all Christian mankind. For the true Church, as we shall see, is still a sort of ideal challenge to the faithful, rather than an already finished institution,—a call upon men for a heavenly quest, rather than a present possession of humanity. "Create me,"—this is the word that the Church, viewed as an idea, addresses to mankind.

Meanwhile the contrast between the letter and the spirit of a fundamental doctrine is nowhere more momentous and more tragic than in case of the doctrine of the nature and the office of the Christian Church. The spirit of this doctrine consists, as we have already seen, in the assertion that there is a certain divinely ordained and divinely significant spiritual community, to which all must belong who are to attain the true goal of life; that is, all who, to use the distinctly religious phraseology, are to be saved.

How profoundly reasonable are the considerations upon which this doctrine is based we have yet to see, and can only estimate in the light of a due study of all the essential Christian ideas. To my own mind these considerations are such as can be interpreted and defended without our needing, for the purposes of such interpretation and defence, any acceptance of traditional dogmas. For these considerations are based upon human nature. They have to do with interests which all reasonable men, whether Christian or non-Christian, more or less clearly recognize, in proportion as men advance to the higher stages of the art of life.

The spirit, then, of the doctrine of the Church is as reasonable as it is universal. It is Christian by virtue of features which, when once understood, also render it simply and impressively human. This, I say, is what our entire study of the three Christian ideas will, in the end, if I am right, bring to our attention.

III

But the letter of the doctrine of the Church has been subject to fortunes such as, in various ways and degrees, attend the visible embodiment of all the great ideals of humanity; only that, as I have just said, the resulting tragedy is, in no other case in which spirit and letter are in conflict, greater than in this case.

In general the risks of temporary disaster which great ideals run appear to be directly proportioned to the value of the ideals. The disasters may be destined to give place to victory; but great truths bear long sorrows. What humanity most needs, it most persistently misunderstands. The spirit of a great ideal may be immortal; its ultimate victory, as we may venture to maintain, may be predetermined by the very nature of things; but that fact does not save such an ideal from the fires of the purgatory of time. Its very preciousness often seems to insure its repeated, its long-enduring, effacement. The comfort that it would bring if it were fully understood and accepted may make all the greater the sorrow of a world that still waits for the light.

In case of the history of the essential idea of the Church, the complications of dogma, the strifes of the sects, the horrors of the religious wars in former centuries, the confusions of controversy in our own day, must not make us despair. Such is the warfare of ideals. Such is this present world.

Least of all may we attempt, as many do, to accuse this or that special tendency or power in the actual Church, past or present, of being mainly responsible for this failure to appreciate the ideal Church. The defect lies deeper than students of such problems usually suppose. Human nature, — not any one party, — yes, the very nature of the processes of growth themselves, and not any particular form of religious or of moral error, must be viewed as the source of the principal tragedies of the history of all the Christian ideals.

In fact, the true idea of the Church has not been forsaken; it is, in a very real sense, still to be found, or rather, to be created. We have to do, in this case, not so much with apostasy as with evolution. To be sure, at the very outset, the ideal of the Church was seen afar off through a glass, darkly. The well-known apocalyptic vision revealed the true Church as the New Jerusalem that was yet to come down from heaven. The expression of the idea was left, by the early Church, as a task for the ages. The spirit of that idea was felt rather than ever adequately formulated, and the vision still remains one of the principal grounds and sources of the hope of humanity.

IV

Such doctrines, and such conflicts of spirit and letter, cannot be understood unless our historical sense is well awakened. On the other hand, they cannot be understood *merely* through a study of history. The values of ideals must be ideally discerned. If viewed without a careful and critical reflection, the history of such processes as the development of the idea of the Church presents a chaos of contending motives and factions. Apart from some understanding of history, all critical reflection upon this idea remains an unfruitful exercise in dialectics. We must therefore first divide our task, and then reunite the results, hoping thereby to win a connected view of the ideal that constitutes our present problem.

Let us, then, first point out certain motives which, when considered quite apart from any specifically Christian ideas or doctrines, may serve to make intelligible the ideal which is here in question. Then let us sketch the way in which the idea of the Christian Church first received expression.

This first expression of the idea of the Church, as we shall find, transformed the very teaching which it most eloquently reënforced and explained, namely, the teaching which the parables of the founder had left for the faith of the Christian community to interpret. This was the teaching about the office and the saving power of Christian love. For such, as we shall see, was the first result of the appearance of the idea of the Church in Christian history.

By sketching, then, some non-Christian developments and then a stage of early Christian life, we shall get two aspects of the ideal of the universal community before us. Hereby we shall not have reached any solution of our problem of Christianity; but we shall have brought together in our minds certain Christian and certain non-Christian ideas whose interrelations will hereafter prove to be of the utmost importance of our whole enterprise.

Next in order, then, comes a brief review of some of those motives which, apart from Christian history and Christian doctrine, make the ideal of the universal community a rationally significant ideal. These motives, in their turn, are of two kinds. Some of them are motives derived from the natural history of mankind. Some of them are distinctively ethical motives. We must become acquainted, through a very general summary, with both of these sorts of motives. Both sorts have interacted. The nature of man as a social being suggests certain ethical ideals. These ideals, in their turn, have modified the natural history of society.

V

As an essentially social being, man lives in communities, and depends upon his communities for all that makes his civilization articulate. His communities, as both Plato and Aristotle already observed, have a sort of organic life of their own, so that we can compare a highly developed community, such as a state, either to the soul of a man or to a living animal. A community is not a mere collection of individuals. It is a sort of live unit, that has organs, as the body of an individual has organs. A community grows or decays, is healthy or diseased, is young or aged, much as any individual member of the community possesses such characters. Each of the two, the community or the individual member, is as much a live creature as is the other. Not only does the community live, it has a mind of its own, — a mind whose psychology is not the same as the psychology of an individual human being. The social mind displays its psychological traits in its characteristic products, — in languages, in customs, in religions,—products which an individual human mind, or even a collection of such minds, when they are not somehow organized into a genuine community, cannot produce. Yet language, custom, religion are all of them genuinely mental products.

Communities, in their turn, tend, under certain conditions, to be organized into composite communities of still higher and higher grades. States are united in empires; languages cooperate in the production of universal literature; the corporate entities of many communities tend to organize that still very incomplete community which, if ever it comes into existence, will be the world-state, the community possessing the whole world's civilization.

So far, I have spoken only of the natural history of the social organization, and not of its value. But the history of thought shows how manifold are the ways in which, if once you grant that a community is or can be a living organic being, with a mind of its own, this doctrine about the natural facts can be used for ideal, for ethical, purposes. Few ideas have been, in fact, more fruitful than this one in their indirect consequences for ethical doctrines as well as for religion.

It is no wonder, then, that many object to every such interpretation of the nature of a community by declaring that, whatever our ethical ideals may demand, a community really has no mind of its own at all, and is no living organism. All the foregoing statements about the mind of a community (as such objectors insist) are metaphorical. A community is a collection of individuals. And the comparison of a community to an animal, or to a soul, is at best a convenient fiction.

Other critics, not so much simply rejecting the foregoing doctrine as hesitating, remark that to call a community an organism, and to speak of its possession of a mind, is to use some form of philosophical mysticism. And such mysticism, they say, stands, in any case, in need of further interpretation.

To such objectors I shall here only reply that one can maintain all the foregoing views regarding the real organic life and regarding the genuine mind of a community, without committing one's self to any form of philosophical mysticism, and without depending upon mere metaphors. For instance, Wundt, in his great book entitled "Volkerpsychologie," treats organized communities as psychical entities. He does so deliberately, and states his reasons. But he does all this purely as a psychologist. Communities, as he insists, behave as if they were wholes, and exhibit psychological laws of their own. Following Wundt, I have already said that it is the community which produces languages, customs, religions. These are, all of them, intelligent mental products, which can be psychologically analyzed, which follow psychological laws, and which exhibit characteristic processes of mental evolution,— processes that belong solely to organized groups of men. So Wundt speaks unhesitatingly of the *Gesammtbewusstsein*, or *Gesammtwille*, of a community; and he finds this mental life of the community to be as much an object for the student of the natural history of mind, as is the consciousness of any being whose life a psychologist can examine. His grounds are not mystical, but empirical,— if you will, pragmatic. A community behaves like an entity with a mind of its own. Therefore it is a fair "working hypothesis" for the psychologist to declare that it is such an entity, and that a community has, or is, a mind.

VI

So far, then, I have merely sketched what, in another context, will hereafter concern us much more at length. For in later lectures we shall have to study the metaphysical problems which we here first touch. A community can be viewed as a real unity. So we have seen, and so far only we have yet gone.

But we have now to indicate why this conception, whether metaphysically sound or not, is a conception that can be ethical in its purposes. And here again only the most elementary and fundamental aspects of our topic can be, in this wholly preparatory statement, mentioned. To all these problems we shall have later to return.

We have said that a community can behave like an unit; we have now to point out that an individual member of a community can find numerous very human motives for behaving towards his community as if it not only were an unit, but a very precious and worthy being. In particular he — the individual member — may love his community as if it were a person, may be devoted to it as if it were his friend or father, may serve it, may live and die for it, and may do all this, not because the philosophers tell him to do so, but because it is his own heart's desire to act thus.

Of such active attitudes of love and devotion towards a community, on the part of an individual member of that community, history and daily life present countless instances. One's family, one's circle of personal friends, one's home, one's village community, one's clan, or one's country may be the object of such an active disposition to love and to serve the community as an unit, to treat the community as if it were a sort of super-personal being, and as if it could, in its turn, possess the value of a person on some higher level. One who thus loves a community, regards its type of life, its form of being, as essentially more worthy than his own. He becomes devoted to its interests as to something that by its very nature is nobler than himself. In such a case he may find, in his devotion to his community, his fulfilment and his moral destiny. In order to view a community in this way it is, I again insist, not necessary to be a mystic. It is only necessary to be a hearty friend, or a good citizen, or a home-loving being.

Countless faithful and dutifully disposed souls, belonging to most various civilizations,—people active rather than fanciful, and earnest rather than speculative,—have in fact viewed their various communities in this way. I know of no better name for such a spirit of active devotion to the community to which the devoted individual belongs, than the excellent old word "Loyalty,"—a word to whose deeper meaning some Japanese thinkers have of late years recalled our attention.

Loyalty, as I have elsewhere defined it, is the willing and thorough-going devotion of a self to a cause, when the cause is something which unites many selves in one, and which is therefore the interest of a community. For a loyal human being the interest of the community to which he belongs is superior to every merely individual interest of his own. He actively devotes himself to this cause.[1]

Loyalty exists in very manifold shapes, and belongs to no one time, or country, or people. Warlike tribes and nations, during the stages of their life which are intermediate between savagery and civilization, have often developed a high type of the loyal consciousness, and hence have defined their virtues in terms of loyalty. Such loyalty may last over into peaceful stages of social life; and the warlike life is not the exclusive originator of the loyal spirit. Loyalty often enters into a close alliance with religion, and from its very nature is disposed to religious interpretations. To the individual the loyal spirit appeals by fixing his attention upon a life incomparably vaster than his own individual life,—a life which, when his love for his community is once aroused, dominates and fascinates him by the

[1]See Lecture I of the "Philosophy of Loyalty" (New York, 1908).

relative steadiness, the strength and fixity and stately dignity, of its motives and demands.

The individual is naturally wayward and capricious. This waywardness is a constant source of entanglement and failure. But the community which he loves is rendered relatively constant in its will by its customs; yet these customs no longer seem, to the loyal individual, mere conventions or commands. For his social enthusiasm is awakened by the love of his kind; and he glories in his service, as the player in his team, or the soldier in his flag, or the martyr in his church. If his religion comes into touch with his loyalty, then his gods are the leaders of his community, and both the majesty and the harmony of the loyal life are thus increased. The loyal motives are thus not only moral, but also æsthetic. The community may be to the individual both beautiful and sublime.

Deep-seated, then, in human nature are the reasons that make loyalty appear to the individual as a solution for the problem of his personal life. Yet these motives tend to still higher and vaster conquests than we have here yet mentioned. Warlike tribes and nations fight together; and in so far loyalty contends with loyalty. But on a more highly self-conscious level the loyal spirit tends to assume the form of chivalry. The really devoted and considerate warrior learns to admire the loyalty of his foe; yes, even to depend upon it for some of his own best inspiration. Knighthood prizes the knightly spirit. The loyalty of the clansmen breeds by contagion a more intense loyalty in other clans; but at the same time it breeds a love for just such loyalty. Kindred clans learn to respect and, ere long, to share one another's loyalty. The result is an ethical motive that renders the alliance and, on occasion, the union of various clans and nationalities not only a possibility, but a conscious ideal.

The loyal are, in ideal, essentially kin. If they grow really wise, they observe this fact. The spirit that loves the community learns to prize itself as a spirit that, in all who are dominated by it, is essentially one, despite the variety of special causes, of nationalities, or of customs. The logical development of the loyal spirit is therefore the rise of a consciousness of the ideal of an universal community of the loyal,—a community which, despite all warfare and jealousy, and despite all varieties of gods and of laws, is supreme in its value, however remote from the present life of civilization.

The tendency towards the formation of such an ideal of an universal community can be traced both in the purely secular forms of loyalty, and in the history of the relations between loyalty and religion in the most varied civilizations. In brief, loyalty is, from the first, a practical faith that communities, viewed as units, have a value which is superior to all the values and interests of detached individuals. And the sort of loyalty which reaches the level of true chivalry and which loves the honor and the loyalty of the stranger or even of the foe, tends, either in company with or apart from any further religious motives, to lead men towards a conception of the brotherhood of all the loyal, and towards an estimation of all the values of life in terms of their relation to the service of one ideally universal community. To this community in ideal all men belong; and to act as if one were a member of such a community is to win in the highest measure the goal of individual life. It is to win what religion calls salvation.

When thus abstractly stated, the ideal of an universal community may appear far away from the ordinary practical interests of the plain man. But the history of the spirit of loyalty shows that there is a strong tendency of loyalty towards such universal ideals. Some such conception of the ideal community of all mankind, actually resulting from reflection upon the spirit of loyalty, received an occasional and imperfect formulation in Roman Stoicism. In this more speculative shape the Stoic conception of the universal community was indeed not fitted to win over the Roman world as a whole to an active loyalty to the cause of mankind.

Yet the conception of universal loyalty, as devotion to the unity of an ideal community, a community whereof all loyal men should be members, has not been left merely to the Stoics, nor yet to any other philosophers to formulate. The conception of loyalty both springs from practical interests and tends of itself, apart from speculation, towards the enlargement of the ideal community of the loyal in the direction of identifying that community with all mankind. The history of the ideals and of the religion of Israel, from the Song of Deborah to the prophets, is a classic instance of the process here in question.

VII

We have thus indicated some of the fundamentally human motives which the ideal of the universal community expresses. We have next to turn in a wholly different direction and to remind ourselves of the way in which this ideal found its place in the early history of the Christian Church.

I cannot better introduce this part of my discussion than by calling attention to a certain contrast between the reported teaching of the Master regarding the Kingdom of Heaven, and some of the best-known doctrines of the Apostle Paul. This contrast is as obvious and as familiar as it has been neglected by students of the philosophy of Christianity. Every word that I can say about it is old. Yet a survey of the whole matter is not common, and I believe that this contrast has never more demanded a clear restatement than it does today.

The particular contrast which I here have in mind is *not* the one which both the apologists and the critics of Pauline Christianity usually emphasize. It is a contrast which does not directly relate to Paul's doctrine of the person and mission of Christ; and nevertheless it is a contrast that bears upon the very core of the Gospel. For it is a contrast that has to do with the doctrine about the nature, the office, the saving power of Christian love itself. I say that just this contrast between Paul's doctrine and the teachings of Jesus, although perfectly familiar, has been neglected by students of our problem. Let me briefly show what I have in mind.

The best-known and, for multitudes, the most directly moving of the words which tradition attributes to Jesus, describe the duty of man, the essence of religion, and the Kingdom of Heaven itself, in terms of the conception of Christian love. I have not here either the time or the power adequately to expound this the chief amongst the doctrines which tradition ascribes directly to Jesus. I must pass over what countless loving and fit teachers have made so familiar. Yet I must remind you of two features of Christ's doctrine of love which at this point especially concern our own enterprise.

First, it is needful for me to point out that, despite certain stubborn and widespread misunderstandings, the Christian doctrine of love, as that doctrine appears in the parables and in the Sermon on the Mount, involves and emphasizes a very positive and active and heroic attitude toward life, and is not, as some have supposed, a negative doctrine of passive self-surrender. And secondly, I must also bring to your attention the fact that the Master's teaching about love leaves unsolved certain practical problems, problems which this very heroism and this positive tendency of the doctrine make by contrast all the more striking.

These unsolved problems of the reported teaching of Jesus about love seem to have been deliberately brought before us by the

Master, and as deliberately left unsolved. The way was thus opened for a further development of what the Master chose to teach. And such further development was presumably a part of what the founder more or less consciously foresaw and intended.

The grain of mustard seed — so his faith assured him — must grow. To that end it was planted. Now a part of the new growth, a contribution to the treatment of the problems which the original teaching about love left unsolved, was, in the sequel, due to Paul. This sequel, whether the Master foresaw it or not, is as important for the further office of Christianity as the original teaching was an indispensable beginning of the process. Jesus awaited in trust a further revelation of the Father's mind. Such a new light came in due season.

Two features, then, of the doctrine of love as taught by Jesus, — its impressively positive and active character, and the mystery of its unsolved problems, — these two we must next emphasize. Then we shall be ready to take note of a further matter which also concerns us, — namely, Paul's new contribution to the solution of the very problems concerning love which the parables and the sayings of Jesus had left unsolved. This new contribution, — Paul himself conceived not as his own personal invention. For he held that the new teaching was due to the spirit of his risen and ascended Lord. What concerns us is that Paul's additional thought was a critical influence in determining both the evolution and the permanent meaning of Christianity.

VIII

The love which Jesus preached has often been misunderstood. Critics, as well as mistaken friends of the Master's teachings, have supposed Christian love to be more or less completely identical with self-abnegation, — with the amiably negative virtue of one who, as the misleading modern phrase expresses the matter, "has no thought of self." Another modern expression, also misleading, is used by some who identify Christian love with so-called "pure altruism." The ideal Christian, as such people interpret his virtue, "lives wholly for others." That is what is meant by the spirit which resists not evil, which turns the other cheek to the smiter, which forgives, and pities, and which abandons all worldly goods.

Now, against such misunderstandings, many of the wiser expounders of Christian doctrine, both in former times and in our own, have taken pains to show that love, as the Jesus of the sayings and of the parables conceived it, does *not* consist in mere self-abnegation, and is not identical with pure altruism, and is both heroic and positive. The feature of the Master's doctrine of love which renders this more positive and heroic interpretation of the sayings inevitable, is the familiar reason which is laid at the basis of his whole teaching. One is to love one's neighbor because God himself, as Father, divinely loves and prizes each individual man. Hence the individual man has an essentially infinite value, although he has this value only in and through his relation to God, and because of God's love for him. Therefore mere self-abnegation cannot be the central virtue. For the Jesus of the sayings not only rejoices in the divine love whereof every man is the object, but also invites every man to rejoice in the consciousness of this very love, and to delight also in all men, since they are God's beloved. The man whom this love of God is to transform into a perfect lover cannot henceforth merely forget or abandon the self. The parable of the servant who, although himself forgiven by his Lord, will not forgive his fellow-servant, shows indeed how worthless self-assertion is when separated from a sense that all are equally dependent upon God's love. But the parable of the talents shows with equal clearness how stern the demands of the divine love are in requiring the individual to find a perfectly positive expression of the unique value which it is his office, and his alone, to return to his Lord with usury. Every man, this self included, has just such an unique value, and must be so viewed. Hence the sayings are full of calls to self-expression, and so to heroism. Love is divine; and therefore it includes an assertion of its own divinity; and therefore it can never be mere self-abnegation. Christian altruism never takes the form of saying, "I myself ought to be or become nothing; while only the others are to be served and saved." For the God who loves me demands not that I should be nothing, but that I should be his own. Love is never merely an amiable tolerance of whatever form human frailty and folly may take. To be sure, the lover, as Jesus depicts him, resists not evil, and turns his cheek to the smiter. Yes, but he does this with full confidence that God sees all and will vindicate his servant. The lover vividly anticipates the positive triumph of all the righteous; and so his love for even the least of the little ones is, in anticipation, an active and strenuous sharing in the final victory of God's will. His very non-resistance is therefore inspired by a divine contempt for the powers of evil. Why should one resist who always has on his side and in his favor the power that is irresistible, that loves him, and that will triumph even through his weakness?

Such a spirit renders pity much more than a mere absorption in attempting to relieve the misery of others. Sympathy for the sufferer, as the sayings of Jesus depict it, is but an especially pathetic illustration of one's serene confidence that the Father who cares for all triumphs over all evil, so that when we feel pity and act pitfully, we take part in this divine triumph. Hence pity is no mere tenderness. It is a sharing in the victory that overcomes the world.

Such, then, in brief, is the doctrine of Christian love as the sayings and the parables contain it, — a doctrine as positive and strenuous as it is humane, and as it is sure of the Father's good will and overruling power. So far I indeed merely remind you of what all the wiser expounders of Christian doctrine, whatever their theology or their disagreements, have, on the whole, and despite popular misunderstandings, agreed in recognizing. And hereupon you might well be disposed to ask: Is not this, in spirit and in essence, the deepest meaning, — yes, is it not really the whole of Christianity? What did Paul do, what could he do, when he spoke of love, but repeat this, the Master's doctrine?

IX

In answer to this question, we must next note that, over against this clear and positive definition of the spiritual attitude that Jesus attributes to the Christian lover, there stand certain problems which come to mind when we ask for more precise directions regarding what the lover is to do for the object of his love. Love is concerned not only with the lover's inner inspiration, but with the services that he is to perform for the beloved. Now, in the world in which the teaching of Jesus places the Christian lover, love has two objects, — God and one's neighbor. What is one to do in order to express one's love for each of these objects?

So far as concerns the lover's relation to God, the answer is clear, and is stated wholly in religious terms. Purity of heart in loving, perfect sincerity and complete devotion, the heroism of spirit just described, — these, with complete trust in God, with utter submission to the Father's will, — these are the services that the lover can render to God. In these there is no merit; for they are as nothing in comparison with one's debt to the Father. But they are required. And in so far the doctrine of love is made explicit and the rule of righteousness is definite.

But now let us return to the relation of love to the services that one is to offer to one's neighbor. What can the lover, — in so far as Jesus describes his task, — what can he do for his fellow-man?

To this question it is, indeed, possible to give one answer which clearly defines a duty to the neighbor; and this duty is emphasized throughout the teaching of Jesus. This duty is the requirement to use all fitting means, — example, precept, kindliness, non-resistance, heroism, patience, courage, strenuousness, — all means that tend to make the neighbor himself one of the lovers. The first duty of love is to produce love, to nourish it, to extend the Kindom of Heaven by teaching love to all men. And *this* service to one's neighbor is a clearly definable service. And so far the love of the neighbor involves no unsolved problems.

But in sharp contrast with this aspect of the doctrine of love stands another aspect, which is indeed problematic. In addition to the extension of the loving spirit through example and precept, the lover of his neighbor has on his hands the whole problem of humane and benevolent practical activity, — the problem of the positively philanthropic life.

The doctrine of love, — so positive, so active, so resolute in its inmost spirit, — might naturally be expected to give in detail counsel regarding what to do for the personal needs of the lover's fellow-man. But, at this point, we indeed meet the more baffling side of the doctrine of love. Jesus has no system of rules to expound for guiding the single acts of the philanthropic life. Apart from insisting upon the loving spirit, apart from the one rule to extend the Kingdom of Heaven and to propagate this spirit of love among men, the Master leaves the practical decisions of the lover to be guided by loving instinct rather than by a conscious doctrine regarding what sort of special good one can do to one's neighbor.

Thus the original doctrine of love, as taught in the parables, involves no definite programme for social reform, and leaves us in the presence of countless unsolved practical issues. This is plainly a deliberate limitation to which the Master chose to subject his explanations about love.

Jesus tells us of many conditions that appear necessary to the practical living of the life of love for one's neighbor. But when we ask: Are these conditions not only necessary but sufficient? we are often left in doubt. Love relieves manifest suffering, when it can; love feeds the hungry, clothes the naked; — in brief, love seems, at first sight, simply to offer to the beloved neighbor whatever that neighbor himself most desires. It is easy to interpret the golden rule in this simple way. Yet we know, and the author of the parables well knows and often tells us, that the natural man desires many things that he ought not to desire and that love ought not to give him. Since the life is more than meat, it also follows that feeding the hungry and clothing the naked are not acts which really supply what man most needs. The natural man does not know his own true needs. Hence the golden rule does not tell us in detail what to do for him, but simply expresses the spirit of love. What is sure about love is that it indeed unites the lover, in spirit, to God's will. What constitutes, in this present world, the pathos, the tragedy of love, is that, because our neighbor is so mysterious a being to our imperfect vision, we do not now know how to make him happy, to relieve his deepest distresses, to do him the highest good; so that most loving acts, such as giving the cup of cold water, and helping the sufferer who has fallen by the wayside, seem, to our more thoughtful moods, to be mere symbols of what love would do if it could, — mere hints of the active life that love would lead if it were directly and fully guided by the Father's wisdom.

Modern philanthropy has learned to develop a technically clearer consciousness about this problem of effective benevolence, and has made familiar the distinction between loving one's neighbor, and finding out how to be practically useful in meeting the neighbor's needs. Hence, sometimes, the modern mind wonders how to apply the spirit of the parables to our special problems of benevolence, and questions whether, and in what sense, the original Gospel furnishes guidance for our own modern social consciousness.

The problems thus barely suggested are indeed in a sense answered, so far as the originally reported teaching of Jesus is concerned, but are answered by a consideration which awakens a new call for further interpretation. The parables and the Sermon on the Mount emphasize, in the present connection, two things: First, that it is indeed the business of every lover of his neighbor to help other men by rendering them also lovers; and secondly that, as to other matters, one who tries to help his neighbor must leave to God, to the all-loving Father, the care for the true and final good of the neighbor whom one loves. Since the judgment day is near, in the belief of Jesus and of his hearers, since the final victory of the Kingdom will erelong be miraculously manifested, the lover, so Jesus seems to hold, can wait. It is his task to use his talent as he can, to be ready for his Lord's appearance, and to be strenuous in the spirit of love. But the God who cares for the sparrows will care for the success of love.

It is simply not the lover's task to set this present world right; it is his only to act in the spirit that is the Father's spirit, and that, when revealed and triumphant, at the judgment day, will set all things right. In this way the heroism of the ideal of the Kingdom is perfectly compatible, in the parables, with an attitude of resignation with regard to the means whereby the ideal is to be accomplished. Serene faith as to the result, strenuousness as to the act, whatever it is, which the loving spirit just now prompts: this is the teaching of the parables.

I have said that the world of the parables contains two beings to whom Christian love is owed: God and the neighbor. Both, as you now see, are mysterious. The serene faith of the Master sets one mystery side by side with the other, bids the disciple lay aside all curious peering into what is not yet revealed to the loving soul, and leaves to the near future, — to the coming end of the world, — the lifting of all veils and the reconciliation of all conflicts.

X

Such, then, are the problems of the doctrine of love which the Master brings to light, but does not answer. Our next question is: What does Paul contribute to this doctrine of love?

Paul indeed repeated many of his Master's words concerning love; and he everywhere is in full agreement with their spirit. And yet this agreement is accompanied by a perfectly inevitable further development of the doctrine of Christian love, — a development which is due to the fact that into the world of Paul's religious life and teaching there has entered, not only a new experience, but a new sort of being, — a real object whereof the Master had not made explicit mention.

God and the neighbor are beings whose general type religion and common sense had made familiar long before Jesus taught, mysterious though God and one's neighbor were to the founder's hearers, and still remain to ourselves. Both of them are conceived by the religious consciousness of the parables as personal beings, and as individuals. God is the supreme ruler who, as Christ conceives him, is also an individual person, and who loves and wills. The neighbor is the concrete human being of daily life.

But the new, the third being, in Paul's religious world, seems to the Apostle himself novel in its type, and seems to him to possess a nature involving what he more than once calls a "mystery." To express, so far as he may, this "mystery," he uses characteristic metaphors, which have become classic.

This new being is a corporate entity,—the body of Christ, or the body of which the now divinely exalted Christ is the head. Of this body the exalted Christ is also, for Paul, the spirit and also, in some new sense, the lover. This corporate entity is the Christian community itself.

Perfectly familiar is the fact that the existence and the idea of this community constitute a new beginning in the evolution of Christianity. But neglected, as I think and as I have just asserted, is the subtle and momentous transformation, the great development which this new motive brings to pass in the Pauline form of the doctrine of Christian love.

What most interests us here, and what is least generally understood, I think, by students of the problem of Christianity, is the fact that this new entity, this corporate sort of reality which Paul so emphasizes, this being which is not an individual man but a community, does not, as one might suppose, render the Apostle's doctrine of love more abstract, more remote from human life, less direct and less moving, than was the original doctrine of love in the parables. On the contrary, the new element makes the doctrine of love more concrete, and, as I must insist, really less mysterious. In speaking of this corporate entity, the Apostle uses metaphors, and knows that they are metaphors; but, despite what the Apostle calls the new "mystery," these metaphors explain much that the parables left doubtful. These metaphors do not hide, as the Master, in using the form of the parable, occasionally intended for the time to hide from those who were not yet ready for the full revelation, truths which the future was to make clearer to the disciples. No, Paul's metaphors regarding the community of the faithful in the Church bring the first readers of Paul's epistles into direct contact with the problems of their own daily religious life.

The corporate entity—the Christian community—proves to be, for Paul's religious consciousness, something more concrete than is the individual fellow-man. The question: Who is my neighbor? had been answered by the Master by means of the parable of the Good Samaritan. But that question itself had not been due merely to the hardness of heart of the lawyer who asked it. The problem of the neighbor actually involves mysteries which, as we have already seen and hereafter shall still further see, the parables deliberately leave, along with the conception of the Kingdom of Heaven itself, to be made clearer only when the new revelation, for which the parables are preparing the way, shall have been granted. Now Paul feels himself to be in possession of a very precious part of this further revelation. He has discovered, in his own experience as Apostle, a truth that he feels to be new. He believes this truth to be a revelation due to the spirit of his Lord.

In fact, the Apostle has discovered a special instance of one of the most significant of all moral and religious truths, the truth that a community, when unified by an active indwelling purpose, is an entity more concrete and, in fact, less mysterious than is any individual man, and that such a community can love and be loved as a husband and wife love; or a father or mother love.

Because the particular corporate entity whose cause Paul represents, namely, the Christian community, is in his own experience something new, whose origin he views as wholly miraculous, whose beginnings and whose daily life are bound up with the influence which he believes to be due to the spirit of his risen and ascended Lord, Paul indeed regards the Church as a "mystery." But, as a fact, his whole doctrine regarding the community has a practical concreteness, a clear common sense about it, such that he is able to restate the doctrine of Christian love so as to be fully just to all its active heroism, while interpreting much which the parables left problematic.

XI

What can I do for my neighbor's good? The parables had answered: "Love him, help him in his obvious and bitter needs, teach him the spirit of love, and leave the rest to God." Does Paul make light of this teaching? On the contrary, his hymn in honor of love, in the first epistle to the Corinthians, is one of Christianity's principal treasures. Nowhere is the real consequence of the teaching of Jesus regarding love more completely stated. But notice this difference: For Paul the neighbor has now become a being who is primarily the fellow-member of the Christian community.

The Christian community is itself something visible; miraculously guided by the Master's spirit. It is at once for the Apostle a fact of present experience and a divine creation. And therefore every word about love for the neighbor is in the Apostle's teaching at once perfectly direct and human in its effectiveness and is nevertheless dominated by the spirit of a new and, as Paul believes, a divinely inspired love for the community.

Both the neighbor and the lover of the neighbor to whom the Apostle appeals are, to his mind, members of the body of Christ; and all the value of each man as an individual is bound up with his membership in this body, and with his love for the community.

Jesus had taught that God loves the neighbor,—yes, even the least of these little ones. Paul says to the Ephesians: "Christ loved the church, and gave himself up for it, that he might sanctify it; . . . that he might present the church to himself a glorious church, not having spot: . . . but that it should be holy and without blemish." One sees: The object of the divine love, as Paul conceives it, has been at once transformed and fulfilled.

In God's love for the neighbor, the parables find the proof of the infinite worth of the individual. In Christ's love for the Church Paul finds the proof that both the community, and the individual member, are the objects of an infinite concern, which glorifies them both, and thereby unites them. The member finds his salvation only in union with the Church. He, the member, would be dead without the divine spirit and without the community. But the Christ whose community this is, has given life to the members,—the life of the Church, and of Christ himself. "You hath he quickened, which were dead in trepasses and sins."

In sum: Christian love, as Paul conceives it, takes on the form of Loyalty. This is Paul's simple but vast transformation of Christian love.

Loyalty itself was, in the history of humanity, already, at that time, ancient. It had existed in all tribes and peoples that knew what it was for the individual so to love his community as to glory in living and dying for that community. To conceive virtue as faithfulness to one's community, was, in so far, no new thing. Loyalty, moreover, had long tended towards a disposition to enlarge both itself and its community. As the world had come together, it had gradually become possible for philosophers, such as the later Stoics, to conceive of all humanity as in ideal one community.

Although this was so far a too abstract conception to conquer the world of contending powers, the spirit of loyalty was also not without its religious relationships, and tended, as religion tended, to make the moral realm appear, not only a world of human communities, but a world of divinely ordained unity. Meanwhile, upon every stage, long before the Christian virtues were conceived, loyalty had inspired nations of warriors with the sternest of their ideals of heroism, and with their noblest visions of the destiny of the individual. And the prophets of Israel had indeed conceived the Israel of God's ultimate triumph as a community in and through which all men should know God and be blessed.

But in Paul's teaching, loyalty, quickened to new life, not merely by hope, but by the presence of a community in whose meetings the divine spirit seemed to be daily working fresh wonders, keeps indeed its natural relation to the militant virtues, is heroic and strenuous, and delights to use metaphors derived from the soldier's life. It appears also as the virtue of those who love order, and who prefer law to anarchy, and who respect worldly authority. And it derives its religious ideas from the prophets.

But it also becomes the fulfilment of what Jesus had taught in the parables concerning love. For the Apostle, this loyalty unites to all these stern and orderly and militant traits, and to all that the prophets had dreamed about Israel's triumph, the tenderness of a brother's love for the individual brother. Consequently, in Paul's mind, love for the individual human being, and loyalty to the divine community of all the faithful; graciousness of sentiment, and orderliness of discipline; are so directly interwoven that each interprets and glorifies the other.

If the Corinthians unlovingly contend, brother with brother, concerning their gifts, Paul tells them about the body of Christ, and about the divine unity of its spirit in all the diversity of its members and of their powers. On the other hand, if it is loyalty to the Church which is to be interpreted and revivified, Paul pictures the dignity of the spiritual community in terms of the direct beauty and sweetness and tenderness of the love of brother for brother,—that love which seeketh not her own.

The perfect union of this inspired passion for the community, with this tender fondness for individuals, is at once the secret of the Apostle's power as a missionary and the heart of his new doctrine. Of loyalty to the spirit and to the body of Christ, he discourses in his most abstruse as well as in his most eloquent passages. But his letters close with the well-known winning and tender messages to and about individual members and about their intimate personal concerns.

As to the question: "What shall I do for my brother?" Paul has no occasion to answer that question *except* in terms of the brother's relations to the community. But just for that reason his counsels can be as concrete and definite as each individual case requires them to be. Because the community, as Paul conceives it,—the small community of a Pauline church,—keeps all its members in touch with one another; because its harmony is preserved through definite plans for setting aside the differences that arise amongst individuals; because, by reason of the social life of the whole, the physical needs, the perils, the work, the prosperity of the individual are all made obvious facts of the common experience of the church, and are all just as obviously and definitely related to the health of the whole body,—Paul's gospel of love has constant and concrete practical applications to the life of those whom he addresses. The ideal of the parables has become a visible life on earth. So live together that the Church may be worthy of Christ who loves it, so help the individual brother that he may be a fitting member of the Church. Such are now the counsels of love.

All this teaching of Paul was accompanied, of course, in the Apostle's own mind, by the unquestioning assurance that this community of the Christian faith, as he knew it and in his letters addressed its various representatives, was indeed a genuinely universal community. It was already, to his mind, what the prophets had predicted when they spoke of the redeemed Israel. By the grace of God, all men belonged to this community, or would soon belong to it, whom God was pleased to save at all.

For the end of the world was very soon to come, and would manifest its membership, its divine head, and its completed mission. According to Paul's expectation, there was to be no long striving towards an ideal that in time was remote. He dealt with the interests of all mankind. But his faith brought him into direct contact with the institution that represented this world-wide interest. What loyalty on its highest levels has repeatedly been privileged to imagine as the ideal brotherhood of all who are loyal, Paul found directly presented, in his religious experience, as his own knowledge of his Master's purpose, and of its imminent fulfilment.

This vision began to come to Paul when he was called to be an apostle; and later, when he was sent to the Gentiles, the ideal grew constantly nearer and clearer. The Church was, for Paul, the very presence of his Lord.

Such, then, was the first highly developed Christian conception of the universal community. That which the deepest and highest rational interests of humanity make most desirable for all men, and that which the prophets of Israel had predicted afar off, the religious experience of Paul brought before his eyes as the daily work of the spirit in the Church. Was not Christ present whenever the faithful were assembled? Was not the spirit living in their midst? Was not the day of the Lord at hand? Would not they all soon be changed, when the last trumpet should sound?

Our sketch, thus far, of the spirit of the ideal of the universal community, solves none of our problems. But it helps to define them. This, the first of our three essential ideas of Christianity, is the idea of a spiritual life in which universal love for all individuals shall be completely blended, practically harmonized, with an absolute loyalty for a real and universal community. God, the neighbor, and the one church: These three are for Paul the objects of Christian love and the inspiration of the life of love.

Paul's expectations of the coming judgment were not realized. Those little apostolic churches, where the spirit daily manifested itself, gave place to the historical church of the later centuries, whose possession of the spirit has often been a matter of dogma rather than of life, and whose unity has been so often lost to human view. The letter has hidden the spirit. The Lord has delayed his coming. The New Jerusalem, adorned as a bride for her husband, remains hidden behind the heavens. The vision has become the Problem of Christianity.

Our sketch has been meant merely to help us towards a further definition of this problem. To such a definition our later lectures must attempt still further to contribute. We have a hint of the sources of the first of our three essential ideas of Christianity. We have still to consider what is the truth of this idea. And in order to move towards an answer to this question, we shall be obliged, in our immediately subsequent lectures, to attempt a formulation of the two other essential ideas of Christianity named in our introductory statement.

III

The Moral Burden
of the
Individual

"All things excellent," says Spinoza, "are as difficult as they are rare;" and Spinoza's word here repeats a lesson that nearly all of the world's religious and moral teachers agree in emphasizing. Whether such a guide speaks simply of "excellence," or uses the distinctively religious phraseology and tells us about the way to "salvation," he is sure, if he is wise, to recognize, and on occasion to say, that whoever is to win the highest goal must first learn to bear a heavy burden. It also belongs to the common lore of the sages to teach that this burden is much more due to the defects of our human nature than to the hostility of fortune. "We ourselves make our time short for our task": such comments are as trite as they are well founded in the facts of life.

I

But among the essential ideas of Christianity, there is one which goes beyond this common doctrine of the serious-minded guides of humanity. For this idea defines the moral burden, to which the individual who seeks salvation is subject, in so grave a fashion that many lovers of mankind, and, in particular, many modern minds, have been led to declare that so much of Christian doctrine, at least in the forms in which it is usually stated, is an unreasonable and untrue feature of the faith. This idea I stated at the close of our first lecture, side by side with the two other ideas of Christianity which I propose, in these lectures, to discuss. The idea of the Church, — of the universal community, — which was our topic in the second lecture, is expressed by the assertion that there is a real and divinely significant spiritual community to which all must belong who are to win the true goal of life. The idea of the moral burden of the individual is expressed by maintaining that (as I ventured to state this idea in my own words): "The individual human being is by nature subject to some overwhelming moral burden from which, if unaided, he cannot escape. Both because of what has technically been called original sin, and because of the sins that he himself has committed, the individual is doomed to a spiritual ruin from which only a divine intervention can save him."

This doctrine constitutes the second of the three Christian ideas that I propose to discuss. I must take it up in the present lecture.

II

To this mode of continuing our discussion you may object that our second lecture left the idea of the Church very incompletely stated, and, in many most important respects, also left that idea uninterpreted, uncriticised, and not yet brought into any clear relation with the creed of the modern man. Is it well, you may ask, to discuss a second one of the Christian ideas, when the first has not yet been sufficiently defined?

I answer that the three Christian ideas which we have chosen for our inquiry are so closely related that each throws light upon the others, and in turn receives light from them. Each of these ideas needs, in some convenient order, to be so stated and so illustrated, and then so made the topic of a thoughtful reflection, that we shall hereby learn: First, about the basis of this idea in human nature; secondly, about its value, — its ethical significance as an interpretation of life; and thirdly, about its truth, and about its relation to the real world. At the close of our survey of the three ideas, we shall bring them together, and thus form some general notion of what is essential to the Christian doctrine of life viewed as a whole. We shall at the same time be able to define the way in which this Christian doctrine of life expresses certain actual needs of men, and undertakes to meet these needs. We shall then have grounds for estimating the ethical and religious value of the connected whole of the doctrines in question.

There will then remain the hardest part of our task: the study of the relation of these Christian ideas to the real world. So far as we are concerned, this last part of our investigation will involve, in the main, metaphysical problems; and the closing lectures of our course will therefore contain an outline of the metaphysics of Christianity, culminating in a return to the problems of the modern man.

Such is our task. On the way toward our goal we must be content, for a time, with fragmentary views. They will, erelong, come into a certain unity with one another; but for that unity we must wait, until each idea has had its own partial and preliminary presentation.

Of the idea of the universal community we have learned, thus far, two things, and no more. First, we have seen that this idea has a broad psychological basis in the social nature of mankind, while it gets its ethical value from its relations to the interests and needs of all those of any time or nation who have learned what is the deeper meaning of loyalty. By loyalty, as you remember, I mean the thoroughgoing, practical, and loving devotion of a self to an united community.

Secondly, we have seen that, in addition to its general basis in human nature, this idea has its specifically Christian form. The significance of this form we have illustrated by the way in which the original doctrine of Christian love, as Jesus taught it in his sayings and parables, received not only an application, but also a new development in the consciousness of the apostolic churches, when the Apostle Paul experienced and moulded their life.

The synthesis of the Master's doctrine of love with the type of loyalty which the life of the spirit in the Church taught Paul to express, makes concrete and practical certain more mysterious aspects of the doctrine of love which the Master had taught in parables, but had left for a further revelation to define. And herewith the spirit of the Christian idea of the universal community entered, as a permanent possession, into the history of Christianity.

This preliminary study of the idea of the universal community leaves us with countless unsolved problems. But it at least shows us where some portion of our main problem lies. The dogmas of the historical Church concerning its own authority we have so far left, in our discussion, almost untouched. That the spirit and the letter of this first of our Christian ideas are still very far apart, all who love mankind, and who regard Christianity wisely, well know. We have not yet tried to show how spirit and letter are to be brought nearer together. It has not been my privilege to tell you where the true Church is today to be found. As a fact, I believe it still to be an invisible Church. And I readily admit that a disembodied idea does not meet all the interests of Christianity, and does not answer all the questions of the modern man.

But we have yet, in due time, to consider whether, and to what extent, the universal community is a reality. That is a problem, partly of dogma, partly of metaphysics. It is not my office to supply the modern man, or any one else, with a satisfactory system of dogmas. But I believe that philosophy has still something to say which is worth saying regarding the sense in which there really is an universal community such as expresses what the Christian idea means. I shall hereafter offer my little contribution to this problem.

III

Let us turn, then, to our new topic. The moralists, as we have already pointed out, are generally agreed that whoever is to win the highest things must indeed learn to bear a heavy moral burden. But the Christian idea now in question adds to the common lore of the moralists the sad word: "*The individual cannot bear this burden.* His tainted nature forbids; his guilt weighs him down. If by salvation one means a winning of the true goal of life, the individual, unaided, cannot be saved. And the help that he needs for bearing his burden must come from some source entirely above his own level,—from a source which is, in some genuine sense, divine."

The most familiar brief statement of the present idea is that of Paul in the passage in the seventh chapter of the epistle to the Romans, which culminates in this cry: "O wretched man that I am!" What the Apostle, in the context of this passage, expounds as his interpretation both of his own religious experience and of human nature in general, has been much more fully stated in the form of well-known doctrines, and has formed the subject-matter for ages of Christian controversy.

In working out his own theory of the facts which he reports, Paul was led to certain often cited statements about the significance and the effect of Adam's legendary transgression. And, as a consequence of these words and of a few other Pauline passages, technical problems regarding original sin, predestination, and related topics have come to occupy so large a place in the history of theology, that, to many minds, Paul's own report of personal experience, and his statements about plain facts of human nature, have been lost to sight (so far as concerns the idea of the moral burden of the individual) in a maze of controversial complications. To numerous modern minds the whole idea of the moral burden of the individual seems, therefore, to be an invention of theologians, and to possess little or no religious importance.

Yet I believe that such a view is profoundly mistaken. The idea of the moral burden of the individual is, as we shall see, not without its inherent complications, and not without its relation to very difficult problems, both ethical and metaphysical. Yet, of the three essential ideas of Christianity which constitute our list, it is, relatively speaking, the simplest, and the one which can be most easily interpreted to the enlightened common sense of the modern man. Its most familiar difficulties are due rather to the accidents of controversy than to the nature of the subject.

The fate which has beset those who have dealt with the technical efforts to express this idea is partly explicable by the general history of religion; but is also partly due to varying personal factors, such as those which determined Paul's own training. This fate may be summed up by saying that, regarding just this matter of the moral burden of the individual, those who, by virtue of their genius or of their experience, have most known what they meant, have least succeeded in making clear to others what they know.

Paul, for instance, grasped the essential meaning of the moral burden of the individual with a perfectly straightforward veracity of understanding. What he saw, as to this matter, he saw with tragic clearness, and upon the basis of a type of experience that, in our own day, we can verify, as we shall soon see, much more widely than was possible for him. But when he put his doctrine into words, both his Rabbinical lore, and his habits of interpreting tradition, troubled his speech; and the passages which embody his theory of the sinfulness of man remain as difficult and as remote from his facts, as his report of these facts of life themselves is eloquent and true.

Similar has been the fortune of nearly all subsequent theology regarding the technical treatment of this topic. Yet growing human experience, through all the Christian ages, has kept the topic near to life; and today it is in closer touch with life than ever. The idea of the moral burden of the individual seems, to many cheerful minds, austere; but, if it is grave and stern, it is grave with the gravity of life, and stern only as the call of life, to any awakened mind, ought to be stern. If the traditional technicalities have obscured it, they have not been able to affect its deeper meaning or its practical significance. Rightly interpreted, it forms, I think, not only an essential feature of Christianity, but an indispensable part of every religious and moral view of life which considers man's business justly, and does so with a reasonable regard for the larger connections of our obligations and of our powers.

IV

If we ourselves are to see these larger connections, we must, for the time, disregard the theological complications of the history of doctrine concerning original sin, and must also disregard the metaphysical problems that lie behind these complications. We must do this; but not as if these theological theories were wholly arbitrary, or wholly insignificant. We must simply begin with those facts of human nature which here most deeply concern us.

These facts have a metaphysical basis. In the end, we ourselves shall seek to come into touch with so much of theology as most has to do with our problem of Christianity. We cannot tell, until our preliminary survey is completed, and our metaphysical treatment of our problem is reached, what form our sketch of a theology will assume. We must be patient with our fragmentary views until we see how to bring them together.

But, for the time being, our question relates not to the legend of Adam's fall, nor to something technically called original sin, but to man as we empirically know him. We ask: How far is the typical individual man weighed down, in his efforts to win the goal of life, by a burden such as Paul describes in his epistle to the Romans? And what is the significance of this burden?

Here, at once, we meet with the obvious fact, often mentioned, not only in ancient, but also in many modern, discussions of our topic,— with the fact that there are, deep-seated in human nature, many tendencies that our mature moral consciousness views as evil. These tendencies have a basis in qualities that are transmitted by heredity.

Viewed as an observant naturalist,—as a disinterested student of the life-process views them, all our inherited instincts are, in one sense, upon a level. For no instincts are, at the outset of life, determined by any purpose,—either good or evil,—of which we are then conscious. But, when trained, through experience and action, our instincts become interwoven into complex habits, and thus are transformed into our voluntary activities. What at the beginning is an elemental predisposition to respond to a specific sensory stimulus in a more or less vigorous but incoherent and generalized way, becomes, in the context of the countless other predispositions upon which is based our later training, the source of a mode of conduct,— of conduct that, as we grow, tends to become more and more definite, and that may be valuable for good or for ill. And, as a fact, many of our instinctive predispositions actually appear, in the sequel, to be like noxious plants or animals. That is, to use a familiar phrase, they "turn out ill." They are expressed in our maturer life in maladjustments, in vices, or perhaps in crimes.

Now Paul, like a good many other moralists, was impressed by the number and by the vigor of those amongst our instinctive predispositions which, under the actual conditions of human training, "turn out ill," and are interwoven into habits that often lead the natural man into baseness and into a maze of evil deeds. Paul summarizes this aspect of the facts, as he saw them, in his familiar picture, first, of the Gentile world, and then of the moral state of the unregenerate who were Jews. This picture we find in the opening chapters of his epistle to the Romans.

The majority of readers appear to suppose that the essential basis of Paul's theory about the moral burden of the individual is to be found in these opening chapters, and in the assertion that the worst vices and crimes of mankind are the most accurate indications of how bad human nature is. For such readers, whether they agree with Paul or not, the whole problem reduces to the question: "Are men, and are human traits and tendencies, naturally as mischievous; are we all as much predisposed to vices and to crimes as Paul's dark picture of the world in which he lived bids us believe that all human characters are? Is man,—viewed as a fair observer from another planet might view him,—is man by nature, or by heredity, predominantly like a noxious plant or animal? Unless some external power, such as the power that Paul conceives to be Divine Grace, miraculously saves him, is he bound to turn out ill, — to be the beast of prey, the victim of lust, the venomous creature, whom Paul portrays in these earlier chapters of his letters to the Romans?"

You well know that, as to the questions thus raised, there is much to be said, both for and against the predominantly mischievous character of the natural and instinctive predispositions of men; and both for and against the usual results of training, in case of the people who make up our social world. Paul's account of this aspect of the life of the natural man has both its apologists and its critics.

I must simply decline, however, to follow the usual controversies as to the natural predispositions of the human animal any further in this place. I have mentioned the familiar topic in order to say at once that none of the considerations which the opening chapters of the epistle to the Romans suggest to a modern reader regarding the noxious or the useful instinctive predispositions of ordinary men, or even of extraordinarily defective or of exceptionally gifted human beings, seem to be of any great importance for the understanding of the genuine Pauline doctrine of the moral burden of the individual.

Paul opened the epistle to the Romans by considerations which merely prepared the way for his main thesis. His argument in the earlier chapters is also chiefly preparatory. But his main doctrine concerning our moral burden depends upon other considerations than a mere enumeration of the vices and crimes of a corrupt society. It depends, in fact, upon considerations which, as I believe, are almost wholly overlooked in most of the technical controversies concerning original sin, and concerning the evil case of the unregenerate man.

I shall venture to translate these more significant considerations which Paul emphasizes into a relatively modern phraseology. I believe that I shall do so in a way that is just to Paul's spirit, and that will enable us soon to return to the text of the seventh chapter of his epistle with a clearer understanding of the main issue.

V

Whoever sets out to study, as psychologist, the moral side of human nature, with the intention of founding upon that study an estimate of the part which good and evil play in our life, must make clear to his mind a familiar, but important, and sometimes neglected distinction. This is the distinction between the conduct of men, upon the one hand, and the grade or sort of consciousness with which, upon the other hand, their conduct, whatever it is, is accompanied.

Conduct, as we have already mentioned, results from the training which our hereditary predispositions, our instinctive tendencies, get, when the environment has played upon them in a suitable way, and for a sufficient time. The environment which trains us to our conduct may be animate or inanimate; although in our case it is very largely a human environment. It is not necessary that we should be clearly aware of what our conduct in a given instance is or means, just as it is not necessary that one who speaks a language fluently should be consciously acquainted with the grammar of that language, or that one who can actually find the way over a path in the mountains should be able to give directions to a stranger such as would enable the latter to find the same way.

In general, it requires one sort of training to establish in us a given form of conduct, and a decidedly different sort of training to make us aware of what that form of conduct is, and of what, for us ourselves, it means.

The training of all the countless higher and more complex grades and types of knowledge about our own conduct which we can find present in the world of our self-knowledge, is subject to a general principle which I may as well state at once. Conduct, as I have just said, can be trained through the action of any sort of tolerable environment, animate or inanimate. But the higher and more complex types of our consciousness about our conduct, our knowledge about what we do, and about why we do it, — all this more complex sort of practical knowledge of ourselves, is trained by a specific sort of environment, namely, by a social environment.

And the social environment that most awakens our self-consciousness about our conduct does so by opposing us, by criticising us, or by otherwise standing in contrast with us. Our knowledge of our conduct, in all its higher grades, and our knowledge of ourselves as the authors or as the guides of our own conduct, our knowledge of how and why we do what we do, — all such more elaborate self-knowledge is, directly or indirectly, a social product, and a product of social contrasts and oppositions of one sort or another. Our fellows train us to all our higher grades of practical self-knowledge, and they do so by giving us certain sorts of social trouble.

If we were capable of training our conduct in solitude, we should not be nearly as conscious as we now are of the plans, of the ideals, of the meaning, of this conduct. A solitary animal, if well endowed with suitable instincts, and if trained through the sort of experimenting that any intelligent animal carries out as he tries to satisfy his wants, would gradually form some sort of conduct. This conduct might be highly skilful. But if this animal lived in a totally unsocial, in a wholly inanimate, environment, he would meet with no facts that could teach him to be aware of what his conduct was, in the sense and degree in which we are aware of our own conduct. *For he, as a solitary creature, would find no other instance of conduct with which to compare his own.* And all knowledge rests upon comparison. It is my knowledge of my fellows' doings, and of their behavior toward me, — it is this which gives me the basis for the sort of comparison that I use whenever I succeed in more thoughtfully observing myself or estimating myself.

If you want to grasp this principle, consider any instance that you please wherein you are actually and clearly aware of how you behave and of why you behave thus. Consider, namely, any instance of a higher sort of skill in an art, in a game, in business, — an instance, namely, wherein you not only *are* skilful, but are fully observant of what your skill is, and of why you consciously prefer this way of playing or of working. You will find that always your knowledge and your estimate of your skill and of your own way of doing, turn upon comparing your own conduct with that of some real or ideal comrade, or fellow, or rival, or opponent, or critic; or upon knowing how your social order in general carries on or estimates this sort of conduct; or, finally, upon remembering or using the results of former social comparisons of the types mentioned.

I walk as I happen to walk, and in general, if let alone, I have no consciousness as to what my manner of walking is; but let my fellow's gait or pace attract my attention, or let my fellow laugh at my gait, or let him otherwise show that he observes my gait; and forthwith, if my interest is stirred, I may have the ground for beginning to observe what my own gait is, and how it is to be estimated.

In brief, it is our fellows who first startle us out of our natural unconsciousness about our own conduct; and who then, by an endless series of processes of setting us attractive but difficult models, and of socially interfering with our own doings, train us to higher and higher grades and to more and more complex types of self-consciousness regarding what we do and why we do it. Play and conflict, rivalry and emulation, conscious imitation and conscious social contrasts between man and man, — these are the source of each man's consciousness about his own conduct.

Whatever occurs in our literal social life, and in company with our real fellows, can be, and often is, repeated with endless variations in our memory and imagination, and in a companionship with ideal fellow-beings of all grades of significance. And thus our thoughts and memories of all human beings who have aroused our interest, as well as our thoughts about God, enrich our social environment by means of a wealth of real and ideal fellow-beings, with whom we can and do compare and contrast ourselves and our own conduct.

And since all this is true, this whole process of our knowledge about our own doings, and about our plans, and about our extimates of ourselves, is a process capable of simply endless variation, growth, and idealization. Hence the variations of our moral self-consciousness have all the wealth of the entire spiritual world. Comparing our doings with the standards that the social will furnishes to us, in the form of customs and of rules, we become aware both of what Paul calls, in a special instance, "the law," and of ourselves either as in harmony with or opposed to this law. The comparison and the contrast make us view ourselves on the one side, and the social will, — that is, "the law," — on the other side, as so related that, the more we know of the social will, the more highly conscious of ourselves we become; while the better we know ourselves, the more clearly we estimate the dignity and the authority of the social will.

So much, then, for a mere hint of the general ways in which our moral self-consciousness is a product of our social life. This self is known to each one of us through its social contrasts with other selves, and with the will of the community. If these contrasts displease us, we try to relieve the tension. If they fascinate, we form our ideals accordingly. But in either case we become conscious of some plan or ideal of our own. Our developed conscience, psychologically speaking, is the product of endless efforts to clear up, to simplify, to reduce to some sort of unity and harmony, the equally endless contrasts between the self, the fellow-man, and the social will in general, —contrasts which our social experience constantly reveals and renders fascinating or agonizing, according to the state of our sensitiveness or of our fortunes.

VI

These hints of the nature of a process which you can illustrate by every higher form and gradation of the moral consciousness of men have now prepared us for one more observation which, when properly understood, will bring us directly in contact with Paul's own comments upon the moral burden of any human being who reaches a high spiritual level.

Our conduct may be, according to our instincts and our training, whatever it happens to be. Since man is an animal that is hard to train, it will often be, from the point of view of the social will of our community, more or less defective conduct. But it might also be fairly good conduct; and, in normal people of good training, it often is so. In this respect, then, it seems unpsychological to assert that the conduct of all natural men is universally depraved, — however ill Paul thought of his Gentiles.

Let us turn, however, from men's conduct to their consciousness about their conduct; and then the simple and general principles just enunciated will give us a much graver view of our moral situation. Paul's main thesis about our moral burden relates not to our conduct, but to our consciousness about our conduct.

Our main result, so far, is that, from a purely psychological point of view, my consciousness about my conduct, and consequently my power to form ideals, and my power to develop any sort of conscience, are a product of my nature as a social being. And the product arises in this way: Contrasts, rivalries, difficult efforts to imitate some fascinating fellow-being, contests with my foes, emulation, social ambition, the desire to attract attention, the desire to find my place in my social order, my interest in what my fellows say and do, and especially in what they say and do with reference to me, — such are the more elemental social motives and the social situations which at first make me highly conscious of my own doings.

Upon the chaos of these social contrasts my whole later training in the knowledge of the good and the evil of my own conduct is founded. My conscience grows out of this chaos, — grows as my reason grows, through the effort to get harmony into this chaos. However reasonable I become, however high the grade of the conscientious ideals to which, through the struggle to win harmony, I finally attain, all of my own conscientious life is psychologically built upon the lowly foundations thus furnished by the troubled social life, that, together with my fellows, I must lead.

VII

But now it needs no great pessimism to observe that our ordinary social life is one in which there is a great deal of inevitable tension, or natural disharmony. Such tension, and such disharmony, are due not necessarily to the graver vices of men. The gravest disharmonies often result merely from the mutual misunderstandings of men. There are so many of us. We naturally differ so much from one another. We comprehend each other so ill, or, at best, with such difficulty. Hence social tension is, so to speak, the primary state of any new social enterprise, and can be relieved only through special and constantly renewed efforts.

But this simple observation leads to another. If our social life, owing to the number, the variety, and the ignorance of the individuals who make up our social world, is prevailingly or primarily one in which strained social situations,—forms of social tension,—social troubles, are present, and are constantly renewed, it follows that every individual who is to reach a high grade of self-consciousness as to his own doings, will be awakened to his observation of himself by one or another form or instance of social tension. As a fact, it is rivalry, or contest, or criticism that first, as we have seen, naturally brings to my notice what I am doing. And the obvious rule is that, within reasonable limits, the greater the social tension of the situation in which I am placed, the sharper and clearer does my social contrast with my fellows become to me. And thus, the greater the social tension is, the more do I become aware, through such situations, both about my own conduct, and about my plans and ideals, and about my will.

In brief, my moral self-consciousness is bred in me through social situations that involve,—not necessarily any physical conflict with my fellows,—but, in general, some form of social conflict,—conflict such as engenders mutual criticism. Man need not be, when civilized, at war with his fellows in the sense of using the sword against them. But he comes to self-consciousness as a moral being through the spiritual warfare of mutual observation, of mutual criticism, of rivalry,—yes, too often through the warfare of envy and of gossip and of scandal-mongering, and of whatever else belongs to the early training that many people give to their own consciences, through taking a more or less hostile account of the consciences of their neighbors. Such things result from the very conditions of high grades of self-consciousness about our conduct and our ideals.

The moral self, then, the natural conscience, is bred through situations that involve social tension. What follows?

VIII

It follows that such tension, in each special case, indeed seems evil to us, and calls for relief. And in seeking for such relief, the social will, in its corporate capacity, the will of the community, forms its codes, its customary laws; and attempts to teach each of us how he ought to deal with his neighbors so as to promote the general social harmony. But these codes,—these forms of customary morality,—they have to be taught to us as conscious rules of conduct. They can only be taught to us by first teaching us to be more considerate, more self-observant, more formally conscientious than we were before. But to accomplish this aim is to bring us to some higher level of our general self-consciousness concerning our own doings. And this can be done, as a rule, only by applying to us some new form of social discipline which, in general, introduces still new and more complex kinds of tension,—new social contrasts between the general will and our own will, new conflicts between the self and its world.

Our social training thus teaches us to know ourselves through a process which arouses our self-will; and this tendency grows with what it feeds upon. The higher the training and the more cultivated and elaborate is our socially trained conscience,—the more highly conscious our estimate of our own value becomes, and so, in general, the stronger grows our self-will.

This is a commonplace; but it is precisely upon this very commonplace that the moral burden of the typical individual, trained under natural social conditions, rests. If the individual is no defective or degenerate, but a fairly good member of his stock, his conduct may be trained by effective social discipline into a more or less admirable conformity to the standards of the general will. But his conduct is not the same as his own consciousness about his conduct; or, in other words, his deeds and his ideals are not necessarily in mutual agreement. Meanwhile, his consciousness about his conduct, his ideals, his conscience, are all trained, under ordinary conditions, by a social process that begins in social troubles, in tensions, in rivalries, in contests, and that naturally continues, the farther it goes, to become more and more a process which introduces new and more complex conflicts.

This evil constantly increases. The burden grows heavier. Society can, by its ordinary skill, train many to be its servants,—servants who, being under rigid discipline, submit because they must. But precisely in proportion as society becomes more skilled in the external forms of culture, it trains its servants by a process that breeds spiritual enemies. That is, it breeds men who, even when they keep the peace, are inwardly enemies one of another; because every man, in a highly cultivated social world, is trained to moral self-consciousness by his social conflicts. And these same men are inwardly enemies of the collective social will itself, because in a highly cultivated social order the social will is oppressively vast, and the individual is trained to self-consciousness by a process which shows him the contrast between his own will and this, which so far seems to him a vast impersonal social will. He may obey. That is conduct. But he will naturally revolt inwardly; and that is his inevitable form of spiritual self-assertion, so long as he is trained to self-consciousness in this way, and is still without the spiritual transformations that some higher form of love for the community, — some form of loyalty, and that alone, — can bring.

This revolt will tend to increase as culture advances. High social cultivation breeds spiritual enmities. For it trains what we in our day call individualism, and, upon precisely its most cultivated levels, glories in creating highly conscious individuals. But these individuals are brought to consciousness by their social contrasts and conflicts. Their very consciences are tainted by the original sin of social contentiousness. The higher the cultivation, the vaster and deeper are precisely the more spiritual and the more significant of these inward and outward conflicts. Cultivation breeds civilized conduct; it also breeds conscious independence of spirit and deeper inner opposition to all mere external authority.

Before this sort of moral evil the moral individual, thus cultivated, is, if viewed merely as a creature of cultivation, powerless. His very conscience is the product of spiritual warfare, and its knowledge of good and evil is tainted by its origin. The burden grows; and the moral individual cannot bear it, unless his whole type of self-consciousness is transformed by a new spiritual power which this type of cultivation can never of itself furnish.

For the moral cultivation just described is cultivation in "the law"; that is, in the rules of the social will. But such cultivation breeds individualism; that is, breeds consciousness of self-will. And the burden of this self-will increases with cultivation.

As we all know, individualism, viewed as a highly potent social tendency, is a product of high cultivation. It is also a relatively modern product of such cultivation. Savages appear to know little about individualism. Where tribal custom is almighty, the individual is trained to conduct, but not to a high grade of self-consciousness. Hence the individual, in a primitive community, submits; but also he has no very elaborate conscience. Among most ancient peoples, individualism was still nearly unknown.

Two ancient peoples, living under special conditions and possessing an extraordinary genius, developed very high grades of individualism. One of these peoples was Israel,—especially that fragment of later Israel to which Judaism was due. Paul well knew what was the nature and the meaning of just that high development of individuality which Judaism had in his day made possible.

The other one of these peoples was the Greek people. Their individualism, their high type of self-consciousness regarding conduct, showed what is meant by being, as every highly individualistic type of civilization since their day has been, characteristically merciless to individuals. Greek individualism devoured its own children. The consciousness of social opposition determined the high grade of self-consciousness of the Greek genius. It also determined the course of Greek history and politics; and so the greatest example of national genius which the world has ever seen promptly destroyed its own life, just because its self-consciousness was due to social conflicts and intensified them. The original sin of its own cultivation was the doom of that cultivation.

In the modern world the habit of forming a high grade of individual consciousness has now become settled. We have learned the lesson that Israel and Greece taught. Hence we speak of personal moral independence as if it were our characteristic spiritual ideal. This ideal is now fostered still more highly than ever before,—is fostered by the vastness of our modern social forces, and by the way in which these forces are to-day used to train the individual consciousness which opposes itself to them, and which is trained to this sort of opposition.

The result is that the training of the cultivated individual, under modern conditions, uses, on the one hand, all the motives of what Paul calls "the flesh,"—all the natural endowment of man the social being,—but develops this fleshly nature so that it is trained to self-consciousness by emphasizing every sort and grade of more skilful opposition to the very social will that trains it. Our modern world is therefore peculiarly fitted to illustrate the thesis of Paul's seventh chapter of the epistle to the Romans. To that chapter let us now, for a moment return.

IX

The difficulty of the argument of Paul's seventh chapter lies in the fact that in speaking of our sinful nature, he emphasizes three apparently conflicting considerations: First, he asserts that sinfulness belongs to our elemental nature, to our flesh as it is at birth; secondly, he insists that sin is not cured but increased by cultivation, unless the power of the Divine Spirit intervenes and transforms us into new creatures; thirdly, he declares that our sinfulness belongs not to especially defective or degenerate sinners, but to the race in its corporate capacity, so that no one is privileged to escape by any good deed of his own, since we are all naturally under the curse.

To the first consideration many modern men reply that at birth we have only untrained instinctive predispositions, which may, under training, turn out well or ill, but which, until training turns them into conduct, are innocent.

This comment is true, but does not touch Paul's main thesis, which is that, being as to the flesh what we are, — that is, being essentially social animals, — all our natural moral cultivation, if successful, can only make us aware of our sinfulness. "Howbeit, I had not known sin but for the law." It is precisely this thesis which the natural history of the training of our ordinary moral self-consciousness illustrates. This training usually takes place through impressing the social will upon the individual by means of discipline. The result must be judged not by the accidental fortunes of this or of that formally virtuous or obviously vicious individual. The true problem lies deeper than we are accustomed to look. It is just that problem which Paul understands.

Train me to morality by the ordinary modes of discipline and you do two things: First, and especially under modern conditions, you teach me so-called independence, self-reliance. You teach me to know and to prize from the depths of my soul, my own individual will. The higher the civilization in which this mode of training is followed, the more I become an individualist among mutually hostile individualists, a citizen of a world where all are consciously free to think ill of one another, and to say, to every external authority: "My will, not thine, be done."

But this teaching of independence is also a teaching of distraction and inner despair. For, if I indeed am intelligent, I also learn that, in a highly cultivated civilization, the social will is mighty, and daily grows mightier, and must, ordinarily and outwardly, prevail unless chaos is to come. Hence you indeed may discipline me into obedience, but it is a distracted and wilful obediance, which constantly wars with the very dignity of spirit which my training teaches me to revere. On the one hand, as reasonable being, I say: "I ought to submit; for law is mighty; and I would not, if I could, bring anarchy." So much I say, if I am indeed successfully trained. But I will not obey with the inner man. For I am the being of inalienable individual rights, of unconquerable independence. I have my own law in my own members, which, however I seem to obey, is at war with the social will. I am the divided self. The more I struggle to escape through my moral cultivation, the more I discern my divided state. Oh, wretched man that I am!

Now this my divided state, this my distraction of will, is no mishap of my private fortune. It belongs to the human race, as a race capable of high moral cultivation. It is the misfortune, the doom of man the social animal, if you train him through the discipline of social tension, through troubles with his neighbors, through opposition and through social conflict, through what Whistler called "the gentle art of making enemies." This, apart from all legends, is Paul's thesis; and it is true to human nature. The more outer law there is in our cultivation, the more inner rebellion there is in the very individuals whom our cultivation creates. And this moral burden of the individual is also the burden of the race, precisely in so far as it is a race that is social in a human sense.

Possibly all this may still seem to you the mere construction of a theorist. And yet an age that, like our own, faces in new forms the conflicts between what we often name individualism and collectivism, — a time such as the present one, when every new enlargement of our vast corporations is followed by a new development of strikes and of industrial conflicts, — a time, I say, such as ours ought to know where the original sin of our social nature lies.

For our time shows us that *individualism and collectivism are tendencies, each of which as our social order grows, intensifies the other.* The more the social will expresses itself in vast organizations of collective power, the more are individuals trained to be aware of their own personal wants and choices and ideals, and of the vast opportunities that would be theirs if they could but gain control of these social forces. The more, in sum, does their individual self-will become conscious, deliberate, cultivated, and therefore dangerously alert and ingenious.

Yet, if the individuals in question are highly intelligent, and normally orderly in their social habits, their self-will, thus forcibly kept awake and watchful through the very powers which the collective will has devised, is no longer, in our own times, a merely stupid attempt to destroy all social authority. It need not be childishly vicious or grossly depraved, like Paul's Gentiles in his earlier chapters of the epistle to the Romans. It is a sensitive self-will, which feels the importance of the social forces, and which wants them to grow more powerful, so that haply they may be used by the individual himself.

And so, when opportunity offers, the individual self-will casts its vote in favor of new devices to enrich or to intensify the expression of the collective will. For it desires social powers. It wants them for its own use. Hence, in its rebellion against authority, when such rebellion arises, it is a consciously divided self-will, which takes in our day no form more frequently than the general form of moral unrest, of discontent with its own most ardent desires. It needs only a little more emphasis upon moral or religious problems than, in worldly people, in our day, it displays, in order to be driven to utter from a full heart Paul's words: "O wretched man that I am!"

For the highly trained modern agitator, or the plastic disciple of agitators, if both intelligent and reasonably orderly in habits, is intensely *both* an individualist and a man who needs the collective will, who in countless ways and cases bows to that will, and votes for it, and increases its power. The individualism of such a man wars with his own collectivism; while each, as I insist, tends to inflame the other. As an agitator, the typically restless child of our age often insists upon heaping up new burdens of social control, — control that he indeed intends to have others feel rather than himself. As individualist, longing to escape, perhaps from his economic cares, perhaps from the marriage bond, such a highly intelligent agitator may speak rebelliously of all restrictions, declare Nietzsche to be his prophet, and set out to be a Superman as if he were no social animal at all. Wretched man, by reason of his divided will, he is; and he needs only a little reflection to observe the fact.

But note: These are no mere accidents of our modern world. The division of the self thus determined, and thus increasing in our modern cultivation, is not due to the chance defects of this or of that more or less degenerate individual. Nor is it due merely to a man's more noxious instincts. This division is due to the very conditions to which the development of self-consciousness is subject, not only in our present social order, but in every civilization which has reached as high a grade of self-consciousness as that which Paul observed in himself and in his own civilization.

X

The moral burden of the individual, as Paul conceives it, and as human nature makes it necessary, has now been characterized. The legend of Adam's transgression made the fall of man due to the sort of self-consciousness, to the knowledge of good and evil, which the crafty critical remarks of the wise serpent first suggested to man, and which the resulting transgression simply emphasized. What Paul's psychology, translated into more modern terms, teaches, is that the moral self-consciousness of every one of us gets its cultivation from our social order through a process which begins by craftily awakening us, as the serpent did Eve, through critical observations, and which then fascinates our divided will by giving us the serpent's counsels. "Ye shall be as gods." This is the lore of all individualism, and the vice of all our worldly social ambitions. The resulting diseases of self-consciousness are due to the inmost nature of our social race.

They belong to its very essence as a social race. They increase with cultivation. The individual cannot escape from the results of them through any deed of his own. For his will is trained by a process which taints his conscience with the original sin of self-will, of clever hostility to the very social order upon which he constantly grows more and more consciously dependent.

What is the remedy? What is the escape? Paul's answer is simple. To his mind a new revelation has been made, from a spiritual realm wholly above our social order and its conflicts. Yet this revelation is, in a new way, social. For it tells us: "There is a certain divinely instituted community. It is no mere collection of individuals, with laws and customs and quarrels. Nor is its unity merely that of a mighty but, to our own will, an alien power. Its indwelling spirit is concrete and living, but is also a loving spirit. It is the body of Christ. The risen Lord dwells in it, and is its life. It is as much a person as he was when he walked the earth. And he is as much the spirit of that community as he is a person. Love that community; let its spirit, through this love, become your own. Let its Lord be your Lord. Be one in him and with him and with his Church. And lo! the natural self is dead. The new life takes possession of you. You are a new creature. The law has no dominion over you. In the universal community you live in the spirit; and hence for the only self, the only self-consciousness, the only knowledge of your own deeds which you possess or tolerate: these are one with the spirit of the Lord and of the community."

Translated into the terms that I ventured to use in our last lecture, Paul's doctrine is that salvation comes through loyalty. Loyalty involves an essentially new type of self-consciousness,—the consciousness of one who loves a community as a person. Not social training, but the miracle of this love, creates the new type of self-consciousness.

Only (as Paul holds) you must find the universal community to which to be loyal; and you must learn to know its Lord, whose body it is, and whose spirit is its life.

Paul is assured that he knows this universal community and this Lord. But, apart from Paul's religious faith, the perfectly human truth remains that loyalty (which is the love of a community conceived as a person on a level superior to that of any human individual)—loyalty,—and the devotion of the self to the cause of the community,—loyalty, is the only cure for the natural warfare of the collective and of the individual will,—a warfare which no moral cultivation without loyalty can ever end, but which all cultivation, apart from such devoted and transforming love of the community, only inflames and increases

Thus the second of the essential ideas of Christianity illustrates the first, and is in turn illumined by the first. This, I believe is the deeper sense and truth of the doctrine of the inherent moral taint of the social individual.

IV

The Realm of Grace

The Christian world has been still more deeply influenced by the apostle Paul's teaching concerning the divine grace that saves, than by his account of the moral burden of the individual. The traditional lore of salvation is more winning, and, in many respects, less technical, than is the Christian teaching regarding our lost state.

The present lecture is to be devoted to a study of some aspects of the doctrine of grace. Yet, since our moral burden, and our escape from that burden, are matters intimately connected, we shall find that both topics belong to the exposition of the same essential Christian idea, and that, at the same time, they throw new light upon the first of the three essential Christian ideas, the idea of the universal community. Our present task will therefore enable us to reach a new stage in our survey of the larger connections of the Christian doctrine of life.

I

Christianity is most familiarly known as a religion of love, and this view, as far as it extends, is a true view of Christianity. Our second lecture has shown us, however, that this characterization is inadequate, because it does not render justly clear the nature of the objects to which, in our human world, Christian love is most deeply and essentially devoted. A man is known by the company that he keeps. In its human relations, and apart from an explicit account of its faith concerning the realm of the gods, or concerning God, a religion can be justly estimated only when you understand what kinds and grades of human beings it bids you recognize, as well as what it counsels you to do in presence of the beings of each grade. Now, as our second lecture endeavored to point out, there are in the human world two profoundly different grades, or levels, of mental beings, — namely, the beings that we usually call human individuals, and the beings that we call communities.

Of the first of these two grades, or levels, of human beings, any one man whom you may choose to mention is an example. His organism is, in the physical world, separate from the organisms of his fellows. The expressive movements of this organism, his behavior, his gestures, his voice, his coherent course of conduct, the traces that his deeds leave behind them, — these, in your opinion, make more or less manifest to you the life of his mind. And, in your usual opinion, his mind is, on the whole, at least as separate from the minds of other men, as his organism, and his expressive bodily movements, are physically sundered from theirs.

Of the second of these two levels of human beings, a well-trained chorus, or an orchestra at a concert; or an athletic team, or a rowing crew, during a contest; or a committee, or a board, sitting in deliberation upon some matter of business; or a high court consisting of several members, who at length reach what legally constitutes "the decision of the court," — all these are good examples. Each one of these is, in its own way, a community. The vaster communities, real and ideal, which we mentioned, by way of illustration, in our second lecture, also serve as instances of real beings with minds, whose grade or level is not that of the ordinary human individuals.

Any highly organized community — so in our second lecture we argued — is as truly a human being as you and I are individually human. Only a community is not what we usually call an individual human being; because it has no one separate and internally well-knit physical organism of its own; and because its mind, if you attribute to it any one mind, is therefore not manifested through the expressive movements of such a single separate human organism.

Yet there are reasons for attributing to a community a mind of its own. Some of these reasons were briefly indicated in our second lecture; and they will call for a further scrutiny hereafter. Just here it concerns my purpose simply to call attention to the former argument, and to say, that the difference between the individual human beings of our ordinary social intercourse, and the communities, is a difference justly characterized, in my opinion, by speaking of these two as *grades* or *levels* of human life.

The communities are vastly more complex, and, in many ways, are also immeasurably more potent and enduring than are the individuals. Their mental life possesses, as Wundt has pointed out, a psychology of its own, which can be systematically studied. Their mental existence is no mere creation of abstract thinking or of metaphor; and is no more a topic for mystical insight, or for fantastic speculation, than is the mental existence of an individual man. As empirical facts, communities are known to us by their deeds, by their workings, by their intelligent and coherent behavior, just as the minds of our individual neighbors are known to us through their expressions.

Considered as merely natural existences, communities, like individuals, may be either good or evil, beneficent or mischievous. The level of mental existence which belongs to communities insures their complexity; and renders them, in general, far more potent and, for certain purposes and in certain of their activities, much more intelligent than are the human individuals whose separate physical organisms we ordinarily regard as signs of so many separate minds.

But a community,—in so far like a fallen angel,—may be as base and depraved as any individual man can become, and may be far worse than a man. Communities may make unjust war, may enslave mankind, may deceive and betray and torment as basely as do individuals, only more dangerously. The question whether communities are or are not real human beings, with their own level of mental existence, is therefore quite distinct from the question as to what worth this or that community possesses in the spiritual world. And, in our study of the doctrine of grace, we shall find how intimately the Christian teaching concerning the salvation of the individual man is bound up with the Christian definition, both of the saving community and of the power which, according to the Christian tradition, has redeemed that community, and has infused divine life into the level of human existence which this community, and not any merely human individual, occupies.

II

To the two levels of human mental existence correspond two possible forms of love: love for human individuals; love for communities. In our second lecture we spoke of the natural fact that communities can be the object of love; and that this love may lead to the complete practical devotion of an individual to the community which he loves. Such vital and effective love of an individual for a community constitutes what we called, in that lecture, Loyalty. And when, in our second lecture, the conception of loyalty as the love of an individual for a being that is one the level of a community first entered our argument, we approached this conception by using, as illustrations, what might be called either the more natural or the more primitive types of loyalty,—types such as grow out of family life, and tribal solidarity, and war. As we pointed out in the second lecture, Christianity is essentially a religion of loyalty. We have learned in our third lecture that, for Christianity, the problem of loyalty is enriched, and meanwhile made more difficult, by the nature of that ideal or universal community to which Paul first invited his converts to be loyal.

Paul and his apostolic Christians were not content with family loyalty, or with clan loyalty, or with a love for any community that they conceived as merely natural in its origin. A miracle, as they held, had created the body of Christ. To this new spiritual being, whose level was that of a community, and whose membership was human, but whose origin was, in their opinion, divine, their love and their life were due. Christianity was the religion of loyalty to this new creation. The idea involved has since remained, with all its problems and tragedies, essential to Christianity.

Our study of the moral burden of the individual has now prepared us for a new insight into the special problem which, ever since Paul's time, Christian loyalty has had to solve. This is no longer anywhere nearly as free from complications as are the problems which family loyalty and clan loyalty present, manifold as those problems of natural loyalty actually are. Even the idea of the rational brotherhood of mankind, of the universal community as the Stoics conceived it, presents no problems nearly as complex as is the problem which the Pauline concept of charity, and of Christian loyalty, has to meet.

For Paul, as you now know, finds that the individual man has to be won over, not to a loyalty which at first seems, to the fleshly mind, natural, but to an essentially new life. The natural man has to be delivered from a doom to which "the law" only binds him faster, the more he seeks to escape. And this escape involves finding, for the individual man, a community to which, when the new life comes, he is to be thenceforth loyal as no natural clan loyalty or family loyalty could make him.

The power that gives to the Christian convert the new loyalty is what Paul calls Grace. And the community to which, when grace saves him, the convert is thenceforth to be loyal, we may here venture to call by a name which we have not hitherto used. Let this name be "The Beloved Community." This is another name for what we before called the Universal Community. Only now the universal community will appear to us in a new light, in view of its relations to the doctrine of grace. And the realm of this Beloved Community, whose relations Christianity conceives, for the most part, in supernatural terms, will constitute what, in our discussion, shall be meant by the term "The Realm of Grace."

III

If we suppose that the two levels of human mental existence have both of them been recognized as real, and that hereupon the problem of finding an ideally lovable community has been, for a given individual, solved, so that this individual is sure of his love and loyalty for the community which has won his service, then, from the point of view of that individual, the two levels of human life will indeed be no longer merely distinguished by their complexity, or by their might, or by their grade of intelligence. Henceforth, for the loyal soul, the distinction between the levels, so far as the object of his loyalty is concerned, will be a distinction in value, and a vast one.

The beloved community embodies, for its lover, *values* which no human individual, viewed as a detached being, could even remotely approach. And in a corresponding way, the love which inspires the loyal soul has been transformed; and is not such as could be given to a detached human individual.

The human beings whom we distinguish in our daily life, and recognize through the seeming and the doings of their separate organisms, are real indeed, and are genuinely distinct individuals. But when we love them, our love, however ideal or devoted, has its level and its value determined by their own. And if this love for human individuals is the only form of human love that we know, both our morality and our religion are limited accordingly, and remain on a correspondingly lower level.

Such human love knows its objects precisely as Paul declared that, henceforth, he would no longer know Christ, — namely, "after the flesh." Loyalty knows its object (if I may again adapt Paul's word) "after the Spirit." For Paul's expression here refers, in so far as he speaks of human objects at all, to the unity of the spirit which he conceived to be characteristic of the Christian community, whereof Christ was, to the Apostle's mind, both the head and the divine life. Hence you see how vastly significant, for our view of Christianity, is a comprehension of what is meant by religion of loyalty.

With this indication of the connections which link the thoughts of our lecture on the universal community with the task which lies next in our path, let us turn, first to Paul's own account of the doctrine of grace, and then to the later development of Paul's teachings into those views about the Realm of Grace which came to be classic for the later Christian consciousness. Our own interest in all these matters is here still an interest, first in the foundation which the Christian ideas possess in human nature, and secondly in the ethical and religious values which are here in question. And we still postpone any effort to pass judgment upon metaphysical problems, or to decide the truth as to traditional dogmas.

IV

Let us next summarily review the original and distinctively Pauline doctrine, both of our fallen state and of the grace which saves.

The last lecture furnished the materials for such a review. The pith of the matter can be expressed, in terms of purely human psychology, thus: Man's fallen state is due to his nature as a social animal. This nature is such that you can train his conscience only by awakening his self-will. By self-will, I here mean, as Paul meant, man's conscious and active assertion of his own individual desires, worth, and undertakings, over against the will of his fellow, and over against the social will. Another name for this sort of conscious self-will is the modern term "Individualism," when it is used to mean the tendency to prefer what the individual man demands to what the collective will requires. In general, and upon high levels of human intelligence, when you train individualism, you also train collectivism; that is, you train in the individual a respect for the collective will. And it belongs to Paul's very deep and searching insight to assert that these two tendencies — the tendency towards individualism, and that towards collectivism — do not exclude, but intensify and inflame each other.

Training, if formally successful in producing the skilful member of human society, breeds respect, although not love, for "the law," that is, for the expression of the collective will. But training also makes the individual conscious of the "other law" in "his members," which "wars against" the law of the social will. The result may be, for his outward conduct, whatever the individual's wits and powers make it. But so far as this result is due to cultivation in intelligent conduct, it inevitably leads to an inner division of the self, a disease of self-consciousness, which Paul finds to be the curse of all merely natural human civilization.

This curse is rooted in the primal constitution which makes man social, and which adapts him to win his intelligence through social conflicts with his neighbors. Hence the curse belongs to the whole "flesh" of man; for by "flesh" Paul means whatever first expresses itself in our instincts and thus lies at the basis of our training, and so of our natural life. The curse afflicts equally the race and the individual. Man is by inheritance adapted for this training to self-will and to inner division.

The social order, in training individuals, therefore breeds conscious sinners; and sins both in them and against them. The natural community is, in its united collective will, a community of sin. Its state is made, by its vast powers, worse than that of the individual. But it trains the individual to be as great a sinner as his powers permit.

If you need illustrations, Paul teaches you to look for them in the whole social order, both of Jews and of Gentiles. But vices and crimes, frequent as they are, merely illustrate the principle. The disease lies much deeper than outward conduct can show; and respectability of behavior brings no relief. All are under the curse. Cultivation increases the curse. The individual is helpless to escape by any will or deed of his own.

The only escape lies in Loyalty. Loyalty, in the individual, is his love for an united community, expressed in a life of devotion to that community. But such love can be true love only if the united community both exists and is lovable. For training makes self-will fastidious, and abiding love for a community difficult.

In fact, no social training that a community can give to its members can train such love in those who have it not, or who do not win it through other aid than their training supplies. And no social will that men intelligently devise, apart from previously active and effective loyalty, can make a community lovable. The creation of the truly lovable community, and the awakening of the highly trained individual to a true love for that community, are, to Paul's mind, spiritual triumphs beyond the wit of man to devise, and beyond the power of man to accomplish. That which actually accomplishes these triumphs is what Paul means by the divine grace.

V

One further principle as to the human workings of this grace must still be mentioned, in order to complete our sketch of the foundations which our actual nature, disordered though it be, furnishes, not for the comprehension of this miracle of saving love, but for an account of the conditions under which the miracle takes place, so far as these conditions can fall under our human observation.

Natural love of individuals for communities, as we saw in our second lecture, appears in case of family loyalty, and in case of patriotism; and seems to involve no miracle of grace. But such love of an individual for a community, in so far as such love is the product of our ordinary human nature, tends to be limited or hindered by the influences of cultivation, and is blindly strongest in those who have not yet reached high grades of cultivation. It arises as mother-love or as tribal solidarity arises, from the depths of our still unconscious social nature. The infant or the child loves its home; the mother, her babe; the primitive man, his group.

But loyalty of the type that is in question when our salvation, in Paul's sense of salvation, is to be won, is the loyalty which springs up *after* the individual self-will has been trained through the processes just characterized. It is the loyalty that conquers us, even when we have become enemies of the law. It finds us as such enemies, and transforms us. It is the love which leads the already alert and rebellious self-will to devote all that it has won to the cause which henceforth is to remain, by its own choice, its beloved.

Such loyalty is not the blind instinctive affection from which cultivation inevitably alienates us, by awakening our self-will. It is the love that overcomes the already fully awakened individual. We cannot choose to fall thus in love. Only when once thus in love, can we choose to remain lovers.

Now such love comes from some previous love which belongs to the same high and difficult grade. The origin of this higher form of loyalty is hard to trace, unless some leader is first there, to be the source of loyalty in other men. If such a leader there is, his own loyalty may become, through his example, the origin of a loyalty in which the men of many generations may find salvation. You are first made loyal through the power of some one else who is already loyal.

But the loyal man must also be, as we have just said, a member of a lovable community. How can such a community originate? The family, as we have also remarked, is lovable to the dependent child. Yet often the wayward youth is socially trained to a point where such dependence, just because he has come to clear self-consciousness, seems to him unintelligible; and herewith his father's house ceases to be, for him, any longer lovable.

Great loyalty — loyalty such as Paul himself had in mind when he talked of divine grace — must be awakened by a community sufficiently lovable to win the enduring devotion of one who, like Paul, has first been trained to possess and to keep an obstinately critical and independent attitude of spirit, — an attitude such as, in fact, Paul kept to the end of his life, side by side with his own loyalty, and in a wondrous harmony therewith.

Such a marvellous union of unconquerable and even wilful self-consciousness, with an absolute loyalty to the cause of his life, breathes in every word of Paul's more controversial outbursts, as well as in all of his more fervent exhortations. Such loyalty is no mere childhood love of home. It comes only as a rushing, mighty wind.

In order to be thus lovable to the critical and naturally rebellious soul, the Beloved Community must be, quite unlike a natural social group, whose life consists of laws and quarrels, of a collective will, and of individual rebellion. This community must be an union of members who first love it. The unity of love must pervade it, before the individual member can find it lovable. Yet unless the individuals first love it, how can the unity of love come to pervade it?

The origin of loyalty, if it is to arise, — not as the childhood love of one's home arises, unconsciously and instinctively; but as Paul's love for the Church arises, consciously and with a saving power, — in the life of one who is first trained to all the conscious enmities of the natural social order, — the origin of loyalty seems thus to resemble, in a measure, the origin of life, as the modern man views that problem. A living being is the offspring of a living being. And, in a similar fashion, highly conscious loyalty presupposes a previous loyalty, only a loyalty of even higher level than its own, as its source. Loyalty needs for its beginnings the inspiring leader who teaches by the example of his spirit. But the leader, in order to inspire to loyalty, must himself be loyal. In order to be loyal, he must himself have found, or have founded, his lovable community. And this, in order to be lovable, and a community, must already consist of loyal and loving members. It cannot win the love of the lost soul who is to be saved, unless it already consists of those who have been saved by their love for it. One moves thus in a circle. Only some miracle of grace (as it would seem) can initiate the new life, either in the individuals who are to love communities, or in the communities that are to be worthy of their love.

VI

If the miracle occurs, and then works according to the rules which, in fact, the contagion of love usually seems to follow, the one who effects the first great transformation and initiates the high type of loyalty in the distracted social world must, it would seem, combine in himself, in some way, the nature which a highly trained social individual develops as he becomes self-conscious, with the nature which a community possesses when it becomes intimately united in the bonds of brotherly love, so that it is "one undivided soul of many a soul."

For the new life of loyalty, if it first appears at all, will arise as a bond linking many highly self-conscious and mutually estranged social individuals in one; but this bond can come to mean anything living and real to these individuals, only in case some potent and loyal individual, acting as leader, first declares that for him it is real. In such a leader, and in his spirit, the community will begin its own life, if the leader has the power to create what he loves.

The individual who initiates this process will then plausibly appear to an onlooker, such as Paul was when he was converted, to be at once an individual and the spirit — the very life — of a community. But his origin will be inexplicable in terms of the processes which he himself originates. His power will come from another level than our own. And of the workings of this grace, when it has appeared, we can chiefly say this: That such love is propagated by personal example, although how, we cannot explain.

We know how Paul conceives the beginning of the new life wherein Christian salvation is to be found. This beginning he refers to the work of Christ. The Master was an individual man. To Paul's mind, his mission was divine. He both knew and loved his community before it existed on earth; for his foreknowledge was one with that of the God whose will he came to accomplish. On earth he called into this community its first members. He suffered and died that it might have life. Through his death and in his life the community lives. *He is now identical with the spirit of this community.* This, according to Paul, was the divine grace which began the process of salvation for man. In the individual life of each Christian this same process appears as a new act of grace. Its outcome is the new life of loyalty to which the convert is henceforth devoted.

VII

With any criticism of the religious beliefs of Paul, and with their metaphysical bearings, we are not here concerned. What we have attempted, in this sketch, is an indication of the foundation which human nature furnishes for the Pauline doctrine of divine grace. The human problem, as you see, when it is viewed quite apart from the realm of the gods, is the problem of the value and the origin of loyalty.

The value of loyalty can readily be defined in simply human terms. Man, the social being, naturally, and in one sense helplessly, depends on his communities. Sundered from them, he has neither worth nor wit, but wanders in waste places, and, when he returns, finds the lonely house of his individual life empty, swept, and garnished.

But, on the other hand, his communities, to which he thus owes all his natural powers, train him by teaching him self-will, and so teach him the arts of spiritual hatred. The result is distraction, — spiritual death. Escape through any mere multitude of loves for other individuals is impossible. For such loves, unless they are united by some supreme loyalty, are capricious fondnesses for other individuals, who, by nature and by social training, are as lonely and as distracted as their lover himself. Mere altruism is no cure for the spiritual disease of cultivation.

No wonder, then, that early Buddhism, fully sensible of the disorders of self-will and of the natural consciousness, sees no escape but through the renunciation of all that is individual, and preaches the passionless calm of knowing only what is no longer a self at all. If birth and training mean only distraction, why not look for the cessation of all birth, and the extinction of desire?

Loyalty, if it comes at all, has the value of a love which does not so much renounce the individual self as devote the self, with all its consciousness and its powers, to an all-embracing unity of individuals in one realm of spiritual harmony. The object of such devotion is, in ideal, the community which is absolutely lovable, because absolutely united, conscious, but above all distractions of the separate self-will of its members. Loyalty demands many members, but one body; many gifts, but one spirit.

The value of this ideal lies in its vision of an activity which is endless, but always at rest in its own harmony. Such a vision, as Mr. F. C. S. Schiller has well pointed out, Aristotle possessed when, in dealing with quite another problem than the one now directly before us, he defined the life of God,—the Energeia of the unmoved mover. Such a vision, but interpreted in terms which were quite as human as they were divine, Paul possessed when he wrote to the Corinthians concerning the spiritual gifts. This was Paul's beatific vision, granted him even while he was in the life of earthly tribulation, the vision of the Charity which never faileth,—the vision of Charity as still the greatest of the Christian graces in the world whereto the saved are to be translated.

The realm of absolute loyalty, of the Pauline charity, is what Christianity opposes to the Buddhistic Nirvana. In Nirvana the Buddha sees all, but is no longer an individual, and neither desires nor wills anything whatever. In Paul's vision of beatitude, when I shall know even as I am known, an endlessly restful spiritual activity, the activity of the glorified and triumphant Church, fills all the scene. It is an activity of individuals who still will, and perform the deeds of love, and endlessly aim to renew what they possess,—the life of the perfected and perfectly lovable community, where all are one in Christ.

Paul's vision unites, then, Aristotle's ideal of the divine beatitude, always active yet always at the goal, with his own perfectly practical and concrete ideal of what the united Church, as a community, should be, and in the perfect state, as he thinks, will be.

Thus the value of the loyal life, and of the love of the ideal community, is expressible in perfectly human terms. The problem of grace is the problem of the origin of loyalty; and is again a perfectly human problem. Paul's solution, in the opening of his letter to the Ephesians, "By grace are ye saved, and that not of yourselves; it is the gift of God," is for him the inevitable translation into religious speech of that comment upon the origin of loyalty which we have just, in summary form, stated. The origin of the power of grace is psychologically inexplicable, as all transforming love is. The object to which grace directs the convert's mind is above the level of any human individual.

The realm of grace is the realm of the powers and the gifts that save, by thus originating and sustaining and informing the loyal life. This realm contains, at the very least, three essentially necessary constituent members: First, the ideally lovable community of many individuals in one spiritual bond; secondly, the spirit of this community, which is present both as the human individual whose power originated and whose example, whose life and death, have led and still guide the community, and as the united spiritual activity of the whole community; thirdly, Charity itself, the love of the community by all its members, and of the members by the community.

To the religion of Paul, all these things must be divine. They all have their perfectly human correlate and foundation wherever the loyal life exists.

VIII

We now may see how the characterization of Christianity as not only a religion of love, but as also, in essence, a religion of loyalty, tends to throw light upon some of the otherwise most difficult aspects of the problem of Christianity. We can already predict how great this light, if it grows, promises to become.

Christianity is not the only religion in whose conceptions and experiences a community has been central. Loyalty has not left itself without a witness in many ages of human life, and in many peoples. And all the higher forms of loyalty are, in their spirit, religious; for they rest upon the discovery, or upon the faith, that, in all the darkness of our earthly existence, we individual human beings, separate as our organisms seem in their physical weakness, and sundered as our souls appear by their narrowness, and by their diverse loves and fortunes, are not as much alone, and not as helpless, in our chaos of divided will, as we seem.

For we are members one of another, and members, too, of a real life that, although human, is nevertheless, when it is lovable, also above the level upon which we, the separate individuals, live our existence. By our organisms and by our individual divisions of knowledge and of purpose, we are chained to an order of nature. By our loyalty, and by the real communities to which we are worthily loyal, we are linked with a level of mental existence such that, when compared with our individual existence, this higher level lies in the direction of the divine. Whatever the origin of men's ideals of their gods, there should be no doubt that these gods have often been conceived, by their worshippers, as the representatives of some human community, and as in some sense identical with that community.

But loyalty exists in countless forms and gradations. Christianity is characterized not only by the universality of the ideal community to which, in its greatest deeds and ages, it has, according to its intent, been loyal; but also by the depth and by the practical intensity and the efficacy of the love towards this community which has inspired its most representative leaders and reformers; and, finally, by the profoundly significant doctrines and customs to which it has been led in the course of its efforts to identify the being of its ideal community with the being of God.

Other religions have been inspired by loyalty. Other religions have identified a community with a divine being. And, occasionally, — yes, as the world has grown wiser and more united, increasingly, — non-Christian thinking and non-Christian religion have conceived an ideal community as inclusive as mankind, or as inclusive as the whole realm of beings with minds, however vast that realm may be.

But, historically speaking, Christianity has been distinguished by the concreteness and intensity with which, in the early stages of its growth, it grasped, loved, and served its own ideal of the visible community, supposed to be universal, which it called its Church. It has further been contrasted with other religions by the skill with which it gradually revised its views of the divine nature, in order to be able to identify the spirit that, as it believed, guided, inspired, and ruled this Church, with the spirit of the one whom it had come to worship as its risen Lord.

IX

If we bear these facts in mind, there is much in the otherwise so difficult history of Christian dogma which we can easily see in a new light. I myself am far from being a technical theologian, and, in coming to the few fragments of an understanding of the meaning of the history of dogma which I possess, I owe much to views such as, in England, Professor Percy Gardner has set forth, both in his earlier discussions, and notably in his recent book on "The Religious Experience of the Apostle Paul." I also owe new light to the remarkable conclusions which Professor Troeltsch of Heidelberg states, at the close of his recently published volume on "The Social Doctrines of the Christian Churches."[1] I shall make no endeavor in this place to deal with those technical aspects of the history of dogma which lie beyond my province as a philosophical student of the Christian doctrine of life. But if I attempt to restate a very few of the results of others in terms of that view of the essence of Christian loyalty which does concern me, my word, at this stage of our discussion, must be as follows: —

Jesus unquestionably taught, in the best-attested, and in the best-known, of his sayings, love for all individual human beings. But he taught this as an organic part of his doctrine of the Kingdom of Heaven. The individual whom you are bidden to love as your brother and your neighbor is, even while Jesus depicts him, transformed before your eyes. For, first, he is no longer the separate organism with a separate mind and a detached being and destiny, whom you ordinarily loathe if he is your enemy, and resist if he endangers or oppresses you. No, — when he asks your aid, — though he be "the least of these my brethren" — he speaks with the voice of the judge of all men, with the voice that you hope to hear saying: "Come ye blessed of my Father, for I was hungered and ye gave me meat." In other words, the real man, whom your eyes only seem to see, but whom on the level of ordinary human intercourse you simply ignore, actually belongs to another level of spiritual existence, above the level of our present life of divisions. The mystery of the

---

[1] *Die sozialen Lehren der Christlichen Kirchen und Gruppen* (Tübingen, 1912).

real being of this man is open only to the divine Love.

If you view your neighbor as your Father would have you view him, you view him not only as God's image, but also as God's will and God's love. If one asks for further light as to how the divine love views this man, the answer of Jesus, in the parables is, in substance, that this man is a member of the Kingdom of Heaven.

The Kingdom of Heaven is obviously a community. But this community is itself a mystery, — soon to be revealed, — but so far in the visible world, of which Jesus speaks, not yet to be discovered. This Kingdom is a treasure hid in a field. Its Master has gone into a far country. Watch and be ready. The Lord will soon return. The doctrine of Christian love, as thus taught by Jesus, so far as the records guide us, implies loyalty to the Kingdom; but expresses itself in forms which demand further interpretation, and which the Master intended to have further interpreted.

Now the apostolic churches held that those visions of the risen Lord, upon the memory and report of which their life as communities was so largely based, had begun for them this further interpretation. For them Christian loyalty soon became explicit; because their community became visible. And they believed their community to be the realization of the Kingdom; because they were sure that their risen Lord, whom the reported and recorded visions had shown, was henceforth in their midst as the spirit of this community.

The realm of grace, thus present to the Christian consciousness, needed to be further explored. The explorers were those who helped to define dogmas. The later development of the principal dogmas of the post-apostolic Church was due to a process in which, as Professor Troeltsch persuasively insists,[2] speculation and the use of the results of ancient philosophy (however skilful and learned such processes might be), were in all the great crises of the history of doctrine wholly subordinate to practical religious motives.[2]

To use the phraseology that I myself am obliged to prefer: The

[2]In the summary of his "Ergebnisse," on p. 967, *op. cit.*, Troeltsch says: —

"Es erhellt die Abhängigkeit der ganzen christlichen Vorstellungswelt und des Dogmas von den soziologischen Grundbedingungen, von der jeweiligen Gemeinschaftsidee. Das einzige besondere christliche Ur-Dogma, das Dogma von der Göttlichkeit des Christus, entsprang erst aus dem Christuskult und dieser wiederum aus der Notwendigkeit der Zusammenscharung der Gemeinde des neuen Geistes. Der Christuskult ist der Organisationspunkt einer christlichen Gemeinschaft und der Schöpfer des christlichen Dogmas. Da der Kultgott der Christen, nicht wie ein anderer Mysteriengott polytheistisch zu verstehen ist, sondern die erlösende Offen-

common sense of the Christian Church had three problems to solve. First: It was loyal to the universal spiritual community; and upon this loyalty, according to its view, salvation depended. But this universal community must be something concrete and practically efficacious. Hence the visible Church had to be organized as the appearance on earth of God's Kingdom. For what the parables had left mysterious about the object and the life of love, an authoritative interpretation, valid for the believers of those times, must be found, and was found in the visible Church.

Secondly, The life, the unity, the spirit of the Church had meanwhile to be identified with the person and with the spirit of the risen and ascended Lord, whom the visions of the first disciples had made henceforth a central fact in the belief of the Church.

The supernatural being whose body was now the Church, whose spirit was thus identified with the will and with the mind of a community, had once, as man, walked the earth, had really suffered and died. But since he had risen and ascended, henceforth—precisely because he was as the spirit whose body was this community, the Church—he was divine. Such was the essential article of the new faith.

Paul had already taught this. This very doctrine, in its further development, must be kept by the Church as concrete as the recorded life of the Master had been, as close to real life as the work of the visible Church was, and as true to the faith in the divine unity and destiny of the universal community, as Christian loyalty in all those formative centuries remained.

And yet all this must also be held in touch with that doctrine of the unity, the personality, and the ineffable transcendence of God,— that doctrine which was the heritage of the Church, both from the religion of Israel and from the wisdom of Greece. Speaking in a purely historical and human sense, the dogma of the Trinity was the psychologically inevitable effort at a solution of this complex but intensely practical problem.

barung des monotheistischen Gottes der Propheten darstellt, so wird aus dem Christusdogma das Trinitätsdogma. Alle philosophischen und mythologischen Entlehnungen sind nur Mittel für diesen aus der inneren Notwendigkeit der christlichen Kultgemeinschaft sich bildenden Gedanken." My own text, at this point, interprets the results which Troeltsch has reached, but also translates them into the terms of my own philosophy of loyalty. Lectures VII, VIII, and XV will show, in much greater fulness than is here possible, how far-reaching are the consequences which follow from accepting the interpretation of Christianity here merely sketched.

Loyalty to the community inspired this solution. The problem of the two natures of Christ, divine and human, was also psychologically forced upon Christianity by the very problem of the two levels of our human existence which I have just sketched.[3]

I speak still, not of the truth, but of the psychological motives of the dogma. The problem of the two levels of human existence is concrete, is practical, and exists for all of us. Every man who learns what the true goal of life is must live this twofold existence,—as separate individual, limited by the flesh of this maladjusted and dying organism,—yet also as member of a spiritual community which, if loyal, he loves, and in which, in so far as he is loyal, he knows that his only true life is hidden, and is lived.

But for Christianity this problem of the two levels was vital, not only for the individual Christian, but also for the interpretation of the person of Christ, and for the life of the Church. Since, for historical and psychological reasons, the solution of this problem could not be, for Christianity, either polytheistic or disloyal in its spirit, the only humanly natural course was, first, to distinguish the transcendent divine being from the concretely active spirit whose daily work was that of the Church, and then also to distinguish both of these from the human individuality of the Master who had taught the mystery of the Kingdom, and who had then suffered and died, and, as was believed, had risen to create his Church. One had, I say, clearly to distinguish all these; to declare them all to be perfectly real facts. And then one had to unite and, in form, to identify them all, by means of dogmas which were much less merely ingenious speculations than earnest resolutions to act and to believe whatever the loyal Christian life and the work of the Church demanded for the unity of humanity and for the salvation of the world.

The result may be estimated philosophically, as one may judge to be reasonable. I have said nothing about the metaphysical truth of these dogmas. But the result should not be judged as due to merely speculative subtleties, or as a practical degeneration of the spirit of the early Church.

The common sense of the Church was simply doing its best to express the meaning of its loyalty. This loyalty had its spiritual community and its human master. And its problems were the problems

---

[3]The relation of the traditional doctrine of the "two natures" to my present thesis regarding the "two levels" is something which I am solely responsible for asserting.

of all loyalty. And it was as a religion of loyalty, with a community, a Lord, and a Spirit to interpret, that Christianity was led to the doctrine of the two natures of Christ, and to the dogma of the Trinity.

X

The psychological motives and the historical background of the capital dogmas of the Church are therefore best to be understood in the light of the conception of the universal community, if only one recognizes the historical fact that the Christian consciousness was by purely human motives obliged to define its community as due to the work of the Master who once walked the earth.

It is not surprising, then, that the Fourth Gospel, wherein the Pauline conception of the Church as the body of Christ, and of Christ as the spirit of the Church, is perfectly united with the idea of the divine Word made flesh, is, of all the Gospels, the one which, although much the farthest from the literal history of the human Master's earthly words and deeds, has been, in its wholeness, the nearest to the heart of the Christian world during many centuries.

The Synoptic Gospels stir the spirits of men by the single word or saying of Jesus, by the recorded parable, or by the impressive incident, be this incident a legend, or a fragment of literally true portrayal (we often know not which).

But the Fourth Gospel impresses us most in its wholeness. This Gospel faces the central practical problem of Christianity, — the problem of grace, the transformation of the very essence of the individual man. This transformation is to save him by making him a dweller in the realm which is at once inaccessibly above his merely natural level as an individual, and yet daily near to whatever gives to his otherwise ruined natural existence its entire value. This realm is the realm of the level of the united and lovable community.

From this realm comes all saving grace. Wherever two or three are gathered together in a genuine unity of spirit, — this realm does indeed begin to display itself. Other religions besides Christianity have illustrated that fact. And whatever, apart from legend on the one hand, and speculative interpretation on the other, we human beings can appreciate, in a vital sense, concerning the meaning of what we call divine, we learn through such love for communities as arises from the companionships of those who are thus joined.

This truth humanity at large has long since possessed in countless expressions and disguises. But the fortune of Christianity led the

Church to owe its foundation to teachings, to events, to visions, and, above all, to a practical devotion, which, from the first, required the faithful to identify a human individual with the saving spirit of a community, and with the spirit of a community which was also conceived as wholly divine.

The union of the concrete and the ineffable which hereupon resulted, — the union of what touches the human heart and stirs the soul as only the voice of a living individual leader can touch it, — the complete union of this with the greatest and most inspiring of human mysteries, — the mystery of loving membership in a community whose meaning seems divine, — this union became the central interest of Christianity.

Apart from what is specifically Christian in belief, such union of the two levels has its place in our daily lives wherever the loyalty of an individual leader shows to other men the way that leads them to the realm of the spirit. And whenever that union takes place, the divine and the human seem to come into touch with each other as elsewhere they never do.

The mystery of loyalty, as Paul well knew, is the typical mystery of grace. It is, in another guise, the mystery of the incarnation. According to the mind of the early Christian Church, one individual had solved that mystery for all men.

He had risen from the shameful death that, for Christianity, as for its greatest rival Buddhism, is not only the inevitable but the just doom of whoever is born on the natural level of the human individual; — he had ascended to the level of the Spirit, and had become, in the belief of the faithful, the spirit of a community whose boundaries were coextensive with the world, and of whose dominion there was to be no end.

The Fourth Gospel conceives this union of the two levels of spiritual existence with a perfect mastery at once of the exalted poetry and of the definitely practical concreteness of the idea, and of the experiences which make it known to us. That the conception of the Logos — a philosophical conception of Greek origin — is used as the vehicle of the portrayal is, for our present purpose, a fact of subordinate importance.

What is most significant is the direct and vital grasp of the new problem, as it appears in the Fourth Gospel. The spirit of the infant Church is here expressed with such unity and such pathos that all the complications of the new ideas vanish; and one sees only the symbol of the perfectly literal and perfectly human triumph of the Spirit,—a triumph which can appear only in this form of the uniting of the level of individuality with the level of perfect loyalty.

In the tale here presented, the dust of our natural divisions is stirred into new life. From the tomb of individual banishment into which the divine has freely descended, from the wreck to which every human individual is justly doomed, the Word made flesh arises.

But "Who is this King of Glory?" He is, in this portrayal, the one who says: "I am the vine. Ye are the branches." The Spirit of the community speaks. The Pauline metaphor appears in a new expression. But it is uttered not by the believer, but by the being who has solved the mystery of the union of the self and the community. He speaks to individuals who have not yet reached that union. He comforts them:—

"Peace I leave with you; my peace I give unto you; not as the world giveth give I unto you." This is the voice of the saving community to the troubled soul of the lonely individual.

"Let not your heart be troubled, neither let it be fearful. Ye have heard how I said to you, I go away, and I come to you." "Abide in me, and I in you. As the branch cannot bear fruit of itself except it abide in the vine; so neither can ye, except ye abide in me."

"These things have I spoken unto you in proverbs: The hour cometh, when I shall no more speak unto you in proverbs, but shall tell you plainly of the Father." "In the world ye shall have tribulation; but be of good cheer; I have overcome the world."

The loyal alone know whose world this is, and for whom. In the prayer with which this farewell closes, the Jesus of the Fourth Gospel prays: "Holy Father, keep them in thy name which thou hast given me, that they may be one, even as we are one."

These are explicitly the words of the spirit of the universal community, whom mortal eyes no longer see, and whom, in a lonely world of tribulation, men who are doomed to die now miss with grief and expect with longing. But: "Hast thou been so long with me, and hast not known me?"

In such words the Fourth Gospel embodies the living spirit of the lovable community. This is what the loyal soul knows.

That is why I venture to say in my own words (though I am neither apologist, nor Christian preacher, nor theologian), that Christianity is a religion not only of love, but also of loyalty. And that is why the Fourth Gospel tells us the essential ideas both of Christianity, and of the Christian Realm of Grace, more fully than do the parables, unless you choose to read the parables as the voice of the Spirit of the Church.

In all this I have meant to say, and have said, nothing whatever about the truth, or about the metaphysical bases of Christian dogma.

I have been characterizing the human motives that lie at the basis of the doctrine of the realm of grace, and have been pointing out the ethical and religious value of these motives.

V

Time and Guilt

In Matthew Arnold's essay on "St. Paul and Protestantism," there is a well-known passage from which I may quote a few words to serve as a text for the present lecture. These words express what many would call a typical modern view of an ancient problem.

I

In this essay, just before the words which I shall quote, Matthew Arnold has been speaking of the relation between Paul's moral experiences and their religious interpretation, as the Apostle formulates it in the epistle to the Romans. Referring to a somewhat earlier stage of his own argument, Arnold here says: "We left Paul in collision with the fact of human nature, but in itself a sterile fact, a fact upon which it is possible to dwell too long, although Puritanism, thinking this impossible, has remained intensely absorbed in the contemplation of it, and indeed has never properly got beyond it, —

the sense of sin." "Sin," continues Matthew Arnold, "is not a monster to be mused on, but an impotence to be got rid of. All thinking about it, beyond what is indispensable for the firm effort to get rid of it, is waste of energy and waste of time. We then enter that element of morbid and subjective brooding, in which so many have perished. This sense of sin, however, it is also possible to have not strongly enough to beget the firm effort to get rid of it; and the Greeks, with all their great gifts, had this sense not strongly enough; its strength in the Hebrew people is one of this people's mainsprings. And no Hebrew prophet, or psalmist felt what sin was more powerfully than Paul." In the sequel, Arnold shows how Paul's experience of the spiritual influence of Jesus enabled the Apostle to solve his own problem of sin without falling into that dangerous brooding which Arnold attributes to the typical Puritan spirit. As a result, Arnold identifies his own view of sin with that of Paul and counsels us to judge the whole matter in the same way.

We have here nothing to do with the correctness of Matthew Arnold's criticism of Protestantism; and also nothing to say, at the present moment, about the adequacy of Arnold's interpretation, either of Paul or of Jesus. But we are concerned with that characteristically modern view of the problem of sin which Arnold so clearly states in the words just quoted.

What constitutes the moral burden of the individual man, — what holds him back from salvation, — may be described in terms of his natural heritage, — his inborn defect of character, — or in terms of his training, — or, finally, in terms of whatever he has voluntarily done which has been knowingly unrighteous. In the present lecture I am not intending to deal with man's original defects of moral nature, nor yet with the faults which his training, through its social vicissitudes, may have bred in him. I am to consider that which we call, in the stricter sense, sin.

Whether correctly or incorrectly, a man often views certain of his deeds as in some specially intimate sense his own, and may also believe that, amongst these his own deeds, some have been wilfully counter to what he believes to be right. Such wrongful deeds a man may regard as his own sins. He may decline to plead ignorance, or bad training, or uncontrollable defect of temper, or overwhelming temptation, as the ground and excuse for just these deeds. Before the forum of his own conscience he may say: "That deed was the result of my own moral choice, and was my sin." For the time being I shall not presuppose, for the purposes of this argument, any philosophical theory about free will. I shall not, in this lecture, assert that, as a fact, there is any genuinely free will whatever. At the moment, I shall provisionally accept only so much of the verdict of common sense as any man accepts when he says: "That was my own voluntary deed, and was knowingly and wilfully sinful." Hereupon I shall ask: Is Matthew Arnold's opinion correct with regard to the way in which the fact and the sense of sin ought to be viewed by a man who believes that he has, by what he calls his own "free act and deed," sinned? Is Arnold's opinion sound and adequate when he says: "Sin is not a monster to be mused on, but an impotence to be got rid of." Arnold praises Paul for having taken sin seriously enough to get rid of it, but also praises him for not having brooded over sin except to the degree that was "indispensable to the effort to get rid of it." Excessive brooding over sin is, in Arnold's opinion, an evil characteristic of Puritanism. Is Arnold right?

II

Most of us will readily agree that Arnold's words have a ring of sound modern sense when we first hear them spoken. Brooding over one's sins certainly appears to be not always,—yes, not frequently,—and surely not for most modern men, a convenient spiritual exercise. It tends not to the edification, either of the one who broods, or of his brethren. Brooding sinners are neither agreeable companions nor inspiring guides. Arnold is quite right in pointing out that Paul's greatest and most eloquent passages—those amongst his words which we best remember and love—are full of the sense of having somehow "got rid" of the very sin to which Paul most freely confesses when he speaks of his own past as a persecutor of the Church and as an unconverted Pharisee. It is, then, the escape from sin, and not the bondage to sin, which helps a man to help his fellows. Ought not, therefore, the thought of sin to be used only under the strict and, so to speak, artistic restraints to which Matthew Arnold advises us to keep it subject? You have fallen into a fault; you have given over your will to the enemy; you have wronged your fellow; or, as you believe, you have offended God in word and deed. What are you now to do about this fact? "Get rid of your sin," says Matthew Arnold. Paul did so. He did so through what he called a loving union with the spirit of Christ. As he expressed the matter, he "died" to sin. He "lived" henceforth to the righteousness of his Master and of the

Christian community. And that was, for him, the end of brooding, unless you call it brooding when his task as missionary required him to repeat the simple confession of his earlier life, — the life that he had lived before the vision of the risen Christ transformed him. Matthew Arnold counsels a repetition of Paul's experience in modern fashion, and with the use of modern ideas rather than of whatever was narrow, and of whatever is now superseded, in Paul's religious opinions and imagery.

The modern version of Paulinism, as set forth by Arnold, would involve, first, a return to the primitive Christianity of the sayings of Jesus; next, a "falling in love" with the person and character of Jesus; and, finally, a "getting rid of sin" through a new life of love, lived in the spirit of Jesus. Matthew Arnold's version of the Gospel is, at the present moment, more familiar to general readers of the literature of the problem of Christianity than it was when he wrote his essays on religion. So far as sin is concerned, is not this version heartily acceptable to the modern mind? Is it not sensible, simple, and in spirit strictly normal, as well as moral and religious? Does it not dispose, once for all, both of the religious and of the practical aspect of the problem of sin?

I cannot better state the task of this lecture than by taking the opportunity which Arnold's clearness of speech gives me to begin the study of our question in the light of so favorite a modern opinion.

III

It would not be useful for us to consider any further, in this place, Paul's own actual doctrine about such sin as an individual thinks to have been due to his own voluntary and personal deed. Paul's view regarding the nature of original sin involves other questions than the one which is at present before us. We speak here not of original sin, but of knowing and voluntary evil doing. Paul's idea of salvation from original sin through grace, and through loving union with the spirit of the Master, is inseparable from his special opinions regarding the Church as the body of Christ, and regarding the supernatural existence of the risen Christ as the Spirit of the Church. These matters also are not now before us. The same may be said of Paul's views concerning the forgiveness of our voluntary sins. For, in Paul's mind, the whole doctrine of the sins which the individual has knowingly and wilfully committed, is further complicated by the Apostle's teachings about predestination. And for an inquiry into those teachings there is, in this lecture, neither space nor motive. Manifold and impressive though Paul's dealings with the problem of sin are, we shall therefore do well, upon this occasion, to approach the doctrine of the voluntary sins of the individual from another side than the one which Paul most emphasizes. Let us turn to aspects of the Christian tradition about wilful sin for which Paul is not mainly responsible.

We all know, in any case, that Arnold's own views about the sense and the thought of sin are not the views which have been prevalent in the past history of Christianity. And Arnold's hostility to the Puritan spirit carries him too far when he seems to attribute to Puritanism the principal responsibility for having made the fact and the sense of sin so prominent as it has been in Christian thought. Long before Puritanism, mediæval Christianity had its own meditations concerning sin. Others than Puritans have brooded too much over their sins. And not all Puritans have cultivated the thought of sin with a morbid intensity.

I have no space for a history of the Christian doctrine of wilful sin. But, by way of preparation for my principal argument, I shall next call to mind a few of the more familiar Christian beliefs concerning the perils and the results of voluntary sin, without caring, at the moment, whether these beliefs are mediæval, or Puritan, or not. Thereafter, I shall try to translate the sense of these traditional beliefs into terms which seem to me to be worthy of the serious consideration of the modern man. After this restatement and interpretation of the Christian doctrine,—not of original sin, but of the voluntary sin of the individual,—we shall have new means of seeing whether Arnold is justified in declaring that no thought about sin is wise except such thought as is indispensable for arousing the effort "to get rid of sin."

IV

The teaching of Jesus concerning wilful sin, as it is recorded in some of the best known of his sayings, is simple and searching, august in the severity of the tests which it uses for distinguishing sinful deeds from righteous deeds, and yet radiant with its familiar message of hope for the sincerely repentant sinner. I have no right to judge as to the authenticity of the individual sayings of Jesus which our Gospels record. But the body of the teachings of the Master concerning sin is not only one of the most frequently quoted portions of the Gospel tradition, but is also an essential part of that doctrine of Christian love which great numbers of Christian souls, both learned and unlearned, find to be the most obviously characteristic expression of what the founder had at heart when he came to seek and to save that which was lost. Searching is this teaching about sin, because of what Matthew Arnold called the *inwardness* of the spirit which Jesus everywhere emphasized in telling us what is the essence of righteousness. August is this teaching in the severity of the tests which it applies; because all seeming, all worldly repute, all outward conformity to rules, avail nothing in the eyes of the Master, unless the interior life of the doer of good works is such as fully meets the requirements of love, both towards God and towards man.

Countless efforts have been made to sum up in a few words the spirit of the ethical teaching of Jesus. I make no new effort, I contribute no novel word or insight, when I now venture to say, simply in passing, that the religion of the founder, as preserved in the sayings, is a religion of Whole-Heartedness. The voluntary good deed is one which, whatever its outward expression may be, carries with it the whole heart of love, both to God and to the neighbor. The special act—whether it be giving the cup of cold water, or whether it be the martyr's heroism in confessing the name of Jesus in presence of the persecutor—matters less than the inward spirit. The Master gives no elaborate code to be applied to each new situation. The whole heart devoted to the cause of the Kingdom of Heaven, —this is what is needed.

On the other hand, whatever wilful deed does not spring from love of God and man, and especially whatever deed breaks with the instinctive dictates of whole-hearted love, is sin. And sin means alienation from the Kingdom and from the Father; and hence, in the end, means destruction. Here again the august severity of the teaching is fully manifested. But from this destruction there is indeed an escape. It is the escape by the road of repentance. That is the only road which is emphatically and repeatedly insisted upon in the sayings of Jesus, as we have them. But this repentance must include a whole-hearted willingness to forgive those who trespass against us. Thus repentance means a return both to the Father and to the whole-hearted life of love. Another name for this wholeheartedness, in action as well as in repentance, is faith. For the true lover of God instinctively believes the word of the Son of Man who teaches these things and is sure that the Kingdom of God will come.

But like the rest of the reported sayings of Jesus, this simple and august doctrine of the peril of sin, and of the way of escape through repentance, comes to us with many indications that some further and fuller revelation of its meaning is yet to follow. Jesus appears in the Gospel reports as himself formally announcing to individuals that their sins are forgiven. The escape from sin is therefore not always wholly due to the repentant sinner's own initiative. Assistance is needed. And Jesus appears in the records, as assisting. He assists, not only as the teacher who announces the Kingdom, but as the one who has "power to forgive sins." Here again I simply follow the well-known records. I am no judge as to what sayings are authentic.

I am sure, however, that it was but an inevitable development of the original teaching of the founder and of these early reports about his authority to forgive, when the Christian community later conceived that salvation from personal and voluntary sin had become possible through the work which the departed Lord had done while on earth. *How* Christ saved from sin became hereupon a problem. But *that* he saved from sin, and that he somehow did so through what he won for men by his death, became a central constituent of the later Christian tradition.

A corollary of this central teaching was a further opinion which tradition also emphasized, and, for centuries, emphasized the more, the further the apostolic age receded into the past. This further opinion was: That the wilful sinner is powerless to return to a whole-hearted union with God through any deed of his own. He could not "get rid of sin," either by means of repentance or otherwise, unless the work of Christ had prepared the way. This, in sum, was long the common tradition of the Christian world. How the saving work of Christ became or could be made efficacious for obtaining the forgiveness of the wilful sin of an individual,—this question, as we well know, received momentous and conflicting answers as the Christian church grew, differentiated, and went through its various experiences of heresy, of schism, and of the learned interpretation of its faith. Here, again, the details of the history of dogma, and the practice of the Church and of its sects in dealing with the forgiveness of sins, concern us not at all.

We need, however, to remind ourselves, at this point, of one further aspect of the tradition about wilful sin. That sin, if unforgiven, leads to "death," was a thought which Judaism had inherited from the religion of the prophets of Israel. It was a grave thought, essential to the ethical development of the faith of Israel, and capable of vast development in the light both of experience and of imagination.

Because of the later growth of the doctrine of the future life, the word "death" came to mean, for the Christian mind, what it could not yet have meant for the early prophets of Israel. And, in consequence, Christian tradition gradually developed a teaching that the divinely ordained penalty of unforgiven sin—the doom of the wilful sinner—is a "second death," an essentially endless penalty. The Apocalypse imaginatively pictures this doom. When the Church came to define its faith as to the future life, it developed a well-known group of opinions concerning this endless penalty of sin. In its outlines this group of opinions is familiar even to all children who have learned anything of the faith of the fathers.

An essentially analogous group of opinions is found in various religions that are not Christian. In its origin this group of opinions goes back to the very beginnings of those forms of ethical religion whose history is at all closely parallel to the history of Judaism or of Christianity. The motives which are here in question lie deeply rooted in human nature; but I have no right and no time to attempt to analyze them now. It is enough for my purpose to remind you that the idea of the endless penalty of unforgiven sin is by no means peculiar to Puritanism; and that it is certainly an idea which, for those who accept it with any hearty faith, very easily leads to many thoughts about sin which tend to exceed the strictly artistic measure which Matthew Arnold assigns as the only fitting one for all such thoughts.

To think of a supposed "endless penalty" as a certain doom for all unforgiven sin, may not lead to morbid brooding. For the man who begins such thoughts may be sedately sure that he is no sinner. Or again, although he confesses himself a sinner, he may be pleasantly convinced that forgiveness is readily and surely attainable, at least for himself. And, as we shall soon see, there are still other reasons why no morbid thought need be connected with the idea of endless penalty. But no doubt such a doctrine of endless penalty tends to awaken thoughts which have a less modern seeming, and which involve a less sure confidence in one's personal power to "get rid of sin" than Matthew Arnold's words, as we have cited them, convey. If, without any attempt to dwell further, either upon the history or the complications of the traditional Christian doctrine of the wilful sin of the individual. we reduce that doctrine to its simplest terms, it consists of two theses, both of which have had a vast and tragic influence upon the fortunes of Christian civilization. The theses are these: First: "By no deed of his own, unaided by the supernatural consequences of the work of Christ, can the wilful sinner win forgiveness." Second: "The penalty of unforgiven sin is the endless second death."

V

The contrast between these two traditional theses and the modern spirit seems manifest enough, even if we do not make use of Matthew Arnold's definition of the reasonable attitude towards sin. This contrast of the old faith and the modern view is one of the most frequently emphasized means of challenging the ethical significance of the Christian tradition.

It is indeed difficult to define just who the "modern man" is, and what views he has to hold in order to be modern. But very many people, I suppose, would be disposed to accept as a partial definition of the modern man, this formulation: "The modern man is one who does not believe in hell, and who is too busy to think about his own sins." If this definition is indeed too trivial to be just, it would still seem to many serious people that, at this point, if at no other, the modern man has parted company with Christian tradition.

And the parting would appear to be not accidental, nor yet due to superficial motives. The deepest ethical interests would be at stake, if the appearances here represent the facts as they are. For the old faith held that the very essence of its revelation concerning righteousness was bound up with its conception of the consequences of unforgiven sin. On the other hand, if the education of the human race has taught us any coherent lesson, it has taught us to respect the right of a rational being to be judged by moral standards that he himself can see to be reasonable.

Hence the moral dignity of the modern idea of man seems to depend upon declining to regard as just and righteous any penalty which is supposed to be inflicted by the merely arbitrary will of any supernatural power. The just penalty of sin, to the modern mind, must therefore be the penalty, whatever it is, which the enlightened sinner, if fully awake to the nature of his deed, and rational in his estimate of his deed, would voluntarily inflict upon himself. And how can one better express that penalty than by following the spirit of Matthew Arnold's advice: "Get rid of your sin"? This advice, to be sure, has its own deliberate sternness. For "the firm effort to get rid of sin" may involve long labor and deep grief. But "endless penalty," a "second death,"—what ethically tolerable meaning can a modern mind attach to these words?

Is not, then, the chasm between the modern ethical view and the ancient faith at this point simply impassable? Have the two not parted company altogether, both in letter and, still more, in their inmost spirit?

To this question some representatives of modern liberal Christianity would at once reply that, as I have already pointed out, the early Gospel tradition does not attribute to Jesus himself the more hopeless aspects of the doctrine of sin, as the later tradition was led to define them. Jesus, according to the reports of his teaching in the Gospels, does indeed more than once use a doctrine of the endless penalty of unforgiven sin,—a doctrine with which a portion of the Judaism of his day was more or less familiar. In well-known parables he speaks of the torments of another world. And in general he deals with wilful sin unsparingly. But, so far as the present life is concerned, he seems to leave the door of repentance always open. The Father waits for the Prodigal Son's return. And the Prodigal Son returns of his own will. We hear nothing in the parables about his being unable effectively to repent unless some supernatural plan of salvation has first been worked out for him. Is it not possible, then, to reconcile the Christian spirit and the modern man by simply returning to the Christianity of the parables? So, in our day, many assert.

I do not believe that the parables, in the form in which we possess them, present to us any complete view of the essence of the Christian doctrine of sin, or of the sinner's way of escape. I do not believe that they were intended by the Master to do so. I have already pointed out how our reports of the founder's teachings about sin indicate that these teachings were intended to receive a further interpretation and supplement. Our real problem is whether the interpretation and supplement which later Christian tradition gave, through its doctrine of sin, and of the endless penalty of sin, was, despite its tragedy, its mythical setting, and its arbitrariness, a

teaching whose ethical spirit we can still accept or, at least, understand. Is the later teaching, in any sense, a just development of the
underlying meaning of the parables? Does any deeper idea inform
the traditional doctrine that the wilful sinner is powerless to save
himself from a just and endless penalty through any repentance, or
through any new deed of his own?

As I undertake to answer these questions, let me ask you to bear
in mind one general historical consideration. Christianity, even in its
most imaginative and in its most tragic teachings, has always been
under the influence of very profound ethical motives, — the motives
which already inspired the prophets of Israel. The founder's doctrine
of the Kingdom, as we now possess that doctrine, was an outline of
an ethical religion. It was also a prologue to a religion that was yet to
be more fully revealed, or at least explained. This, as I suppose, was
the founder's personal intention. When the early Church sought to
express its own spirit, it was never knowingly false; it was often
most fluently, yet faithfully, true to the deeper meaning of the
founder. Its expressions were borrowed from many sources. Its
imagination was constructive of many novelties. Only its deeper
spirit was marvelously steadfast. Even when, in its darker moods, its
imagination dwelt upon the problem of sin, it saw far more than it
was able to express in acceptable formulas. Its imagery was often of
local, or of heathen, or even of primitive origin. But the truth which
the imagery rendered edifying and teachable, — this often bears and
invites an interpretation whose message is neither local nor primitive. Such an interpretation I believe to be possible in case of the
doctrine of sin and of its penalty; and to my own interpretation I
must now ask your attention.

VI

There is one not infrequent thought about sin upon which Matthew Arnold's rule would surely permit us to dwell; for it is a
thought which helps us, if not wholly "to get rid of sin," still, in
advance of decisive action, to forestall some temptations to sin which
we might otherwise find too insistent for our safety. It is the thought
which many a man expresses when he says, of some imagined act:
"If I were to do that, I should be false to all that I hold most dear; I
should throw away my honor; I should violate the fidelity that is to
me the very essence of my moral interest in my existence." The
thought thus expressed may be sometimes merely conventional; but

it may also be very earnest and heartfelt.

Every man who has a moral code which he accepts, not merely as the customary and, to him, opaque or senseless verdict of his tribe or of his caste, but as his own chosen personal ideal of life, has his power to formulate what for him would seem (to borrow the religious phraseology) his "sin against the Holy Ghost,"—his own morally "impossible" choice, so far as he can now predetermine what he really means to do.

Different men, no doubt, have different exemplary sins in mind when they use such words. Their various codes may be expressions of quite different and largely accidental social traditions; their diverse examples of what, for each of them, would be his own instance of the unpardonable sin, may be the outcome of the *tabus* of whatever social order you please. I care for the moment not at all for the objective ethical correctness of any one man's definition of his own moral code. And I am certainly here formulating no ethical code of my own. I am simply pointing out that, when a man becomes conscious of his own rule of life, of his own ideal of what makes his voluntary life worth while, he tends to arrange his ideas of right and wrong acts so that, for him at least, *some* acts, when he contemplates the bare possibility of doing them himself, appear to him to be acts such that they would involve for him a kind of moral suicide,—a deliberate wrecking of what makes life, for himself, morally worthwhile.

One common-sense way of expressing such an individual judgment upon these extreme acts of wrong-doing, is to say: "If I were to do that of my own free will, I could thereafter never forgive myself."

Since I am here not undertaking any critical discussion of the idea of the "Ought," I do not now venture the thesis that every man who is a reasonable being at all, or who, as they say, "has a conscience," must needs be able to name instances of acts which, if he knowingly chose to do them, would make his life, in his own eyes, a moral chaos,—a failure,—so that he would "never forgive" himself for those acts. If a student of ethics asks me to prove that a man ought to view his own life and his own will in this way, I am not here concerned to offer such a proof in philosophical terms.

But this I can point out: In case a man thinks of his own possible actions in this way, he need not be morbidly brooding over sins of which it is well not to think too much. He *may* be simply surveying his plan of life in a resolute way, and deciding, as well as he can, where he stands; what his leading ideas are, and what makes his voluntary life, from his own point of view, worth living. To be resolute, is at all events no weakness; and nobody "perishes" merely because he has his mind clearly made up regarding what, for him, would be his own unpardonable sin. There is no loss for one's manhood in knowing how one's "sin against the Holy Ghost," one's possible act for which one is resolved never to ask one's own forgiveness, is defined. Such thoughts tend to clear our moral air, if only we think them in terms of our own personal ideals, and do not, as is too often the case, apply them solely to render more dramatic our judgments about our neighbors.

VII

In order to be able to formulate such thoughts, one must have an "ideal," even if one cannot state it in an abstract form. One must think of one's voluntary life in terms of fidelity to some such "ideal," or set of ideals. One must regard one's self as a creature with a purpose in living. One must have what they call a "mission" in one's own world. And so, whether one uses philosophical theories or religious beliefs, or does not use them, one must, when one speaks thus, actually have some sort of spiritual realm in which, as one believes, one's moral life is lived, a realm to whose *total* order, as one supposes, one could be false if one chose. One's mission, one's business, must ideally extend, in some fashion, to the very boundaries of this spiritual realm, so that, if one actually chose to commit one's supposed unpardonable sin, one could exist in this entire realm only as, in some sense and degree, an outcast, — estranged, so far as that one unpardonable fault estranged one, from one's own chosen moral hearth and fireside. At least this is how one resolves, in advance of decisive action, to view the matter, in case one has the precious privilege of being able to make such resolves. And I say that so to find one's self resolving, is to find *not* weakness and brooding, but resoluteness and clearness. Life seems simply blurred and dim if one can nowhere find in it such sharp moral outlines. And if one becomes conscious of such sharp outlines, one is not saying: "Behold me, the infallible judge of moral values for all mankind. Behold me with the absolute moral code precisely worked out." For one is so far making no laws for one's neighbors. One is accepting no merely traditional *tabus*. One is simply making up one's mind so as to give a more coherent sense to one's choices. The penalty of *not* being able to make such resolves regarding what would be one's own unpardonable sin, is simply the penalty of flabbiness and irresoluteness. To remain unaware of what we propose to do, never helps us to live. To be aware of our coherent plan, to have a moral world and a business that, in ideal, extends to the very boundaries of this world, and to view one's life, or any part of it, as an expression of one's own personal will, is to assert one's genuine freedom, and is not to accept any external bondage. But it is also to bind one's self, in all the clearness of a calm resolve. It is to view certain at least abstractly possible deeds as moral catastrophes, as creator of chaos, as deeds whereby the self, *if* it chose them, would, at least in so far, banish itself from its own country.

To be able to view life in this way, to resolve thus deliberately what genuine and thoroughgoing sin would mean for one's own vision, requires a certain maturity. Not all ordinary misdeeds are in question when one thinks of the unpardonable sin. Blunders of all sorts fill one's childhood and youth. What Paul conceived as our original sin may have expressed itself for years in deeds that our social order condemns, and that our later life deeply deplores. And yet, in all this maze of past evil-doing and of folly, we may have been, so far, either helpless victims of our nature and of our training, or blind followers of false gods. What Paul calls sin may have "abounded." And yet, as we look back, we may now judge that all this was merely a means whereby, henceforth, "grace may more abound." We may have learned to say, — it may be wise, and even our actual duty to say: "I will not brood over these which were either my ignorant or my helpless sins. I will henceforth firmly and simply resolve 'to get rid of them.' That is for me the best. Bygones are bygones. Remorse is a waste of time. These 'confusions of a wasted youth' must be henceforth simply ignored. That is the way of cheer. It is also the way of true righteousness. I can live wisely only in case I forget my former follies, except in so far as a memory of these follies helps me not to repeat them."

One may only the more insist upon this cheering doctrine of Lethe and forgiveness for the past, and of "grace abounding" for the future, when there comes into one's life those happenings which Paul viewed as a new birth, and as a "dying to sin." These workings of "grace," if they occur to us, may transform our "old man" of inherited defect, of social waywardness, of contentiousness, and of narrow hatred for our neighbors and for "the law" into the "new life." It is a new life to us because we now seem to have found our own cause, and have learned to love our sense of intimate companionship with the universe. Now, for the first time, we have found a life that seems to us to have transparent sense, unity of aim, and an abiding and sustaining inspiration about it.

If this result has taken place, then, whatever our cause, or our moral opinions, or our religion may be, we shall tend to rejoice with Paul that we have now "died" to the old life of ignorance and of evil-working distractions. Hereupon we may be ready to say, with him, and joyously: "There is no condemnation" for us who are ready to walk after what we now take to be "the spirit." The past is dead. Grace has saved us. Forgiveness covers the evil deeds that were done. For those deeds, as we now see, were *not* done by our awakened selves. They were not our own "free acts" at all. They were the workings of what Paul called "the flesh." "Grace" has blotted them out.

I am still speaking not of any one faith about the grace that saves, or about the ideal of life. Let a man find his salvation as it may happen to him to find it. But the main point that I have further to insist upon is this: Whenever and however we have become morally mature enough to get life all colored through and through by what seems to us a genuinely illuminating moral faith, so that it seems to us as if, in every deed, we could serve, despite our weakness, our one highest cause, and be faithful to all our moral world at every moment, — then this inspiration has to be paid for. The abundance of grace means, henceforth, a new gravity of life.

For we now have to face the further fact that, if we have thus won vast ideals, and a will that is now inspired to serve them, we can imagine ourselves becoming false to this our own will, to this which gives our life its genuine value. We can imagine ourselves breaking faith with our own world-wide cause and inspiration. One who has found his cause, if he has a will of his own, can become a conscious and deliberate traitor. One who has found his loyalty is indeed, at first, under the obsession of the new spirit of grace. But if, henceforth, he lives with a will of his own, he can, by a wilful closing of his eyes to the light, *become* disloyal.

Our actual voluntary life does not bear out any theory as to the fatally predestined perseverance of the saints. For our voluntary life seems to us as if it was free either to persevere or not to persevere.

The more precious the light that has seemed to come to me, the deeper is the disgrace to which, in my own eyes, I can condemn myself, if I voluntarily become false to this light.

Now it is indeed not well to brood over such chances of falsity. But it is manly to face the fact that they are present.

I repeat that, in all this statement, I have presupposed no philosophical theory of free will, and have not assumed the truth of any one ethical code or doctrine. I have been speaking simply in terms of moral experience, and have been pointing out how the world seems to a man who reaches sufficient moral maturity to possess, even if but for a season, a pervasive and practically coherent ideal of life, and to value himself as a possible servant of his cause, but a servant whose freedom to choose is still his own.

What I point out is that, if a man has won practically a free and conscious view of what his honor requires of him, the reverse side of this view is also present. This reverse side takes the form of knowing what, for this man himself, it would mean to be wilfully false to his honor. One who knows that he freely serves his cause knows that he could, if he chose, become a traitor. And if indeed he freely serves his cause, he knows whether or no he could forgive himself if he wilfully became a traitor. Whoever, through grace, has found the beloved of his life, and now freely lives the life of love, knows that he could, if he chose, betray his beloved. And he knows what estimate his own free choice now requires him to put upon such betrayal.

Choose your cause, your beloved, and your moral ideal as you please. What I now point out is that so to choose is to imply your power to define what, for you, would be the unpardonable sin if you committed it. This unpardonable sin would be betrayal.

VIII

So far I have spoken of the moral possibility of treason. We seem to be free. Therefore it seems to us as if treason were possible. But now, *do* any of us ever actually thus betray our own chosen cause? Do we ever actually turn traitor to our own flag,—to the flag that we have sworn to serve,—after taking our oath, not as unto men, but as unto ourselves and our cause? Do any of us ever really commit that which, in our own eyes, is the unpardonable sin?

Here, again, let every one of us judge for himself. And let him also judge rather himself than his neighbor. For we are here speaking, not of customary codes, nor of outward seeming, but of how a man who knows his ideal and knows his own will finds that his inward deed appears to himself.

Still, apart from all evil speaking, the common experience of mankind *seems* to show that such actual and deliberate sin against the light, such conscious and wilful treason, occasionally takes place.

So far as we know of such treason at all, or reasonably believe in its existence, it appears to us to be, on the whole, the worst evil with which man afflicts his fellows and his social order in this distracted world of human doings. The blindness and the naïve cruelty of crude passion, the strife and hatred with which the natural social order is filled, often seem to us mild when we compare them with the spiritual harm that follows the intentional betrayal of great causes once fully accepted, but then wilfully forsaken, by those to whom they have been intrusted.

"If the light that is in thee be darkness, how great is that darkness." This is the word which seems especially fitted for the traitor's own case. For he has seen the great light. The realm of the spirit has been graciously opened to him. He has willingly entered. He has chosen to serve. And then he has closed his eyes; and by his own free choice, a darkness far worse than that of man's primal savagery has come upon him. And the social world, the unity of brotherhood, the beloved life which he has betrayed, — how desolate he has left what was fairest in it. He has reduced to its primal chaos the fair order of those who trusted and who lived and loved together in one spirit!

But we are here little concerned with what others think of the traitor, if such traitor there be. We are interested in what (if the light against which he has sinned returns to him), the traitor henceforth is to think of himself. Matthew Arnold would say, "Let him think of his sin," — that is, in this case, of his treason, — only in so far as is indispensable to the "firm resolve to get rid of it." We ask whether, — now that the traitor has first won his own light, and has defined by his own will his own unpardonable sin, and has then betrayed his cause, has sinned against his light and has done his little best to make chaos of his own chosen ideal and of his moral order, — we ask, I say, whether Arnold's rule seems any longer quite adequate to meet the situation.

Of course I am not venturing to assign to the supposed traitor any penalties *except* those which his own will really intends to assign to him. I am not acting in the least as his Providence. I am leaving him quite free to decide his own fate. I am certainly not counselling him to feel any particular kind or degree of the mere emotion called remorse. For all that I now shall say, he is quite free, if that is his desire, to forget his treason once for all, and to begin his business afresh with a new moral ideal, or with no ideal at all, as he may choose.

What I ask, however, is simply this: *If* he resumes his former position of knowing and choosing an ideal, if he also remembers what ideal he formerly chose, and what and how and how deliberately he betrayed, and knows himself for what he is, what does he judge regarding the now inevitable and endless consequences of his deed? And what answer will be now make to Matthew Arnold's kind advice: — "Get rid of your sin." He need not answer in a brooding way. He need be no Puritan. He may remain as cheerful in his passing feelings as you please. He may quite calmly rehearse the facts. He may decline to shed any tear, either of repentance or of terror. My only hypothesis is that he sees the facts as they are, and confesses, however coolly and dispassionately, the moral value which, as a matter of simple coherence of view and opinion, he now assigns to himself.

IX

He will answer Matthew Arnold's advice, as I think, thus: "'Get rid of my sin?' How can I get rid of it? It is done. It is past. It is as irrevocable as the Archæan geological period, or as the collision of stellar masses, the light of whose result we saw here on earth a few years ago, when a new star flamed forth in the Constellation Perseus. I am the one who, at such a time, with such a light of the spirit shining before me, with my eyes thus and thus open to my business and to my moral universe, first, so far as I could freely act at all, freely closed my eyes, and then committed what my own will had already defined to be my unpardonable sin. So far as in me lay, in all my weakness, but yet with all the wit and the strength that just then were mine, I was a traitor.

"That fact, that event, that deed, is irrevocable. The fact that I am the one who then did thus and so, not ignorantly, but knowingly, — that fact will outlast the ages. That fact is as endless as time.

"And, in so far as I continue to value myself as a being whose life is coherent in its meaning, this fact that then and there I was a traitor will always consitute a genuine penalty, — my own penalty, — a penalty that no god assigns to me, but that I, simply because I am myself, and take an interest in knowing myself, assign to myself, precisely in so far as and whenever I am awake to the meaning of my own life. I can never undo that deed. If I ever say, 'I have undone that deed,' I shall be both a fool and a liar. Counsel me, if you will, to forget that deed. Counsel me to do good deeds without number to set over against that treason. Counsel me to be cheerful, and to despise Puritanism. Counsel me to plunge into Lethe. All such counsel may be, in its way and time, good. Only do not counsel me 'to get rid of' just that sin. That, so far as the real facts are concerned, cannot be done. For I am, and to the end of endless time shall remain, the doer of that wilfully traitorous deed. Whatever other value I may get, that value I retain forever. My guilt is as enduring as time."

But hereupon a bystander will naturally invite our supposed traitor to repent, and to repent thoroughly of his treason. The traitor, now cool and reasonable once more, can only apply to his own case Fitzgerald's word in the Omar Khayyam stanzas: —

> The moving finger writes, and having writ,
> Moves on: nor all your piety nor wit
> Can lure it back to cancel half a line,
> Nor all your tears wash out a word of it.

These very familiar lines were sometime viewed as Oriental fatalism. But they are, in fact, fully applicable to the freest of deeds when once that deed is done.

We need not further pursue any supposed colloquy between the traitor and those who comment upon the situation. The simple fact is that each deed is *ipso facto* irrevocable; that our hypothetical traitor, in his own deed, has been false to whatever light he then and there had and to whatever ideal he then viewed as his highest good. Hereupon no new deed, however good or however faithful, and however much of worthy consequences it introduces into the future life of the traitor or of his world, can annul the fact that the one traitorous deed was actually done. No question as to whether the traitor, when he first chose the cause which he later betrayed, was then ethically correct in his choice, aids us to estimate just the one matter which is here in question, — namely, the value of the traitor as the doer of that one traitorous deed. For his treason consists not in his blunders in the choice of his cause, but in his sinning against such light as he then and there had. The question is, furthermore, not one as to his general moral character, apart from this one act of treason. To condemn at one stroke the whole man for the one deed is, of course, absurd. But it is the one deed which is now in question. This man may *also* be the doer of countless good deeds. But our present question is solely as to his value as the doer of that one traitorous deed. This value he has through his own irrevocable choice. Whatever other values his other deeds may give him, this one value remains, never to be removed. By no deed of his own can he ever escape from that penalty which consists in his having introduced into the moral world the one evil which was, at the time, as great an evil as he could then, of his own will, introduce.

In brief, by his own deed of treason, the traitor has consigned himself, — not indeed his *whole* self, but his self as the doer of this deed, — to what one may call the *hell of the irrevocable*. *All* deeds are indeed irrevocable. But only the traitorous sin against the light is such that, in advance, the traitor's own free acceptance of a cause has stamped it with the character of being what his own will had defined as his own unpardonable sin. Whatever else the traitor may hereafter do, — and even if he becomes and remains, through all his future life, in this or any other world, a saint, — the fact will remain: There was a moment when he freely did whatever he could to wreck the cause that he had sworn to serve. The traitor can henceforth do nothing that will give to himself, precisely in so far as he was the doer of that one deed, any character which is essentially different from the one determined by his treason.

The hell of the irrevocable: all of us know what it is to come to the border of it when we contemplate our own past mistakes or mischances. But we can enter it and dwell in it only when the fact "This deed is irrevocable," is combined with the further fact "This deed is one that, unless I call treason my good, and moral suicide my life, I cannot forgive myself for having done."

Now to use these expressions is not to condemn the traitor, or any one else, to endless emotional horrors of remorse, or to any sensuous pangs of penalty or grief, or to any one set of emotions whatever. It is simply to say: If I morally value myself at all, it remains for me a genuine and irrevocable evil in my world, that ever I was, even if for that one moment only and in that one deed, with all my mind and my soul and my heart and my strength, a traitor. And if I ever had any cause, and then betrayed it, — such an evil not only was my deed, but such an evil forever remains, so far as that one deed was done, the *only* value that I can attribute to myself precisely *as* the doer of that deed at that time.

What the pungency of the odors, what the remorseful griefs, of the hell of the irrevocable may be, for a given individual, we need not attempt to determine, and I have not the least right or desire to imagine. Certainly remorse is a poor companion for an active life; and I do not counsel any one, traitor or not traitor, to cultivate remorse. Our question is not one about one's feelings, but about one's genuine value as a moral agent. Certainly forgetfulness is often useful when one looks forward to new deeds. I do not counsel any one uselessly to dwell upon the past. Still the fact remains, that the more I come to take large and coherent views of my life and of its meaning, the more will the fact that, by my own traitorous deed, I have banished myself to the hell of the irrevocable, appear to me both a vast and a grave fact in my world. I shall learn, if I wisely grow into new life, neither to be crushed by any sort of facing of that fact, nor to brood unduly over its everlasting presence as a fact in my life. But so long as I remain awake to the real values of my life, and to the coherence of my meaning, I shall know that while no god shuts me, or could possibly shut me, if he would, into this hell, it is my own will to say that, for this treason, just in so far as I wilfully and knowingly committed this treason, I shall permit none of the gods to forgive me. For it is my precious privilege to assert my own reasonable will, by freely accepting my place in the hell of the irrevocable, and by never forgiving myself for this sin against the light. If any new deed can assign to just that one traitorous deed of mine any essentially novel and reconciling meaning, — that new deed will in any case certainly *not* be mine. I can do good deeds in future; but I cannot revoke my individual past deed. If it ever comes to appear as anything but what I myself then and there made it, that change will be due to no deed of mine. Nothing that I myself can do will ever really reconcile me to my own deed, so far as it was that treason.

This, then, as I suppose, is the essential meaning which underlies the traditional doctrine of the endless penalty of wilful sin. This deeper meaning is that, quite apart from the judgment of any of the gods, and wholly in accordance with the true rational will of the one who has done the deed of betrayal, the guilt of a free act of betrayal is as enduring as time. This doctrine so interpreted is, I insist, *not* cheerless. It is simply resolute. It is the word of one who is ready to say to himself, "Such was my deed, and I did it." No repentance, no pardoning power can deprive us of the duty and, — as I repeat, — the precious privilege of saying that of our own deed.

VI

Atonement

The human aspect of the Christian idea of atonement is based upon such motives that, if there were no Christianity and no Christians in the world, the idea of atonement would have to be invented, before the higher levels of our moral existence could be fairly understood. To the illustration of this thesis the present lecture is to be largely devoted. The thesis is not new; yet it seems to me to have been insufficiently emphasized even in recent literature; although, as is well known, modern expositors of the meaning of the Christian doctrine of atonement have laid a constantly increasing stress upon the illustrations and analogies of that doctrine which they have found present in the common experience of mankind, in non-theological literature, and the history of ethics.

I

The treatment of the idea of atonement in the present lecture, if it in any respect aids towards an understanding of our problem, will depend for whatever it accomplishes upon two deliberate limitations.

The first limitation is the one that I have just indicated. I shall emphasize, more than is customary, aspects of the idea of atonement which one could expound just as readily in a world where the higher levels of moral experience had somehow been reached by the leaders of mankind, but where Christians and Christianity were as yet wholly unknown.

My second limitation will be this: I shall consider the idea of atonement in the light of the special problems which the close of the lecture on "Time and Guilt" left upon our hands. The result will be a view of the idea of atonement which will be intentionally fragmentary, and which will need to be later reviewed in its connection with the other great Christian ideas.

It is true that the history of the Christian doctrine of the atonement has inseparably linked, with the topics that I shall here most emphasize, various religious beliefs, and theological interpretations, with which, under my chosen limitations and despite these limitations, I shall endeavor to keep in touch. But, in a great part of what I shall have to say, I shall confine myself to what I may call "the problem of the traitor," — an ethical problem which, on the basis laid in the fore-going lecture, I now choose arbitrarily as my typical instance of the human need for atonement, and of a sense in which, in purely human terms, we are able to define what an atoning act would be, if it took place, and what it could accomplish, as well as what it could not accomplish.

Our last lecture familiarized us with the conception of the being whom I shall now call, throughout this discussion, "the traitor." We shall soon learn new reasons why our present study will gain, in definiteness of issue and in simplicity, by using the exemplary moral situation in which our so-called "traitor" has placed himself, as our means for bringing to light what relief, what possible, although always imperfect, reconciliation of the traitor with his own moral world, and with himself, this situation permits.

Perhaps I can help you to anticipate my further statement of my reasons for dwelling upon the unlovely situation of the hypothetical traitor, if I tell you what association of ideas first conducted me to the choice of the exemplary type of moral tragedy which I shall use as the vehicle whereby we are here to be carried nearer to our proposed view of the idea of atonement.

In Bach's Matthew Passion Music, whose libretto was prepared under the master's own guidance, there is a great passage wherein, at the last supper, Christ has just said: "One of you shall betray me." "And they all begin to say," so the recitative first tells us, although at once passing the words over into the mouths of the chorus, "Is it I? Is it I? Is it I?" And then there begins (with the use of the recurrent chorale), the chorus of "the Believers": "'Tis I, *My* sins betray thee, who died to make me whole." The effect of this, as well as of other great scenes in the Passion Music,—the dramatic and musical workings in their unity, as Bach devised them, transport the listener to a realm where he no longer hears an old story of the past retold, but, looking down, as it were, upon the whole stream of time, sees the betrayal, the divine tragedy, and the triumph, in one,—not indeed timeless, but time-embracing vision. In this vision all flows and changes and passes from the sorrows of a whole world to the hope of reconciliation. Yet all this fluent and passionate life is one divine life, and is also the listener's, or, as we can also say, the spectator's own life. Judas, the spectator knows as himself, as his own ruined personality; the sorrow of Gethsemane, the elemental and perfectly human passion of the chorus: "Destroy them, destroy them, the murderous brood,"—the waiting and weeping at the tomb, —these things belong to the present life of the believer who witnesses the passion. They are all the experiences of us men, just as we are. They are also divine revelations, coming as if from a world that is somehow inclusive of our despair, and that yet knows a joy which, as Bach depicts it in his music drama, is not so much mystical, as simply classic in the perfection of its serene self-control.

What the art of Bach suggests, I have neither the right nor the power to translate into "matter-moulded forms of speech." I have here to tell you only a little about the being whom Mephistopheles calls "der kleine Gott der Welt," about the one who, as the demon says:—

Bleibt stets von gleichem Schlag,
Und ist so wunderlich, als wie am ersten Tag.

And I am forced to limit myself in this discourse to choosing,—as my exemplary being who feels the need of some form of atonement, —man in his most unlovely and drearily discouraging aspect,—man in his appearance as a betrayer. The justification of this repellent choice can appear, if at all, then only in the outcome of our argument, and in its later relation to the whole Christian doctrine of life. But you may now see what first suggested my using this choice in this lecture.

So much, however, it is fair to add as I introduce my case. The "traitor" of my discourse shall here be the creature of an ideal definition based upon facts set forth in the last lecture. I shall soon have to speak again of the sense in which all observers of human affairs have a right to say that there are traitors, and that we well know some of their works. But we have in general no right to say with assurance, when we speak of our individual neighbors, that we know who the traitors are. For we are no searchers of hearts. And treason, as I here define it, is an affair of the heart, — that is, of the inner voluntary deed and decision.

While my ideal definition of the traitor of whom we are now to speak thus depends, as you see, upon facts already discussed in our discourse on "Time and Guilt," our new relation to the being defined as a traitor consists in the fact that, at the last time, we considered the nature of his guilt, while now we mean to approach an understanding of his relation to the idea of atonement.

II

Two conditions, as you will remember from our last lecture, determine what constitutes, for the purposes of my definition, a traitor. The first condition is that a traitor is a man who has had an ideal, and who has loved it with all his heart and his soul and his mind and his strength. His ideal must have seemed to him to furnish the cause of his life. It must have meant to him what Paul meant by the grace that saves. He must have embraced it, for the time, with full loyalty. It must have been his religion, his way of salvation. It must have been the cause of a Beloved Community.

The second condition that my ideal traitor must satisfy is this. Having thus found his cause, he must, as he now knows, in at least some one voluntary act of his life, have been deliberately false to his cause. So far as in him lay, he must, at least in that one act, have betrayed his cause.

Such is our ideal traitor. At the close of the last lecture we left him condemned, in his own sight, to what we called the "hell of the irrevocable."

We now, for the moment, still confine ourselves to his case, and ask: Can the idea of atonement mean anything that permits its application, in any sense, however limited, to the situation of this traitor? Can there be any reconciliation, however imperfect, between this traitor and his own moral world, — any reconciliation which, from his own point of view, and for his own consciousness, can make his situation in his moral world essentially different from the situation in which his own deed has so far left him?

In the hell of the irrevocable there may be, as at the last time we pointed out, no sensuous penalties to fear. And there may be, for all that we know, countless future opportunities for the traitor to do good and loyal deeds. Our problem lies in the fact that none of these deeds will ever undo the supposed deed of treason. In that sense, then, no good deeds of the traitor's future will ever *so* atone for his one act of treason, that he will become clear of just that treason, and of what he finds to be its guilt. He had his moral universe; and his one act of treason did the most that he then and there could do to destroy that world and to wreck his own relation to its meaning. His irrevocable deed is, for his moral consciousness, its own endless penalty. For that deed he can never forgive himself, so long as he knows himself. And nothing that we can now say will change just these aspects of the matter. So much in the traitor's situation is irrevocably fixed.

But it is still open to us to ask whether anything could occur in the traitor's moral world which, without undoing his deed, could still add some new aspect to this deed, — an aspect such that, when the traitor came to view his own deed in this light, he could say: "Something in the nature of a genuinely reconciling element has been added, not only to my world and to my own life, but also to the inmost meaning even of my deed of treason itself. My moral situation has hereby been rendered genuinely better than my deed left it. And this bettering does not consist merely in the fact that some new deed of my own, or of some one else, has been simply a good deed, instead of a bad one, and has thus put a good thing into my world to be henceforth considered side by side with the irrevocable evil deed. No, this bettering consists in something more than this, — in something which gives to my very treason itself a new value; so that I can say, not: 'It is undone;' but 'I am henceforth in some measure, in some genuine fashion, morally reconciled to the fact that I did this evil.' "

Plainly, if any such reconciliation is possible, it will be at best but an imperfect and tragic reconciliation. It cannot be simply and perfectly destructive of guilt. But the great tragic poets have long since taught us that there are indeed tragic reconciliations even when there are great woes. These tragic reconciliations may be infinitely pathetic; but they may be also infinitely elevating, and even, in some unearthly and wondrous way, triumphant.

Our question is: Can such a tragic reconciliation occur in the case of the traitor? If it can occur, the result would furnish to us an instance of an atonement. This atonement would not mean, and could not mean, a clearing away of the traitor's guilt as if it never had been guilt. It would still remain true that the traitor could never rationally forgive himself for his deed. But he might in some measure, and in some genuine sense, become, not simply, but tragically, — sternly, — yet really, reconciled, not only to himself, but to his deed of treason, and to its meaning in his moral world.

Let us consider, then, in what way, and to what degree, the traitor might find such an atonement.

III

The Christian idea of atonement has always involved an affirmative answer to the question: Is an atonement for even a wilful deed of betrayal possible? Is a reconciliation of even the traitor to himself and to his world a possibility? The help that our argument gets from employing the supposed traitor's view of his own case as the guide of our search for whatever reconciliation is still possible for him, shows itself, at the present point of our inquiry, by simplifying the issue, and by thus enabling us at once to dispose, very briefly — not indeed of the Christian idea of atonement (for that, as we shall see, will later reveal itself in a new and compelling form), but of a great number of well-known theological theories of the nature of atonement, so far as they are to help our traitor to get a view of his own case.

These theological theories stand at a peculiar disadvantage when they speak to the now fully awakened traitor, when he asks what measure of reconciliation is still for him possible. Our traitor has his own narrow, but for that very reason, clearly outlined problem of atonement to consider. We here confine ourselves to his view.

Calmly reasonable in his hell of the irrevocable, he is dealing, not with the "angry God" of a well-known theological tradition, but with himself. He asks, not indeed for escape from the irrevocable, but for what relative and imperfect tragic reconciliation with his world and with his past, his moral order can still furnish to him, by any new event or deed or report. Shall we offer him one of the traditional theological comforts and say: "Some one, — namely, a divine being, — Christ himself, has accomplished a full 'penal satisfaction' for your deed of treason. Accept that satisfying sacrifice of Christ, and you shall be reconciled."

The traitor need not pause to repeat any of the now so well-known theological and ethical objections to the "penal satisfaction" theories of atonement. He needs no long dispute to clear his head. The cold wintry light of his own insight into what was formerly his moral home and into what he has by his own deed lost, is enough to show him the mercilessly unchangeable outlines of his moral landscape. He sees them; and that is so far enough. "Penal satisfaction?" *"That,"* he will say, "may somehow interest the 'angry God' of one or another theologian. If so, let this angry God be content, if he chooses. That does not reconcile me. So far as penalty is concerned: —

I was my own destroyer and will be my own hereafter.

I asked for reconciliation with my own moral universe, not for the accidental pacification of some angry God. The 'penal satisfaction' offered by another is simply foreign to all the interests in the name of which I inquire."

But hereupon let a grander, — let a far more genuinely religious and indeed truly Christian chord be sounded for the traitor's consolation. Let the words of Paul be heard: "There is now no condemnation for them that are in Christ Jesus, who walk not after the flesh, but after the spirit." The simply human meaning of those immortal words, if understood quite apart from Paul's own religious beliefs, is far deeper than is any merely technical theological theory of atonement. And our traitor will well know what those words of Paul mean. Their deepest human meaning has long since entered into his life. Had it not so entered, he would be no traitor; for he would never have known that there is what, for his own estimate, has been a Holy Spirit, — a cause to which to devote one's life, — a love that is indeed redeeming, and, when it first comes to us, compelling, — the love that raises, as if from the dead, the man who becomes the lover, — the love that also forces the lover, with its mysterious power, to die to his old natural life of barren contentions, and of distractions, and to live in the spirit. That love, — so the traitor well knows, redeems the lover from all the helpless natural wretchedness of the, as yet, unawakened life. It frees from "condemnation" all who remain true to this love.

The traitor knows all this by experience. And he knows it not in terms of mere theological formulas. He knows it as a genuinely human experience. He knows it as what every man knows to whom a transforming love has revealed the sense of a new life.

All this is familiar to the traitor. In his own way, he has heard the voice of the Spirit. He has been converted to newness of life. And *therefore* he has known what his own sin against the Holy Ghost meant. And, thereafter, he has deliberately committed that very sin. Therefore Paul's words are at once, to his mind, true in their most human as well as in their most spiritual sense. And just for that very reason they are to him now, in his guilt, as comfortless and as unreconciling as a death knell. For they tell him of precisely *that* life which once was his, and which, so far as his one traitorous deed could lead to such a result, he himself has deliberately slain.

If there is to be any, even the most tragic, reconciliation for the traitor, there must be other words to be heard besides just these words of Paul.

IV

Yet there are expositors of the Christian idea of the atonement who have developed the various so-called "moral theories" of the atoning work of Christ. And these men indeed have still many things to tell our traitor. One of the most clearly written and, from a purely literary point of view, one of the most charming of recent books on the moral theory of the idea of atonement, namely, the little book with which Sabatier ended his life work, very effectively contrasts with all the "penal satisfaction" theories of atonement, the doctrine that the work of Christ consisted in such a loving sacrifice for human sin and for human sinners that the contemplation of this work arouses in the sinful mind a depth of saving repentance, as well as of love,—a depth of glowing fervor, such as simply purifies the sinner's soul. For love and repentance and new life,—these constitute reconciliation. These, for Sabatier, and for many other representatives of the "moral theories" of atonement,—these are in themselves salvation.

I need not dwell upon such opinions in this connection. They are nowadays well known to all who have read any notable portion of the recent literature of the atonement. They are present in this recent literature in almost endless variations. In general these views are deep, and Christian, and cheering, and unquestionably moral. And their authors can and do freely use Paul's words; and on occasion supplement Paul's words by a citation of the parables. In the parables there is no definite doctrine of atonement enunciated. But there is a doctrine of salvation through loving repentance. Cannot our traitor, in view of the loving sacrifice that constitutes, according to tradition, Christ's atoning work, repent and love? Does *that* not reconcile him? May not the love of Christ both constrain and console him?

V

Once more, speaking still from his own purely human point of view, our traitor sadly simplifies the labor of considering in detail these various moral theories of atonement. The traitor seeks the possible, the relative, the inevitable imperfect reconciliation which, for one in his case, is still rationally definable. He discounts all that you can say as to the transforming pathos and the compelling power of love, and of the sacrifices. All this he long since knows. And, as I must repeat, all this constitutes the very essence of his own tragedy. He knew love before he became a traitor. He knew the love that has inspired heroes, martyrs, prophets, and saviours of mankind. All this he knew. And in his one traitorous deed he thrust it forth. That is the very heart of his problem. Repentance? Yes,—so far as he now has insight,—he has repentance for his traitorous deed. He has this repentance, if not as in the form of passionate remorse, still in the form of an irrevocable condemnation of his own deed. He has this repentance as the very breath of what is now his moral existence in the hell of the irrevocable.

As for amendment of life, and good deeds yet to come, he well knows the meaning of all these things. He is ready to do whatever he can. But none of all this doing of good works, none of this repentance, no love, and no tears will "lure back" the "moving finger" to "cancel half a line," or wash out a word of what is written. Once, when the great light first came, and the one who is now the traitor saw what life meant, his repentance—as he then indeed repented—reconciled him with his own life, and did so for precisely the reasons which Paul has explained. But that was his repentance for the former deeds of his folly, for the misadventures and the passions of his helpless natural sinfulness. He then repented, namely, of what he had done before the light came.

But *now* his state is quite other. We know *why* it is other. And we know, too, why the parables no longer can comfort the traitor. Their words can at most only remind him of what he himself best knows.

"Thou knewest," says the returning Lord to the traitor-servant in the parable of the talents; "thou knewest that I was a hard master." And as for our traitor, — so far as his one deed of treason could express his will, — it was the deed of one who not merely hid his talent in a napkin, but betrayed his Lord as Judas betrayed. Therefore if atonement is to mean for the traitor anything that shall be in any sense reconciling, he must hear of it in some new form. He is no mere prodigal son. His problem is that of the sin against the Holy Ghost.

Let us leave, then, both the "penal satisfaction" theories and the "moral theories" to address themselves to other men. Our traitor knows too well the sad lesson of his own deed to be aided either by the vain technicalities of the more antiquated of these theological types of theories, or by the true, but to him no longer applicable, comforts which the theories of the other — the moral type — open to his view.

Plainly, then, the traitor himself can suggest nothing further as to his own reconciliation with the world where, by his deed of betrayal, he once chose to permit the light that was in him to become darkness. We must turn in another direction.

VI

We have so far considered the traitor's case as if his treason had been merely an affair of his own inner life, — a sort of secret impious wish. But of course, while we are indeed supposing the traitor, — now enlightened by the view of his own deed, — to be the judge of what he himself has meant and done, — we well know that his false deed was, in his own opinion, no mere thought of unholiness. He had a cause. That is, he lived in a real world. And he was false to his cause. He betrayed. Now betrayal is something objective. It breaks ties. It rends asunder what love has joined in dear unity.

What human ties the traitor broke, we leave to him to discover for himself. Why they were to his mind holy, we also need not now inquire. Enough, — since he was indeed loyal, — he had found his ties; — they were precious and human and real; and he believed them holy; — and he broke them. That is, so far as in him lay, he destroyed by his deed the community in whose brotherhood, in whose life, in whose spirit, he had found his guide and his ideal. His deed, then, concerns not himself only, but that community whereof he was a voluntary member. The community knows, or in the long run must learn, that the deed of treason has been done, even if, being itself no searcher of hearts, it cannot identify the individual traitor. We often know not who the traitors are. But if ours is the community that is wrecked, we may well know by experience that there has been treason.

The problem of reconciliation, then,—if reconciliation there is to be,—concerns not only the traitor, but the wounded or shattered community. Endlessly varied are the problems—the tragedies, the lost causes, the heartbreaks, the chaos, which the deeds of traitors produce. All this we merely hint in passing. But all this constitutes the heart of the sorrow of the higher regions of our human world. And we here refer such countless, commonplace, but crushing tragedies to these ruins which are the daily harvest-home of treason, merely in order to ask the question: Can a genuinely spiritual community, whose ideals are such as Paul loved to portray when he wrote to his churches,—can such a loving and beloved community in any degree reconcile itself to the existence of traitors in its world, and to the deeds of individual traitors? Can it in any wise find in its world something else, over and above the treason,—something which atones for the spiritual disasters that the very being of treason both constitutes and entails? Must not the existence of traitors remain, for the offended community, an evil that is as intolerable and irrevocable and as much beyond its powers of reconciliation as is, for the traitor himself, his own past deed, seen in all the light of its treachery? Can any soul of good arise or be created out of this evil thing, or as an atonement therefor?

You see, I hope, that I am in no wise asking whether the community which the traitor has assailed, desires, or does well either to inflict or to remit any penalties said to be due to the traitor for his deed. I am here speaking wholly of the possibility of inner and human reconciliations. The only penalty which, in the hell of the irrevocable, the traitor himself inevitably finds, is the fact: "I did it." The one irrevocable fact with which the community can henceforth seek to be reconciled, if reconciliation is possible, is the fact: "This evil was done." That is, "These invaluable ties were broken." This unity of brotherhood was shattered. The life of the community,—as it was before the blow of treason fell,—can never be restored to its former purity of unscarred love. This is the fact. For this let the community now seek,—not oblivion, for that is a mere losing of the truth; not annulment, for that is impossible; *but* some measure of reconciliation.

For the community, as I am now viewing its ideal but still distinctly human life, the question is *not* one of what we usually call "forgiveness." If "forgiveness" means simply an affectionate remission of penalty, that is something which, for a given community, may be not only humanly possible, but obviously both wise and desirable. Penalty is no remedy for the irrevocable. Forgiveness is often both reasonable and convenient. Nor need the question be raised as to whether the community could ever trust the traitor with the old hearty human, although always fallible, confidence. What the community can know is—not the traitor's heart, but the fact—manifest through the shattered ties and the broken spiritual life,—the fact that a deed of treason has been done. That the deed was the voluntary work of just this traitor, the community can learn only as a matter of probable opinion, or perhaps through the traitor's confession. But, just as the community cannot now search the traitor's heart, or know whether he will hereafter repeat his treason in some new form,—just so, too, it never has been able, before the deed of treason was committed, to search the hearts of any of its free and loyal members, and to know whether, in fact, its trust was wholly well founded when it believed, or hoped, that just this treason would never be committed by any one of the members whom it fondly trusted.

All the highest forms of the unity of the spirit, in our human world, constantly depend, for their very existence, upon the renewed free choices, the sustained loyalty, of the members of communities. Hence the very best that we know, namely, the loyal brotherhood of the faithful who choose to keep their faith,—this best of all human goods, I say,—is simply inseparable from countless possibilities of the worst of human tragedies,—the tragedy of broken faith. At such cost must the loftiest of our human possessions in the realm of the spirit be purchased,—at the cost, namely, of knowing that some deed of wilful treason on the part of some one whom we trusted as brother or as beloved may rob us of this possession. And the fact that we are thus helplessly dependent on human fidelity for some of our highest goods, and so may be betrayed,—this fact is due not to the natural perversity of men, nor to the mere weakness of those who love and trust. This fact is due to something which, without any metaphysical theory, we ordinarily call man's freedom of choice. We do not want our beloved community to consist of puppets, or of merely fascinated victims of a mechanically insistent love. We want the free loyalty of those who, whatever fascination first won them to their cause, remain faithful because they choose to remain faithful. Of such is the kingdom of good faith. The beloved community demands for itself such freely and deliberately steadfast members. And for that very reason, in a world where there is such free and good faith,—there can be treason. Hence the realm where the spirit reaches the highest human levels is the region where the worst calamities can, and in the long run do, assail many who depend upon the good faith of their brethren.

The community, therefore, never had any grounds, before the treason, for an absolute assurance about the future traitor's perseverance in the faith. After his treason, if indeed he repents and now begins once more to act loyally,—it may acquire a relative assurance that he will henceforth abide faithful. The worst evil is not, then, that a trust in the traitor, which once was rightly serene and perfectly confident, is now irrevocably lost. It is not *this* which constitutes the irreconcilable aspect of the traitor's deed. All men are frail. And especially must those who are freely loyal possess a certain freedom to become faithless if they choose. This evil is a condition of the highest good that the human world contains. And so much the community, in presence of the traitor, ought to recognize as something that was always possible. It also ought to know that a certain always fallible trust in the traitor can indeed be restored by his future good deeds, if such are done by him with every sign that he intends henceforth to be faithful.

But what is indeed irrevocably lost to the community through the traitor's deed is precisely what I just called "unscarred love." The traitor remains — for the community as well as for himself — the traitor,—just so far as his deed is confessed, and just so far as his once unsullied fidelity has been stained. *This* indeed is irrevocable. It is perfectly human. But it is unutterably comfortless to the shattered community.

It is useless, then, to say that the problem of reconciliation, so far as the community is concerned, is the problem of "forgiveness," not now as remission of penalty, but of forgiveness, in so far as forgiveness means a restoring of the love of the community, or of its members, towards the one who has now sinned, but repented. Love may be restored. If the traitor's future attitude makes that possible, human love ought to be restored to the now both repentant and well-serving doer of the past evil deed. But alas! this restored love will be the love for the member who *has been a traitor;* and the tragedy of the treason will permanently form part in and of this love. Thus, then, up to this point, there appears for the community as well as for the traitor, no ground for even the imperfect reconciliation of which we have been in search. Is there, then, any other way, still untried, in which the community may hope, if not to *find*, then to *create* something which, in its own strictly limited fashion, will reconcile the community to the traitor and to the irrevocable, and irrevocably evil, deed.

VII

Such a way exists. The community cannot undo the traitor's deed, and cannot simply annul the now irrevocable fact of the evil which has been accomplished. Penalty, even if called for, annuls nothing of all that has been done. Repentance does not turn backwards the flow of time. Restored and always fallible human confidence in the traitor's good intentions regarding his future deeds, is not true reconciliation. Forgiveness does not wash out a word of the record that the moving finger of treason has written. The love of the forgiving community, or of its members, for the repentant and now well-doing traitor, is indeed a great good; but it is a love that has forever lost one of its most cherished possessions, — the possession of a loyal member who, in the old times before the treason, not only loved, but, so far, *had steadfastly kept his faith*. By all these means, then, *no* atonement is rendered to the community. Neither hatred nor penalty need be, from the side of the community, in any wise in question. But the fact remains: The community has lost its treasure; its once faithful member who, until his deed of treason came, had been wholly its own member. And it has lost the ties and the union which he destroyed by his deed. And, for all this loss, it lovingly mourns with a sorrow for which, thus far, we see no reconciliation. Who shall give to it its own again?

The community, then, can indeed *find* no reconciliation. But can it *create* one? At the worst, it is the traitor, and it is not the community, that has done this deed. New deeds remain to be done. The community is free to do them, or to be incarnate in some faithful servant who will do them. Could any possible new deed, done by, or on the behalf of, the community, and done by some one who is *not* stained by the traitor's deed, introduce into this human world an element which, as far as it went, would be, in whatever measure, genuinely reconciling?

VIII

We stand at the very heart and centre of the human problem of atonement. We have just now nothing to do with theological opinion on this topic. I insist that our problem is as familiar and empirical as is death or grief. That problem of atonement daily arises not as between God and man (for we here are simply ignoring, for the time being, the metaphysical issues that lie behind our problem). That problem is daily faced by all those faithful lovers of wounded and shattered communities who, going down into the depths of human sorrow, either as sufferers or as friends who would fain console, or who, standing by hearths whose fires burn no more, or loving their country through all the sorrows which traitors have inflicted upon her, or who, not weakly, but bravely grieving over the woe of the whole human world, are still steadily determined that no principality and no power, that no height and no depth, shall be able to separate man from his true love, which is the triumph of the spirit. That human problem of atonement is, I say daily faced, and faced by the noblest of mankind. And for these our noblest, despite all our human weakness, that problem is, in principle and in ideal, daily solved. Let us turn to such leaders of the human search after greatness, as our spiritual guides.

Great calamities are, for all but the traitor himself, — so far as we have yet considered his case, — great opportunities. Lost causes have furnished, times without number, the foundations and the motives of humanity's most triumphant loyalty.

When treason has done its last and most cruel work, and lies with what it has destroyed, — dead in the tomb of the irrevocable past, — there is now the opportunity for a triumph of which I can only speak weakly and in imperfectly abstract formulas. But, as I can at once say, this of which I now speak is a human triumph. It forms part of the history of man's earthly warfare with his worst foes. Moreover, whenever it occurs at all, this is a triumph, *not* merely of stoical endurance, nor yet of kindly forgiveness, nor of the mystical mood which, seeing all things in God, feels them all to be good. It is a triumph of the creative will. And what form does it take amongst the best of men, who are here to be our guides?

I answer, this triumph over treason can only be accomplished by the community, or on behalf of the community, through some steadfastly loyal servant who acts, so to speak, as the incarnation of the very spirit of the community itself. This faithful and suffering servant of the community may answer and confound treason by a work whose type I shall next venture to describe, in my own way, thus: First, this creative work shall include a deed, or various deeds, for which only just this treason furnishes the opportunity. Not treason in general, but just this individual treason shall give the occasion, and supply the condition of the creative deed which I am in ideal describing. Without just that treason, this new deed (so I am supposing) could not have been done at all. And hereupon the new deed, as I suppose, is so ingeniously devised, so concretely practical in the good which it accomplishes, that, when you look down upon the human world after the new creative deed has been done in it, you say, first, "This deed was made possible by that treason; and, secondly, *The world, as transformed by this creative deed, is better than it would have been had all else remained the same, but had that deed of treason not been done at all.*" That is, the new creative deed has made the new world better than it was before the blow of treason fell.

Now such a deed of the creative love and of the devoted ingenuity of the suffering servant, on behalf of his community, breaks open, as it were, the tomb of the dead and treacherous past, and comes forth as the life and the expression of the creative and reconciling will. It is this creative will whose ingenuity and whose skill have executed the deed that makes the human world better than it was before the treason.

To devise and to carry out some new deed which makes the human world better than it would have been had just that treasonable deed *not* been done;—is that not, in its own limited way and sense, a reconciling form, both of invention and of conduct? Let us forget, for the moment, the traitor. Let us now think only of the community. We know why and in what sense it cannot be reconciled to the traitor or to his deed. But have we not found, without any inconsistency, a new fact which furnishes a genuinely reconciling element? It indeed furnishes no perfect reconciliation with the irrevocable; but it transforms the meaning of that very past which it cannot undo. It cannot restore the unscarred love. It does supply a new triumph of the spirit,—a triumph which is not so much a mere compensation for what has been lost, as a transfiguration of the very loss into a gain that, without this very loss, could never have been won. The traitor cannot thus transform the meaning of his own past. But the suffering servant can thus transfigure this meaning; can bring out of the realm of death a new life that only this very death rendered possible.

The triumph of the spirit of the community over the treason which was its enemy, the rewinning of the value of the traitor's own life, when the new deed is done, involves the old tragedy, but takes up that tragedy into a life that is now more a life of triumph than it would have been if the deed of treason had never been done.

Therefore, if indeed you suppose or observe that, in our human world, such creative deeds occur, you see that they indeed do not remove, they do not annul, either treason or its tragedy. But they do show us a genuinely reconciling, a genuinely atoning, fact in the world and in the community of the traitor. Those who do such deeds solve, I have just said, not the impossible problem of undoing the past, but the genuine problem of finding, even in the worst of tragedies, the means of an otherwise impossible triumph. They meet the deepest and bitterest of estrangements by showing a way of reconciliation, and a way that only this very estrangement has made possible.[1]

IX

This is the human aspect of the idea of atonement. Do we need to solve our theological problems before we decide whether such an idea has meaning, and is ethically defensible? I must insist that this idea comes to us, not from the scholastic quiet of theological speculation, but stained with the blood of the battlefields of real life. For myself, I can say that no theological theory suggested to me this interpretation of the essential nature of an atoning deed. I cannot call the interpretation new, simply because I myself have learned it from observing the meaning of the lives of some suffering servants,—plain

[1] The view with regard to Atonement stated in the test was reached by me quite independently of any knowledge on my part of the remarkable book of Mr. Charles Allen Dinsmore: *Atonement in Literature and Life* (Boston, 1906). I am glad to find myself in close agreement with some of the essential features of Mr. Dinsmore's position. He has especially called my attention to Milton's illustration of this view of Adam's case.

human beings,—who never cared for theology, but who incarnated in their own fashion enough of the spirit of their community to conceive and to accomplish such new and creative deeds as I have just attempted to characterize. To try to describe to you, at all adequately, the life or the work of any such persons, I have neither the right nor the power. Here is no place for such a collection and analysis of the human form of the atoning life as only a William James could have justly accomplished. And upon personal histories I could dwell, in this place, only at the risk of intruding upon lives which I have been privileged sometimes to see afar off, and briefly, but which I have no right to report as mere illustrations of a philosophical argument. It is enough, I think, for me barely to indicate what I have in mind when I say that such things are done amongst men.

All of us well know of great public benefactors whose lives and good works have been rendered possible through the fact that some great personal sorrow, some crushing blow of private grief first descended, and seemed to wreck their lives. Such heroic souls have then been able, in these well-known types of cases, not only to bear their own grief, and to rise from the depths of it (as we all in our time have to attempt to do). They have been able also to use their grief as the very source of the new arts and inventions and labors whereby they have become such valuable servants of their communities. Such people indeed often remind us of the suffering servant in Isaiah; for their life work shows that they are willing to be wounded for the sake of their community. Indirectly, too, they often seem to be suffering because of the faults as well as because of the griefs of their neighbors, or of mankind. And it indeed often occurs to us to speak of these public or private benefactors as living some sort of atoning life, as bearing in a sense, not only the sorrows, but the sins of other men.

Yet it is *not* of such lives, noble as they are, that I am now thinking—nor of *such* vicarious suffering, of such sympathizing helpfulness in human woe, of such rising from private grief to public service,—that I am now speaking, when I say that atoning deeds, in the more precise sense just described, are indeed done in our human world. Sharply contrasted with these beneficent lives and deeds, which I have just mentioned, are the other lives of which I am thinking, and to which, in speaking of atonement, I have been referring. These are the lives of which I have so little right to give more than a bare hint in this place.

One's private grief *may be* the result of the deed of a traitor. That again is something which often seems to happen in our human world. One may rally from the despair due to even such a blow, and may later become a public benefactor. We all know, I suppose, people who have done that, and whose lives are the nobler and more serviceable because they have conquered such a grief, and have learned great lessons through such a conquest. Yet even *such* lives do not show exactly the reconciling and atoning power that I now most have in mind. Let me next state a mere supposition.

Suppose a community, — a modern community, — to be engaged with the ideals and methods of modern reform, in its contests with some of those ills which the natural viciousness, the evil training, and the treasonable choices of very many people combine to make peculiarly atrocious in the eyes of all who love mankind. Such evils need to be met, in the good warfare, not only by indignant reformers, not only by ardent enthusiasts, but also by calmly considerate and enlightened people, who distinguish clearly between fervor and wisdom, who know what depths of woe and of wrong are to be sounded, but who also know that only self-controlled thoughtfulness and well-disciplined self-restraint can devise the best means of help. As we also well know, we look, in our day, to highly trained professional skill for aid in such work. We do not hope that those who are merely well-meaning and loving can do what most needs to be done. We desire those who know. Let us suppose, then, such a modern community as especially needing, for a very special purpose, one who *does* know.

Hereupon let us suppose that one individual exists whose life has been wounded to the core by some of treason's worst blows. Let us suppose one who, always manifesting true loyalty and steadfastly keeping strict integrity, has known, not merely what the ordinary professional experts learn, but also what it is to be despised and rejected of men, and to be brought to the very depths of lonely desolation, and to have suffered thus through a treason which also deeply affected, not one individual only, but a whole community. Let such a soul, humiliated, offended, broken, so to speak, through the very effort to serve a community, forsaken, long daily fed only by grief, yet still armed with the grace of loyalty and of honor, and with the heroism of dumb suffering, — let such a soul not only arise, as so many great sufferers have done, from the depths of woe, — let such a soul not only triumph, as so many have done, over the grief that treason caused; but let such a soul also use the very lore which just this treason had taught, in order to begin a new life work. Let this life work be full of a shrewd, practical, serviceable, ingenious wisdom which only that one individual experience of a great treason could have taught. Let this new life work be made possible only because of that treason. Let it bring to the community, in the contest with great public evils, methods and skill and judgment and forethought which only that so dear-bought wisdom could have invented. Let these methods have, in fact, a skill that the traitor's own wit has taught, and that is now used for the good work. Let that life show, not only what treason can do to wreck, but what the free spirit can learn from and through the very might of treason's worst skill.

If you will conceive of such a life merely as a possibility, you may know why I assert that genuinely atoning deeds occur, and what I believe such deeds to be. For myself, any one who should supply the facts to bear out my supposition (and such people, as I assert, there are in our human world) would appear henceforth to me to be a sort of symbolic personality, — one who had descended into hell to set free the spirits who are in prison. When I hear those words, "descended into hell," repeated in the creed, I think of such human beings, and feel that I know at least some in our human world to whom the creed in these words refers.

X

Hereupon, you may very justly say that the mere effects of the atoning deeds of a human individual are in this world apparently petty and transient; and that even the most atoning of sacrificial human lives can devise nothing which, within the range of our vision, *does* make the world of the community better, in any of its most tragic aspects, than it would be if no treason had been committed.

If you say this, you merely give me the opportunity to express the human aspect of the idea of the atonement in a form very near to the form which, as I believe, the Christian idea of atonement has always possessed when the interests of the religious consciousness (or, if I may use the now favorite word, the subconsciousness) of the Church, rather than the theological formulations of the theory of atonement, have been in question. Christian feeling, Christian art, Christian worship, have been full of the sense that *somehow* (and *how* has remained indeed a mystery) there was something so precious about the work of Christ, something so divinely wise (so skilful and divinely beautiful?) about the plan of salvation,—that, as a result of all this, after Christ's work was done, the world as a whole was a nobler and richer and worthier creation than it would have been if Adam had not sinned.

This, I insist, has always been felt to be the sense of the atoning work which the faith has attributed to Christ. A glance at a great Madonna, a chord of truly Christian music, ancient or modern, tells you that this is so. And this sense of the atoning work cannot be reduced to what the modern "moral" theories of the Christian atonement most emphasize.

For what the Christian regards as the atoning work of Christ is, from this point of view, *not* something about Christ's work which merely arouses in sinful man love and repentance.

No, the theory of atonement which I now suggest, and which, as I insist, is subconsciously present in the religious sentiment, ritual, and worship of all Christendom, is a perfectly "objective" theory,—quite as "objective" as any "penal satisfaction" theory could be. Christian religious feeling has always expressed itself in the idea that what atones is something perfectly "objective," namely, Christ's work. And this atoning work of Christ was for Christian feeling a deed that was made possible only through man's sin, but that somehow was so wise and so rich and so beautiful and divinely fair that, after this work was done, the world was a better world than it would have been had *man* never sinned.

So the Christian consciousness, I insist, has always felt. So its poets have often, in one way or another, expressed the matter. The theologians have disguised this simple idea under countless forms. But every characteristically Christian act of worship expresses it afresh. Treason did its work (so the legend runs) when man fell. But Christ's work was so perfect that, in a perfectly objective way, it took the opportunity which man's fall furnished to make the world better than it could have been had man not fallen.

But this is indeed, as an idea concerning God and the universe and the work of Christ, an idea which is as human in its spirit, and as deep in its relation to truth, as it is, in view of the complexity of the values which are in question, hard either to articulate or to defend. How should we know, unless some revelation helped us to know, whether and in what way Christ's supposed work made the world better than it would have been had man not sinned?

But in this discussion I am speaking of the purely human aspect of the idea of atonement. *That* aspect is now capable of a statement which does not pretend to deal with any but our human world, and which fully admits the pettiness of every human individual effort to produce such a really atoning deed as we have described.

The human community, depending, as it does, upon its loyal human lovers, and wounded to the heart by its traitors, and finding, the farther it advances in moral worth, the greater need of the loyal, and the greater depth of the tragedy of treason, — utters its own doctrine of atonement as this postulate, — the central postulate of its highest spirituality. This postulate I word thus: *No baseness or cruelty of treason so deep or so tragic shall enter our human world, but that loyal love shall be able in due time to oppose to just that deed of treason its fitting deed of atonement.* The deed of atonement shall be so wise and so rich in its efficacy, that the spiritual world, after the atoning deed, shall be better, richer, more triumphant amidst all its irrevocable tragedies, than it was before that traitor's deed was done.

This is the postulate of the highest form of human spirituality. It cannot be proved by the study of mankind as they are. It can be asserted by the creative will of the loyal. Christianity expressed this postulate in the symbolic form of a report concerning the supernatural work of Christ. Humanity must express it through the devotion, the genius, the skill, the labor of the individual loyal servants in whom its spirit becomes incarnate.

As a Christian idea, the atonement is expressed in a symbol, whose divine interpretation is merely felt, and is viewed as a mystery. As a human idea, atonement is expressed (so far as it can at any one time be expressed) by a peculiarly noble and practically efficacious type of human deeds. This human idea of atonement is also expressed in a postulate which lies at the basis of all the best and most practical spirituality. The Christian symbol and the practical postulate are two sides of the same life, — at once human and divine.

VII

The Christian Doctrine

of Life

Throughout these lectures, both the contrast and the close connection between ethical and religious ideas have been illustrated. Ethical ideas define the nature of righteous conduct. Religious ideas have to do with bringing us into union with some supremely valuable form or level of life. Morality gives us counsel as to our duty. Religion, pointing out to us the natural poverty and failure which beset our ordinary existence, undertakes to show us some way of salvation. Ethical teachings direct us to a better mode of living. Religion undertakes to lead us to a home-land where we may witness, and, if we are successful, may share some supreme fulfilment of the purpose for which we live. In the Sermon on the Mount, the counsel, "Judge not that ye be not judged," is ethical; the beatitudes are religious. When Paul rebukes the Corinthians for their disputes, his teaching is, in so far, ethical. When he writes the great chapter on Charity, his doctrine is religious.

187

Now what I here mean by a "doctrine of life" comprises both ethical and religious elements. It brings these elements into unity, and, if it is a sound doctrine, it gives us both a connected survey of some notable portion of our duty, and an insight into the nature and source of the supreme values of our existence.

A religious doctrine very generally includes some assertions about the real world such that they can be elaborately tested only in case one is willing to undertake a metaphysical inquiry. But, as we have repeatedly seen in these lectures, both ethical and religious doctrines also deal with many matters which we can test, sufficiently for some of our most serious purposes, without raising issues which are technically and formally metaphysical. And that is why we have so far postponed any metaphysical study of the foundations which the various essential ideas of Christianity possess in the nature of the real universe. Both the ethical significance and the religious spirit which these ideas assure, we could in large measure estimate merely by taking account of the acknowledged facts of human nature.

A doctrine of life — that is, a coherent and comprehensive teaching concerning both the moral conduct of life, and the realm wherein the highest good is to be hoped for, sought, and, haply, won — will therefore, like the various ethical and religious ideas which inform such a general survey and estimate of human life, arouse many metaphysical questions. But, in large part, it can be both stated and estimated without answering these metaphysical questions in a technical way.

The present lecture is to be devoted to bringing together the essential Christian ideas which we have considered in the foregoing discussions, and to stating, as the result of a synthesis of these ideas, some aspects of the Christian doctrine of life.

I

This lecture will presuppose, and will not attempt to repeat, many of the most familiar of the moral precepts which characterize the Christian view of conduct. What I have time to dwell upon ought so to be selected that essential and weighty matters come to our notice. But if any one finds that my sketch omits much that is also of importance for the Christian definition of our duty, let him know from the start that I aim at certain larger connections, and endeavor to set down here genuinely Christian teachings about duty, but that I do not hope to be exhaustive in any part of my report.

Such moral teachings of Christianity as I can restate will be intimately connected with Christian views about life which are also religiously important. I shall make no effort to keep asunder, in my sketch, the ethical teachings and the religious interests of Christianity. In our study of the ethical value of the separate ideas, I have unhesitatingly passed from the strictly ethical to the obviously religious aspect of these ideas, whenever it was convenient to do so, always postponing, for reasons which I have repeatedly explained, the technically metaphysical problems which both the ethical and the religious sides of the questions at issue have involved.

You can, for convenience, sunder your treatment, both of ethical and of religious problems, from your technical metaphysics. But ethics and religion, in a case such as that of Christianity, can indeed be contrasted; but cannot profitably be kept apart in your exposition. This, I suppose, has been manifest at each stage of our foregoing discussion of the different Christian ideas. It will be more than ever manifest in the present portrayal of the connected whole to which they belong.

II

What is essential to the Christian doctrine of life can be brought to mind, at this point, more readily than in any other way known to me, by a very brief contrast between some features of the Christian religion, and the corresponding features of the greatest historical rival of Christianity, namely, Buddhism. Of the latter religion I know, like most philosophical students of my type of training, only very superficially, and mainly at second hand. What I mention regarding that matter has therefore merely the value of emphasizing the contrast to which I am to direct attention, and of thus illustrating the position of Christianity.

Let me begin my sketch by pointing out some features wherein these two great religions agree.

Both Christianity and Buddhism are products of long and vast processes of religious evolution. Both of them originally appealed to mature and complex civilizations. Yet both of them intended that their appeal should, in the end, be made to all mankind. Both of them deliberately transcended the limits of caste, of rank, of nation, and of race, and undertook to carry their message to all sorts and conditions of men. Both showed, as missionary religions, an immense power of assimilation. Both freely used, so far as they could do so without sacrificing essentials, the religious ideas which they found present in the various lands that their missionaries reached; and, like Paul, both of them became all things to all men, if haply they might thereby win any man to the faith that they thought to be saving.

Both were redemptive religions, which condemned both the mind and the sins of the natural man; and taught salvation through a transformation of the innermost being of this natural man. Each developed a great variety of sects and of forms of social life. Each made use of religious orders as a means of separating those who, while desirous of salvation, were able, in their present existence, to live only in a close contact with the world, from those who could aim directly at the highest grades of perfection.

Each of these two religions attempts, by a frank exposure of the centrally important facts of our life, to banish the illusions which bind us fast to earth, and, as they both maintain, to destruction. Each is therefore, in its own way, austere and unsparing in the speech which it addresses to the natural man. Each shuns mere popularity, and is transparently honest in its estimate of the vanities of the world. Each aims at the heart of our defects. Each says: "What makes your life a wreck and a failure, is that your very essence as a human self is, in advance of the saving process, a necessary source of woe and wrong. Each of the two religions insists upon the inmost life of the heart as the source whence proceeds all that is evil, and whence may proceed all that can become good about man. Each rejects the merely outward show of our deeds as a means for determining whether we are righteous or not. Each demands absolute personal sincerity from its followers. Each blesses the pure in heart, requires strict self-control, and makes an inner concentration of mind upon the good end an essential feature of piety. Each preaches kindliness toward all mankind, including our enemies. Each condemns cruelty and malice. Each, in fact, permits no human enmities. Each is a religion that exalts those who, in the world's eyes, are weak.

And not only in these more distinctly ethical ideas do the two religions agree. Each of them has its own world of spiritual exaltation; its realm that is not only moral, but deeply religious; its home-land of deliverance, where the soul that is saved finds rest in communion with a peace that the world can neither give nor take away.

In these very important respects, therefore, the distinctly religious features of the two faiths are intimately related. In case of each of the two religions, but in the case of Buddhism rather more than in the case of Christianity, it is possible, and in fact just and requisite, to distinguish its ideas of the nature and the means and the realm of salvation from the metaphysical opinions which a more or less learned exposition of the doctrines of the faith almost inevitably uses.

Buddhism has its ideas of the moral order of the universe, of Nirvana, and of the Buddhas,—the beings who attain supreme enlightenment,—and who thereby save the world. These ideas invite metaphysical speculation, and furnish motives that tended towards the building up of a theology, and that, in the end, produced a theology. But each of these religious ideas, in the case of Buddhism, can be defined without defining either a metaphysical or a theological system. The original teaching of Gotama Buddha rejected all metaphysical speculation, and insisted solely upon the ethical foundations of the doctrine, and upon those distinctly religious, but non-metaphysical, views of salvation, and of the higher spiritual life, which Buddha preferred to depict in parables, rather than to render needlessly abstruse through discussions such as, in his opinion, did not tend to edification.

The common ethical and religious features of Christianity and Buddhism are thus both many and impressive. Some of the greatest life questions are faced by both religions, and, in the respects which I have now pointed out, are answered in substantially the same way. Moreover, in several of the ethical and religious ideas in which these two religions agree with each other, they do not closely agree with any other religion. So far as I can venture to judge, no other religions that have attempted to appeal to the deepest and most universal interests of mankind have been so free as both Buddhism and Christianity are from bondage to national, to racial, and to worldly antagonisms and prejudices. No others have made so central, as they both have done, the conception of a personal saviour of mankind, whose dignity depends both upon the moral merits of his teaching and of his life, and upon the religious significance of the spiritual level to which he led the way, thus moulding both the thoughts and the lives of his followers.

When we add to all these parallels the fact that each of these religions had an historical founder, whose life later came to be the object of many legendary reports; and that the legends, in each case, were so framed by the religious imagination of the early followers of the faith in question that they include a symbolism, whereby a portion of the true meaning of each faith is expressed in the stories about the

founder,—when, I say, we add this fact to all the others, we get some
hint of the very genuine community of spirit which belongs to
these two great world religions. That the imaginative Buddha-
legends show an unrestrained and often helpless disposition to adorn
the religion with an edifying body of miraculous tales, while the relative self-restraint of the early Christian Church in holding in check,
as much as it did, its vigorous myth-making tendencies, remains, in
many respects, a permanent marvel,—all this constitutes a very
notable contrast between the two faiths. But this is, in part, a contrast
between the two civilizations (so remote, in many ways, from each
other) whose development lay at the basis of the two religions.
Buddhism was more surrounded by an atmosphere of magic than the
Christian Church ever was. Yet in those essentials which I have just
reported, the agreements and analogies between the two faiths are
both close and momentous. So far the two seem to be genuine coworkers in the same vast task of the ages,—the salvation of man,
through the transformation of a natural life into a life whose dwelling-place lies beyond human woe and sin.

III

Wherein, then, lies the most essential contrast between the Christian and the Buddhistic doctrines of life? This contrast, when it once
comes to light, is, to my mind, far more impressive than are the
agreements. It has often been discussed. What I say about it is the
word of one who cannot decide problems of the comparative
history of religion. But I must venture my own statement at this
point, despite my comparative ignorance of Buddhism; because the
contrast in question seems to me so illuminating for one who wishes
clearly to grasp the essence of Christianity.

The most familiar way of stating this contrast is to say that Buddhism is pessimistic, while Christianity is a religion of hope. This is,
in part, true; but it is not very enlightening, unless the spirit of
Christian hopefulness is more fully explained, and unless the Buddhistic pessimism is quite justly appreciated. Both religions hope for
salvation; and, for each of them, salvation means an overcoming of
the world. Each deplores humanity as it is, and means to transform
us. The contrast is, therefore, hardly to be defined as a contrast of
hope with despair. For each undertakes to overcome the world, and
assures us that we can be transformed. And each regards our natural
state as one worthy of despair, were not the way of salvation opened.

Nearer to the whole truth seems to be that frequently repeated statement of the matter which insists upon the creative attitude which Christianity requires the will to take, as against the quietism of Buddha. Buddhism, as we mentioned in a former lecture, has as its goal a certain passionless contemplation, in which the distinction of one individual from another is of no import, so that the self, as *this* self, vanishes. Christianity conceives love as positively active, and dwells upon a hope of immortality.

Nevertheless, the concept of beatitude, as the Christian thought of the Middle Ages formulated that concept, sets the contemplative life nearer the goal than the active life, even when the active life is one of charity. Hence, in their more mystical moods and expressions, the two religions are, once more, much more largely in agreement than our own very natural partisanship, determined by our Christian traditions, tends to make us admit.

It is also true that Buddhism aims at the extinction of the individual self; while Christianity assigns to the human individual an infinite worth. And this is indeed a vastly important difference. Yet this very importance remains unexplained, and a mere formula, until you see what it is about the human individual which constitutes, for the Christian view, his importance. One may answer, in simple terms, that, according to the teachings of Jesus, the individual is infinitely important, because the Father loves him; while Buddhism, in its original Southern form, has nothing to offer that is equivalent to this love of God for the individual man. Yet the further question has to be faced: Why and for what end does the God of Christianity love the individual? And it is here, at last, that you come face to face with the deepest contrast.

For God's love towards the individual is, from the Christian point of view, a love for one whose destiny it is to be a *member of the Kingdom of Heaven.* The Kingdom of Heaven is essentially a community. And the idea of this community, as the founder in parables prophetically taught that idea, developed into the conception which the Christian Church formed of its own mission; and through all changes, and despite all human failures, this conception remains a sovereign treasure of the Christian world.

IV

The Individual *and* the Community: this, if I may so express a perfectly human antithesis in religious and deliberately symbolic speech,—this pair of terms and of ideas is, so to speak, the *sacred pair*, to whose exposition and to whose practical application the whole Christian doctrine of life is due. This pair it is which, in the first place, enables Christianity to tell the individual why, in his natural isolation and narrowness, he is essentially defective,—is inevitably a failure, is doomed, and must be transformed. This, if you choose, is the root and core of man's original sin,—namely, the very form of his being as a morally detached individual. This is the bondage of his flesh; this is the soul of his corruption; this is his alienation from true life; this fact, namely, that by nature, as a social animal, he is an individual who, though fast bound by ties which no man can rend, to the community wherein he chances to be born or trained, never-theless, *until* the true love of a community, and *until* the beloved community itself appear in his life, is a stranger in his father's house, a hater of his only chance of salvation, a worldling, and a worker of evil deeds, a miserable source of misery. *This* is why, for Christianity, the salvation of man means the destruction of his natural self,—the sacrifice of what his flesh holds dearest,—the utter transformation of the primal core of the social self. I say: it is the merely natural rela-tion of the individual to the community which, for Christianity, explains all this. Here are the two levels of human existence. The individual, born on his own level, is naturally doomed to hatred for what belongs to the other level. Yet there, on that higher level, his only salvation awaits him.

Buddhism fully knows, and truly teaches, where the root of bit-terness is to be found,—not in the outward deed, but in the inmost heart of the individual self. But what, so far as I know, the original Southern Buddhism *never* clearly made a positive part of its own plan of the salvation of mankind, is a transformation of the self, *not* through the *mere* destruction of the narrow and corrupt flesh which alienates it from the true life, *but by the simple and yet intensely positive* DEVOTION *of the self to a new task,—to its creative office as a loyal member of a beloved community*. Early Buddhism never, so far as I know, clearly defined its ideal of the beloved community in terms which make that community, viewed simply as an ideal, one conscious unity of the business, of the eager hopes, and of the patiently ingenious and endlessly constructive love, of all mankind.

The ideal Christian community is one in which compassion is a mere incident in the realization of the new life, not only of brotherly concord, but also of an interminably positive creation of new social values, all of which exist for many souls in one spirit. The ideal Christian community of all mankind is to be as intimate in its enthusiasm of service as the daily life of a Pauline church was intended by the apostle to be, — and as novel in its inventions of new arts of common living as the gifts of the spirit in the early Christian Church were believed to be novel. The ideal Christian community is to be the community of all mankind, — as completely united in its inner life as one conscious self could conceivably become, and as destructive of the natural hostilities and of the narrow passions which estrange individual men, as it is skilful in winning from the infinite realm of bare possibilities concrete arts of control over nature and of joy in its own riches of grace. This free and faithful community of all mankind, wherein the individuals should indeed die to their own natural life, but should also enjoy a newness of positive life, — this community never became, so far as I can learn, a conscious ideal for early Buddhism.

How far the Japanese religion of loyalty, in its later forms of modified Buddhism, or in its other phases, has approached, or will hereafter approach, to an independent and original definition of the positive and constructive ideal of a conscious and universal human community which is here in question, I am quite unable to judge. The Japanese Buddhist sects well know what salvation by grace is. They well conceive and accept the doctrine of the incarnation of the divine being in a supernatural individual man; and are certainly universal in their general conceptions of some sort of human brotherhood. And they have reached these religious ideas quite apart from any dependence upon Christianity.

But what I miss in their religious conceptions, so far as I have read reports of these conceptions, is such a solution of the problem of human life in terms of loyalty, as *at once* demands the raising of the human self from the level of its natural narrowness, to the level of a complete and conscious personal membership in a beloved community, and *at the same time* defines the ideal community to whose level and in whose spirit we are to live, as the community of all mankind, and as one endlessly creative and conscious human spirit, whose life is to be lived upon its own level, and of whose dominion there is to be, in ideal and in meaning, no end.

The familiar article in the Christian creed which expresses this perfectly concrete and practical and also religious ideal, and expresses it in terms whose ethical and whose religious value you can test by personal and social experience, whatever may be your own definition of the dogmas of the Church, and whatever your meta-physical opinions may be, and whatever form of the visible or invis-ible Church chances best to seem to meet this your interpretation, —the familiar article of the Christian creed which expresses, I say, this ideal, just as an ideal, uses the words: "I believe in the Holy Ghost, the holy Catholic Church, the communion of saints." My earlier exposition of this idea sadly failed if I did not show you how one can understand and accept the spirit of this article of the creed, without accepting the dogmas or the obedience or the practice of any one form of the visible Christian Church. But it was this which I had in mind when I said, in our opening lecture, that Christianity has furnished mankind with its most impressive and inspiring vision of the home-land of the spirit.

V

Ethically speaking, the counsels which this Christian idea of the community implies, include all the familiar maxims of the Sermon on the Mount and all the lessons of the parables, but tend to give them such sorts of development as the ideals of the early Church, in Pauline and post-Pauline times, gradually gave to them. Always what I have called the difference between the two levels of our human existence must be borne in mind, if the interpretation of Christian love is to become as concrete as Paul made it in his epistles, and as concrete as later ages have attempted to keep it, even while developing its meaning.

You love your neighbor, first, because God loves him. Yes, but how and why does God love him? Because God loves the Kingdom of Heaven; and the Kingdom of Heaven is a perfectly live unity of individual men joined in one divine chorus—an unity of men who, *except* through their attachment to this life which exists on the level of the beloved community of the Kingdom of Heaven, would be miserable breeders of woe, and would be lost souls. Let your love for them be a love for your fellow-members in this Kingdom of Heaven.

Yes; but *this* neighbor is your enemy; or he belongs to the wrong tribe or caste or sect. Do not consider these unhappy facts as having any bearing on your love for him. For the ethical side of the doc-trine of life concerns not what you *find*, but what you are to *create*. Now God means this man to become a member of the community which constitutes the Kingdom of Heaven; and God loves this man accordingly. View him, then, as the soldier views the comrade who serves the same flag with himself, and who dies for the same cause. In the Kingdom you, and your enemy, and yonder stranger, are one. For the Kingdom is the community of God's beloved.

As for the way in which you are to love, make that way of loving, to your own mind, more alive, by recalling the meaning of your own dearest friendships. Think of the *closest* unity of human souls that you know. Then conceive of the Kingdom in terms of such love. When friends really join hands and hearts and lives, it is not the mere collection of sundered organisms and of divided feelings and will that these friends view as their life. Their life, as friends, is the unity which, while above their own level, wins them to itself and gives them meaning. This unity is the vine. They are the branches.

Now of such unity is the Kingdom of Heaven. See, then, in every man the branch of such a vine, — the outflowing of such a purpose, — the beloved of such a spirit, the incarnation of such a divine concern for many in one. And then your Christian love will be much more than mere pity, — will be greater than any amiable sympathy with the longings of those poor creatures of flesh could, of itself, become. Your love will then become the Charity that never faileth. For its object is the Beloved Community, and the individual as, ideally, a member of that community.

Is such a regard for individuals too impersonal to meet the spirit of the parables? No, — it does not destroy, it fulfils, as the early Christian Church, in ideal, fulfilled the spirit of the parables. Paul spoke thus, and thereby made Christian love more rather than less personal.

If by person you merely mean the morally detached individual man, then the community, — the Kingdom of Heaven, is indeed superpersonal. If, by person, you mean a live unity of knowledge and of will, of love and of deed, — then the community of the Kingdom of Heaven is a person on a higher level than is the level of any human individual; and the Kingdom of Heaven is at once within you, and above you, — a human life, and yet a life whose tabernacles are built up on a Mount of Transfiguration.

Reconsider familiar parables in the light of such an interpretation, — an interpretation as old and familiar as it is persistently ignored or misunderstood. That, I insist, is a useful way of restating the Christian moral doctrine of life.

Over what does the Father in the parable of the Prodigal Son rejoice? Over the mere delight that his son's presence now gives him, and over the feasting and the merriment that his own forgiving power supplies to the repentant outcast? No, the Father has won again, not merely his son as a hungry creature who can repent and be fed. The Father has won again the unbroken community of his family. It is the Father's house that rejoices. It is this community which makes merry; and the father is, for the moment, simply the incarnation of the spirit of this community.

Why is there more joy in heaven over one sinner that repenteth than over ninety and nine just persons? *Why* is the lost sheep sought in the wilderness? Because the individual soul has its infinite meaning in and through the unity of the Kingdom. The one lost sheep, found again, — or the one repentant sinner, — symbolizes the restoration of the unity of this community, as the keystone stands for the sense of the whole arch, as the flag symbolizes the country.

And *why*, in the parable of the judgement, does the judge of all the earth identify himself with "the least of these my brethren," — with the stranger, with the sick, with the captive? Because the judge of all the earth is explicitly the spirit of the universal community, who speaks in the name of all who are one in the light and in the life of the Kingdom of Heaven.

VI

These things remind us how ill those interpret the teachings of the Master who see in them a merely amiable fondness for what any any morally detached individual happens to love or to suffer or seem. It is the ideal oneness of the life of the Kingdom of Heaven which glorifies and renders significant every human individual who loves the Kingdom, or whom God views as such a lover. And because Paul had before him the life of the churches, while the Master left the Kingdom of Heaven for the future to reveal, Paul's account of Christian morals is an enrichment, and a further fufilment of what the parables began to tell, and left to the coming of the Kingdom to make manifest.

In such wise, then, are the familiar precepts to be interpreted, if the Christian doctrine of the moral life is to be what it was intended to be, — not a body of maxims and of illustrations, but a living and growing expression of the life-spirit of Christianity.

For the doctrine, if thus interpreted, points you not only backwards to the reported words of the Master, but endlessly forwards into the region where humanity, as it continues through the coming ages, must, with an unwearied patience, labor and experiment, and invent and create. The true moral code of Christianity has always been and will remain fluent as well as decisive. Only so could it express the Master's true spirit. It therefore must not view either the parables or the sayings as a storehouse of maxims, or even as a treasury of individual examples and of personal expressions of the Master's mind, expressions such that these maxims, these examples, and these personal sayings of the Master can never be surpassed in their ethical teachings. The doctrine of the sayings and of the parables actually cries out for reinterpretation, for the creation of a novel life. That seems to me precisely what the founder himself intended. The early apostolic Churches fulfilled the Master's teaching by surpassing it, and were filled with the spirit of their Master just because they did so. This, to my mind, is a central lesson of the early development of Christianity.

All morality, namely, is, from this point of view, to be judged by the standards of the Beloved Community, of the ideal Kingdom of Heaven. Concretely stated, this means that you are to test every course of action *not* by the question: What can we find in the parables or in the Sermon on the Mount which seems to us more or less directly to bear upon this special matter? The central doctrine of the Master was: "So act that the Kingdom of Heaven may come." This means: So act as to help, however you can, and whenever you can, towards making mankind one loving brotherhood, whose love is not a mere affection for morally detached individuals, but a love of the unity of its own life upon its own divine level, and a love of individuals in so far as they can be raised to communion with this spiritual community itself.

VII

Now if we speak in purely human, and still postpone any speaking in metaphysical, terms, the community of all mankind is an ideal. Just now, just in this year or on this day, there exists no human community that is adequately conscious of its own unity, adequately creative of what it ought to create, adequately representative, on its own level, of the real and human communion of the spirit. Our best communities of to-day either take account of caste or of nation or of race, as all the political communities do, or else, when deliberately aiming at universality and at religious unity, they exclude one another; and are therefore not, in an ideal sense and degree, beloved communities. Two things, if no other, stand between even the best of the churches as they are, — between them, I say, and the attainment of the goal of the truly beloved and the universal human community.

The one thing is their sectarian character, — excluding, as they do, the one the other. The other thing is their official organization, which cultivates, in each of the more highly developed communities of this type, a respect for the law at precisely the expense of that which Paul experienced in case of the legal aspect of the Judaism in which he was trained.

No, — the universal and beloved community is still hidden from our imperfect human view, and will remain so, how long we know not.

Nevertheless, the principle of principles in all Christian morals remains this: — "Since you cannot *find* the universal and beloved community, — *create* it." And this again, applied to the concrete art of living, means: Do whatever you can to take a step towards it, or to assist anybody, — your brother, your friend, your neighbor, your country, — mankind, — to take steps towards the organization of that coming community.

That, I say, is the principle of principles for Christian morals. But, for that very reason, there can be no code of Christian morals, nor any one set of personal examples, or of sayings, or of parables, or of other narratives, which will do more than to arouse us to create something new on our way towards the goal. Christian morality will not, either suddenly or gradually, conquer the world. But, if Christianity, conceived in its true spirit retains its hold upon mankind, humanity will go on creating new forms of Christian morality; whose only persistent feature will be that they intend to aid men to make their personal, their friendly, their social, their political, their religious orders and organizations such that mankind comes more and more to resemble the ideal, the beloved, the universal community. And the ethical aspect of the creed of the Christian world always will include this article: "I believe in the beloved community and in the spirit which makes it beloved, and in the communion of all who are, in will and in deed, its members. I see no such community as yet; but none the less my rule of life is: Act so as to hasten its coming."

Now such an ethical creed is not a vague humanitarian enthusiasm. For it simply requires that we work with whatever concrete human materials we have for creating both the organization of communities and the love of them. The work is without any human conclusion that we can foresee. But it can be made always definite, simply by resoluteness, in union with devotion. *That* is the type of work which always has been characteristically Christian, and which promises to remain so.

VIII

The Christian idea of the community and of its relation to the way of salvation requires for its complete appreciation a comparison and synthesis which shall also include the idea of Atonement.

In the foregoing lecture we endeavored to set the religious value of the idea of atonement in a light which must be, for many minds, somewhat novel; for otherwise the idea of atonement would not have been so long and so variously rendered more mysterious by the technically theological treatment which has been freely devoted to it. Nevertheless, in its deepest spirit, this very idea of atonement has been so dear to the religious mind of Christendom, and so familiar in art, in worship, and in comtemplation, that it simply ought not to appear so mysterious. The fate of the Christian idea of atonement has been, that what Christian piety felt to be the head of the corner, the Christian intellect has either rejected, or else, even in trying to defend the atonement, has made a stone of stumbling, and a rock of offence.

Between the idea of the saving community and the idea of atonement, lie the gravest of Christian ideas,—those which many optimists find too discouraging to face, or too austere to be wholesome. These are: the idea of sin, the idea of our original bondage to sin, and the idea of the consequences involved in defining sin as an inner voluntary inclination of the mind, rather than as an outwardly manifest evil deed. These ideas about sin are in part common, as we have said, to Christianity and to Buddhism.

But, as a fact, Christianity has so developed these very ideas, has so united them with the conception of the grace and of the loyalty which save men from their natural sinfulness, that just these conceptions regarding sin, despite the fact that Matthew Arnold thought them too likely to lead to a brooding wherein "many have perished," are ideas such that their rightful definition renders Christianity what, for Paul, it became a religion of spiritual freedom.

In our studies of the moral burden of the individual, and of the

realm of grace, we have seen how Christianity is a religion dependent, for its conception of original sin, upon the most characteristic
features of that social cultivation whereby we are brought to a high
level of self-consciousness. Early Buddhism had, so far as I am aware,
no views about the nature of the social self as clear as those which
Paul attained and, in his own way, expressed. But this very doctrine
about "the law,"—that is, about the social origin of the individual
self, and about that which "causes sin to abound," is a theory which
lies at the root of the power and the right of Christianity to say, to
the self which has first attained sinful cultivation in self-will, and
which has then been transformed by "grace" into a loyal self, precisely what Paul said to his converts: "All things are yours." For the
doctrine of Paul is, that the escape from original sin comes through
the acceptance of a service which is perfect freedom. Out of the
Christian doctrine of sin grows the Christian teaching about the freedom of the faithful,—a teaching which, in its turn, lies at the basis
of some of the most important developments of the modern mind.
The doctrine of sin need not lead, then, to brooding. It may lead to
spiritual self-possession.

The doctrine of atonement enables us to extend the Pauline theory
of salvation by grace, so that not merely our originally helpless bondage to the results of our social cultivation is removed by the grace
of loyalty, but the saddest of all the forms and consequences of wilful
sin,—namely, the deed and the result of conscious disloyalty, can
be brought within the range which the grace of the will of the community can reach. The result of our discussion in the last lecture
has been that, if we are right, the idea of atonement has a perfectly
indispensable office, both in the ethical and in the religious task
which the Christian doctrine of life has to accomplish.

IX

Let me try to make a little more obvious the interpretation of the
idea of atonement which, in the last lecture, I stated in outline. Let
me use for this purpose another illustration.

If my view about the essence of the idea of atonement is correct,
the first instance of an extended account of an atoning process which
the Biblical narratives include, would be the story of Joseph and his
brethren. Let us treat this story, of course, as obviously a little
romance. We study merely its value as an illustration. The brethren
sin against Joseph, and against their father. Their deed has some of

the characteristics, not of mere youthful folly, but of maturely wilful treason. They assail not merely their brother, but their father's love for the lost son. Their crime is carefully considered, and is deeply treacherous. But it goes still farther. The treason is directed against their whole family community. Now, in the long run, according to the beautiful tale, Joseph not only comforts his father and is able to be a forgiving benefactor to his brethren, but in such wise atones for the sin of his brethren that the family unity is restored. Here, then, is felt to be a genuine atonement. Wherein does it consist?

Does it consist in this, that the brethren have earned a just penalty which, as a fact, they never adequately suffer; while Joseph, guilt-less of their wilful sin, vicariously suffers a penalty which he has not deserved? Does the atonement further consist in the fact that Joseph is able and willing freely to offer, for the good of the family, both the merits and the providential good fortune which this vicarious endur-ance of his has won?

No,—this "penal satisfaction" theory of the atoning work of Joseph, if it were proposed as an example of a doctrine of atonement, certainly would not meet that sense of justice, and of the fitness of things, and of the true value of Jospeh's life and deeds,—that sense, I say, which every child who first hears the story readily feels,— without in the least being able to tell what he feels. If one magnified the deed of Joseph to the infinite, and said, as many have said, "Such a work as Joseph did for his brethren, even such a work, in his own divinely supreme way and sense Christ did for sinful man,"—would *that* theory of the matter make the nature of atonement obvious? Would a vicarious "penal satisfaction" help one to understand either one or the other of these instances of atonement?

But let us turn from such now generally discredited "penal satis-faction" theories to the various forms of modern moral theories. Let us say, applying our explanations once more to the story of Joseph: "God's Providence sent Joseph into captivity, through the sin of his brethren, but still under a divine decree. Joseph was obedi-ent and faithful and pure-minded. God rewarded his patience and fidelity by giving him power in Egypt. Then Joseph, having suffered and triumphed, set before his brethren (not with a due measure of gently stern rebuke for their past misdeeds), an example of love and forgiveness so moving, that they deeply repented, confessed their sins, and loved their brother as never before. *That* was Joseph's atonement. And that, if magnified to the infinite, gives one a view of the sense in which the work of Christ atones for man's sin." Would such an account help us to understand atonement, either in Joseph's case, or in the other?

I should reply that such moral theories of atonement, applied to the story of Joseph, miss the most obvious point and beauty of the tale; and also show us in no wise what genuine atoning work the Joseph of the story did. Would the mere repentance, or the renewed love of the treacherous brethren for Joseph, or their wish to be forgiven, or their confession of their sin, constitute a sufficient ground for the needed reconciliation, in view of their offence against their brother, their father, or their family? If this was all the atonement which Joseph's labors supplied, he failed in his supposed office. Something more is needed to satisfy even the child who enjoys the story.

But now, let us become as little children ourselves. Let us take the tale as a sensitive child takes it, when its power first enters his soul. Let us simply articulate what the child feels. Here, according to the tale, is a patriarchial family invaded by a wilful treason, wounded to the core, desolated, broken. The years go by. The individual who was most directly assailed by the treason is guiltless himself of any share in that treason. He is patient and faithful and obedient. When power comes to him, he uses that power (which only just this act of treason could have put into his hands), first, to accomplish a great work of good for the community of a great kingdom. Herewith, according to the tale, he provides for the future honor and glory of his own family for all time to come. And then, being brought once more into touch with his family, he behaves with such clemency, and justice, and family loyalty; he shows such transient but amiable brotherly severity towards the former traitors, he shows also such tender filial devotion; his weeping when the family unity is restored is so rich in pathos; his care in providing for his father and for the future is so wise; his creative skill in making again into one fair whole what treason had shattered is so wonderful, that all these things together make the situation one whereof the child says without definite words, what we now say: "Through Joseph's work all is made, in fact, better than it would have been had there been no treason at all." Now I submit that Joseph's atoning work consists simply in this triumphantly ingenious creation of good out of ill. That the brethren confess and repent is inevitable, and is a part of the good result; but by itself that is only a poor offering on their part.

It is Joseph who atones. His atonement is, of course, vicarious. But it is perfectly objective. And it is no vicarious "penal satisfaction" whatever. It is simply the triumph of the spirit of the family through the devoted loyalty of an individual. This, in fact, is, in substance, what Joseph himself says in his closing words to his brethren.

Joseph turns into a good, for the family, for the world, for his father, for the whole community involved, what his brothers had made ill. In his deed, through his skill, as well as through his suffering, the world is made better than it would have been had the treason never been done. This, I insist, constitutes his atoning work.

As to the brethren, — their treason is, of course, irrevocable. Joseph's deed does not wipe out that guilt of their own. But they can stand in the presence of their community and hear the distinctly reconciling word: "You have been the indirect cause of a good that, by the grace and the ingenuity of the community and of its faithful servant, has now been created, while, but for your treason, this good could not have been created. Your sin cannot be cancelled. Nor are you in any wise the doers of the atoning deed. But the community welcomes you to its love again, — not as those whose irrevocable deed has been cancelled, but as those whom love has so overruled that you have been made a source whence a spring of good flows."

The repentant and thankful brothers can now accept this reconciliation, — never as a destruction of their guilt, but as a new and an objective fact whose significance they are willing to lay at the basis of a new loyalty. The community is renewed; the spirit has triumphed; and the traitors are glad that the irrevocable deed which they condemn has been made a source of a good which never could have existed without it. They are in a new friendship with their community, since the ends that have triumphed unite the new will with the old and evil will, through a new conquest of the evil.

Let my illustration pass for what it is worth. I still insist that an atonement of this sort, if it occurs at all, is a perfectly objective fact, namely, the creation by somebody of a definite individual good on the basis of a definite previous evil. That the total result, in a given case, such as that of Joseph, is something better than would have existed, or than would have been possible, had not that evil deed first been done, to which the atoning deed is the response, — all this, I say, is a perfectly proper matter for a purely objective study. Such a study has the difficulties which attend all inquiries into objective values. But these difficulties do not make the matter one of arbitrary whim.

Moreover, if the atoning deed has brought, as a fact, such good out of evil that, despite the evil deed, the world is better than it could have been if the evil deed had not been done, — then this very fact has its own reconciling value, — a value limited but precious. The repentant sinner, seeing what, in Adam's vision, Milton makes the first human sinner foresee, will rightly find a genuine consolation, and a true reunion with his community, in thus being aware that his iniquity has been overruled for good.

A theory of atonement, founded upon this basis, is capable of as technical treatment as any other, and deals with facts and values which human wit can investigate, so far as the facts in question are accessible to us. Such a theory of atonement could be applied to estimate the atoning work of Christ, by any one who believed himself to be sufficiently in touch with the facts about Christ's supposed work. It would be capable of as technical a statement as our knowledge warranted.

This then, in brief, is my proposal looking towards an interpretation of the idea of atonement.

X

Turning once more to view, in the light of this interpretation, the Christian doctrine of life in its unity, we may see how all the ideas now unite to give to this doctrine a touch both with the ethical and with the religious interests of humanity.

To sum up: As individuals we are lost; that is, are incapable of attaining the true goal of life. This our loss is due to the fact that we have not love. So the Master taught. But the problem is also the problem: For what love shall I seek? What love will save me? Here, if we restrict our answer to human objects, and deliberately avoid theology, the Christian answer is: Love the Community. That is, be Loyal.

Yet one further asks: What community shall I love? The answer to this question has been lengthily discussed. We need not here, at any length, repeat it. Speaking still in human terms, we are to love a community which, in ideal, is identical with all mankind, but which can never exist on earth until man has been transfigured and unified, as Paul hoped that his churches would soon witness this transfiguration and this union, at the end of the world.

So far as this ideal indeed takes possession of us, we can direct our human life in the spirit of this love for the community, far away as the goal may seem and be.

Yet what stands in the way of our being completely absorbed by this ideal? The answer is: Our enemy is what Paul called the flesh, and found further emphasized by "the law." This enemy is due to our nature as social beings, so far as this nature is cultivated by social conditions which, while training our self-consciousness, even thereby inflame our self-will. *This our social nature*, then, is the basis of our natural enmity both towards the law, and towards the spirit.

How can this natural enmity be overcome? The answer is: By the means of those unifying social influences which Paul regarded as due to grace. Genius, and only genius, — the genius which, in the extreme cases, founds new religions, and which, in the better known cases, creates great social movements of a genuinely saving value, can create the communities which arouse love, which join the faithful into one, and which transform the old man into the new. When once we have come under the spell of such creative genius, and of the communities of which some genius appears to be the spirit, — only then can we too die to the old life, and be renewed in the spirit. The early Christian community is (still speaking in human terms) one great historical instance of such a source of salvation. To be won over to the level of *such* a community is, just in so far, to be saved.

But the will of the loyal is, in the purely human and practical sense, a will that we call free. The higher the spiritual gifts in question are, the greater is the opportunity for wilful treason to the community to which we have once given faith. The consequences of every deed include the great fact that each deed is irrevocable. And the penalty of wilful treason, therefore, is, for the traitor, — precisely in so far as he knows himself, and values his life in its larger connections, — an essentially endless penalty, — the penalty which he assigns to himself, — the fact of his sin.

For such penalty is there any aid that can come to us through the atoning deed of another? There is such aid possible. *In the human world we can never count upon it. But it is possible.* And sometimes, by the grace of the community, and by the free will of a noble soul, such aid comes. As a fact, the whole life of man gets its highest — one is often disposed to say, its only real and abiding — goods, from the conquest over ill. Atoning deeds, deeds that, through sacrifices, win again the lost causes of the moral world, not by undoing the irrevocable, nor by making the old bitterness of defeat as if it never had been, but by creating new good out of ancient ill, and by producing a total realm of life which is better than it would have been had the evil not happened, — atoning deeds express the most nearly absolute loyalty which human beings can show. The atoning deeds are the most creative of the expressions which the community gives, through the deed of an individual, to its will that the unity of the spirit should triumph, not only despite, but *through*, the greatest trag- edies, — the tragedies of deliberate sin.

Through the community, or on its behalf, the atoning deeds are done. The individual who has sinned, but who knows of free atoning deeds that indeed have been done, — deeds whereby good comes out of his evil, — can be not wholly reconciled to his own past, but truly restored to the meaning of the loyal life. Upon the hope that such atoning deeds, if they have not been done because of our sins, may yet be done, all of us depend for such rewinning of our spiritual rela- tions to our community as we have sinned away. And thus the idea of the community and the idea of atonement, — both of them, still interpreted in purely human fashion, but extended in ideal through the whole realm that the human spirit can ever conquer, form in their inseparable union, and in their relation to the other Christian ideas, the Christian doctrine of life. The Christian life is one that first, as present in the individual, offers to the community practical devotion and absorbing love. This same life, also present in the indi- vidual, looks to the community for the grace that saves and for the atonement that, so far as may be, reconciles. As incorporate in the community, or as incarnate in those who act as the spirit of the com- munity, and who create new forms of the community, and originate atoning deeds, — as thus present in the community and in its crea- tively loyal individual members, the Christian life expresses the postulate, the prayer, the world-conquering will, whose word is: Let the spirit triumph. Let no evil deed be done so deep in its treachery but that creative love shall find the way to make the world better than it would have been had that evil deed not been done.

The Christian doctrine of life consists in observing and asserting that these ideas have their real and distinctly human basis. This doctrine also consists in the purely voluntary assertion that, in so far as these ideals are not yet verifiable in human life as it is, this life is to be lived as if they were verifiable, or were sure to become so in the fulness of time. For that fulness of time, for that coming of the Kingdom, we both labor and wait.

VIII

The Modern Mind
and the
Christian Ideas

Throughout our exposition of the ideas which, in their unity, constitute the Christian doctrine of life, we have intended to bring to light the relations of these ideas to the modern mind. Whenever we have attempted to define what we mean by the modern mind, we have been guided by two considerations. First, certain opinions and mental attitudes seem to be characteristic of leading teachers and of representative tendencies in our own day. Secondly, these prominent ideas of our day express general lessons which the history of mankind appears to us to have taught. We have accepted the postulate that history includes a more or less coherent education of the human race; and then have we viewed the modern mind as the present heir to this wisdom. And therefore some at least of the prominent ideas of our day have seemed to deserve their prominence because they express part of the lesson of history.

How vague the resulting general conception of the modern mind and of its opinions necessarily is, we have acknowledged. But the conception is useful, simply because it enables us to summarize a type of convictions that possess indeed no supreme authority, but that are signs which men must interpret, and leadings which they must attempt to follow, if they are to take part in that collective human life which is to record itself in future history, and if our age is to teach any lesson to those who shall come after us.

The present lecture will be devoted to a summary of some of the lessons which the hostory of religion seems to have taught mankind, and to a general study of the bearing of these lessons upon our estimate of the present and the future of the Christian religion.

I

There are three lessons of religious history, and three views prominent in recent discussion, which may be said to form part of the characteristically modern view of the meaning and destiny of religion.

First, religion is, historically speaking, a product of certain human needs; and its endurance depends upon its power to meet those needs. A religion which ceases to strengthen hearts and to fulfil the just demands of the human spirit for guidance through the wilderness of this world, is doomed; and in due time passes away; as the religion of Greco-Roman antiquity decayed and died; and as countless tribal and national religions have died, along with the social orders and cultures which they, in their day, sustained and inspired.

To use a metaphor which I believe to be neither trivial nor unjust: The gods, as man conceives the gods, live upon spiritual food; but, viewed in the light of history, they appear as beings who must earn their bread by supplying, in their turn, the equally spiritual sustenance which their worshippers need. And unless they thus earn their bread, the gods die; and the holy places that have known them, know them no more forever. Let the ruins of ancient temples suggest the meaning that lies behind my figure of speech.

To make this assertion concerning the inevitable fortunes of all religions, is not to reduce the conception of religious truth to that which current pragmatism emphasizes. The relation between the two conceptions of religious truth which are in question will concern us in our later lectures. Here it is enough to say that I am not now deciding whether or no any religious truth is absolute; but am expressly limiting myself to the forms under which religious truth and error enter human history.

The needs of the worshippers determine, in the long run, the historical fate of religions. It is just, however, to add, that worshippers actually need an everlasting gospel; and that, if such a gospel were to be revealed to man, it would not only satisfy human needs, but also contain absolute religious truth.

What I thus point out is simply meant to emphasize the assertion that the realm of religion is a realm, not of merely natural facts, but of will and of need, of desire, of longing, and of satisfaction. In other words, as it is now customary to state the case, religion is mainly concerned, not with facts that belong to the material world, but with values. Religion, meanwhile, aims at the absolute, but has no vehicle to carry its message to ourselves except the vehicle of human experience. The goal of religion is something beyond all our transient strivings. But its path lies through the realm of human needs.

And so, when a religion loses touch with human needs, it dies.

II

Such is the first of the three modern opinions about religion to which I wish to call attention. The second may be stated in well-known terms. We live in an age when there have already occurred great recent changes in the spiritual needs whereof men are conscious. And in the near future still greater changes in these needs are likely to be felt.

Those changes in the needs of mankind which led to the decay and death of the religions of antiquity were petty in contrast to the vast transformations of the human spirit to which our modern conditions seem likely to lead within the next few centuries. Physical science and the industrial arts are altering the very foundations of our culture, of our social order, and of our opinions regarding nature. This alteration is now taking place at a rate for which no previous age of human history furnishes any parallel. Apart from chance catastrophes, which seem unlikely to happen, these processes of mental and of social change are likely to continue at a constantly increasing rate. In consequence, man's whole spiritual outlook will probably soon become different from any outlook that men have ever before experienced. This law of constantly accelerated change promises to dominate the most essential interests of the civilization of the near future.

Concerning this second thesis which I here attribute to the modern mind, there is likely to be little difference of opinion amongst us. Many of us fear or deplore great spiritual changes. We all feel sure that such will soon occur. We know that, regarding all such matters, we have indeed no right to predict the future of humanity in any but the most general terms. Yet the prospect of very rapid and vast mental and social transformations, in the near future of civilization, is emphasized in our minds by innumerable considerations. Few of us are disposed to believe that, were we permitted to return to earth a very few centuries from now, we should find that even the dearest and oldest of the traditional features of our civilization had remained exempt from momentous and, to our minds, bewildering alterations.

The wildest flights of imagination regarding such possibilities often seem to us instructive, just because they help us to read one great warning which the modern world gives us. This is the warning that nothing in human affairs is so sacred as to be sure of escaping the workings of this law of accelerated change.

III

The third of the modern opinions which I here have in mind is closely associated with the two foregoing theses.

In ancient civilizations the religious institutions were often supported by the whole social power of the peoples concerned, so that the religious life of a nation belonged to whatever was most characteristic and most conservative about the civilization in question. In the Middle Ages, despite the enormous complexity of the Christian social order, the religious institutions still formed a very large part of what was most essential to European culture. But in recent times religious institutions — institutions of the nature of churches, of sects, or of religious orders — stand in a much less central position in our organized social life than ever before. The tangible social importance of these institutions grows constantly less rather than greater. Had all the temples of a typical ancient city, and had all its priests and sacred places, been suddenly destroyed, so that none of the customary festivals and sacrifices could be carried on, we know how tragically the whole life of that city would have been disturbed, if not wholly paralyzed. But our modern industrial arts, our world-wide commerce, our daily business, our international relations, grow constantly more and more independent of any ecclesiastical and, in fact, of any public religious activities or institutions; so that, if all churches and priesthoods and congregations were temporarily to suspend their public functions and their visible doings, our market-places and factories and merchants and armies would continue to go on, for the time, much as usual.

In consequence, in the modern world, religion no longer has the effective institutional support of the whole collective social will, but lives more apart from the other great social interests, and dwells more in a realm where internal faith rather than publicly administered law determines the range of its control. Hence when the social world is subject to forces which tend towards change, religion no longer stands at the point where the most conservative powers of society are massed. Religion must depend for its ability to resist change upon new weapons. Conservatism will no longer stand as its potent and natural defender. The human needs that it is to meet will be in a state of constant growth. The visible social organizations which have been its closest allies in the past can no longer be counted upon to preserve its visible forms. Once, when the temples and the gods were threatened, all the state rose as one man to defend them. For they were the centre of the social order. But henceforth commerce and industry will tend to take the place in men's minds which religious institutions once occupied. The things of the spirit must now be defended with the sword of the spirit. Worldly weapons can no longer be used either to propagate or to preserve religion. Religion must find its own way to the hearts of the coming generations. And these hearts will be stirred by countless new cares and hopes. The human problem of religion will grow constantly more complicated.

Our three assertions of the modern mind regarding religion define for us, then, the religious problem of the future. No religion can survive unless it keeps in touch with men's conscious needs. In the future men's needs will be subject to vastly complex and rapidly changing social motives. In the future, religion, as a power aiming to win and to keep a place in men's hearts, can no longer permanently count on the institutional forces which have in the past been amongst its strongest supports. Its own institutions will tend, with the whole course of civilization, to come increasingly under the sway of the law of accelerated change. The non-religious institutions of the future, the kingdoms and the democracies of this world, the social structures which will be used for the purposes of production, of distribution, and of political life, will certainly exemplify the law of accelerated change. And these social structures will not be under the control of religious institutions.

IV

Such are some of the lessons which history and the present day teach to the modern mind. Such are the conditions which determine the religious problems of the future. What shall we say of these problems, in their bearing upon Christianity?

In answer we can only take account of what we have gained for an understanding of our situation through our study of the Christian ideas. What we need is to look again at the sword of the spirit which is still in the hands of religion.

Were the strength of the Christian religion, in its contest with the coming modern world, mainly the strength of its already existing religious institutions, we can see at once that all the three considerations which we have just emphasized would combine to make the prospects of the contest doubtful. It is true that no reasonable man ought for a moment to underestimate the actual vitality of the religious institutions of the Christian world, viewed simply as institutions. Assertions are indeed sometimes made to the effect that the Church, in all its various forms and divisions, or in very many of them, is already very rapidly losing touch, or has already hopelessly lost touch, with the modern world; and that here the process of estrangement between the Church and modern life is constantly accelerated. Some observers even venture to predict a rapid dwindling of all or most of the ecclesiastical institutions of Christendom in the near future. I suppose all such extreme assertions to be hasty and unwarranted. What we can see is merely this: that if the future of Christianity depended upon its institutions rather than upon its ideas, the result of changes that lie before us would be doubtful.

But our study of the Christian ideas has shown that the deepest human strength of this religion lies precisely in these ideas themselves. By the might of these ideas early Christianity conquered the Roman world. In the light of these ideas European civilization has since been transformed; and by their spirit it still guides its life. These Christian ideas, — not their formulations in the creeds, — not their always inadequate institutional embodiment, — and of course not any abstract statement of them such as our philosophical sketch has attempted,—these ideas constitute the sword of the spirit with which the Christian religion has to carry on its warfare. What makes its contest with the world of the future hopeful is simply the fact that, whatever creed or institution or practice may lose its hold on the modern mind, the Christian doctrine of life is the expression of universal human needs,—and of the very needs upon whose satisfaction the very life of every social order depends for its worth and for its survival. No progress in the industrial arts, and no massing of population or of wealth, and no scheme of political reform, can remove from the human mind and the human heart these needs, and the ideas that alone can satisfy them. As for social changes, they will inevitably mean vast social tragedies. But such tragedies can only emphasize the very longings to which the Christian doctrine of life appeals. Whatever happens to any of the visible forms and institutions of Christianity, the soul of this religion can always defiantly say to itself:—

> Stab at thee then who will;
> No stab the soul can kill.

With this interpretation of its mission present to its mind, it can face all its enemies with all the might of the spirit upon its side. It is this view of the relation between the Christian ideas and the modern world which I here wish to emphasize.

To accomplish this end, we have merely to sum up what our whole study has already taught us, and to contrast our views with those which some other accounts of the problem of Christianity have defended.

V

Many, in our day, are disposed to think that the true, or perhaps also the last, refuge of religion is some form of mystical piety. Retire from the world; seek rest in what Meister Eckhart called the wilderness of the Godhead; win an immediate experience of the presence of the divine; surrender your individuality; let God be all in all to you; and then,—so such lovers of religion declare,—you will indeed win the peace that the world can neither give nor take away. By such a flight into Egypt the defenders of mystical religion hope to save the divine life from the hands of the Herod of modern worldliness. If you thus flee, they say, you may find what the saints of old found in their deserts and their cloisters. Modern civilization, with all its restlessness, will then become to you, so the partisans of mystical religion insist, a matter of indifference. Time, with all its mysterious futures and its endless changes, will for you simply pass away. You will behold the end of all things. You will, so to speak, witness the judgment day. If Christianity is to triumph at all, such minds hold that it must triumph in the form of the mystical and utterly unworldly piety thus suggested. Such solutions of the problem of Christianity are at this moment freely offered for our need. Such solutions in plenty will be offered in the future.

Now I have, personally, a profound respect for the mystical element in religion. The problem of justly estimating that element is a problem as inexhaustible as it is fascinating. And I have no doubt that the mystics have indeed contributed indispensable religious values to our experience. I am eager to bring to light, in our future discussion, what some of those values are. But of this I am sure: Mystical piety can never either exhaust or express the whole Christian doctrine of life. For the Christian doctrine of life, in its manifoldness, in the intensity and variety of the human interests to which it appeals, is an essentially social doctrine. Private individual devotion can never justly interpret it.

Paul was a mystic; but he was a mystic with a community to furnish the garden where the mystical flowers grew; and where the fruits of the spirit were ripened, and where all the gifts of the spirit found their only worthy expression.

Without his community, without his brethren to be edified, and without charity to furnish the highest of the spiritual gifts, Paul, as he expressly tells us, would have accounted all his other gifts as making him but as sounding brass and as a tinkling cymbal. In all this he displayed that sound judgment, that clear common sense, to which the Christian doctrine of life has always been true. If Christianity, in the future, triumphs, that will be because some active and beloved community comes gradually more and more to take control of human affairs, and not because religion has fled to the recesses of any wilderness of the Godhead.

As a fact, the mystical tendency in religion is not the last, the mature, result, not yet the last refuge, of piety. Mysticism is the always young, it is the childlike, it is the essentially immature aspect of the deeper religious life. Its ardor, its pathos, its illusions, and its genuine illuminations have all the characters of youth about them, characters beautiful but capricious. Mature religion of the Christian type takes, and must take, the form of loyalty, — the loyalty which Paul lived out, and described. Loyalty fulfils the individual, not by annulling or quenching his individual self-expression, but by teaching him to assert himself through an active and creative devotion to his community. Hence, while one may be thoroughly loyal, and therefore thoroughly religious, without having the gift or the grace of mystical illumination, no mystic can become truly religious unless, like all the really greatest of the mystics,—beyond all his illuminations, and besides all his mere experiences of fulfilment, or of the immediate presence of the Divine,—he attains to a strenuous, active loyalty which can overcome the world only by living in the community. The strength of Christianity, in its conflict with the future world of our changing social order, will therefore depend upon the fact that its doctrine of life permits it, and indeed requires it, to be as practical and constructive in its dealing with the problems of social life as the industrial arts are practical and constructive in their production of material goods. It is the Christian will, and not Christian mysticism, which must overcome the world.

VI

If many thus suppose that the only solution of the problem of Christianity is a solution in terms of inner religious experience, and if they hold that the modern man should seek to interpret his religion mainly or wholly in a mystical sense, and should regard Christianity as a religion of private individual illumination,—there are many others who indeed vigorously reject this view. And some such defenders of the faith declare that, if Christianity is to survive at all, it can survive only in the form of a literal acceptance of the principal dogmas of the historical Church.

Those Christian apologists who view our problem in this way declare that the modern man, and the civilization of the future, must face an old and well-known choice between alternatives. "Christianity," so they say, "declares itself to be a revealed religion. This declaration forms a part of its very essence. If one rejects the thesis that Christianity is a revelation of God's will, the only alternative is to view Christian doctrine as a mere system of ethical teachings, and thus to transform the Christian religion into bare morality. The future of Christianity depends wholly upon how this choice is made."

Our previous discussion now enables us to answer this frequent assertion of the apologists of Christian tradition, by insisting that, whatever the final truth about Christianity may be, the choice between alternatives which lies before the modern man is *not* justly to be stated in any such way as the one upon which these apologists so often insist.

In fact, the most significant choice for the modern man, in dealing with Christianity, lies between accepting and rejecting the Christian doctrine of life. And the Christian ideas whereof this doctrine of life consists can be both estimated and put into practice without presupposing any one view of God or of revelation, although such an estimate may indeed lead, in the end, to a theology. When stated in human terms, as we have thus far stated them in these lectures, the Christian ideas do not constitute merely an ethical system. Nor is their spirit that of a mere morality. For they relate to the salvation of man. That is, they include the assertion that human life ought to be guided in the light of a highest good which is not a merely worldly or natural good, and which cannot be obtained through mere skill in winning good fortune, or in successfully living the life of a human individual. For the Christian doctrine of life insists that the human individual, as he is naturally constituted, simply cannot live a successful life, but must first be transfigured.

The Christian ideas depend upon acknowledging what we have called the distinction between the two levels of human existence, and upon defining the highest good of man in terms of a transformation of our individual nature. A loving union of the individual with a level of existence which is essentially above his own grade of being is what the Christian doctrine of life defines as the way that leads towards the highest good. The whole of Christianity, as we have seen, grows out of this doctrine of the two levels.

But, from the very nature of the case, the vista which this doctrine of the two levels opens before us is at once human and illimitable. Man the individual is essentially insufficient to win the goal of his own existence. Man the community is the source of salvation. And by man the community I mean, *not* the collective biological entity called the human race, and not the merely natural community which gives to us, as social animals, our ordinary moral training. Nor by man the community do I mean the series of misadventures and tragedies whereof the merely external history of what is called humanity consists. By man the community I mean man in the sense in which Paul conceived Christ's beloved and universal Church to be a community,—man viewed as one conscious spiritual whole of life. And I say that this conscious spiritual community is the sole possessor of the means of grace, and is the essential source of the salvation of the individual. This, in general, is what the Christian doctrine of life teaches. The essential problem for the modern man is the question: Is this doctrine of life true?

Now the conception of man the spiritual community comes to our knowledge, *not*, in the first place, by means of any revelation from the world of the gods; nor yet through metaphysical reflection; although, when once we have this conception, it easily suggests to us dogmas, and easily seems to us as if it were a superhuman revelation, and also awakens an inexhaustible metaphysical interest.

The saving idea of man the community comes to us through two kinds of perfectly human experience. First, it comes to us through the experience of the failure both of our natural self-will and of our mere morality to save us. This failure is due to the essential defect of the level upon which, by nature, man the social individual lives. Buddhism was founded upon this experience of the inevitable failure of the human individual to win his own goal. Paul, before his vision of the risen Lord converted him, learned in another form, and by perfectly human experience, the same negative lesson. Individual self-will is due to our insatiable natural greed, and is only inflamed by our merely moral cultivation.

Secondly, however, when such experience of the failure of a merely individual human existence has done its work, another sort of experience is needed to reveal to us the meaning of the life which belongs to the other human level, — to the level of the beloved community. This experience is the experience of the meaning of loyalty. It is this experience which, while always essentially human in the facts that it brings to our notice, opens up its endless vistas, suggests to us countless interpretations in terms of our relations to a supernatural world, and justly seems to be a revelation of something not ourselves which is worthy to be our guide and salvation. This experience of grace and of loyalty it is which awakens an inexhaustible metaphysical interest.

Since these ethical and religious and metaphysical vistas and interests are indeed endless, and since the life work and the insight to which they call us are constantly growing, there is no one way of defining in dogmatic formulas that view of God or of revelation to which they will always require us to adhere. Man the community, without ceasing to be genuinely human, may also prove to be divine. That is a matter for further inquiry. Loyalty, without ceasing to be a spirit that we learn through our human relations, may also prove to be a revelation from a realm of life which is infinitely superior to any human life that we now experience. In other words, the higher of the two levels of human existence may prove to be, not only essentially above our individual level, but endlessly and quite divinely above that level. Man the community may prove to be God, as the traditional doctrine of Christ, of the Spirit, and of the Church seems to imply. But all such possible outcomes and interpretations, to which the Christian doctrine of life may lead, must be discovered for themselves. It is vain to narrow the choice that lies before the modern man and before the future social order to a choice between any one set of traditional dogmas on the one hand, and a mere morality on the other.

VII

The Christian doctrine of life is therefore no mere morality, any more than it is a mere mysticism. And yet it does not depend upon first accepting any one form of theology or any one view about revelation. For one who wishes to judge fairly the Christian doctrine of life, the choice which is to be faced is therefore this: *Either* a doctrine that individuals can work out their own salvation, *or else* a recognition that salvation comes through loyalty to the beloved community and through the influence of the realm of grace. Loyalty,— the beloved community,— the realm of grace,— these are indeed essential features of Christian doctrine.

The various views about revelation which have taken part in Christian history can be understood only in case this contrast between the two levels, and the practical significance of grace, of salvation, and of loyalty, have first been made clear in human terms. But if these human aspects of the Christian ideas have been grasped, one may then go on to the comprehension of what the Christian views about God have been trying, with varied symbolism, to present to the minds of men. One who approaches the problem of Christianity with the lore of the two levels of human existence well in mind will be ready for spiritual novelties. He will not limit himself to any simple pair of alternatives. His creed will be neither a narrow moralism nor an equally narrow traditional dogmatism. He will perceive that we have endlessly new things yet to learn about what were, and still are, the sources of Christian doctrine and life,— the sources of the inspirations which guide humanity into novel undertakings, and the sources, also, of those traditions of the Church which symbolized so much more then they made explicit. He will also be quite ready to see that, despite all the changes of doctrine, the unity of the Christian doctrine of life has been and can be retained, — and retained just because Christianity is a doctrine of life, and hence a doctrine of that which preserves its meaning through change, and by virtue of change, so that the doctrine also must change its form as the life changes, but must nevertheless keep its unity precisely in so far as the changing life means something coherent and worthy.

And therefore, when we ask how the modern man, and how the future social order, stands related to the Christian ideas, our question really concerns the worth and the coherence which the Christian doctrine of life still retains, and will retain, in the midst of our vast and distracted modern world. Such a question is at best not easy to answer. But our foregoing studies have furnished a preparation for an attempt towards such an answer. I believe that some such preparation is needed, and will grow more and more necessary the more complex the situation of modern civilization becomes.

VIII

Closely related to the effort to reduce our problem of Christianity to the simple choice of alternative, "Either Christianity is a revealed religion, or else it is a mere system of morality," there stands another interpretation of the same problem with which you are all familiar. This interpretation often expresses itself thus: "The modern man's relation to a Christian creed must depend upon his answer to the question, "Is, or is not the man Jesus, the founder of Christianity, identical with the Christ, the God-Man, whom Christian tradition has acknowledged as Lord?" The modern man's choice, when thus interpreted, lies between the two alternative theses: — "*Either* Jesus, the founder of Christianity, was a man, and only a man; *or else* Jesus was the Christ, that is, was the God-Man."

Many apologists insist that this one choice between alternatives may be said to cover *all* that is most important in the problem of Christianity. For if the modern man, in presence of this choice, decides that in his opinion Jesus was the Christ, the decision brings him into close touch with all the best-known traditions of historical Christianity. The Christian religion is then acknowledged to be a divine process; and the work of the divine founder becomes the one source of human salvation. On the other hand, if Jesus was a man

and only a man, then, however exalted his human life, or his doctrine, may have been, he stands upon essentially the same level as
Socrates or as Confucius. For in that case he taught as an individual
man, addressing his individual fellow-men; and the worth of his
teaching must vary with the needs of persons and of periods. So the
problem of the modern man is stated by many Christian apologists.

As a fact, the choice between alternatives which is thus formulated
can be neglected by no serious student of our problem of Christianity. It is also true, however, that the choice cannot justly be made
unless one takes account of considerations which tend greatly to
widen our vista, and which define possibilities whereof those who
believe in Christian tradition seldom take adequate account.

In answer, then, to the challenge: "*Either* you must believe that the
founder of Christianity was only a man, *or else* you must accept
Jesus as the Christ, the divine man,"—we must first reply, I think,
by an assertion which is as capable of a reasonable historical confirmation as it is often, at the present moment, neglected. It is indeed
no new assertion, and many in the past have made it. But our foregoing study, I think, helps us to view this assertion in a new light.

IX

Whatever may be the truth about the person of Christ, and about
the supposed supernatural origin of Christianity, the human source
of the Christian doctrine of life, and also the human source of all the
later Christologies, must be found in the early Christian community
itself. The Christian religion, in its early form, is the work and
expression of the Christian Church.

By the early Christian community I mean, first of all, the company
of disciples who, after the Master's death, assembled in Galilee, and
who, a little later, returned to Jerusalem. This community was
absorbed, at first, in what it knew of the earliest visions of the risen
Lord; and it narrated these visions in forms which the well-known
gospel legends preserved for later Christian ages. This community
also cherished the memory and the reported sayings of the Master.
Erelong this same community began to experience those phenomena
of collective religious fervor which it regarded as the work of the
divine Spirit. It began its own task of propagating its faith. It made
converts. Of these converts the greatest was the apostle Paul. Now
this community,—not Paul himself as an individual,—not any one
man, but this community, acting under the inspiration of its leaders,

—is the source of all later forms of Christian life and faith. In this sense it is true that this community is the real human founder of Christianity.

It is of course also true that Jesus during his life had, as an individual man, taught a doctrine, and done a work, which made this first Christian community possible. In this sense it is correct to say that the man Jesus, in so far as he was merely an individual man, is the founder of Christianity. But when we say this, we must add that, so far as we know of the teachings of the man Jesus, they did not make explicit what proved to be precisely the most characteristic feature of Christianity,—namely, the mission and the doctrine of the Christian community itself. The doctrine of Christian love, as the Master taught it, is not yet, in explicit form, the whole Christian doctrine of life. For the Christian doctrine of life is a doctrine which is unintelligible apart from the ideal of the universal community.

It is of course true, that had it not been for the life and for the teachings of Jesus, and had not the visions of the risen Lord been seen and held in memory, there would have been no Christian religion, and nothing for Paul to discover or to teach.

But it is also true that Christianity not only is a religion founded upon the idea of the divine community,—the Church,—but also is a religion whose human founder was rather the community itself, acting as a spiritual unity,—than it was any individual man whatever. Our doctrine of the two levels of human existence has explained what such a view of the matter means.

We know how the Church interpreted its own origin when it held that its actual originator was no mere individual man at all. In this opinion the Church was, as I hold, literally right, however you interpret the human person of Jesus.

The modern man, therefore, need not accept the early Christology of the Church in order to recognize that, since the founding of Christianity was due to the united spirit of the early Christian community, this founding was not wholly, or mainly, due to any individual man whatever.

Meanwhile, since the human founder Jesus gave the stimulus, the signal,—or, to use the now current Bergsonian language, set in motion the vital impetus, without which the Christian community, as this potent and creative human and spiritual union, would never have come into existence,—we can indeed also say that the man Jesus was, in this sense, the founder of Christianity. But we cannot say that, speaking of Jesus as an individual man, we know that he explicitly intended to found the Christian Church. For he simply did not make explicit what he taught about the Kingdom of Heaven as a divine community. And the foundation of the Church, as a community, depends, humanly speaking, upon psychological motives — upon motives belonging not merely to individual but also to social psychology — upon motives which we cannot fathom by means of any soundings that our historical materials or our knowledge of social psychology permit us to make. We shall presumably never know the true sources of the Easter visions until we have learned the whole truth about that second, that higher, level of human existence upon whose reality I have insisted. *The psychology of the origins of Christian experience is thus social, and is not an individual psychology.*

These considerations with regard to Christian origins teach us that, deep as the historical mystery of the Christian origins remains, and will presumably for countless ages remain, neither the modern man of to-day, nor the men of the future, can be limited to the simple choice which the apologists emphasize.

X

But, as you will say, What bearing have such historical comments upon the future prospects of the Christian faith?

I answer: These considerations tend to show us: first, that the Christian ideas do not demand for their interpretation and appreciation any one theory regarding the natural or supernatural origin of this religion; and secondly, that, in consequence, these ideas run no risk of being neglected or forgotten in consequence of the inevitable modern transformations of our ideas regarding nature and the supernatural.

Without sinking to the level of a mere moralism, Christianity presents to us a view of life which indeed arouses profound metaphysical inquiries; but which yet appeals to the most concrete and vital and present moral and religious interests. And without staking its existence upon the truth of any legends, Christianity, when fairly interpreted, presents to us, in the symbolism of its Christological myths, a doctrine which is capable of the most manifold religious and metaphysical interpretations, but which also expresses the perfectly human and the verifiable experiences that the loyal life everywhere illustrates.

We have seen that the social motives to which Christianity appeals are rooted in the very depths of our nature. They are the motives which make us naturally dependent upon life in communities, and morally lost and helpless without loyalty. These motives will not pass away. Christianity was that one among the religions which first invented an effective way of making the ideal of loyalty to the universal community not only impressive, but so transforming that for centuries the European world was under the sway of the institutions which gave expression to this ideal.

These institutions are now threatened; and the historical outcome of the vast conflicts upon which they are now entering cannot be foreseen. Moreover, in order to give to its doctrine of life not only a social expression, but an internal consistency and intensity of religious meaning, Christianity, in its early days, recorded its legends and framed its creeds. Many of the resulting groups of ideas already seem strangers in our modern world; and they will probably seem to future generations, — as time goes on, — less and less literally acceptable. But now that we have seen something of what momentous and literally true, and permanently needed, spiritual discoveries concerning human life and its salvation the symbolism of these legends and of these creeds originally expressed, we are able to judge the Christian doctrine of life upon its own immortal merits, and to separate this judgment from any one theory, either about metaphysical or about historical truth.

Christianity will always arouse new critical and philosophical inquiries; its creeds will probably change unceasingly; its present institutions may in time wholly pass away. But in the new human life of the future ages, love and loyalty will not lose, but grow in human value, so long as man remains alive.

And the calm stern conscience wherewith the Christian faith has always condemned both our natural chaos of passion and our graver disloyalties, — this conscience will be increasingly needed; needed, not because men fear, but because men grow more self-possessed and clear in vision. The more reasonable, the more critical, the more far-seeing, and the more humane men become, the more will the ideas of the moral burden of the individual and of the irrevocable guilt of disloyalty appeal, not to the morbid moods, but to the resolute will and the clear self-consciousness of the enlightened man of the future.

Furthermore, as the spirit of science extends its influence, loyalty to the common insight and to the growth of knowledge will become prominent in the consciousness of the civilized man. For the scientific spirit is indeed one of the noblest and purest forms of loyalty.

The Christian virtues, then, will flourish in the civilization of the future, if indeed that civilization itself flourishes. For the more complex its constitution, and the swifter and vaster its social changes, the more will that civilization need love, and loyalty, and the grace of spiritual unity, and the will and the conscience which the Christian ideas have defined, and counselled, and that atoning conflict with evil wherein the noblest expression of the spirit must always be found.

The Christian virtues will survive if humanity triumphs in its contest with its own deepest needs and in its struggle after its own highest goods. But if the Christian virtues survive, they will find their religious expression. And this expression will be attended with the knowledge that, in its historical origins, the religion of the future will be continuous with and dependent upon the earliest Christianity; so that the whole growth and vitality of the religion of the future will depend upon its harmony with the Christian spirit. Whatever becomes of the present creeds and the present institutions, the man of the future, looking out over the wide vista of the ages, will know how near he is, despite all time and change, to the spirit of Christianity.

So much, and only so much, our survey of the Christian doctrine of life permits us to assert concerning the relation of the Christian spirit to the modern mind, without essaying the grave tasks of a philosophical theory of the real world. Herewith the first part of our task is done. The second part calls for another method.

Part II

The Real World
and the
Christian Ideas

IX

The Community
and the
Time-Process

The present situation of the Philosophy of Religion is dominated by motives and tendencies which are at once inspiring and confusing. It is the task of a student of this branch of philosophy to do whatever he can towards clarifying our outlook. Some of our recent leaders of opinion have turned our attention to new aspects of human experience, and have enriched philosophy with a wealth of fascinating intuitions. These contributions to the philosophy of our time have obvious bearings upon the interests of religion. If religion depended solely upon intuition and upon novelty, our age would already have proved its right to be regarded as a period of great advances in religious insight.

In fact, however, religion is concerned, not merely with our experience, but also with our will. The true lover of religion needs a conscience, as well as a joy in living—a coherent plan of action as well as a vital impulse. Now, in the present phase of the philosophy of religion, the religious aspect of the conscience is, as I believe, too seldom made a central object of inquiry. The interests of a coherent plan of life are too much neglected. I believe that both our ethical and our distinctly religious concerns tend to suffer in consequence of these tendencies of recent thought to which I thus allude. I believe that much can be done to profit by the novelties and by the intuitions of our day, without losing ourselves in the wilderness of caprices into which recent discussion has invited us to make the future home of our philosophy.

I

Because I view the problems of the philosophy of religion in this general way, I have undertaken, in the foregoing lectures, a study of the problem of Christianity which has been intended to accomplish three distinct, but closely connected tasks: —

First, in a fashion that has shown, as I hope, some genuine sympathy with the tendencies now prevalent, both in the whole field of philosophy, and, in particular, in the study of religion, I have tried to interpret some of the more obviously human and practical aspects of the religious beliefs of our fathers. In other words, I have approached the problem of Christianity from the side, not of metaphysics and of traditional dogmas, but of religious life and of human experience.

Secondly, even in using this mode of approach, I have laid stress upon the fact that Christianity — viewed as a doctrine of life — is not merely a religion of experience and of sentiment, but also a religion whose main stress is laid upon the unity and the coherence of the common experience of the faithful, and upon the judgment which a calm and farseeing conscience passes upon the values of life. The freedom of spirit to which Christianity, in the course of its centuries of teaching, has trained the civilizations which it has influenced, has been the freedom which loves both a wide outlook and a well-knit plan of action. In brief, I have insisted that Christianity, whatever its metaphysical basis may be, and however rich may be the wealth of intuitions which it has opened to its followers, has all the seriousness of purpose, and all the strenuousness of will, which make it indeed a religion of loyalty.

Thirdly, I have, from the outset, said that our view of the mission and the truth of the Christian doctrine of life would not be complete without a study of the metaphysical basis of the Christian ideas.

In the last two lectures we have considered how the modern mind stands related to the human interests which the Christian doctrine of life expresses. Our fathers, however, held Christianity to be, not merely a plan for the salvation of man, but a revelation concerning the origin and fate of the whole cosmos. From this point onwards, in our study, we must face anew the problem which the old faith regarded as solved. We, too, must take account of the universe. We must consider what is the consistent position for the modern mind to accept when the inquiry arises: Has the Christian doctrine of life a more than human meaning and foundation? Does this doctrine express a truth, not only about man, but about the whole world, and about God?

II

The modern man has long since learned not to confine himself to a geocentric view of the universe, nor to an anthropocentric view of the affairs of this planet of ours. For minds trained as ours now are, it has become inevitable to imagine how human concerns would seem to us if we heard of them from afar, as dwellers in other solar or stellar systems might be supposed to hear of them. We have been taught to remember that at some time, — a time not nearly so distant from us in the future as the Miocene division of the Tertiary period is now distant from us in the past, man will probably be as extinct as is now the sabre-toothed tiger. But such considerations as these arouse further queries about Christian doctrine — queries which no modern mind can wholly ignore. Let all be admitted which we urged at the last time regarding the close relation of the Christian doctrine of life to the deepest needs of humanity. Then this will indeed show that Christianity, viewed simply *as* such a doctrine of life, need not fear social changes, so long as civilized man endures; and will remain as a spiritual guide of future generations, however vast the revolutions to which they may be subject, so long as the future generations view life largely and seriously.

But such considerations will not meet all the legitimate questions of a philosophy of religion. For religion, although it need not depend for its appeal to the human heart upon solving the problems of the cosmos, inevitably leads to a constantly renewed interest in those problems. Let it be granted that the salvation of mankind indeed requires some form of religion whose essential ideas are in harmony with the Christian ideas which we have examined; still, that fact will not quite supply an answer to our natural inquiries, if indeed mankind is destined simply to fail, — as the sabre-toothed tiger failed. And if mankind, in the vast cosmos, is as much alone amongst the beings that people the universe as the earth seems to be alone amongst the countless worlds, — what shall it profit us if we seem to be saving our own souls for a time, but actually remain, after all, what we were before, — utterly insignificant incidents in a world-process that neither needs men nor heeds them?

Traditional theology could long ignore such considerations, because it could centre all the universe about the earth and man. But the modern man must think of his kind as thus really related to an immeasurably vast cosmic process, at whose centre our planet does not stand, and in whose ages our brief human lives play a part as transient, relatively speaking, as is, for our own eyes, the flickering of the northern lights.

The task to which we must now devote ourselves is thus determined, for our age, and for the modern man, by the enlarged perspective in which we have to view human history. Our doctrine of life is not so readily to be connected with our picture of the universe as would be the case if we still lived under the heavenly spheres of an ancient cosmology. Yet we shall find that the difference which is here in question will not prove to be so great in its meaning as the quantitative differences between the ancient and modern world seem, at first, to imply. Our fathers also faced the problem of the infinity of the universe, much as they often tried to ignore or to minimize that problem. And, in the spiritual world, mere quantity, however vast, is not the hardest of obstacles to overcome.

III

In any case, however, the part of our undertaking upon which we thus enter, corresponds to those chapters of traditional theology which dealt with the esistence and nature of God, and with God's relation to the world, and with the origin and destiny of the human individual. Our own attempt to study these well-worn problems begins with one, and perhaps with only one, advantage over the best-known traditional modes of expounding a philosophical theology. We, namely, set out under the guidance of our foregoing study of the Christian ideas. Central among these ideas is that of the Universal Community. For us, then, theology, if we are to define any theology at all, must depend upon the metaphysical interpretation and foundation of the community. If that ideal of one beloved and united community of all mankind whose religious value we have defended, has a basis, not merely in the transient interests of us mortals, but also in whatever is largest and most lasting in the universe, then indeed the doctrine of the community will prove to be a doctrine about the being and nature and manifestation of God; and our estimate of the relation of the modern mind to the spirit of a Christian creed will be altered and completed accordingly. This one doctrine will indeed not suffice to make us literal followers of tradition; but it will bring us into a sympathy with some of the most essential features of the Christian view of the divine being.

IV

What interests are at stake when this aspect of the problems of theology is emphasized, I can best remind you by recalling the fact which we mentioned in comparing Buddhism and Christianity in a former lecture. The most characteristic feature by which the Christian doctrine of life stands contrasted with its greatest religious rival, we found to be the one summarized in the words of the creed: "I believe in the Holy Ghost, the Holy Catholic Church, the communion of saints." In our former lecture, when we commented upon these words we laid no stress upon the special traditions of the historical Church. We considered only the universally human significance of the ideal which has always constituted the vital principle of the historical Church, — far away as the adequate embodiment of that ideal in any visible human institution still seems to be. At the present stage of our inquiry, — since we are, of necessity, entering for the time the world of metaphysical abstractions, we have also to abstract from still another aspect of the meaning which the words of the creed intend to convey. For neither the historical Church, nor the distinctively human ideal which it expresses, shall be, in these metaphysical lectures, at the centre of our attention. We are here to ask: For what truth, if any, regarding the whole nature of things, does that article of the creed stand? Our answer must be found, if at all, in some metaphysical theory of the community and of its relation, if such relation it possesses, to the divine being. In other words, the central problem in our present attempt at a theology must be that problem which traditional Christian theology has so strangely neglected, — the problem of what the religious consciousness has called the Holy Spirit.

V

The philosophy of religion, in dealing with the problem of Christianity, has often elaborately expounded and criticised the arguments for the existence of God. Such philosophical arguments have in general to do with the concept of the Deity viewed quite apart from the Christian doctrine of the Trinity. In other cases, and for obvious historical reasons, the philosophy of religion has had much to say about the doctrine of the Logos. This doctrine, when treated as a part of Christian theology, is usually taken to be the theory of the second person of the Trinity. But the traditional doctrine of the Holy Spirit, neglected by the early theologians of the Church, even when the creeds were still in the formative period of their existence, has remained until this day in the background of inquiry, both for the theologians and for the philosophers. A favorite target for hostile, although often inarticulate, criticism on the part of the opponents of tradition, and a frequent object of reverential, but confessedly problematic and often very vague, exposition on the part of the defenders of the faith, — the article of the creed regarding the Holy Spirit is, I believe, the one matter about which most who discuss the problem of Christianity have least to say in the way of definite theory.

Yet, if I am right, — this is, in many respects, the really distinctive and therefore the capital article of the Christian creed, so far as that creed suggests a theory of the divine nature. This article, then, should be understood, if the spirit of Christianity, in its most human and vital of features, is to be understood at all. And this article should be philosophically expounded and defended, if any distinctively Christian article of the creed is to find a foundation in a rationally defensible metaphysical theory of the universe.

Apart from the doctrine of the ideal community, and of the divine Spirit as constituting the unity and the life of this community, Theism can be, as for many centuries it has been, defined and defended. But such theism, which "knows not so much as whether there is any Holy Ghost," is not distinctively Christian in its meaning. And the Logos-doctrine, except when viewed in unity with the doctrine of the Spirit, is indeed what some of its recent hostile critics (such as Harnack) have taken it to be, — a thesis of Greek philosophy, and not a characteristically Christian opinion. The Logos-doctrine of the Fourth Gospel, as we earlier saw, is indeed no mere following of Greek metaphysics; for the Fourth Gospel identifies the Logos with the spirit of the community. Here, then, in this doctrine of the spirit, lies the really central idea of any distinctively Christian metaphysic.

To approach the problems of the philosophy of religion from the side of the metaphysical basis of the idea of the community is therefore, I believe, to undertake a task as momentous as it is neglected.

VI

Moreover, as we shall soon find, this mode of beginning the metaphysical part of our task promises to relieve us, for the time, from the need of using some terms and of repeating some discussions, which recent controversy may well have made wearisome to many of us. The altogether too abstractly stated contrast between Monism and Pluralism — a contrast which fills so large a place in the polemical metaphysical writings of the day, does not force itself to the front, in our minds and in our words, when we set out to inquire into the real basis of the idea of the community. For a community immediately presents itself to our minds both as one and as many; and unless it is both one and many, it is no community at all. This fact does not, by itself, solve the problem of the One and the Many. But it serves to remind us how untrue to life is the way in which that problem is frequently stated.

In fact, as I believe, the idea of the community, suggested to us by the problems of human social life, but easily capable of a generalization which possesses universal importance, gives us one of our very best indications of the way in which the problem of the One and the Many is to be solved, and of the level of mental life upon which the solution is actually accomplished.

So much may serve as a general indication of the nature of our undertaking. Let me next attempt to define the problem of the community more precisely.

VII

Motives which are as familiar as they are hard to analyze have convinced us all, before we begin to philosophize, that our human world contains a variety of individually distinct minds or selves, and that some, for us decisively authoritative, principle of individuation, keeps these selves apart, and forbids us to regard their various lives merely as incidents, or as undivided phases of a common life. This conviction — the stubborn pluralism of our present and highly cultivated social consciousness — tends indeed, under criticism, to be subject to various doubts and modifications, — the more so as, in case we are once challenged to explain who we are, none of us find it easy to define the precise boundaries of the individual self, or to tell wherein it differs from the rest of the world, and, in particular, from the selves of other men.

But to all such doubts our social common sense replies by insisting upon three groups of facts. These facts combine to show that the individual human selves are sundered from one another by gaps which, as it would seem, are in some sense impassable.

First, in this connection, our common sense insists upon the empirical sundering of the feelings, — that is, of the immediate experiences of various human individuals. One man does not feel, and, speaking in terms of direct experience, cannot feel, the physical pains of another man. Sympathy may try its best to bridge the gulf thus established by nature. Love may counsel me to view the pangs of my fellow *as if they were* my own. But, as a fact, my sensory nerves do not end in my fellow's skin, but in mine. And the physical sundering of the organisms corresponds to a persistent sundering of our streams of immediate feeling. Even the most immediate and impressive forms of sympathy with the physical pangs of another human being only serve the more to illustrate how our various conscious lives are thus kept apart by gulfs which we cannot cross. When a pitiful man shrinks, or feels faint, or is otherwise overcome with emotion, at what is called "the sight" of another's suffering, — how unlike are the sufferings of the shrinking or terrified or overwhelmed spectator, and the pangs of the one with whom he is said to sympathize. As a fact, the sympathizer does not feel the sufferer's pain. What he feels is his own emotional reverberation at the sight of its symptoms. That is, in general, something very different, both in quality and in intensity, from what the injured man feels.

We appear, then, to be individuated by the diversity and the separateness of our streams of immediate feeling. My toothache cannot directly become an item in my neighbor's mind. Facts of this sort form the first group of evidences upon which common sense depends for its pluralistic view of the world of human selves.

The facts of the second group are closely allied to the former, but lie upon another level of individual life, — namely, upon the level of our more organized ideas.

"One man," so says our social common sense, "can only indirectly

discover the intentions, the thoughts, the ideas, of another man."
Direct telepathy, if it ever occurs at all, is a rare and, in most of our
practical relations, a wholly negligible fact. By nature, every man's
plans, intents, opinions, and range of personal experience are secrets,
except in so far as his physical organism indirectly reveals them. His
fellows can learn these secrets only through his expressive movements. Control your expression, keep silence, avoid the unguarded
look and the telltale gesture; and then nobody can discover what is
in your mind. No man can directly read the hearts of his fellows.
This seems, for our common sense, to be one of the deepest-seated
laws of our social experience. It is often expressed as if it were not
merely an empirical law, but a logical necessity. How could I possibly possess or share or become conscious of the thoughts and purposes of another mind, unless I were myself identical with that
mind? So says our ordinary common sense. The very supposition
that I could be conscious of a thought or of an intent which was all
the while actually present to the consciousness of another individual
man, is often regarded as a supposition not only contrary to fact,
but also contrary to reason. Such a supposition, it is often said, would
involve a direct self-contradiction.

Otherwise expressed, the facts of this second group, and the principles which they exemplify, are summed up by asserting, as our
social common sense actually asserts: We are individuated by the
law that our trains of conscious thought and purpose are mutually
inaccessible through any mode of direct intuition. Each of us lives
within the charmed circle of his own conscious will and meaning, —
each of us is more or less clearly the object of his own inspection,
but is hopelessly beyond the direct observation of his fellows.

Of separate streams of feeling, — of mutually inaccessible and essentially secret trains of ideas, — we men are thus constituted. By
such forms and by such structure of mental life, by such divisions
which no human power can bring into one unity of insight, individual human minds are forced to exist together upon terms which
make them, in so far, appear to resemble Leibnizian monads. Their
only windows appear to be those which their physical organisms
supply.

The third group of facts here in question is the group upon which
our cultivated social common sense most insists whenever ethical
problems are in question; and therefore it is precisely this third
group of facts which has most interest in its bearings upon the idea
of the community.

"We are all members one of another." So says the doctrine of the community. "On the contrary," so our social common sense insists: "We are beings, each of whom has a soul of his own, a destiny of his own, rights of his own, worth of his own, ideals of his own, and an individual life in which this soul, this destiny, these rights, these ideals, get their expression. No other man can do my deed for me. When I choose, my choice coalesces with the voluntary decision of no other individual." Such, I say, is the characteristic assertion to which this third group of facts leads our ordinary social pluralism.

In brief: We thus seem to be individuated by our deeds. The will whereby I choose my own deed, is not my neighbor's will. My act is my own. Another man can perform an act which repeats the type of my act, or which helps or hinders my act. But if the question arises concerning any one act: Who hath done this? — such a question admits of only one true answer. Deeds and their doers stand in one-one correspondence. Such is the opinion of our cultivated modern eithical common sense.

Upon this individuation of the selves by their deeds appear to rest all the other just mentioned ethical aspects of our modern social pluralism. As we mentioned in an earlier lecture, primitive man is not an individualist. The clear consciousness of individual rights, dignity, worth, and responsibility seems to be a product of that moral cultivation of which we have now frequently spoken. According to the primitive law of blood revenge, it is the community and not the individual that suffers for a deed. The consciousness that my deed is peculiarly my own also forms the basis for that cultivated idea of sin of which we found Paul making use. At all events, this ethical aspect of individual self-consciousness is frequently used by common sense as one of the most impressive grounds for doubting any philosophy which appears to make light of the distinctness of the social individuals.

VIII

Nevertheless, all these varieties of individual experience, these chasms which at any one present moment seem to sunder mind and mind, and these ethical considerations which have taught us to think of one man as morally independent of another, do not tell us the whole truth about the actual constitution of the social realm. There are facts that seem to show that these many are also one. These, then, are facts which force upon us the problem of the community.

As we have now repeatedly seen, social coöperation unquestionably brings into existence languages, customs, religions. These, as Wundt declares, are indeed psychological creations. Yet a language, a custom, or a religion is not a collection of discrete psychological phenomena, each of which corresponds to some separate individual mind to which that one mental fact belongs, or is due. Thus, the English language is a mental product, — and a product possessing intelligent unity. Its creator must be regarded as also, in some sense, a single intelligence. But the creator of the English language was no mere collection of Englishmen, each of whom added his word or phrase or accent, or other linguistic fact. The creator of English speech is the English people. Hence the English people is itself some sort of mental unit with a mind of its own.

The countless phenomena which Wundt in his Völkerpsychologie brings to our attention, constitute a philosophical problem which ought to be only the more carefully studied in case one regards the facts upon which our ordinary social pluralism rests as both unquestionable and momentous.

For if indeed men are sundered in their individual lives by the chasms which our social common sense seems to make so obvious; if they live in mutually inaccessible realms of conscious solitude; how comes it to pass that, nevertheless, in their social life, large and small bodies of men can come to act as if one common intelligence and one common will were using the individuals as its almost helpless instruments? Here is indeed a great problem. The theories of Wundt's type have the advantage of emphasizing and defining that problem.

Our ordinary social pluralism leads us to conceive the individual streams of consciousness as if they were unable to share even a single pang of pain. No one of them, we have said, can directly read the secret of a single idea that floats in another stream. Each conscious river of individual life is close shut between its own banks, like the Oregon of Bryant's youthful poem that rolls, "and hears no sound but his own waves."

But in our actual social life, — in the market-place, or at the political gathering, or when mobs rage and imagine a vain thing, in the streets of a modern city, the close shut-in streams of consciousness now appear as if they had lost their banks altogether. They seem to flow together like rivers that are lost in the ocean, and to surge into tumultuous unity, as if they were universal tides.

Or, again, our ordinary social pluralism makes us view the individual selves as if they were Leibnizian monads that had no windows. The social phenomena of the lives of communities, on the contrary, make these monads appear as if they had no walls, or as if they became mere drops that coalesce. Our ethical pluralism makes us proudly declare, each for himself, "My deed is my own." But our collective life often seems to advise us to say, not, "I act thus;" but, "Thus the community acts in and through me." Or again, our cultivated independence declares, "I think thus and thus." But, when the ethnologist Bastian uses the formula, "Ich denke nicht; sondern es denkt in mir," the social facts, especially of primitive human thought, go far to give this formula a meaning. In Europe the discovery of individual thinking began in some sense with the early Greek philosophers. Before them, tribes and communities did the thinking.

Now such considerations are emphasized by the theories of the type which Wundt favors.

Such theories, without being able to tell us all that we should like to know regarding what constitutes the unity of a community, have in common the tendency to insist that in many cases a community behaves as an unit, and therefore must be an unit, however its inner coherence may be constituted. If, however, we admit the facts which Wundt emphasizes, it is natural to seek for some further and perhaps more concrete way of conceiving what the mental life of a community may be, and how its unity is constituted. Wundt himself has hardly done all, I think, that we could desire in this direction, and it is natural to supplement his views by others.

Such a further approach towards an insight into the problem of the community is suggested by William James's discussion of what, in his lectures here at Oxford on "The Pluralistic Universe," he called the "compounding of consciousness."

The main interests which guided James in the lectures to which I refer were indeed not the interests which I have emphasized in the early part of this course. James was not dealing with the problems which Christianity presents; nor was he interested in the idea of the community, in the form in which I am approaching that problem. But he was concerned with general religious and metaphysical issues; and questions relating to pluralism were explicitly in the foreground of his inquiry. He was also led to take account of manifold motives which tend to show that our mental world does not merely consist of sundered fields or streams of consciousness with barriers that part them.

Those who hear me will well remember how James emphasized, in the course of his argument, the difficulties which, as he explained, had so long held him back from any form of philosophy which should involve believing that a "compounding of consciousness" occurs, or is real. How should any one conscious mind be inclusive of another, or such that it was compounded with that other? This question, as James declared, had long seemed to him incapable of any answer in terms which should involve admitting the possibility of such "co-consciousness," if indeed our philosophy were to be permitted to remain rational at all. But James actually reached at length a point in his own reflections where, as he said, this compounding of consciousness, this Bergsonian interpenetration of the various selves, came to appear to him in certain cases an empirically verifiable fact, —or, at all events, an irresistible hypothesis. When this point was reached, James felt that, for him, a philosophical crisis had come.

James faced and passed this crisis. He did so upon the basis of his own well-known anti-intellectualism. The mental world, he said, must not be interpreted in rational terms. If the compounding of consciousness occurs, it is irrational, although real. James was rejoiced, however, to feel that, in this matter, he stood in alliance with Bergson. And so, henceforth, for James, the many selves interpenetrated, or, at all events, might do so. It was merely the sterile intellect (so he now affirmed) which was responsible for the conceptual abstractions that had seemed to sunder various minds, not only empirically, but absolutely, and to make the compounding of consciousness impossible. It still remained for James true that we are indeed many. But this assertion no longer implied: We are sundered from one another by divisions that are absolutely impassable. We may be many selves; and yet, from these many selves, a larger self may be compounded,—a self such as one of Fechner's planetary consciousnesses was, or such as some still vaster cosmical form of mental life may be. This larger self may from above, as it were, bridge what is for us an impassable chasm. Interpenetration, which for us seems impossible, may come to pass for some higher sort of intuition.

With this treatment of the problem of the one and the many in the form in which social psychology presents it to our attention, James's account of the great cosmological questions and of their religious bearings came to an end,—just at the point where we all most needed to know what his next step in philosophy would be.

In substance, this outcome of a long series of efforts to deal with the problems of the one and the many in the world of the mental beings was based, in the case of James, partly upon empirical phenomena, of the type reported in his "Varieties of Religious Experience," and partly upon hypothetical extensions of these empirical phenomena. These hypothetical extensions themselves were again suggested to him, partly by Fechner's speculations on the cosmical enlargements of consciousness; partly by the general voluntaristic tendencies which so long characterized James's religious thought; and partly by Bergson's use of the new category of "interpenetration" as the one especially suited to aid us in the perception of the mental world. The results brought James, at the very close of his career, into new relations with the idealistic tradition in philosophy, —a relation which I ought not here to attempt to characterize at all extensively.

But in any case, the sort of compounding of consciousness which James favored differed in many respects from what I have in mind when I speak of the idea of the community. When the minds of James's world began to interpenetrate in earnest, as they did in this last phase of his religious speculation, they behaved much like drops of mercury that, falling, may form a pool, until, moved by one impulse or another, they break away from their union again, and flow and glitter until the next blending occur. Paul's conception of the spirit in the Church never appealed, I think, to James's mind.

But, in any case, James's final opinions, although only indirectly bearing upon our own main problem, tended to show, better than would otherwise have been possible, where the true problem lies.

IX

We may be aided in making a more decisive advance towards understanding what a community is by emphasizing at this point a motive which we have not before mentioned, and which no doubt plays a great part in the psychology of the social consciousness.

Any notable case wherein we find a social organization which we can call, in the psychological sense, either a highly developed community or the creation or product of such a community, is a case where some process of the nature of a history—that is, of coherent social evolution—has gone on, and has gone on for a long time, and is more or less remembered by the community in question. If, ignoring history, you merely take a cross-section of the social order at any one moment; and if you thus deal with social groups that have little or no history, and confine your attention to social processes which occur during a short period of time,—for example, during an hour, or a day, or a year,—what then is likely to come to your notice takes either the predominantly pluralistic form of the various relatively independent doings of detached individuals, or else the social form of the confused activities of a crowd. A crowd, whether it be a dangerous mob, or an amiably joyous gathering at a picnic, is not a community. It has a mind, but no institutions, no organization, no coherent unity, no history, no traditions. It may be an unit, but is then of the type which suggests James's mere blending of various consciousnesses,—a sort of mystical loss of personality on the part of its members. On the other hand, a group of independent buyers at market, or of the passers-by in a city street, is not a community. And it also does not suggest to the onlooker any blending of many selves in one. Each purchaser seeks his own affairs. There may be gossip, but gossip is not a function which establishes the life of a community. For gossip has a short memory. But a true community is essentially a product of a time-process. A community has a past and will have a future. Its more or less conscious history, real or ideal, is a part of its very essence. A community requires for its existence a history and is greatly aided in its consciousness by a·memory.

If you object that a Pauline church, such as I have so often used as an ideal instance of a community, was an institution that had been but very recently founded when the apostle wrote his epistles, then I reply at once that a Pauline church was instructed by the apostle to regard its life as a phase in the historical process of the salvation of mankind. This process, as conceived by Paul and his churches, had gone on from Adam unto Moses, from Moses unto Christ; and the very life of the community was bound up with its philosophy of history. That the memory of this community was in part legendary is beside the point. Its memory was essential to its life, and was busy with the fate of all mankind and with the course of all time.

The psychological unity of many selves in one community is bound up, then, with the consciousness of some lengthy social process which has occurred, or is at least supposed to have occurred. And the wealthier the memory of a community is, and the vaster the historical processes which it regards as belonging to its life, the richer —other things being equal—is its consciousness that it *is* a community, that its members are somehow made one in and through and with its own life.

The Japanese are fond of telling us that their imperial family, and their national life, are coeval with heaven and earth. The boast is cheerfully extravagant; but its relation to a highly developed form of the consciousness of a community is obvious. Here, then, is a consideration belonging to social psychology, but highly important for our understanding of the sense in which a community is or can be possessed of one mental life.

X

If we ask for the reason why such a real or fancied history, possessing in general a considerable length and importance, is psychologically needed in case a group consisting of many individual human beings is to regard itself as an united community, our attention is at once called to a consideration which I regard as indeed decisive for the whole theory of the reality of the community. Obvious as it is, however, this consideration needs to be explicitly mentioned, because the complexity of the facts often makes us neglect them.

The rule that time is needed for the formation of a conscious community is a rule which finds its extremely familiar analogy within the life of every individual human self. Each one of us knows that he just now, at this instant, cannot find more than a mere fragment of himself present. The self comes down to us from its own past. It needs and is a history. Each of us can see that his own idea of himself as this person is inseparably bound up with his view of his own former life, of the plans that he formed, of the fortunes that fashioned him, and of the accomplishments which in turn he has fashioned for himself. A self is, by its very essence, a being with a past. One must look lengthwise backwards in the stream of time in order to see the self, or its shadow, now moving with the stream, now eddying in the currents from bank to bank of its channel, and now strenuously straining onwards in the pursuit of its own chosen good.

At this present moment I am indeed here, as this creature of the moment,—sundered from the other selves. But nevertheless, if considered simply in this passing moment of my life, I am hardly a self at all. I am just a flash of consciousness,—the mere gesticulation of a self,—not a coherent personality. Yet memory links me with my own past,—and not, in the same way, with the past of anyone else. This joining of the present to the past reveals a more or less steady tendency,—a sense about the whole process of my remembered life. And this tendency and sense of my individual life agree, on the whole, with the sense and the tendencies that belong to the entire flow of the time-stream, so far as it has sense at all. My individual life, my own more or less well-sundered stream of tendency, not only is shut off at each present moment by various barriers from the lives of other selves,—but also constitutes an intelligible sequence in itself, so that, as I look back, I can say: "What I yesterday intended to pursue, that I am to-day still pursuing." "My present carries farther the plan of my past." Thus, then, I am one more or less coherent plan expressed in a life. "The child is father to the man." My days are "bound each to each by mutual piety."

Since I am this self, not only by reason of what now sunders me from the inner lives of other selves, but by reason of what links me, in significant fashion, to the remembered experiences, deeds, plans, and interests of my former conscious life, I need a somewhat extended and remembered past to furnish the opportunity for my self to find, when it looks back, a long process that possesses sense and coherence. In brief, my idea of myself is an interpretation of my past,—linked also with an interpretation of my hopes and intentions as to my future.

Precisely as I thus define myself with reference to my own past, so my fellows also interpret the sense, the value, the qualifications, and the possessions of my present self by virtue of what are sometimes called my antecedents. In the eyes of his fellow-men, the child is less of a self than is the mature man; and he is so not merely because the child just now possesses a less wealthy and efficient conscious life than a mature man possesses, but because the antecedents of his present self are fewer than are the antecedents of the present self of the mature man. The child has little past. He has accomplished little. The mature man bears the credit and the burden of his long life of deeds. His former works qualify his present deeds. He not only possesses, but in great part is, for his fellow-men, a record.

These facts about our individual self-consciousness are indeed well known. But they remind us that our idea of the individual self is no mere present datum, or collection of data, but is based upon an interpretation of the sense, of the tendency, of the coherence, and of the value of a life to which belongs the memory of its own past. And therefore these same facts will help us to see how the idea of the community is also an idea which is impressed upon us whenever we make a sufficiently successful and fruitful effort to interpret the sense, the coherent interest, and the value of the relations in which a great number of different selves stand to the past.

XI

Can many different selves, all belonging to the present time, possess identically the same past as their own personally interesting past life? This question, if asked about the recent past, cannot be answered in the affirmative, unless one proposes either to ignore or in some way to set aside the motives which, in our present consciousness, emphasize, as we have seen, the pluralism of the social selves. Quite different, however, becomes the possible answer to this question if, without in the least ignoring our present varieties and sunderings, one asks the question concerning some past time that belongs to previous generations of men. For then each of two or more men may regard the same fact of past life as, in the same sense, a part of his own personal life. Two men of the present time may, for instance, have any number of ancestors in common. To say this is not to ignore the pluralistic view of the selves, but only to make mention of familiar facts of descent. But now if these men take great interest in their ancestors, and have a genuine or legendary tradition concerning the ancestors, each of the two men of the present time may regard the lives, the deeds, the glory, and perhaps the spiritual powers or the immortal lives of certain ancestors, now dwelling in the spirit-world, as a part of his own self. Thus, when the individual Maori, in New Zealand, in case he still follows the old ways, speaks of the legendary canoes in which the ancestors of old came over from the home land called Hawaiki to New Zealand, he says, choosing the name of the canoe according to his own tribe and tradition, "*I* came over in the canoe Tai-Nui." Now any two members of a tribe whose legendary ancestors came over in Tai-Nui, possess, from their own point of view, identically the same past, in just this respect. Each of the two men in question has the same reason, good or bad, for extending himself into the past, and for saying, "I came over in that canoe." Now the belief in this identity of the past self of the ancestor of the canoe, belonging to each of the two New Zealanders, does not in the least depend upon ignoring, or upon minimizing, the present difference between these two selves. The present consciousnesses do not in the least tend to interpenetrate. Neither of the two New Zealanders in question need suppose that there is now any compounding of consciousness. Each may keep aloof from the other. They may be enemies. But each has a reason, and an obvious reason, for extending himself into the ancestral past.

My individual self extends backwards, and is identified with my remembered self of yesterday, or of former years. This is an interpretation of my life which in general turns upon the coherence of deeds, plans, interests, hopes, and spiritual possessions in terms of which I learn to define myself. Now my remembered past is in general easily to be distinguished from the past of any other self. But if I am so interested in the life or in the deeds of former generations that I thus extend, as the Maori extends, my own self into the ancestral past, the self thus extended finds that the same identical canoe or ancestor is part of my own life, and also part of the ideally extended life of some fellow-tribesman who is now so different a being, and so sharply sundered from my present self.

Now, in such a case, how shall I best describe the unity that, according to this interpretation of our common past, links my fellow-tribesmen and myself? A New Zealander says, "We are of the same canoe." And a more general expression of such relations would be to say, in all similar cases, "We are of the same community."

In this case, then, the real or supposed identity of certain interesting features in a past which each one of two or of many men regards as belonging to his own historically extended former self, is a ground for saying that all these many, although now just as various and as sundered as they are, constitute, with reference to this common past, a community. When defined in such terms, the concept of the community loses its mystical seeming. It depends indeed upon an interpretation of the significance of facts, and does not confine itself to mere report of particulars; but it does not ignore the present varieties of experience. It depends also upon an interpretation which does not merely say, "These events happened," but adds, "These events belong to the life of this self or of this other self." Such an interpretation we all daily make in speaking of the past of our own familiar individual selves. The process which I am now using as an illustration, — the process whereby the New Zealander says, "I came over in that canoe," — extends the quasi-personal memory of each man into an historical past that may be indefinitely long and vast. But such an extension has motives which are not necessarily either mystical or monistic. We all share those motives, and use them, in our own way, and according to our ideals, whenever we consider the history of our country, or of mankind, or of whatever else seems to us to possess a history that is significantly linked with our personal history.

XII

Just as each one of many present selves despite the psychological or ethical barriers which now keep all of these selves sundered, may accept the same past fact or event as a part of himself, and say,"That belonged to my life," even so, each of many present selves, despite these same barriers and sunderings, may accept the same future event, which all of them hope or expect, as part of his own personal future. Thus, during a war, all of the patriots of one of the contending nations may regard the termination of the war, and the desired victory of their country, so that each one says: "I shall rejoice in the expected surrender of that stronghold of the enemy. That surrender will be my triumph."

Now when many contemporary and distinct individual selves so interpret, each his own personal life, that each says of an individual past or of a determinate future event or deed: "That belongs to my life;" "That occurred, or will occur, to me," then these many selves may be defined as hereby constituting, in a perfectly definite and objective, but also in a highly significant, sense, a community. They may be said to constitute a community *with reference* to that particular past or future event, or group of events, which each of them accepts or interprets as belonging to his own personal past or to his own individual future. A community constituted by the fact that each of its members accepts as part of his own individual life and self the same *past* events that each of his fellow-members accepts, may be called a *community of memory.* Such is any group of persons who individually either remember or commemorate the same dead, —each one finding, because of personal affection or of reverence for the dead, that those whom he commemorates form for him a part of his own past existence.

A community constituted by the fact that each of its members accepts, as part of his own individual life and self, the same expected *future* events that each of his fellows accepts, may be called a *community of expectation,* or upon occasion, a *community of hope.*

A community, whether of memory or of hope, exists relatively to the past or future facts to which its several members stand in the common relation just defined. The concept of the community depends upon the interpretation which each individual member gives to his own self, — to his own past, — and to his own future. Every one of us does, for various reasons, extend his interpretation of his own individual self so that from his own point of view, his life includes many faraway temporal happenings. The complex motives of such interpretations need not now be further examined. Enough, — these motives may vary from self to self with all the wealth of life. Yet when these interests of each self lead it to accept any part or item of the same past or the same future which another self accepts as its own, — then pluralism of the selves is perfectly consistent with their forming a community, either of memory or of hope. How rich this community is in meaning, in value, in membership, in significant organization, will depend upon the selves that enter into the community, and upon the ideals in terms of which they define themselves, their past, and their future.

With this definition in mind, we see why long histories are needed in order to define the life of great communities. We also see that, if great new undertakings enter into the lives of many men, a new community of hope, unified by the common relations of its individual members to the same future events, may be, upon occasion, very rapidly constituted, even in the midst of great revolutions.

The concept of the community, as thus analyzed, stands in the closest relation to the whole nature of the time-process, and also involves recognizing to the full both the existence and the significance of individual selves. In what sense the individual selves constitute the community we can in general see, while we are prepared to find that, for the individual selves, it may well prove to be the case that a real community of memory or of hope is necessary in order to secure their significance. Our own definition of a community can be illustrated by countless types of political, religious, and other significant communities which you will readily be able to select for yourselves. Without ignoring our ordinary social pluralism, this definition shows how and why many selves may be viewed as actually brought together in an historical community. Without presupposing any one metaphysical interpretation of experience, or of time, our definition shows where, in our experience and in our interpretation of the time-process, we are to look for a solution of the problem of the community. Without going beyond the facts of human life, of human memory, and of human interpretation of the self and of its past, our definition clears the way for a study of the constitution of the real world of the spirit.

X

*The Body
and the
Members*

Henceforth, in these lectures, I shall restrict the application of the term "community" to those social groups which conform to the definition stated at the close of our last lecture. Not every social group which behaves so that, to an observer, it seems to be a single unit, meets all the conditions of our definition. Our new use of the term "community" will therefore be more precise and restricted than was our earlier employment of the word. But our definition will clear the way for further generalizations. It will enable us to express our reasons for much that, in our study of the Christian doctrine of life, had to be stated dogmatically, and illustrated rather than intimately examined.

We have repeatedly spoken of two levels of human life, the level of the individual and the level of the community. We have now in our hands the means for giving a more precise sense to this expression, and for furnishing a further verification of what we asserted about these two levels of life. We have also repeatedly emphasized the ethical and religious significance of loyalty; but our definition will help us to throw clearer light upon the sources of this worth. And by thus sharpening the outlines of our picture of what a real community is, we shall be made ready to consider whether the concept of the community possesses a more than human significance. Let us recall our new definition to mind, and then apply it to our main problems.

I

Our definition presupposes that there exist many individual selves. Suppose these selves to vary in their present experiences and purposes as widely as you will. Imagine them to be sundered from one another by such chasms of mutual mystery and independence as, in our natural social life, often seem hopelessly to divide and secrete the inner world of each of us from the direct knowledge and estimate of his fellows. But let these selves be able to look beyond their present chaos of fleeting ideas and of warring desires, far away into the past whence they came, and into the future whither their hopes lead them. As they thus look, let each one of them ideally enlarge his own individual life, extending himself into the past and future, so as to say of some far-off event, belonging, perhaps, to other generations of men, "I view that event as a part of my own life." "That former happening or achievement so predetermined the sense and the destiny which are now mine, that I am moved to regard it as belonging to my own past." Or again: "For that coming event I wait and hope as an event of my own future."

And further, let the various ideal extensions, forwards and backwards, include at least one common event, so that each of these selves regards that event as a part of his own life.

Then, *with reference to the ideal common past and future in question, I say that these selves constitute a community.* This is henceforth to be our definition of a community. The present variety of the selves who are the members of the spiritual body so defined, is not hereby either annulled or slighted. The motives which determine each of them thus ideally to extend his own life, may vary from self to self in the most manifold fashion.

Our definition will enable us, despite all these varieties of the members, to understand in what sense any such community as we have defined exists, and is one.

Into this form, which, when thus summarily described, seems so abstract and empty, life can and does pour the rich contents and ideals which make the communities of our human world so full of dramatic variety and significance.

II

The *first* condition upon which the existence of a community, in our sense of the word, depends, is the power of an individual self to extend his life, an ideal fashion, so as to regard it as including past and future events which lie far away in time, and which he does not now personally remember. That this power exists, and that man has a self which is thus ideally extensible in time without any definable limit, we all know.

This power itself rests upon the principle that, however a man may come by his idea of himself, the self is no mere datum, but is in its essence a life which is interpreted, and which interprets itself, and which, apart from some sort of ideal interpretation, is a mere flight of ideas, or a meaningless flow of feelings, or a vision that sees nothing, or else a barren abstract conception. How deep the process of interpretation goes in determining the real nature of the self, we shall only later be able to estimate.

There is no doubt that what we usually call our personal memory does indeed give us assurances regarding our own past, so far as memory extends and is trustworthy. But our trust in our memories is itself an interpretation of their data. All of us regard as belonging, even to our recent past life, much that we cannot just now remember. And the future self shrinks and expands with our hopes and our energies. No one can merely, from without, set for us the limits of the life of the self, and say to us: "Thus far and no farther."

In my ideal extensions of the life of the self, I am indeed subject to some sort of control,—to what control we need not here attempt to formulate. I must be able to give myself some sort of reason, personal, or social, or moral, or religious, or metaphysical, for taking on or throwing off the burden, the joy, the grief, the guilt, the hope, the glory of past and of future deeds and experiences; but I must also myself personally share in this task of determining how much of the past and the future shall ideally enter into my life, and shall contribute to the value of that life.

And if I choose to say, "There is a sense in which *all* the tragedy and the attainment of an endless past and future of deeds and of fortunes enter into my own life," I say only what saints and sages of the most various creeds and experiences have found their several reasons for saying. The fact and the importance of such ideal extensions of the self must therefore be recognized. Here is the first basis for every clear idea of what constitutes a community.

The ideal extensions of the self may also include, as is well known, not only past and future events and deeds, but also physical things, whether now existent or not, and many other sorts of objects which are neither events nor deeds. The knight or the samurai regarded his sword as a part of himself. One's treasures and one's home, one's tools, and the things that one's hands have made, frequently come to be interpreted as part of the self. And any object in heaven or earth may be thus ideally appropriated by a given self. The ideal self of the Stoic or of the Mystic may, in various fashions, identify its will, or its very essence, with the whole universe. The Hindoo seer seeks to realize the words: "I am Brahm;" "That art thou."

In case such ideal extensions of the self are consciously bound up with deeds, or with other events, such as belong to the past or future life which the self regards as its own, our definition of the community warrants us in saying that many selves form one community when all are ideally extended so as to include the same object. But unless the ideal extensions of the self thus consciously involve past and future deeds and events that have to do with the objects in question, we shall not use these extensions to help us to define communities.

For our purposes, the community is a being that attempts to accomplish something in time and through the deeds of its members. These deeds belong to the life which each member regards as, in ideal, his own. It is in this way that both the real and the ideal Church are intended by the members to be communities in our sense. An analogous truth holds for such other communities as we shall need to consider. The concept of the community is thus, for our purposes, a practical conception. It involves the idea of deeds done, and ends sought or attained. Hence I shall define it in terms of members who themselves not only live in time, but conceive their own ideally extended personalities in terms of a time-process. In so far as these personalities possess a life that is for each of them his own, while it is, in some of its events, common to them all, they form a community.

Nothing important is lost, for our conception of the community, by this formal restriction, whereby common objects belong to a community only when these objects are bound up with the deeds of the community. For, when the warrior regards his sword as a part of himself, he does so because his sword is the instrument of his will, and because what he does with his sword belongs to his literal or ideal life. Even the mystic accomplishes his identification of the self and the world only through acts of renunciation or of inward triumph. And these acts are the goal of his life. Until he attains to them, they form part of his ideal future self. Whenever he fully accomplishes these crowning acts of identification, the separate self no longer exists. When knights or mystics form a community, in our sense, they therefore do so because they conceive of deeds done, in common, with their swords, or of mystical attainments that all of them win together.

Thus then, while no authoritative limit can be placed upon the ideal extensions of the self in time, those extensions of the self which need be considered for the purposes of our theory of the community are indeed extensions in time, past or future; or at all events involve such extensions in time.

Memory and hope constantly incite us to the extensions of the self which play so large a part in our daily life. Social motives of endlessly diverse sort move us to consider "far and forgot" as if to us it were near, when we view ourselves in the vaster perspectives of time. It is, in fact, the ideally extended self, and not, in general, the momentary self, whose life is worth living, whose sense outlasts our fleeting days, and whose destiny may be worthy of the interest of beings who are above the level of human individuals. The present self, the fleeting individual of to-day, is a mere gesticulation of a self. The genuine person lives in the far-off past and future as well as in the present. It is, then, the ideally extended self that is worthy to belong to a significant community.

III

The *second* condition upon which the existence of a community depends is the fact that there are in the social world a number of distinct selves capable of social communication, and, in general, engaged in communication.

The distinctness of the selves we have illustrated at length in our previous discussion. We need not here dwell upon the matter further, except to say, expressly, that a community does *not* become one, in the sense of my definition, by virtue of any reduction or melting of these various selves into a single merely present self, or into a mass of passing experience. That mystical phenomena may indeed form part of the life of a community, just as they may also form part of the life of an individual human being, I fully recognize.

About such mystical or quasi-mystical phenomena, occurring in their own community, the Corinthians consulted Paul. And Paul, whose implied theory of the community is one which my own definition closely follows, assured them in his reply that mystical phenomena are not essential to the existence of the community; and that it is on the whole better for the life of such a community as he was addressing, if the individual member, instead of losing himself "in a mystery," kept his own individuality, in order to contribute his own edifying gift to the common life. Wherein this common life consists we have yet further to see in what follows.

The *third* of the conditions for the existence of the community which my definition emphasizes consists in the fact that the ideally extended past and future selves of the members include at least some events which are, for all these selves, identical. This third condition is the one which furnishes both the most exact, the most widely variable, and the most important of the motives which warrant us in calling a community a real unit. The Pauline metaphor of the body and the members finds, in this third condition, its most significant basis, — a basis capable of exact description.

IV

In addition to the instance which I cited at the last time, when I mentioned the New Zealanders and their legendary canoes, other and much more important illustrations may here serve to remind us how a single common past or future event may be the central means of uniting many selves in one spiritual community. For the Pauline churches the ideal memory of their Lord's death and resurrection, defined in terms of the faith which the missionary apostle delivered to them in his teaching, was, for each believer, an acknowledged occurrence in his own past. For each one was taught the faith, "In that one event my individual salvation was accomplished."

This faith has informed ever since the ideal memory upon which Christian tradition has most of all depended for the establishment and the preservation of its own community. If we speak in terms of social psychology, we are obliged, I think, to regard this belief as the product of the life of the earliest Christian community itself. But once established, and then transmitted from generation to generation, this same belief has been ceaselessly recreative of the communities of each succeeding age. And the various forms of the Christian Church,—its hierarchical institutions, its schisms, its reformations, its sects, its heresies, have been varied, differentiated, or divided, or otherwise transformed, according as the individual believers who made up any group of followers of Christian tradition have conceived, each his own personal life as including and as determined by that one ideal event thus remembered, namely, his Lord's death and resurrection.

Since the early Church was aware of this dependence of its community upon its memory, it instinctively resisted every effort to deprive that memory of definiteness, to explain it away as the Gnostic heresies did, or to transform it from a memory into any sort of conscious allegory. The idealized memory, the backward looking faith of an individual believer, must relate to events that seem to him living and concrete. Hence the early Church insisted upon the words, "Suffered under Pontius Pilate." The religious instinct which thus insisted was true to its own needs. A very definite event must be viewed by each believer as part of the history of his own personal salvation. Otherwise the community would lose its coherence.

Paul himself, despite his determination to know Christ, not "after the flesh," but "after the Spirit," was unhesitating and uncompromising with regard to so much of the ideal Christian memory as he himself desired each believer to carry clearly in mind. Only by such common memories could the community be constituted. To be sure, the Apostle's Christology, on its more metaphysical side, cared little for such more precise technical formulations as later became historically important for the Church that formulated its creeds. But the events which Paul regarded as essential to salvation must be, as he held, plainly set down.

Since human memory is naturally sustained by commemorative acts, Paul laid the greatest possible stress upon the Lord's Supper, and made the proper ordering thereof an essential part of his ideal as a teacher. In this act of commemoration, wherein each member recalled the origin of his own salvation, the community maintained its united life.

V

The early Church was, moreover, not only a community of memory, but a community of hope. Since, if the community was to exist, and to be vigorously alive, each believer must keep definite his own personal hope, while the event for which all hoped must be, for all, an identical event, something more was needed, in Paul's account of the coming end of the world, than the more dimly conceived common judgment had hitherto been in the minds of the Corinthians to whom Paul wrote. And therefore the great chapter on the resurrection emphasizes equally the common resurrection of all, and the very explicitly individual immortality of each man. Paul uses both the resurrection of Christ, and the doctrine of the spiritual body, to give the sharpest possible outlines to a picture which has ever since dominated not only the traditional Christian religious imagination, but the ideal of the united Church triumphant.

Nowhere better than in this very chapter can one find an example of the precise way in which the fully developed consciousness of a community solves its own problem of the one and the many, by clearly conceiving both the diversity of the members and the unity of the body in terms of the common hope for the same event.

The Apostle had to deal with the doctrine of the immortality of the individual man, and also with the corporate relations of humanity and of the Church to death and to the end of all things. The most pathetic private concerns and superstitions of men, the most conflicting ideas of matter, of spirit, and of human solidarity, had combined, in those days, to confuse the religious ideas which entered into the life of the early Church, when the words "death and resurrection" were in question. The Apostle himself was heir to a seemingly hopeless tangle of ancient and more or less primitive opinions regarding the human self and the cosmos, regarding the soul and the future.

A mystery-religion of Paul's own time might, and often did, assure the individual initiate of his own immortality. The older Messianic hope, or its successor in the early Christian consciousness, might be expressed, and was often expressed, in a picture wherein all mankind were together called before the judgment seat at the end. But minds whose ideas upon such topics came from various and bewildering sources,—minds such as those of Paul's Corinthians, might, and did, inquire: "What will personally happen to me? What will happen to all mankind?" The very contrast between these two questions was, at that time, novel. The growing sense of the significance of the individual self was struggling against various more or less mystical identifications of all mankind with Adam, or with some one divine or demonic power or spirit. Such a struggle still goes on to-day.

But Paul's task it was, in writing this chapter, to clarify his own religious consciousness, and to guide his readers through the mazes of human hope and fear to some precise view, both of human solidarity and individual destiny. His method consisted in a definition of his whole problem in terms of the relations between the individual, the community, and the divine being whom he conceived as the very life of this community. He undertook to emphasize the individual self, and yet to insist upon the unity of the Church and of its Lord. He made perfectly clear in each believer's mind the idea: "I myself, and not another, am to witness and to take part in this last great change." To this end Paul made use of the conception of the individual spiritual body of each man. But Paul also dwelt with equal decisiveness upon the thought, "The last event of the present world is to be, for all of us, *one* event; for we shall all together arise."

These two main thoughts of the great chapter are in the exposition clearly contrasted and united; and against this well-marked background Paul can then place statements about humanity viewed as one corporate entity, — monistic formulations, so to speak, — and can do this without fear of being misunderstood: "The first man Adam became a living soul. The last Adam became a quickening spirit. The first man is of the earth, earthy; the second man is the Lord from heaven." What these more monistic statements about mankind as one corporate entity are to mean, is made clear simply by teaching each believer to say, "I shall myself arise, with my own transformed and incorruptible body;" and also to say, "This event of the resurrection is one for all of us, for we shall arise together."

In such expressions Paul uses traditions whose sources were indeed obscure and whose meaning was, as one might have supposed, hopelessly ambiguous. The interpretations of these traditions on Paul's part might have been such as to lose sight of the destiny of the individual human being through a more or less mystical blending of the whole race. That would have been natural for a mind trained to think of Adam and of mankind as Paul was trained. Or, again, the interpretation might have taken the form of assuring the individual believer that he could win his own immortality, while leaving him no further ground for special interest in the community. Paul's religious genius aims straight at the central problem of clearing away this ambiguity, and of defining the immortal life, both of the individual and of the community. In the expected resurrection, as Paul pictures it, the individual finds his own life, and the community its common triumph over all the world-old powers of death. And the hope is referred back again to the memory. Was not Christ raised? By this synthesis Paul solves his religious problem, and defines sharply the relation of the individual and the community.

And therefore, whenever, upon the familiar solemn occasions, this chapter is read, not only is individual sorrow bidden to transform itself into an unearthly hope; but even upon earth the living and conscious community of the faithful celebrates the present oneness of spirit in which it triumphs. And the death over which it triumphs is the death of the lonely individual, whom faith beholds raised to the imperishable life in the spirit. This life in the spirit is also the life of the community For the individual is saved, according to Paul, only in and through and with the community and its Lord.

VI

Our present interest in these classic religious illustrations of the idea of the community is not directly due to their historical importance as parts of Christian tradition; but depends upon the help which they give us in seeing how a community, whether it be Christian or not, can really constitute a single entity, despite the multiplicity of its members. Our illustrations have brought before us the fact that hope and memory constitute, in communities, a basis for an unquestionable consciousness of unity, and that this common life in time does not annul the variety of the individual members at any one present moment.

We have still to see, however, the degree to which this consciousness of unity can find expression in an effectively united common life which not only contains common events, but also possesses common deeds and can arouse a common love — a love which passes the love wherewith individuals can love one another.

And here we reach that aspect of the conception of the community which is the most important, and also the most difficult aspect.

VII

A great and essentially dramatic event, such as the imagined resurrection of the bodies of all men, — an event which interests all, and which fixes the attention by its miraculous apparition, — is well adapted to illustrate the union of the one and the many in the process of time. When Paul's genius seized upon this picture, — when, to use the well-known later scholastic phraseology, the spirits of men were thus "individuated by their bodies," even while the event of the resurrection fixed the eye of faith upon one final crisis through which all were to pass "in a moment, in the twinkling of an eye," — when the Apostle thus instructed the faithful, a great lesson was also taught regarding the means whereby the ideal of a community and the harmonious union of the one and the many can be rendered brilliantly clear to the imagination, and decisively fascinating to the will.

But the lives of communities cannot consist of miraculous crises. A community, like an individual self, must learn to keep the consciousness of its unity through the vicissitudes of an endlessly shifting and often dreary fortune. The monotony of insignificant events, the chaos of lesser conflicts, the friction and the bickerings of the members, the individual failures and the mutual misunderstandings which make the members of a community forget the common past and future, — all these things work against the conscious unity of the life of a community. Memory and hope are alike clouded by multitudes of such passing events. The individual members cannot always recall the sense in which they identify their own lives and selves with what has been, or with what is yet to come.

And — hardest task of all — the members, if they are to conceive clearly of the common life, must somehow learn to bear in mind not merely those grandly simple events which, like great victories, or ancestral feats, or divine interferences, enter into the life of the community from without, and thus make their impression all at once.

No, the true common life of the community consists of deeds which are essentially of the nature of processes of coöperation. That is, the common life consists of deeds which many members perform together, as when the workmen in a factory labor side by side.

Now we all know that coöperation constantly occurs, and is necessary to every form and grade of society. We also know that commerce and industry and art and custom and language consist of vast complexes of coöperations. And in all such cases many men manage in combination to accomplish what no one man, and no multitude of men working separately, could conceivably bring to pass. But what we now need to see is the way in which such coöperations can become part, not only of the life, but of the consciousness of a community.

VIII

Every instance of a process of coöperation is an event, or a sequence of events. And our definition of a community requires that, if such coöperative activities are to be regarded as the deeds of a community, there must be individuals, each one of whom says: "That coöperation, in which many distinct individuals take part, and in which I also take part, is, or was, or will be, an event in my life." And many coöperating individuals must agree in saying this of the same process in which they all coöperate.

And all must extend such identifications of the self with these social activities far into the past, or into the future.

But it is notoriously hard — especially in our modern days of the dreary complexity of mechanical labor — for any individual man so to survey, and so to take interest in a vast coöperative activity that he says: "In my own ideally extended past and future that activity, its history, its future, its significance as an event or sequence of events, all have their ideally significant part. That activity, as the coöperation of many in one work, is also my life." To say such things and to think such thoughts grow daily harder for most of the coworkers of a modern social order.

Hence, as is now clear, the existence of a highly organized social life is by no means identical with the existence of what is, in our present and restricted sense, the life of a true community. On the contrary, and for the most obvious reasons, there is a strong mutual opposition between the social tendencies which secure coöperation on a vast scale, and the very conditions which so interest the individual in the common life of his community that it forms part of his own ideally extended life. We met with that opposition between the more or less mechanically coöperative social life, — the life of the social will on the one side, and the life of the true community on the other side, — when we were considering the Pauline doctrine of the law in an earlier lecture. In fact, it is the original sin of any highly developed civilization that it breeds coöperation at the expense of a loss of interest in the community.

The failure to see the reason why this opposition between the tendency to coöperation and the spirit of the community exists; the failure to sound to the depths the original sin of man the social animal, and of the natural social order which he creates; — such failure, I repeat, lies at the basis of countless misinterpretations, both of our modern social problems, and of the nature of a true community, and of the conditions which make possible any wider philosophical generalizations of the idea of the community.

IX

Men do not form a community, in our present restricted sense of that word, merely in so far as the men coöperate. They form a community, in our present limited sense, when they not only coöperate, but accompany this coöperation with that ideal extension of the lives of individuals whereby each coöperating member says: "This activity which we perform together, this work of ours, its past, its future, its sequence, its order, its sense, — all these enter into my life, and are the life of my own self writ large."

Now coöperation results from conditions which a social psychology such as that of Wundt or of Tarde may analyze. Imitation and rivalry, greed and ingenuity, business and pleasure, war and industry, may all combine to make men so coöperate that very large groups of them behave, to an external observer, as if they were units. In the broader sense of the term "community," all social groups that behave as if they were units are regarded as communities. And we ourselves called all such groups communities in our earlier lectures before we came to our new definition.

But we have now been led to a narrower application of the term "community." It is an application to which we have restricted the term simply because of our special purpose in this inquiry. Using this restricted definition of the term "community," we see that groups which coöperate may be very far from constituting communities in our narrower sense. We also see how, in general, a group whose coöperative activities are very highly complex will require a correspondingly long period of time to acquire that sort of tradition and of common expectation which is needed to constitute a community in our sense, — that is, a community conscious of its own life.

Owing to the psychological conditions upon which social coöperation depends, such cooperation can very far outstrip, in the complexity of its processes, the power of any individual man's wit to understand its intricacies. In modern times, when social cooperation both uses and is so largely dominated by the industrial arts, the physical conditions of coöperative social life have combined with the psychological conditions to make any thorough understanding of the coöperative processes upon which we all depend simply hopeless for the individual, except within some narrow range. Experts become well acquainted with aspects of these forms of coöperation which their own callings involve. Less expert workers understand a less range of the coöperative processes in which they take part. Most individuals, in most of their work, have to coöperate as the cogs coöperate in the wheels of a mechanism. They work together; but few or none of them know how they coöperate, or what they must do.

But the true community, in our present restricted sense of the word, depends for its genuine common life upon such coöperative activities that the individuals who participate in these common activities understand enough to be able, first, to direct their own deeds of coöperation; secondly, to observe the deeds of their individual fellow workers, and thirdly to know that, without just this combination, this order, this interaction of the coworking selves, just this deed could not be accomplished by the community. So, for instance, a chorus or an orchestra carries on its coöperative activities. In these cases coöperation is a conscious art. If hereupon these coöperative deeds, thus understood by the individual coworker, are viewed by him as linked, through an extended history with past and future deeds of the community, and if he then identifies his own life with this common life, and if his fellow members agree in this identification, then indeed the community both has a common life, and is aware of the fact. For then the individual coworker not only says: "This past and future fortune of the community belongs to my life;" but also declares: "This past and future deed of coöperation belongs to my life." "This, which none of us could have done alone,—this, which all of us together could not have accomplished unless we were ordered and linked in precisely this way,—this we together accomplished, or shall yet accomplish; and this deed of all of us belongs to my life."

A community thus constituted is essentially a community of those who are artists in some form of coöperation, and whose art constitutes, for each artist, his own ideally extended life. But the life of an artist depends upon his love for his art.

The community is made possible by the fact that each member includes in his own ideally extended life the deeds of coöperation which the members accomplish. When these deeds are hopelessly complex, how shall the individual member be able to regard them as genuinely belonging to his own ideally extended life? He can no longer understand them in any detail. He takes part in them, willingly or unwillingly. He does so because he is social, and because he must. He works in his factory, or has his share, whether greedily or honestly, in the world's commercial activities. And his coöperations may be skilful; and this fact also he may know. But his skill is largely due to external training, not to inner expansion of the ideals of the self. And the more complex the social order grows, the more all this coöperation must tend to appear to the individual as a mere process of nature, and not as his own work,—as a mechanism and not as an ideal extension of himself,—unless indeed love supplies what individual wit can no longer accomplish.

X

If a social order, however complex it may be, actually wins and keeps the love of its members; so that,—however little they are able to understand the details of their present coöperative activities,—they still—with all their whole hearts and their minds and their souls, and their strength—desire, each for himself, that such coöperations should go on; and if each member, looking back to the past, rejoices in the ancestors and the heroes who have made the present life of this social group possible; and if he sees in these deeds of former generations the source and support of his present love; and if each member also looks forward with equal love to the future,—then indeed love furnishes that basis for the consciousness of the community which intelligence, without love, in a highly complex social realm, can no longer furnish. Such love—such loyalty—depends not upon losing sight of the variety of the callings of individuals, but upon seeing in the successful coöperation of all the members precisely that event which the individual member most eagerly loves as his own fulfilment.

When love of the community, nourished by common memories, and common hope, both exists and expresses itself in devoted individual lives, it can constantly tend, despite the complexity of the present social order, to keep the consciousness of the community alive. And when this takes place, the identification of the loyal individual self with the life of the community will tend, both in ideal and in feeling, to identify each self not only with the distant past and future of the community, but with the present activities of the whole social body.

Thus, for instance, when the complexities of business life, and the dreariness of the factory, have, to our minds, deprived our present social coöperations of all or of most of their common significance, the great communal or national festivity, bringing to memory the great events of past and future, not only makes us, for the moment, feel and think as a community with reference to those great past and future events, but in its turn, as a present event, reacts upon next day's ordinary labors. The festivity says to us: "We are one because of our common past and future, because of the national heroes and victories and hopes, and because we love all these common memories and hopes." Our next day's mood, consequent upon the festivity, bids us say: "Since we are thus possessed of this beloved common past and future, let this consciousness lead each of us even to-day to extend his ideal self so as to include the daily work of all his fellows, and to view his fellow members' life as his own."

Thus memory and hope tend to react upon the present self, which finds the brotherhood of present labor more significant, and the ideal identification of the present self with the self of the neighbor easier, because the ideal extension of the self into past and future has preceded.

And so, first, each of us learns to say: "This beloved past and future life, by virtue of the ideal extension, is my own life." Then, finding that our fellows have and love this past and future in common with us, we learn further to say: "In this respect we are all one loving and beloved community." Then we take a further step and say: "Since we are all members of this community, therefore, despite our differences, and our mutual sunderings of inner life, each of us can, and will, ideally extend his present self so as to include the present life and deeds of his fellow."

So it is that, in the ideal church, each member not only looks backwards to the same history of salvation as does his fellow, but is even thereby led to an ideal identification of his present self with that of his fellow member that would not otherwise be possible. Thus, then, common memory and common hope, the central possessions of the community, tend, when enlivened by love, to mould the consciousness of the present, and to link each member to his community by ideal ties which belong to the moment as well as to the stream of past and future life.

XI

Love, when it exists and triumphs over the complexities which obscure and confuse the common life, thus completes the consciousness of the community, in the forms which that consciousness can assume under human conditions. Such love, however, must be one that has the common deeds of the community as its primary object. No one understands either the nature of the loyal life, or the place of love in the constitution of the life of a real community, who conceives such love as merely a longing for the mystical blending of the selves or for their mutual interpenetration, and for that only. Love says to the individual: "So extend yourself, in ideal, that you aim, with all your heart and your soul and your mind and your strength, at *that* life of perfectly definite deeds which never can come to pass unless all the members, despite their variety and their natural narrowness, are in perfect coöperation. Let this life be your art and also the art of all your fellow members. Let your community be as a chorus, and not as a company who forget themselves in a common trance."

Nevertheless, as Paul showed in the great chapter, such love of the self for the community can be and will be not without its own mystical element. For since we human beings are as narrow in our individual consciousness as we are, we cannot ideally extend ourselves through clearly understanding the complicated social activities in which the community is to take part. Therefore our ideal extensions of the self, when we love the community, and long to realize its life with intimacy, must needs take the form of *acting as if we could survey*, in some single unity of insight, that wealth and variety and connection which, as a fact, we cannot make present to our momentary view. Since true love is an emotion, and since emotions are present affections of the self, love, in longing for its own increase, and for its own fulfilment, inevitably longs to find what it loves as a fact of experience, and to be in the immediate presence of its beloved. Therefore, the love of a community (a love which, as we now see, is devoted to desiring the realization of an overwhelmingly vast variety and unity of coöperations), is, as an emotion, discontent with all the present sundering of the selves, and with all the present problems and mysteries of the social order. Such love, then, restless with the narrowness of our momentary view of our common life, desires this common life to be an immediate presence for all of us. Such an immediate presence of all the community to all the members would be indeed, if it could wholly and simply take place, a mere blending of the selves,—an interpenetration in which the individuals vanished, and in which, for that very reason, the real community would also be lost.

Love,—the love of Paul's great chapter,—the loyalty which stands at the centre of the Christian consciousness,—is, as an emotion, a longing for such a mystical blending of the selves. This longing is present in Paul's account. It is in so far not the whole of charity. It is simply the mystical aspect of the love for the community.

But the Pauline charity is not merely an emotion. It is an interpretation. The ideal extension of the self gets a full and concrete meaning only by being actively expressed in the new deeds of each individual life. Unless each man knows how distinct he is from the whole community and from every member of it, he cannot render to the community what love demands,—namely, the devoted work. Love may be mystical, and work should be directed by clearly outlined intelligence; but the loyal spirit depends upon this union of a longing for unity with a will which needs its own expression in works of loyal art.

XII

The doctrine of the two levels of human existence; the nature of a real community; the sense in which there can be, in individual human beings, despite their narrowness, their variety, and their sundered present lives, a genuine consciousness of the life of a community whereof they are members:—these matters we have now, within our limits, interpreted. The time-process, and the ideal extensions of the self in this time-process, lie at the basis of the whole theory of the community. The union and the contrast of the one and the many in the community, and the relation of the mystical element in our consciousness of the community to the active interpretation of the loyal life, these things have also been reviewed. Incidentally, so to speak, we have suggested further reasons why loyalty, whether in its distinctively Christian forms, or in any others, is a saving principle whenever it appears in an individual human life. For in the love of a community the individual obtains, for his ideally extended self, precisely the unity, the wealth, and the harmony of plan which his sundered natural existence never supplies.

Yet it must be not merely admitted, but emphasized, that all such analyses of the sort of life and of interpretation upon which communities and the loyalty of their members depend, does not and cannot explain the origin of loyalty, the true sources of grace, and the way in which communities of high level come into existence.

On the contrary, all the foregoing account of what a community is shows how the true spirit of loyalty, and the highest level of the consciousness of a human community, is at once so precious, and so difficult to create.

The individual man naturally, but capriciously, loves both himself and his fellow-man, according as passion, pity, memory, and hope move him. Social training tends to sharpen the contrasts between the self and the fellow-man; and higher cultivation, under these conditions of complicated social coöperation which we have just pointed out, indeed makes a man highly conscious that he depends upon his community, but also renders him equally conscious that, as an individual, he is much beset by the complexities of the social will, and does not always love his community, or any community. Neither the origin nor the essence of loyalty is explained by man's tendencies to love his individual fellow-man.

It is true that, within the limits of his power to understand his social order, the conditions which make a man conscious of his community also imply that the man should in some respects identify his life with that. But I may well know that the history, the future, the whole meaning of my community are bound up with my own life; and yet it is not necessary that on that account I should wholeheartedly love my own life. I may be a pessimist. Or I may be simply discontented. I may desire to escape from the life that I have. And I may be aware that my fellows, for the most part, also long to escape.

That the community is above my own individual level I shall readily recognize, since the community is indeed vastly more skilful and incomparably more powerful than I can ever become. But what is thus above me I need not on that account be ready wholly to love. To be sure, that man is indeed a sad victim of a misunderstood life who is himself able to be clearly aware of his community, to identify its history and its future, at least in part, with his own ideally extended life, and who is yet *wholly* unable ever to love the life which is thus linked with his own. Yet there remains the fate which Paul so emphasized, and which has determined the whole history of the Christian consciousness: Knowledge of the community is not love of the community. Love, when it comes, comes as from above.

Especially is this true of the love of the ideal community of all mankind. I can be genuinely in love with the community only in case I have somehow fallen in love with the universe. The problem of love is human. The solution of the problem, if it comes at all, will be, in its meaning, superhuman, and divine, if there be anything divine.

What our definition of the community enables us to add to our former views of the meaning of loyalty is simply this: If the universe proves to be, in any sense, of the nature of a community, then love for this community, and for God, will not mean merely love for losing the self, or for losing the many selves, in any interpenetration of selves. If one can find that all humanity, in the sense of our definition, constitutes a real community, or that the world itself is, in any genuine way, of the nature of a community such as we have defined; and *if* hereupon we can come to love this real community, —then the one and the many, the body and the members, our beloved and ourselves, will be joined in a life in which we shall be both preserved as individuals, and yet united to that which we love.

XIII

Plainly a metaphysical study of the question whether the universe is a community will be as powerless as the foregoing analysis of the real nature of human communities to explain the origin of love, or to make any one fall in love with the universe. Yet something has been gained by our analysis of the problem which, from this point onwards, determines our metaphysical inquiry. If our results are in any way positive, they may enable us to view the problem of Christianity, that is, the problem of the religion of loyalty, in a larger perspective than that which human history, when considered alone, determines. The favorite methods of approaching the metaphysical problems of theology end by leaving the individual alone with God, in a realm which seems, to many minds, a realm of merely concepts, of intellectual abstractions, of barren theories. The ways which are just now in favor in the philosophy of religion seem to end in leaving the individual equally alone with his intuitions, his lurid experiences of sudden conversion, or his ineffable mysteries of saintly peace.

May we not hope to gain by a method which follows the plan now outlined? This method, first, encourages a man to interpret his own individual self in terms of the largest ideal extension of that self in time which his reasonable will can acknowledge as worthy of the aims of his life. Secondly, this method bids a man consider what right he has to interpret the life from which he springs, in the midst of which he now lives, as a life that in any universal sense coöperates with his own and ideally expresses its own meaning so as to meet with his own, and to have a history identical with his own. Thirdly, this method directs us to inquire how far, in the social order to which we unquestionably belong, there are features such as warrant us in hoping that, in the world's community, our highest love may yet find its warrant and its fulfilment.

Whatever the fortunes of the quest may be, we have now defined its plan, and have shown its perfectly definite relation to the historical problem of Christianity.

XI

Perception
Conception
and Interpretation

In defining what constitutes a community I have repeatedly mentioned processes of Interpretation. The word "interpretation" is well known; and students of the humanities have special reasons for using it frequently. When one calls an opinion about the self an interpretation, one is not employing language that is familiar only to philosophers. When a stranger in a foreign land desires the services of an interpreter, when a philologist offers his rendering of a text, when a judge construes a statute, some kind of interpretation is in question. And the process of interpretation, whatever it is, is intended to meet human needs which are as well known as they are vital. Such needs determine, as we shall see, whatever is humane and articulate in the whole conduct and texture of our lives.

I

Yet if we ask, What is an interpretation? — the answer is not easy. Nor is it made much easier by stating the question in the form: What does one desire who seeks for an interpretation? What does one gain, or create, or acknowledge who accepts an interpretation?

Our investigation has reached the point where it is necessary to face these questions, as well as some others closely related to them. For, as a fact, to inquire what the process of interpretation is, takes us at once to the very heart of philosophy, throws a light both on the oldest and on the latest issues of metaphysical thought, and has an especially close connection with the special topics to which this course is devoted.

II

First, then, let me briefly recall the ways in which we have already been brought into contact with questions involving the nature of interpretation.

Our whole undertaking is an effort to interpret vital features of Christianity. Each of the three ideas which I have viewed as essential to the Christian doctrine of life had to be interpreted first for itself, and then in its connection with the others. You might have supposed that, when we turned to our metaphysical problems, we should henceforth have to do with questions of fact, and not with interpretation. But we have found that we could not decide how the Christian doctrine of life is related to the real world without defining what we mean by a community. A community, as we have seen, depends for its very constitution upon the way in which each of its members interprets himself and his life. For the rest, nobody's self is either a mere datum or an abstract conception. A self is a life whose unity and connectedness depend upon some sort of inter- pretation of plans, of memories, of hopes, and of deeds. If, then, there are communities, there are many selves who, despite their variety, so interpret their lives that all these lives, taken together, get the type of unity which our last lecture characterized. Were there, then, no interpretations in the world, there would be neither selves nor communities. Thus our effort to study matters of fact led us back to problems of interpretation. These latter problems obviously dominate every serious inquiry into our problem of Christianity.

What, however, is any philosophy but an interpretation either of life, or of the universe, or of both? Does there exist, then, any student of universally interesting issues who is not concerned with an answer to the question. What is an interpretation?

Possibly these illustrations of our topic, few as they are, seem already so various in their characters as to suggest that the term "interpretation" may be too vague in its applications to admit of precise definition. A rendering of a text written in a foreign tongue; a judge's construction of a statute; a man's interpretation of himself and of his own life; our own philosophical interpretation of this or of that religious idea; and the practical interpretation of our destiny, or of God, which a great historical religion itself seems to have taught to the faithful; or, finally, a metaphysical interpretation of the universe,—what—so you may ask—have all these things in common? What value can there be in attempting to fix by a definition such fluent and uncontrollable interests as inspire what various people may call by the common name interpretation?

III

I reply that, beneath all this variety in the special motives which lead men to interpret objects, there exists a very definable unity of purpose. Look more closely, and you shall see that to interpret, or to attempt an interpretation, is to assume an attitude of mind which differs, in a notable way, from the other attitudes present in the intelligent activities of men; while this attitude remains essentially the same amidst very great varieties, both in the individual interpreters and in the interpretations which they seek, or undertake, or accept. Interpretation, viewed as a mental process, or as a type of knowledge, differs from other mental processes and types of knowledge in the objects to which it is properly applied, in the relations in which it stands to these objects, and in the ends which it serves.

In order to show you that this is the case, I must summarize in my own way some still neglected opinions which were first set forth, in outline, more than forty years ago by our American logician, Mr. Charles Peirce, in papers which have been little read, but which, to my mind, remain of very high value as guides of inquiry, both in Logic and in the Theory of Knowledge.[1]

[1]Of the early papers of Mr. Charles Peirce to which reference is here made, the most important are:—

1. In the *Proceedings of the American Academy of Arts and Sciences*, a paper: "On a New List of Categories," May 14, 1867.

2. In the *Journal of Speculative Philosophy*, vol. 2 (1868–1869): "Questions concerning

Mr Charles Peirce has become best known to the general public by the part which William James assigned to him as the inventor of the term "Pragmatism," and as, in some sense, the founder of the form of Pragmatism which James first made his own, and then developed so independently and so significantly. But by a small and grateful company of philosophical students, Mr. Peirce is prized, not solely, and not, I think, mainly for his part in the early history of Pragmatism, but for his contribution to Logic, and for those remarkable cosmological speculations which James also, in his lectures on the *Pluralistic Universe* (as some of you will remember), heartily acknowledged.

Those ideas of Charles Peirce about Interpretation to which I shall here refer, never, so far as I know, attracted William James's personal attention at any time. I may add that, until recently, I myself never appreciated their significance. In acknowledging here my present indebtedness to these ideas, I have to add that, in this place, there is no room to expound them at length. The context in which these views appear, both in the earliest of the published logical papers of Peirce (about 1868), and in many of his later discussions, is always very technical, and is such that no adequate discussion of the issues involved could be presented in a brief statement. Moreover, it is proper to say that Charles Peirce cannot be held responsible for the use that I shall here make of his opinions, or for any of the conclusions that I base upon them.

There is one additional matter which should be emphasized at the outset. Peirce's opinions as to the nature of interpretation were in no wise influenced by Hegel, or by the tradition of German idealism. He formed them on the basis of his own early scientific studies, and of his extensive, although always very independent, interest in the history of scholastic logic. With recent idealism this "father of Pragmatism" has always felt only a very qualified sympathy, and has frequently expressed no little dissatisfaction. Some twelve years ago, just after I had printed a book on general philosophy, Mr. Charles Peirce wrote to me, in a letter of kindly acknowledgment,

Certain Faculties claimed for Man."

3. *Id.:* "Some Consequences of Four Incapacities."

4. *Id.:* "Grounds of the Validity of the Laws of Logic; Further Consequences of Four Incapacities."

In addition to these early papers we may mention:—

5. Article "Sign" in Baldwin's "Dictionary of Philosophy and Psychology,"—a brief statement regarding an important point of Peirce's theory.

the words: "But, when I read you, I do wish that you would study logic. You need it so much."

Abandoning, then, any effort to state Peirce's case as he stated it, let me next call any attention to matters which I should never have viewed as I now view them without his direct or indirect aid.

IV

The contrast between the cognitive processes called, respectively, perception and conception, dominates a great part of the history of philosophy. This contrast is usually so defined as to involve a dual classification of our cognitive processes. When one asks which of the two processes, perception or conception, gives us the more significant guidance, or is the original from which the other is derived, or is the ideal process whereof the other is the degenerate fellow, such a dual classification is in possession of the field.

This classic dual opposition was expressed, in characteristically finished fashion, at the outset of the lectures which Professor Bergson read, in May of last year, at the invitation of the University of Oxford. You all remember his words: "If our power of external and internal perception were unlimited, we should never make use of our power to conceive, or of our power to reason. To conceive is a makeshift in the cases where one cannot perceive; and one reasons only in so far as one needs to fill gaps in our outer or inner perception, or to extend the range of perception."

Here, as is obvious, there is no recognition of the possible or actual existence of a third type of cognitive process, which is neither perception nor conception. The assertion that conception is our makeshift when perception is limited, and that unlimited perception, by rendering conception superfluous, would supply us with that grade of intuition which we, in ideal, attribute to a divine being, involves the postulate that we face the alternative: Either perception, or else conception.

But if one were to oppose the thesis just cited by declaring in favor of conception as against perception; if one were to assert that perception deceives us with vain show, and that conception alone can bring us face to face with reality; if, in short, one were to prefer Plato to Bergson,—one would not thereby necessarily be led to abandon,—one might, on the contrary, all the more emphasize this dual classification of the possible cognitive processes. In such a predominatly dualistic view of the classification of knowledge, both rationalism and empiricism have, on the whole, agreed, throughout the history of thought. Kant and James, Bergson and Mr. Bertrand Russell, are, in this respect, at one.

To be sure, in addition to perception and conception, reason and the reasoning process have been very frequently recognized as having some sort of existence for themselves, over and above the processes of simple perception and conception. Yet when Bergson speaks of reasoning, in the passage just cited from his Oxford lecture, reasoning, for him, means a special form or grade of the conceptual process itself, and is therefore no third type of cognition. When Kant made his well-known triadic distinctions of sense, under-standing, and reason, assigning to sense the power of perceiving, to understanding the power to form and to use concepts, and to reason a third function which Kant did not always define in the same way, —he did not really succeed in escaping from the classical dualism with regard to the processes of cognition. For Kant's account of reason assigns to it, in general, a high grade of conceptual functions, as opposed to perceptual functions; and thus still depends upon the dual contrast between perception and conception. Kant is nearest to defining a third type of cognitive process in many of his accounts of what he calls the *Urtheilskraft*. But he never consistently maintains a triadic classification of the cognitive processes.

V

Despite this prevalence of the dual classification of our cognitive processes, most of us will readily acknowledge that, in our real life, we human beings are never possessed either of pure perception or of pure conception. In ideal, we can define an intuitive type of knowl-edge, which should merely see, and which should never think. In an equally ideal fashion, we can imagine the possibility of a pure thought, which should be wholly absorbed in conceptions, which should have as its sole real object a realm of universals, and which should ignore all sensible data. But we mortals live the intelligent part of our lives through some sort of more or less imperfect union or synthesis of conception and perception.

In recent discussion it has become almost a commonplace to recognize this union as constantly exemplified in human experience. In this one respect, to-day, empiricists and rationalists, pragmatists and intellectualists, are accustomed to agree, although great dif-ferences arise with regard to *what* union of perception and conception constitutes such knowledge as we human beings can hopefully pursue or actually possess.

Kant, assuring us that conceptions without perceptions are "empty," and that perceptions without conceptions are "blind," sets forth, in his theory of knowledge, the well-known account of how the "spontaneity" of the intellect actively combines the perceptual data, and brings the so-called "manifold of sense" to "unity of conception."

Recent pragmatism, laying stress upon the "practical" character of every human cognitive process, depicts the life of knowledge as a dramatic pursuit of perceptions, — a pursuit guided by the "leadings" which our conceptions determine, and which, in some sense, simply constitute our conceptions, in so far as these have genuine life.

When, a number of years ago, I began a general metaphysical inquiry by defining an idea as a "plan of action," and thereupon developed a theory of knowledge and of reality, upon bases which this definition helped me to formulate, I was making my own use of thoughts which, in their outlines, are at the present day common property. The outcome of my own individual use of this definition was a sort of absolute pragmatism, which has never been pleasing either to rationalists or to empiricists, either to pragmatists or to the ruling type of absolutists. But in so far as I simply insisted upon the active meaning of ideas, my statement had something in common with many forms of current opinion which agree with one another in hardly any other respect. Only the more uncompromising of the mystics still seek for knowledge in a silent land of absolute intuition, where the intellect finally lays down its conceptual tools, and rests from its pragmatic labors, while its works do not follow it, but are simply forgotten, and are as if they never had been. Those of us who are not such uncompromising mystics, view accessible human knowledge neither as pure perception nor as pure conception, but always as depending upon the marriage of the two processes.

VI

Yet such a recognition of an active synthesis of perception and conception does not by itself enable us to define a genuinely triadic classification of the types of knowing processes. Let me illustrate this fact by another quotation from Bergson. In a passage in the first of his two Oxford lectures, our author says: "I do not deny the usefulness of abstract and general ideas, — any more than I question the value of bank-notes. But just as the note is only a promise to pay cash, so a conception has value only by virtue of the eventual perceptions for which it stands."

In these words, as you see, the antithesis, "conception," "perception," corresponds to the antithesis, "bank-note" and "cash," and the other antithesis, "credit-value," "cash-value." All these corresponding antitheses involve or depend upon dual classifications. Now it is true, and is expressly pointed out by Bergson, that the members of each of these pairs,—the credit-value, and the cash-value,—as well as the bank-note and its equivalent in gold,—are brought into a certain synthesis by the existence of a process of promising, and of redeeming the promise. A promise, however, involves a species of activity. In case of the bank-note, this activity may express whatever makes some vast commercial system solvent, or may be based upon the whole power of a great modern state.

In very much the same way, many philosophers of otherwise widely different opinions recognize that conception and perception are, in live cognitive processes, brought into synthesis by some sort of activity,—the activity of the mind whose cognitions are in question. This activity may be one of attention. Or it may consist of a series of voluntary deeds.

But in each of these cases, the members of a pair, "bank-note and cash," or "conception and perception," are first antithetically opposed to each other; and then a third or active element, a promise, a volition, or what you will, is mentioned as that which brings the members of the pair into synthesis. But this third or synthetic factor is not thus coordinated with the two opposed members of the pair.

If action, or activity, is the name given to whatever brings perceptions and conceptions into synthesis, then this third factor is not hereby set side by side, both with perception and with conception as a third form of cognitive activity. For action may be viewed as a non-cognitive function,—and classified as "conation." Or, on the contrary, action may be viewed as that grade of cognition which, being neither conception alone, nor perception alone, but the synthesis of the two, is the *only* mature and successfully completed cognitive process. Both of these views have been asserted. We need not discuss them here. But, in any case, "action" or "activity" is not itself hereby defined as a third type of cognition; any more than the activity of promising to pay, in Bergson's illustration, is defined as a third sort of currency which is neither gold nor bank-notes.

Thus far, then, the classification of the cognitive processes as being either perceptions or else conceptions remains triumphant, and is not superseded by regarding genuine knowledge as a synthesis of these two. For the dual contrast between perception and conception dominates all such opinions.

VII

Yet cognition may be considered from a slightly different point of view.

It is natural to classify cognitive processes by their characteristic objects. The object of a perception is a datum of some sort, a *thing*, or perhaps, as Bergson insists, a *change*, or whatever else we may be able immediately to apprehend. The object of a conception is an *universal* of some sort, a *general* or *abstract character*, a *type*, a *quality*, or some complex object based upon such universals. Now do all objects of cognition belong to one of these two classes? If so, in which of these classes will you place your neighbor's mind, or any of the conscious acts of that mind? Is your neighbor's mind a *datum* that you could, were your perception "unlimited," simply find *present* to you, as *red* or as a "change" can be present? Is your neighbor's mind, on the contrary, an abstraction, a mere *sort* of being, an *universal* which you merely conceive? If a conception resembles a bank-note in being a promise to pay, which needs to be redeemed in the gold of percep-tion,—then what immediate perception of your own could ever render to you the "cash-value" of your idea of your neighbor's mind? On the other hand, your present and personal idea of your neigh-bor's mind is certainly not itself such a perceptual "cash-value" for you. Your neighbor's mind is no mere *datum* to your sense at any time.

If, then, there be any cognitive process whose proper object is your neighbor's mind, this process is neither a mere conception nor yet a mere perception. Is it, then, some synthesis or combination of perceptions and conceptions? Or is it, finally, some third form of cognitive process, which is neither perception nor conception, and which cannot be completely describable in terms of combined perceptions and conceptions? Now it appears that the word "interpretation" is a convenient name for a process which at least aims to be cognitive. And the proper object of an interpretation, as we usually employ the name, is either something of the nature of a mind, or else is a process which goes on in a mind, or, finally, is a sign or expression whereby some mind manifests its existence and its processes. Let us consider, then, more closely, whether the process of interpretation, in so far as its proper object is a mind, or is the sign of a mind, can be reduced to a pure perception, or to pure conception, or to any synthesis which merely involves these two.

VIII

We shall here be aided by a very familiar instance, suggested by the very illustration which Bergson uses in pointing out the contrast between perception and conception, and in emphasizing the secondary and purely instrumental character of the process of conception. Gold coin, as Bergson reminds us, corresponds, in its value for the ordinary business of buying and selling, to perceptions as they appear in our experience. Bank-notes correspond, in an analogous fashion, to conceptions. The notes are promises to pay cash. The conceptions are useful guides to possible perceptions. The link between the note and its cash-value is the link which the activity of making and keeping the promises of a solvent bank provides. The link between the conception and its corresponding perception is the link which some active synthesis, such as voluntary seeking, or creative action, or habitual conduct, or intention, supplies. The illustration is clear. In a special way perceptions do indeed correspond to cash-values, and conceptions to credit-values. But in the world of commercial transaction there are other values than simple cash-values and credit-values. Perhaps, therefore, in the realm of cognitive processes there may be analogous varieties.

Recall the familiar case wherein a traveller crosses the boundary of a foreign country. To the boundary he comes provided, let us say, with the gold and with bank-notes of his own country, but without any letter of credit. This side of the boundary his bank-notes are good because of their credit-value. His gold is good because, being the coinage of the realm, it possesses cash-value and is legal tender. But beyond the boundary, in the land to which he goes, the coin which he carries is no longer legal tender, and possibly will not pass at all in ordinary transactions. His bank-notes may be, for the moment, valueless, not because the promise stamped upon their face is irredeemable, but because the gold coin itself into which they could be converted upon presentation at the bank in question, would not be legal tender beyond the boundary.

Consequently, at the boundary, a new process may be convenient, if not, for the traveller's purpose, indispensable. It is the process of exchanging coin of the realm which he leaves for that of the foreign land which he enters. The process may be easy or difficult, may be governed by strict rules or else may be capricious, according to the conditions which prevail at the boundary. But it is a third process, which consists neither in the presentation of cash-values nor in the offering or accepting of credit-values. It is a process of interpreting the cash-values which are recognized by the laws and customs of one realm in terms of the cash-values which are legal tender in another country. It is also a process of proceeding to act upon the basis of this interpretation. We are not concerned with the principles which make this interpretation possible, or which guide the conduct either of the traveller or of the money-changer at the boundary. What interests us here is simply the fact that a new type of transaction is now in question. It is a process of money-changing,—a special form of exchange of values, but a form not simply analogous to the type of the activities whereby conceptions are provided with their corresponding perceptions. And this form is not reducible to that of the simple contrast between credit-values and cash-values.

IX

Each of us, in every new effort to communicate with our fellow-men, stands, like the traveller crossing the boundary of a new country, in the presence of a largely strange world of perceptions and of conceptions. Our neighbor's perceptions, in their immediate presence, we never quite certainly share. Our neighbor's conceptions, for various reasons which I need not here enumerate, are so largely communicable that they can often be regarded, with a high degree of probability, as identical, in certain aspects of their meaning, with our own. But the active syntheses, the practical processes of seeking and of construction, the volitions, the promises, whereby we pass from our own concepts to our own percepts, are often in a high degree individual. In that case it may be very difficult to compare them to the corresponding processes of our neighbors; and then a mutual understanding, in respect of our activities and their values, is frequently as hard to obtain as is a direct view of one another's sensory perceptions. "I never loved you," so says Hamlet to Ophelia. "My lord, you made me believe so." Here is a classic instance of a problem of mutual interpretation. Who of us can solve this problem for Hamlet and Ophelia?

Therefore, in our efforts to view the world as other men view it, our undertaking is very generally analogous to the traveller's financial transactions when he crosses the boundary. We try to solve the problem of learning how to exchange the values of our own lives into the terms which can hope to pass current in the new or foreign spiritual realms whereto, when we take counsel together, we are constantly attempting to pass. Both the credit-values and the cash-values are not always easily exchanged.

I have no hope of showing, in the present discussion, how and how far we can make sure that, in a given case of human social intercourse, we actually succeed in fairly exchanging the coinage of our perceptions and the bank-notes of our conceptions into the values which pass current in the realm beyond the boundary. What measure of truth our individual interpretations possess, and by what tests we verify that truth, I have not now to estimate. But I am strongly interested in the fact that, just as the process of obtaining cash for our bank-notes is not the same as the process of exchanging our coins for foreign coins when we pass the border, precisely so the process of verifying our concepts through obtaining the corresponding percepts is not the same as the process of interpreting our neighbors' minds.

A philosophy which, like that of Bergson, defines the whole problem of knowledge in terms of the classic opposition between conception and perception, and which then declares that, if our powers of perception were unlimited, the goal of knowledge would be reached, simply misses the principal problem, both of our daily human existence and of all our higher spiritual life, as well as of the universe. And in bidding us seek the solution of our problems in terms of perception, such a doctrine simply forbids us to pass any of the great boundaries of the spiritual world, or to explore the many realms wherein the wealth of the spirit is poured out. For neither perception nor conception, nor any combination of the two, nor yet their synthesis in our practical activities, constitutes the whole of any interpretation. Interpretation, however, is what we seek in all our social and spiritual relations; and without some process of interpretation, we obtain no fulness of life.

X

It would be wrong to suppose, however, that interpretation is needed and is used only in our literal social relations with other individual human beings. For it is important to notice that one of the principal problems in the life of each of us is the problem of interpreting himself. The bare mention of Hamlet's words reminds us of this fact. Ophelia does not understand Hamlet. But does he understand himself?

In our inner life it not infrequently happens that we have — like the traveller, or like Hamlet in the ghost-scene, or like Macbeth when there comes the knocking on the gate — to pass a boundary, to cross into some new realm, not merely of experience, but of desire, of hope, or of resolve. It is then our fortune not merely that our former ideas, as the pragmatists say, no longer "work," and that our bank-notes can no longer be cashed in terms of the familiar inner perceptions which we have been accustomed to seek. Our situation is rather this: that *both* our ideas *and* our experiences, both our plans and our powers to realize plans, both our ideas with their "leadings" and our intuitions, are in process of dramatic transformation. At such times we need to know, like Nebuchadnezzar, both our dream and its interpretation.

Such critical passing of a boundary in one's own inner world is a well-known event in youth, when what Goethe called: —

> Neue Liebe, neues Leben,
> Neue Hoffnung, neues Sehnen,

makes one say to one's heart: —

> Ich erkenne dich nicht mehr.

Yet, not only youth, but personal calamity, or other "moving accident," or, in a more inspiring way, the call of some new constructive task, or, in the extreme case, a religious conversion, may at any time force one or another of us to cross a boundary in a fashion similar to those just illustrated.

At such times we are impressed with the fact that there is no royal road to self-knowledge. Charles Peirce, in the earliest of the essays to which I am calling your attention, maintained (quite rightly, I think) that there is no direct intuition or perception of the self. Reflection, as Peirce there pointed out, involves what is, in its essence, an interior conversation, in which one discovers one's own mind through a process of inference analogous to the very modes of inference which guide us in a social effort to interpret our neighbors' minds. Such social inference is surely no merely conceptual process. But it cannot be reduced to the sort of perception which Bergson invited you, in his Oxford lectures, to share. Although you are indeed placed in the "interior" of yourself, you can never so far retire into your own inmost recesses of intuition as merely to find the true self presented to an inner sense.

XI

So far I have merely sketched, with my own illustrations, a few notable features of Peirce's early opinions about interpretation. We are now ready for his central thesis, which, with many variations in detail, he has retained in all his later discussions of the processes in question. I beg you not to be discouraged by the fact that, since Peirce has always been, first of all, a logician, he states this central thesis in a decidedly formal fashion, which I here somewhat freely imitate. We shall soon see the usefulness of this formal procedure.

Interpretation always involves a relation of three terms. In the technical phrase, interpretation *is* a triadic relation. That is, you cannot express any complete process of interpreting by merely naming two terms,—persons, or other objects,—and by then telling what dyadic relation exists between one of these two and the other.

Let me illustrate: Suppose that an Egyptologist translates an inscription. So far two beings are indeed in question: the translator and his text. But a genuine translation cannot be merely a translation in the abstract. There must be some language into which the inscription is translated. Let this translation be, in a given instance, an English translation. Then the translator interprets something; but he interprets it only to one who can read English. And if a reader knows no English, the translation is for such a reader no interpretation at all. That is, a triad of beings—the Egyptian text, the Egyptologist who translates, and the possible English reader—are equally necessary in order that such an English interpretation of an Egyptian writing should exist. Whenever anybody translates a text, the situation remains, however you vary texts or languages or translators, essentially the same. There must exist some one, or some class of beings, to whose use this translation is adapted; while the translator is somebody who expresses himself by mediating between two expressions of meanings, or between two languages, or between two speakers or two writers. The mediator or translator, or interpreter, must, in cases of this sort, himself know both languages, and thus be intelligible to both the persons whom his translation serves. The triadic relation in question is, in its essence, non-symmetrical,—that is, unevenly arranged with respect to all three terms. Thus somebody (let us say A) — the translator or interpreter — interprets somebody (let us say B) to somebody (let us say C). If you transpose the order of the terms, — A, B, C, — an account of the happening which constitutes an interpretation must be altered, or otherwise may become either false or meaningless.

Thus an interpretation is a relation which not only involves three terms, but brings them into a determinate order. One of the three terms is the interpreter; a second term is the object — the person or the meaning or the text — which is interpreted; the third is the person to whom the interpretation is addressed.

This may, at first, seem to be a mere formality. But nothing in the world is more momentous than the difference between a pair and a triad of terms may become, if the terms and the relations involved are themselves sufficiently full of meaning.

You may observe that, when a man perceives a thing, the relation is dyadic. A perceives B. A pair of members is needed, and suffices, to make the relation possible. But when A interprets B to C, a triad of members (whereof, as in case of other relations, two or all three members may be wholly, or in part, identical) must exist in order to make the interpretation possible. Let illustrations show us how important this formal condition of interpretation may become.

When a process of conscious reflection goes on, a man may be said to interpret himself to himself. In this case, although but one personality, in the usual sense of the term, is in question, the relation is still really a triadic relation. And, in general, in such a case, the man who is said to be reflecting remembers some former promise or resolve of his own, or perhaps reads an old letter that he once wrote, or an entry in a diary. He then, at some present time, interprets this expression of his past self.

But, usually, he interprets this bit of his past self to his future self. "This," he says, "is what I meant when I made that promise." "This is what I wrote or recorded or promised." "Therefore," he continues, addressing his future self, "I am now committed to doing thus," "planning thus," and so on.

The interpretation in question still constitutes, therefore, a triadic relation. And there are three men present in and taking part in the interior conversation: the man of the past whose promises, notes, records, old letters, are interpreted; the present self who interprets them; and the future self to whom the interpretation is addressed.

Through the present self the past is so interpreted that its counsel is conveyed to the future self.

XII

The illustration just chosen has been taken from the supposed experience of an individual man. But the relations involved are capable of a far-reaching metaphysical generalization. For this generalization I cannot cite the authority of Peirce. I must deal with just this aspect of the matter in my own way.

The relations exemplified by the man who, at a given present moment, interprets his own past to his own future, are precisely analogous to the relations which exist when any past state of the world is, at any present moment, so linked, through a definite historical process, with the coming state of the world, that an intelligent observer who happened to be in possession of the facts could, were he present, interpret to a possible future observer the meaning of the past. Such interpretation might or might not involve definite predictions of future events. History or biography, physical or mental processes, might be in question; fate or free will, determinism or chance, might rule the region of the world which was under consideration. The most general distinctions of past, present, and future appear in a new light when considered with reference to the process of interpretation.

In fact, what our own inner reflection exemplifies is outwardly embodied in the whole world's history. For what we all mean by past time is a realm of events whose historical sense, whose records, whose lessons, we may now interpret, in so far as our memory and the documents furnish us the evidences for such interpretation. We may also observe that what we mean by future time is a realm of events which we view as more or less under the control of the present will of voluntary agents, so that it is worth while to give to ourselves, or to our fellows, counsel regarding this future. And so, wherever the world's processes are recorded, wherever the records are preserved, and wherever they influence in any way the future course of events, we may say that (at least in these parts of the world) the present potentially interprets the past to the future, and continues so to do *ad infinitum.*

Such, for instance, is the case when one studies the crust of a planet. The erosions and the deposits of a present geological period lay down the traces which, if read by a geologist, would interpret the past history of the planet's crust to the observers of future geological periods.

Thus the Colorado Cañon, in its present condition, is a geological section produced by a recent stream. Its walls record, in their stratification, a vast series of long-past changes. The geologist of the present may read these traces, and may interpret them for future geologists of our own age. But the present state of the Colorado Cañon, which will ere long pass away as the walls crumble, and as the continents rise or sink, will leave traces that may be used at some future time to interpret these now present conditions of the earth's crust to some still more advanced future, which will come to exist after yet other geological periods have passed away.

In sum, if we view the world as everywhere and always recording its own history, by processes of aging and weathering, or of evolution, or of stellar and nebular clusterings and streamings, we can simply define the time order, and its three regions, — past; present, future, — as an order of possible interpretation. That is, we can define the present as, potentially, the interpretation of the past to the future. The triadic structure of our interpretations is strictly analogous, both to the psychological and to the metaphysical structure of the world of time. And each of these structures can be stated in terms of the other.

This analogy between the relational structure of the whole time-process and the relations which are characteristic of any system of acts of interpretation seems to me to be worthy of careful consideration.

XIII

The observation of Peirce that interpretation is a process involving, from its very essence, a triadic relation, is thus, in any case, no mere logical formalism.

Psychologically speaking, the mental process which thus involves three members differs from perception and conception in three respects. First, interpretation is a conversation, and not a lonely enterprise. There is some one, in the realm of psychological happenings, who addresses some one. The one who addresses interprets some object to the one addressed. In the second place, the interpreted object is itself something which has the nature of a mental expression. Peirce uses the term "sign" to name this mental object which is interpreted. Thirdly, since the interpretation is a mental act, and is an act which is expressed, the interpretation itself is, in its turn, a Sign. This new sign calls for further interpretation. For the interpretation is addressed to somebody. And so, — at least in ideal, — the social process involved is endless. Thus wealthy, then, in its psychological consequences, is the formal character of a situation wherein any interpretation takes place.

Perception has its natural terminus in some object perceived; and therewith the process, as would seem, might end, were there nothing else in the world to perceive. Conception is contented, so to speak, with defining the universal type, or ideal form which chances to become an object of somebody's thought. In order to define a new universal, one needs a new act of thought whose occurrence seems, in so far, an arbitrary additional cognitive function. Thus both perception and conception are, so to speak, self-limiting processes. The wealth of their facts comes to them from without, arbitrarily.

But interpretation both requires as its basis the sign or mental expression which is to be interpreted, and calls for a further interpretation of its own act, just because it addresses itself to some third being. Thus interpretation is not only an essentially social process, but also a process which, when once initiated, can be terminated only by an external and arbitrary interruption, such as death or social separation. By itself, the process of interpretation calls, in ideal, for an infinite sequence of interpretations. For every interpretation, being addressed to somebody, demands interpretation from the one to whom it is addressed.

Thus the formal difference between interpretation on the one hand, and perception and conception on the other hand, is a difference involving endlessly wealthy possible psychological consequences.

Perception is indeed supported by the wealth of our sensory processes; and is therefore rightly said to possess an endless fecundity.

But interpretation lives in a world which is endlessly richer than the realm of perception. For its discoveries are constantly renewed by the inexhaustible resources of our social relations, while its ideals essentially demand, at every point, an infinite series of mutual interpretations in order to express what even the very least conversational effort, the least attempt to find our way in the life that we would interpret, involves.

Conception is often denounced, in our day, as "sterile." But perception, taken by itself, is intolerably lonesome. And every philosophy whose sole principle is perception invites us to dwell in a desolate wilderness where neither God nor man exists. For where either God or man is in question, interpretation is demanded. And interpretation, — even the simplest, even the most halting and trivial interpretation of our daily life, — seeks what eye hath not seen, and ear hath not heard, and what it hath not entered into the heart of man to conceive, — namely, the successful interpretation of somebody to somebody.

Interpretation seeks an object which is essentially spiritual. The abyss of abstract conception says of this object: It is not in me. The heaven of glittering immediacies which perception furnishes answers the quest by saying: It is not in me. Interpretation says: It is nigh thee, — even in thine heart; but shows us, through manifesting the very nature of the object to be sought, what general conditions must be met if any one is to interpret a genuine Sign to an understanding mind. And withal, interpretation seeks a city out of sight, the homeland where, perchance, we learn to understand one another.

XIV

Our first glimpse of Charles Peirce's neglected doctrine of the logic of signs and of interpretations necessarily gives us extremely inadequate impressions. But in pointing out the parallelism between the relational characters of the time-process and those of the process of interpretation, I have already shown that the questions at issue are neither merely intellectual, nor purely conceptual, and concern many matters which are confined neither to logic nor to descriptive psychology. As a fact, to conceive the cognitive process in terms of such a threefold division, and also in terms of such a triadic relation, as the division and the relation which Peirce brings to our attention, — to view cognition thus throws light, I believe, upon all the principal issues which are now before us.

Recent pragmatism, both in the form emphasized by James and (so far as I know) in all its other now prominent forms, depends upon conceiving two types of cognitive processes, perception and conception, as mutually opposed, and as in such wise opposed that conception merely defines the bank-notes, while only perception can supply the needed cash. In consequence of this dualistic view of the cognitive process, and in view of other considerations recently emphasized, the essential doctrine of pragmatism has come to include the two well-known theses: That truth is mutable; and that the sole criterion of the present state of the truth is to be found in the contents of particular perceptions.

Corresponding to this form of epistemology we have, in the metaphysic of Bergson, a doctrine of reality based upon the same dual classification of the cognitive processes, and upon the same preference for perception as against its supposed sole rival.

But if we review the facts in the new light which Peirce's views about interpretation enable us, I think, to use, we shall reach results, that, as I close, I may yet barely hint.

XV

Reality, so Bergson tells us, — Reality, which must be perceived just as artists perceive its passing data, and thereby teach us to perceive what we never saw before, — Reality is essentially change, flow, movement. In perceptual time, if you abstract from the material limitations which the present bondage of our intellect forces upon us, both present and past interpenetrate, and all is one ever present duration, consisting of endless qualitatively various but coalescing changes.

But a recognition of the existence, and a due understanding of the character of the process of interpretation, will show us, I believe, that the time-order, in its sense and interconnection, is known to us through interpretation, and is neither a conceptual nor yet a perceptual order. We learn about it through what is, in a sense, the conversation which the present, in the name of the remembered or presupposed past, addresses to the expected future, whenever we are interested in directing our own course of voluntary action, or in taking counsel with one another. Life may be a colloquy, or a prayer; but the life of a reasonable being is never a mere perception; nor a conception; nor a mere sequence of thoughtless deeds; nor yet an active process, however synthetic, wherein interpretation plays no part. Life is essentially, in its ideal, social. Hence interpretation is a necessary element of everything that, in life, has ideal value.

But when the time-process is viewed as an interpretation of the past to the future by means of our present acts of choice, then the divisions and the successions which are found in the temporal order are not, as Bergson supposes, due to a false translation of the perceived temporal flow into a spatial order. For every present deed interprets my future; and therefore divides my life into the region of what I have already done, and the region of what I have yet to accomplish. This division is due, not to the geometrical degeneration which Bergson refers to our intellect, but to one of the most significant features of the spiritual world,—namely, to the fact that we interpret all past time as irrevocable. So to interpret our past is the very foundation of all deliberate choice. But the irrevocable past changes no more. And the stupendous spiritual significance which this interpretation introduces into our view of our lives, of history, of nature, and of God, we have already had occasion to consider in the first part of this course. The philosophy of change, the perception of an universe where all is fluent, can be interpreted only through recognizing that the past returns not; that the deed once done is never to be recalled; that what has been done is at once the world's safest treasure, and its heaviest burden.

Whoever insists upon the mutability of truth, speaks in terms of the dual classification of cognitive processes. But let one learn to know that our very conception of our temporal experience, as of all happenings, is neither a conception nor a perception, but an interpretation. Let one note that every present judgment bearing upon future experience is indeed, as the pragmatists tell us, a practical activity. But let one also see that, for this very reason, every judgment, whose meaning is concrete and practical, so interprets past experience as to counsel a future deed. Let one consider that when my present judgment, addressing my future self, counsels: "Do this," this counsel, if followed, leads to an individual deed, which henceforth irrevocably stands on the score of my life, and can never be removed therefrom.

Hence, just as what is done cannot be undone, just so what is truly or falsely counselled by any concrete and practical judgment remains permanently true or false. For the deed which a judgment counsels remains forever done, when once it has been done.

XVI

Let me summarize the main results of this lecture:—

1. In addition to the world of conception and to the world of perception, we have to take account of a world of interpretation.

2. The features that distinguish from one another the three processes—perception, conception, and interpretation—have to do with their logical and formal characteristics, with their psychological motives and accompaniments, and with the objects to which they are directed.

3. Logically and formally considered, interpretation differs from perception and from conception by the fact that it involves relations which are essentially triadic.

4. Psychologically, interpretation differs from perception and from conception by the fact that it is, in its intent, an essentially social process. It accompanies every intelligent conversation. It is used whenever we acknowledge the being and the inner life of our fellow-men. It transforms our own inner life into a conscious interior conversation, wherein we interpret ourselves. Both of ourselves and of our neighbors we have no merely intuitive knowledge, no complete perception, and no adequate conception. Reflection is an effort at self-interpretation.

5. Both logically and psychologically, interpretation differs from perception and from conception in that each of these latter processes derives the wealth of its facts from a world which, at least in seeming, is external to itself. Were there but one object to perceive, and one universal to conceive, one act of perception and one of conception would be, in the abstract, possible and required. The need for new acts of perception and of conception seems to be, in so far, arbitrarily determined by the presence of new facts which are to be perceived or conceived. But interpretation, while always stimulated to fresh efforts by the inexhaustible wealth of the novel facts of the social world, demands, by virtue of its own nature, and even in the simplest conceivable case, an endless wealth of new interpretations. For every interpretation, as an expression of mental activity, addresses itself to a possible interpreter, and demands that it shall be, in its turn, interpreted. Therefore it is not the continuance, but the interruption, of the process of interpretation which appears to be arbitrary; and which seems to be due to sources and motives foreign to the act of interpretation.

6. Metaphysically considered, the world of interpretation is the world in which, if indeed we are able to interpret at all, we learn to acknowledge the being and the inner life of our fellow-men; and to understand the constitution of temporal experience, with its endlessly accumulating sequence of significant deeds. In this world of interpretation, of whose most general structure we have now obtained a glimpse, selves and communities may exist, past and future can be defined, and the realms of the spirit may find a place which neither barren conception nor the chaotic flow of interpenetrating perceptions could ever render significant.

7. Bergson has eloquently referred us to the artists, as the men whose office it is to teach us how to perceive. Let the philosophers, he tells us, learn from the methods of the artists. In reply we can only insist, in this place, that the sole office of the artists has always been to interpret. They address us, so as to interpret to us their own perceptions, and thereby their own lives and deeds. In turn, they call upon us to renew the endless life of the community of the spirits who interpret. The artists do not do their work for "nothing," nor yet for "pleasure." They do their work because they love the unity of spirit which, through their work, is brought into the life of mankind. The artists are in this respect not alone.

The prophets, the founders of religions, the leaders of mankind: they do not merely see; nor do they merely think; nor yet are they mere pragmatists hovering between abstract conceptions which they dislike, and particular experiences which they indeed desire, but so view that therein they find *only* the particular. Those for whom the sole contrast in the world of cognitions is that between conception and perception, stand in Faust's position. Their conceptions are indeed mere bank-notes. But alas! their perceptions are, at best, mere cash. So in desire they hasten to enjoyment, and in enjoyment pine to feel desire.

Such find indeed their "cash" of experience in plenty. But they never find what has created all the great religions, and all the deathless loyalties, and all the genuinely true insights of the human world, —namely, that interpretation of life which sends us across the borders both of our conceptual and of our perceptual life, to lay up treasures in other worlds, to interpret the meaning of the processes of time, to read the meaning of art and of life.

8. Do you ask what this process is which thus transcends both perception and conception, I answer that it is the process in which you engage whenever you take counsel with a friend, or look in the eyes of one beloved, or serve the cause of your life. This process it is which touches the heart of reality. Let the philosophers, then, endeavor to avoid "sterile" conceptions. Let them equally avoid those wanton revels in mere perception which are at present the bane of our art, of our literature, of our social ideals, and of our religion. Let the philosophers learn from those who teach us, as the true artists do, the art of interpretation.

A few fragmentary indications of the principles of this art we may hope, at the next time, to set forth upon the bases which Charles Peirce's theory has suggested.

XII

The Will to
Interpret

We have seen some of the contrasts whereby the three cognitive processes: Perception, Conception, and Interpretation, are distinguished from one another. Our next task is to become better acquainted with the work and the value of Interpretation.

I

In this undertaking we shall be guided by the special problems to which our lectures are devoted. The metaphysical inquiry concerning the nature and the reality of the community is still our leading topic. To this topic whatever we shall have to say about interpretation is everywhere subordinate. But, since, if I am right, interpretation is indeed a fundamental cognitive process, we shall need still further to illustrate its nature and its principal forms. Every apparent digression from our main path will quickly lead us back to our central issues. Interpretation is, once for all, the main business of philosophy.

The present lecture will include two stages of movement towards our goal. First, we shall study the elementary psychology of the process of interpretation. Secondly, we shall portray the ideal that guides a truth-loving interpreter. The first of these inquiries will concern topics which are both familiar and neglected. The second part of our lecture will throw light upon the ethical problems with which our study of the Christian ideas has made us acquainted. At the close of the lecture our preparation for an outline of the metaphysics of interpretation will be completed.

II

I have called interpretation an essentially social cognitive process; and such, in fact, it is. Man is an animal that interprets; and therefore man lives in communities, and depends upon them for insight and for salvation.

But the elementary psychological forms in which interpretation appears find a place in our lives whether or no we are in company; just as a child can sing when alone, although singing is, on the whole, a social activity. We shall need to consider how an interpreter conducts his mental processes, even when he is taking no explicit account of other minds than his own.

In looking for the psychological foundations of interpretation, we shall be directed by Charles Peirce's formal definition of the mental functions which are involved. Wherever an interpretation takes place, however little it seems to be an explicit social undertaking, a triadic cognitive process can be observed. Let us look, then, for elementary instances of such triadic processes.

In the earliest of the logical essays to which, at the last time, I referred, Charles Peirce pointed out that every instance of conscious and explicit Comparison involves an elementary form of interpretation. This observation of Peirce's enables us to study interpretation in some of its simplest shapes, relieved of the complications which our social efforts to communicate with other minds usually involve.

Yet, even in this rudimentary form, interpretation involves the motives, which, upon higher levels, make its work so wealthy in results, and so significant in its contrasts with perception and conception.

III

The most familiar instances of the mental process known as Comparison seem, at first sight, to consist of a consciousness of certain familiar dyadic relations, — relations of similarity and difference. Red contrasts with green; sound breaks in upon silence; one sensory quality collides, as it were, with another. The "shock of difference" awakens our attention. In other cases, an unexpected similarity of colors and tones attracts our interest. Or perhaps the odors of two flowers, or the flavors of two fruits, resemble one the other. Pairs of perceived objects are, in all these cases, in question. We express our observations in such judgments as: "A resembles B;" "D is unlike E."

Now Peirce's view of the nature of comparison depends upon noticing that, familiar as such observations of similarity and dissimilarity may be, no one of them constitutes the whole of any complete act of comparison. Comparison, in the fuller sense of the word, takes place when one asks or answers the question: What constitutes the difference between A and B?" "*Wherein* does A resemble B?" "*Wherein* consists their distinction?" Let me first illustrate such a question in a case wherein the answer is easy.

If you write a word with your own hand, and hold it up before a mirror, your own handwriting becomes more or less unintelligible to you, unless you are already accustomed to read or to write mirror-script. Suppose, however, that instead of writing words yourself, you let some one else show you words already written. And suppose, further, that two words have been written side by side on the same sheet of paper, neither of them by your own hand. Suppose one of them to have been written upright, while the other is the counterpart of the first, except that it is the first turned upside down, or else is the first in mirror-script. If, without knowing how these words have been produced, you look at them, you can directly observe that the two written words differ in appearance, and that they also have a close resemblance. But, unless you were already familiar with the results of inverting a handwriting or of observing it in a mirror, you could not thus directly observe wherein consist the similarities and the differences of the two words which lie before you on the paper.

Since you are actually familiar with mirror-script, and with the results of turning a sheet of paper upside down, you will indeed no doubt be able to name the difference of the two supposed words. But in order to compare the two words thus presented side by side on the same sheet of paper, and to tell wherein they are similar and wherein they differ, you need what Peirce calls a mediating idea, or what he also calls "a third," which, as he phrases the matter, shall "represent" or "interpret" one of the two written words to, or in terms of, the other. You use such a "third" idea when you say, "This word is the mirror-script representative of that word." For now the difference is interpreted.

Thus a complete act of comparison involves such a "third," such a "mediating" image or idea,—such an "interpreter." By means of this "third" you so compare a "first" object with a "second" as to make clear to yourself wherein consists the similarity and the difference between the second and the first. Comparison must be triadic in order to be both explicit and complete. Likenesses and differences are the signs that a comparison is needed. But these signs are not their own interpretation.

Let us observe another instance of the same general type. One may be long acquainted with the difference between his own right and left hands before one learns to interpret this difference, and so to complete one's comparison, in terms of the third idea that the one hand is a more or less imperfect mirror-image of the other hand, the imperfections being due to the lack of symmetry in our bodily structure.

Still another familiar instance of comparison will show how needful it is to choose the right "third" in order to complete one's view of the matter. One may long have observed that a friend's face, when seen in a mirror, contrasts with the same face if seen apart from the mirror. Yet it may be very hard for a given person to tell why this difference exists, or wherein it consists. I have asked the question of various intelligent and observant people, who could only reply: "It is true that in general a man's face, as I see it before me, does not perfectly resemble that man's face as it appears when I look at it in a mirror. But I cannot define the reason for this difference, or tell wherein the difference consists." The answer to the question is that, since the features of a human face are usually, in their finer details, more or less unsymmetrically disposed with reference to the vertical axis of the body, the mirror picture, even of a fairly regular countenance, must be altered to suit these vertical asymmetries. The idea of the vertical asymmetries is here the needed "third" which interprets the difference between the man's face when seen in the mirror and when seen out of the mirror.

A lady who had passed part of her life in Australia, and part in

England, once told me that, for years, she had never been able to understand the difference which, to her eyes, existed between the full moon as seen in England and as observed by her during her years in Australia. At last she found the right mediating idea, when she came to notice how Orion also gradually became partially inverted during her journeys from English latitudes to those of the far southern seas. For the full moon, as she thus came to know, must be subject to similar apparent inversions; and this was the reason why the "man in the moon" had therefore been undiscoverable when she had heretofore looked for him in Australian skies.

IV

When processes of comparison grow complicated, new "third" terms or "mediators" may be needed at each stage of one's undertaking. So it is when a literary parallel between two poets or two statesmen is in question. Now one and now another trait or event or fortune or deed may stand out as the mediating idea. But always, in such parallels, it is by means of the use of a "third" that each act of comparison is made possible,—whether the case in question be simple or complex. And the mediator plays each time the part which Peirce first formally defined.

Let there arise the problem of drawing a literary parallel between Shakespeare and Dante. The task appears hopelessly complex and indeterminate until, perhaps, the place which the sonnet occupied in the creative activity of each poet comes to our minds. Then indeed, although the undertaking is still vastly complicated, it is no longer quite so hopeless. If "with this key Shakespeare unlocked his heart," yet held fast its deepest mysteries; while Dante accompanied each of the sonnets of the *Vita Nuova* with a comment and an explanation, yet left unspoken what most fascinates us in the supernatural figure of his beloved,—then "the sonnet," viewed as an idea of a poetical form, mediates between our ideas of the two poets, and represents or interprets each of these ideas to the other.

This last example suggests an endless wealth of complexities. And the interpretation in question is also endlessly inadequate to our demands. But on its highest levels, as in its simplest instances, the process of explicit comparison is thus triadic, and to notice this fact is, for the purpose of our study of comparison, illuminating.

For when we merely set pairs of objects before us, and watch their resemblances and differences, we soon lose ourselves in mazes.

Yet even when the mazes are indeed not to be penetrated by any skill, still a triadic comparison is much more readily guided towards the light. "How does A differ from C?" If you can reply to this question by saying that, by means of B, A can be altogether transformed into C, or can, at least, be brought into a close resemblance to C, then the comparison of A to C is made definite.

Let me choose still one more illustration of such a comparison. This time the illustration shall not come from the literary realm; yet it shall be more complex than is the instance of the comparison between a written word and its image in the mirror.

If you cut a strip of paper,—perhaps an inch wide and ten inches long,—you can bring the two ends together and fasten them with glue. The result will be a ring-strip of paper, whose form is of a type very familiar in case of belts, finger-rings, and countless other objects. But this form can be varied in an interesting way. Before bringing the ends of the strip together, let one end of the paper be turned 180°. Holding the twisted end of the strip fast, glue it to the other. There now results an endless strip of paper having in it a single twist. Lay side by side an ordinary ring-strip that has no twist, and a ring-strip of paper that has been made in the way just indicated. The latter strip has a single twist in it. Hereupon ask a person who has not seen you make the two ring-strips, to compare them, and to tell you wherein they agree and wherein they differ.

To your question an ordinary observer, to whom this new form of ring-strip is unfamiliar, will readily answer that they obviously differ because one of them has no twist in it, while the other certainly has some kind of twist belonging to its structure. So far the one whom you question indeed makes use of a "third" idea. But this idea probably remains, so far, vague in his mind, and it will take your uninformed observer some time to make his comparison at all complete and explicit.

In order to aid him in his task, you may hereupon call his attention to the further fact that the ring-strip which contains the single twist has two extraordinary properties. It has, namely, but one side; and it also has but one edge. The mention of this fact will at first perplex the uninitiated observer. But when he has taken the trouble to study the new form, he will find that the idea of a "one-sided strip of paper" enables him to compare the new and the old form, and to interpret his idea of the new ring-form to his old idea of an ordinary ring such as has no twist, and possesses two sides.

V

In all the cases of explicit comparison which we have just considered, what takes place has, despite the endless varieties of circumstance, an uniform character.

Whoever compares has before him what we have called two distinct ideas; perhaps his ideas of these two printed or written words; or again, his ideas of these two ring-strips of paper; or, in another instance, his ideas of Dante and of Shakespeare.

And the term "idea" is used, in the present discussion, in the sense which James and other representative pragmatists have made familiar in current discussion. Let us then hold clearly in mind this definition of the term "idea." For we shall even thereby be led to note facts which will lead us beyond what this definition emphasizes.

An idea, in this sense, is a more or less practical and active process, a "leading" as James calls it, whereby some set of conceptions and perceptions tend to be brought into desirable connections. An idea may consist mainly of some effort to characterize the data of perception through the use of fitting conceptions. Or, again, an idea may be a prediction of future perceptions. Or, an idea may be an active seeking for a way to translate conceptual "bank-notes" into perceptual cash. In any one idea, either the perceptual or the conceptual elements may, at any one moment, predominate. If the conceptual element is too marked for our purposes, the idea stands in need of perceptual fulfilment. If the perceptual element is too rich for our momentary interests, the idea needs further conceptual clarification. In any case, however, according to this view, the motives of an idea are practical, and the constituents of an idea are either the data of perception, or the conceptual processes whereby we characterize or predict or pursue such data.

But when, in Peirce's sense of the word, we have to make an explicit comparison, we have before us two distinct and contrasting ideas. It is their distinctness, it is their contrast, which determines our task. And these ideas involve, in general, not only different perceptual and different conceptual constituents, but also different and sometimes conflicting "leadings," different and sometimes mutually clashing interests, various and mutually estranged motives, activities, or constructions. These two ideas may contrast as do two forms of art. Or they may stand out the one over against the other as if they were two geometrical structures. They may collide as do two warring passions. They may first meet as simple strangers in our inner world. Their relations may resemble those of plaintiff and defendant in a suit at law. Or they may be as interestingly remote from one another as are the spiritual realms of two great poets. In such endlessly various fashions may the two ideas come before us.

The essential fact for our present study is that, in case of the comparisons which Peirce discusses, the problem, whether you call it a theoretical or a practical problem, is not that of linking percepts to their fitting concepts, nor that of paying the bank bills of conception in the gold of the corresponding perceptions. On the contrary, it is the problem either of arbitrating the conflicts; or of bringing to mutual understanding the estrangements; or of uniting in some community the separated lives of these two distinct ideas, — of ideas which, when left to themselves, decline to coalesce or to coöperate, or to enter into one life.

This problem, in the cases of comparison with which Peirce deals, is solved through a new act. For this act originality and sometimes even genius may be required. This new act consists in the invention or discovery of some third idea, distinct from both the ideas which are to be compared. This third idea, when once found, interprets one of the ideas which are the objects of the comparison, and interprets it to the other, or in the light of the other. What such interpretation means, the instances already considered have in part made clear. But the complexity and the significance of the processes involved require a further study. And this further study may here be centred about the question: What is gained by the sort of comparison which Peirce thus characterizes? And, since we have said that all such comparison involves an activity of interpreting one idea in the light of another, we may otherwise state our question thus: What, in these cases of comparison, is the innermost aim of the Will to Interpret which all these processes of comparison manifest?

VI

The rhythm of the Hegelian dialectic, wherein thesis, antithesis, and higher synthesis play their familiar parts, will here come to the minds of some who follow my words; and you may ask wherein Peirce's processes of comparison and interpretation differ from those dialectical movements through division into synthesis, which Hegel long since used as the basis of his philosophy. I reply at once that

Peirce's theory of comparison, and of the mediating idea or "third" which interprets, is, historically speaking, a theory not derived from Hegel, by whom at the time when he wrote these early logical papers, Peirce had been in no notable way influenced. I reply, further, that Peirce's concept of interpretation defines an extremely general process, of which the Hegelian dialectical triadic process is a very special case. Hegel's elementary illustrations of his own processes are ethical and historical. Peirce's theory of comparison is quite as well illustrated by purely mathematical as by explicitly social instances. There is no essential inconsistency between the logical and psychological motives which lie at the basis of Peirce's theory of the triad of interpretation, and the Hegelian interest in the play of thesis, antithesis, and higher synthesis. But Peirce's theory, with its explicitly empirical origin and its very exact logical working out, promises new light upon matters which Hegel left profoundly problematic.

Returning, however, to those illustrations of Peirce's theory of comparison which I have already placed before you, let us further consider the motives which make a comparison of distinct and contrasting ideas significant for the one who compares.

An idea, as I have said, is, in James's sense, a practical "leading." An idea, if, in James's sense, successful, and if successfully employed, leads through concepts to the desirable or to the corresponding percepts. But a comparison of ideas — that, too, is no doubt an active process. To what does it lead? It leads, as we have seen, to a new, to a third, to an interpreting idea. And what is this new idea? Is it "cash," or has it only "credit-value"? What does it present to our view? What does it bring to our treasury?

One must for the first answer this question in a very old-fashioned way. The new, the third, the interpreting idea, in these elementary cases of comparison, shows us, as far as it goes, ourselves, and also creates in us a new grade of clearness regarding what we are and what we mean. First, I repeat, the new or third idea shows us ourselves, as we are. Next, it also enriches our world of self-consciousness. It at once broadens our outlook and gives our mental realm definiteness and self-control. It teaches one of our ideas what another of our ideas means. It tells us how to know our right hand from the left; how to connect what comes to us in fragments; how to live as if life had some coherent aim. All this is indeed, thus far, very elementary information about what one gains by being able to hold three ideas at once in mind. But, in our own day, such information is important information. For our age, supposing that the contrast between perception and conception exhausts the possible types of cognitive processes, is accustomed to listen to those who teach us that self-knowledge also must be either intuitive (and, in that case, merely fluent and transient) or else conceptual (and, in that case, abstract and sterile).

But a dual antithesis between perceptual and conceptual knowledge is once for all inadequate to the wealth of the facts of life. When you accomplish an act of comparison, the knowledge which you attain is neither merely conceptual, nor merely perceptual, nor yet merely a practically active synthesis of perception and conception. It is a third type of knowledge. It interprets. It surveys from above. It is an attainment of a larger unity of consciousness. It is a conspectus. As the tragic artist looks down upon the many varying lives of his characters, and sees their various motives not interpenetrating, but coöperating, in the dramatic action which constitutes his creation, — so any one who compares distinct ideas, and discovers the third or mediating idea which interprets the meaning of one in the light of the other, thereby discovers, or invents, a realm of conscious unity which constitutes the very essence of the life of reason.

Bergson, in his well-known portrayal, has glorified instinct in its contrast with the intellect. The intellect, as he holds, is a mere user of tools. Its tools are concepts. It uses them in its practical daily work to win useful percepts. It loves to be guided in its daily industries by rigid law. It is therefore most at home in the realm of mechanism and of death. Life escapes its devices. Its concepts are essentially inadequate. Instinct, on the contrary, so far as man still preserves that filmy cloud of luminous instinct and of intuition which, in Bergson's opinion, constitutes the most precious resource of genius, perceives, and sympathizes, and so comes in touch with reality.

That this account of the cognitive process is inadequate, both the artist and the prophets combine with the scientific observers of nature, with the mathematicians, and with the great constructive statesmen, to show us. Comparison is the instrument of what one may call, according to one's pleasure, either the observant reason, or the rational intuition whereby the world's leading minds have always been guided. And it is comparison, it is interpretation, which teaches us how to deal with the living, with the significant, and with the genuinely real.

Darwin, for instance, as a naturalist, saw, compared, and mediated. We all know how the leading ideas of Malthus furnished the mediating principle, the third, whereby Darwin first came to conceive how the contrasting ideas with which his hypotheses had to deal could be brought into unity. And that such comparison is peculiarly adapted to deal with the phenomena of life, let not only the genesis of Darwin's ideas, but the place of the process of comparison in the development of all the organic sciences, show.

If we turn to the other extreme of the world of human achievement, in order to learn what is the sovereign cognitive process, we shall find the same answer. For let us ask, — By means of what insight did Amos the prophet meet the religious problems of his own people and of his own day? He faced tragic contrasts, moral, religious, and political. Warring ideas were before him, — ideas, each of which sought its own percepts, through its own concepts of God, of worship, and of success. But Amos introduced into the controversies of his time the still tragic, but inspiring and mediating, idea of the God who, as he declared, delights not in sacrifices but in righteousness. And by this one stroke of religious genius the prophet directed the religious growth of the centuries that were to follow.

Think over the burial psalm, or the Pauline chapters on Charity and the Resurrection, if you would know what part comparison and mediation play in the greatest expressions of the religious consciousness. Remember Lear or the Iliad, if you wish to recall the functions of contrast and of mediation in poetry. Let the Sistine Madonna or Beethoven's Fifth Symphony illustrate the same process in other forms of the artistic consciousness.

If once you have considered a few such instances, then, summing up their familiar lessons, you may note that in none of these cases is it conception, in none of them is it bare perception, least of all is it inarticulate intuition, which has won for us the greatest discoveries, the incomparable treasures in science, in art, or in religion.

The really creative insight has come from those who first compared and then mediated, who could first see two great ideas at once, and then find the new third idea which mediated between them, and illumined.

We often use the word "vision" for this insight which looks down upon ideas as from above, and discovers the "third," thereby uniting what was formerly estranged. If by the word "intuition" one chooses to mean this grade of insight, then one may indeed say that creative mental prowess depends, in general, upon such intuition. But such intuition is no mere perception. It is certainly not conception. And the highest order of genius depends upon reaching the stage of Peirce's "third" type of ideas. Comparison, leading to the discovery of that which mediates and solves, and to the vision of unity, is the psychological basis of poetry, as Shakespeare wrote, and of such prophecy as Paul praised when he estimated the spiritual gifts. Comparison, then, and interpretation constitute the cognitive function whereby we deal with life. Instinct and bare perception, left to themselves, can never reach this level.

VII

When we consider the inner life of the individual man, the Will to Interpret appears, then, as the will to be self-possessed. One who compares his own ideas, views them as from above. He aims to pass from blind "leadings" to coherent insight and to resolute self-guidance. What one wins as the special object of one's insight depends, in such cases, upon countless varying psychological conditions, and upon one's success in finding or in inventing suitable mediators for the interpretation of one idea in the light of another. It may therefore appear as if in this realm of interior comparisons, where the objects compared are pairs of ideas, and where results of comparison consist in the invention of a third, there could be no question of attaining fixed or absolute truth. If anywhere pragmatism could be decisively victorious; if anywhere the purely relative and transient would seem in possession of the field,—one might suppose that comparison would constantly furnish us with instances of relative, shifting, and fluent truth.

As a fact, however, this is not the case. Comparison, which is so powerful an instrument in dealing with life, and with the fluent and the personal, is also perfectly capable of bringing us into the presence of the exact and of the necessary. All depends upon what ideas are compared, and upon the purpose for which they are compared, and upon the skill with which the vision of unity is attained.

Let the comparison of the two ring-strips of paper show what I here have in mind. The difference between a ring-strip which contains a single twist, and another which is constructed in the usual way, seems at first sight to be both insignificant and inexact. A closer study shows that the geometry of surfaces that possess but a single side can be developed into as exact a branch of pure mathematics as you can mention. The development in question would depend upon assuming, quite hypothetically, a few simple principles which are suggested, although not indeed capable of being proved, by experience of the type which recent pragmatism has well analyzed. The branch of pure mathematics in question would consist of deductions from these few simple principles. The deductions would interpret these principles, viewed in some sort of unity and compared together.

But recent pragmatism has not well analyzed the process whereby, in pure mathematics, the consequences which follow from a set of exactly stated hypotheses are determined. This process, the genuine process of deduction, depends upon a series of ideal experiments. These experiments are performed by means of putting together ideas, two and two, by comparing the ideas that are thus brought together, by discovering mediators, and by reading the results of the combination. This process may lead to perfectly exact results which are absolutely true.

I know of no writer who has better or more exactly analyzed the way in which such ideal experiments can lead to novel and precise results than Peirce has done. His analysis of the deductive process was first made a good while since, and anticipated results which Mr. Bertrand Russell and others have since reached by other modes of procedure.

Peirce has shown that, when you interpret your combinations of ideas through ideal experiments, using, for instance, diagrams and symbols as aids, the outcome may be a truth as exact as the ideas compared are themselves exact. It may also be in your own experience as novel a result as your ideal experiment is novel. It may also be an absolute and immutable truth.

What you discover, in a case of deduction, is not that certain conclusions are, in themselves, considered true, but that they follow from, that they are implied by, certain hypothetically assumed premises. But a discovery that certain premises imply a certain conclusion, is the discovery of a fact. This fact may be found, not by perception, nor by conception, but by interpretation. None the less, it is a fact and it may be momentous.

It is customary to imagine that such a deductive process can get out of given premises nothing novel, but only (as people often say)— only what was already present in the premises. This customary view of deduction is incorrect. As Peirce repeatedly pointed out (long before any other writer had explicitly dealt with the matter), you can write out upon a very few sheets of paper all the principles which are actually used as the fundamental hypotheses that lie at the basis of those branches of pure mathematics which have thus far been developed. Yet the logical consequences which follow from these few mathematical hypotheses are so numerous that every year a large octavo volume in fine print is needed to contain merely the titles, and very brief abstracts, of the technical papers containing novel results which have been, during that year, published as researches in pure mathematics.

The mathematical papers in question embody, in general, consequences already implied by the few fundamental hypotheses which I have just mentioned. An infinite wealth of still unknown consequences of the same principles remains yet to be explored and stated. All of these consequences can be won, in pure mathematics, by a purely deductive procedure.

Thus endlessly wealthy, thus possessed of an inexhaustible fecundity, is the genuine deductive process. Peirce long ago showed why. And while the mathematical procedure which is in question cannot here be further discussed, it is enough for our present purpose to indicate why this fecundity of deduction exists.

VIII

Deduction, in the real life of the exact sciences, is a process that recent pragmatism has no means of describing, simply because recent pragmatism is the prey of the dual classification of the cognitive processes, and views what it calls the "workings" of ideas merely in terms of the relations between conceptions and perceptions,—between "credit-values" and "cash-values."

Pragmatism, as James defined it, regards an idea as a "leading," whereby one pursues or seeks particulars; and whereby one sometimes obtains, and sometimes fails to obtain, the "cash-values" which one aims to get. Such a doctrine has no place for the understanding of what happens when, looking down as it were from above, one compares two ideas, and looks for a mediating idea. But just this is what happens in all cases of explicit comparison.

Now in the individual case, an interpretation, a mediating idea, may come to mind through almost any play of association, or as the result of almost any degree of skill in invention, or as the outcome either of serious or of playful combinations. In consequence, an interpretation may prove to be, in the single case, of purely relative and momentary truth and value.

But this, on the other hand, need not be the fortune of interpretation. The results of a comparison may express absolute truths,—truths which once seen can never be reversed. This absoluteness itself may be due to either one of two reasons.

In pure mathematics, a deduction, if correct at all, leads to an absolutely correct and irrevocably true discovery of a relation of implication between exactly stated premises and some conclusion. Deduction does this because deduction results from a comparison, and because the ideas compared may be, and in pure mathematics are, exact enough to suggest, at some moment, to the observant reasoner, an interpretation which, if it applies at all, applies universally to every pair of ideas identical in meaning with the pair of ideas here compared.

The act of comparison may be momentary, and may even be as an event, an accident. The inventive watcher of his own ideas may have been led to his deduction by whatever motive you please. But the interpretation, once discovered, may nevertheless represent a truth which is absolute precisely *because* it is hypothetical. For the assertion: "P implies Q," or "If P, then Q," is an assertion about a matter of fact. And this assertion, if true at all, is always and irrevocably true about the same pair of ideas or propositions: P and Q.

Or again, the result of an interpretation may be absolutely true, because, for whatever reason, the interpretation in question counsels the one who makes the interpretation to do some determinate and individual deed. This deed may be such as to accomplish, at the moment when it is done, some ideally valuable result. But deeds once done are irrevocable. If, by interpreting your ideas in a certain way, at a certain moment, you have been led to do a worthy deed,—then the interpretation remains as irrevocably true as the good deed remains irrevocably done.

The principle, then, relating to the value and to the truth of one's acts of interior and conscious comparison, is that they express an insight which surveys, as from above, an unity wherein are combined various ideas. These ideas, as they first come, are pragmatic leadings which may be mutually estranged, or mutually hostile, or widely contrasted, or intimately interconnected. But, whatever the ideas may have been before they were compared,—as a result of the comparison of the two ideas, one of them is interpreted in the light of the other. The interpretation may possess all the exactness of mathematics, or all the transiency of a chance observation of the play of one's inner life. It may result in Paul's vision of the charity that never faileth, ruling supreme over the contrasts and the bickerings of passing passion; or it may solve a problem of comparative natural history or of comparative philology. Whatever the varieties of the cases in question, comparison can occur, and can reach truth, simply because we are wider than any of our ideas, and can win a vision which shall look down upon our own inner warfare, and upon our own former self-estrangements, as well as upon our own inner contrasts of exact definition. This vision observes not data of sense and not mere abstract concepts. Nor does it consist simply in our pragmatic leadings, and in their successes and failures. It observes what may interpret ideas to other ideas; as prophets and poets interpret to us what otherwise would remain, in seeming, hopelessly various and bewilderingly strange. It is not more intuition that we want. It is such interpretation which alone can enlighten and guide and significantly inspire. Upon the comparisons which thus interpret, our spiritual triumphs depend. Such triumphs are not merely the pragmatic successes of single ideas. They are the attainment of mastery over life.

IX

Our lengthy study of comparison and interpretation, as they are present in the inner life of the individual man, has prepared us for a new view of the social meaning of the Will to Interpret. Here I must once more take a temporary leave of Peirce's guidance, and trust to my own resources.

One who compares a pair of his own ideas may attain, if he is successful, that vision of unity, that grade of self-possession, which we have now illustrated. But one who undertakes to interpret his neighbor's ideas is in a different position.

In general, as we have seen, an interpreter, in his social relations with other men, deals with two different minds, neither of which he identifies with his own. His interpretation is a "third" or mediating idea. This "third" is aroused in the interpreter's mind through signs which come to him from the mind that he interprets. He addresses this "third" to the mind to which he interprets the first. The psychology of the process of social interpretation, so far as that process goes on in the interpreter's individual mind, is identical with that psychology of comparison which we have now outlined. Nobody can interpret, unless the idea which he interprets has become more or less clearly and explicitly one of his own ideas, and unless he compares it with another idea which is, in some sense, his own.

But, from the point of view of the interpreter, the essential difference between the case where he is interpreting the mind of one of his neighbors to the mind of another neighbor, and the case wherein he is comparing two ideas of his own, is a difference in the clearness of vision which is, under human conditions, attainable.

When I compare two ideas of my own, the luminous self-possession which then, for a time, may come to be mine, forms for me an ideal of success in interpretation. This ideal I can attain only at moments. But these moments set a model for all my interpretations to follow.

When I endeavor to interpret my neighbor's mind, my interpretation has to remain remote from its goal. The luminous vision of the results of comparison comes to me, at best, only partially and with uncertainty. My neighbor's ideas I indeed in a measure grasp, and compare with other ideas, and interpret; but, as I do this, I see through a glass darkly. Only those ideas whose comparisons with other ideas, and whose resulting triadic interpretations I can view face to face, can appear to me to have become in a more intimate and complete sense my own individual ideas. When I possess certain ideas sufficiently to enable me to seek for their interpretation, but so that, try as I will, I can never clearly survey, as from above, the success of any of my attempted interpretations,—then these ideas remain, from my own point of view, ideas that never become wholly my own. Therefore these relatively alien ideas can be interpreted at all only by using the familiar hypothesis that they belong to the self of some one else. Under ordinary social conditions this other mind is viewed as the mind of my neighbor. Neither of my neighbor nor of myself have I any direct intuition. But of my own ideas I can hope to win the knowledge which the most successful comparisons exemplify. Of my neighbor's ideas I can never win, under human conditions, any interpretation but one which remains hypothetical, and which is never observed, under these human conditions, as face to face with its own object, or with the idea of the other neighbors to whom the interpretation is addressed.

The Will to Interpret is, in our social relations, guided by a purpose which we are now ready to bring into close relations with the most significant of all the ethical ideals which, in our foregoing lectures, we have portrayed.

The interpreter, the mind to which he addresses his interpretation, the mind which he undertakes to interpret, — all these appear, in our explicitly human and social world, as three distinct selves, — sundered by chasms which, under human conditions, we never cross, and contrasting in their inner lives in whatever way the motives of men at any moment chance to contrast.

The Will to Interpret undertakes to make of these three selves a Community. In every case of ideally serious and loyal effort truly to interpret this is the simplest, but, in its deepest motives, the most purely spiritual of possible communities. Let us view that simple and ideal community as the interpreter himself views it, precisely in so far as he is sincere and truth-loving in his purpose as interpreter.

X

I, the interpreter, regard you, my neighbor, as a realm of ideas, of "leadings," of meanings, of pursuits, of purposes. This realm is not wholly strange and incomprehensible to me. For at any moment, in my life as interpreter, I am dependent upon the results of countless previous efforts to interpret. The whole past history of civilization has resulted in that form and degree of interpretation of you and of my other fellow-men which I already possess, at any instant when I begin afresh the task of interpreting your life or your ideas. You are to me, then, a realm of ideas which lie outside of the centre which my will to interpret can momentarily illumine with the clearest grade of vision. But I am discontent with my narrowness and with your estrangement. I seek unity with you. And since the same will to interpret you is also expressive of my analogous interests in all my other neighbors, what I here and now specifically aim to do is this: I mean to interpret you to somebody else, to some other neighbor, who is neither yourself nor myself. Three of us, then, I seek to bring into the desired unity of interpretation.

Now if I could succeed in interpreting you to another man as fully as, in my clearest moments, I interpret one of my ideas to another, my process of interpretation would simply reduce to a conscious comparison of ideas. I should then attain, as I succeeded in my interpretation, a luminous vision of your ideas, of my own, and of the ideas of the one to whom I interpret you. This vision would look down, as it were, from above. In the light of it, we, the selves now sundered by the chasms of the social world, should indeed not inter-penetrate. For our functions as the mind interpreted, the mind to whom the other is interpreted, and the interpreter, would remain as distinct as now they are. There would be no melting together, no blending, no mystic blur, and no lapse into mere intuition. But for me the vision of the successful interpretation would simply be the attainment of my own goal as interpreter. This attainment would as little confound our persons as it would divide our substance. We should remain, for me, many, even when viewed in this unity.

Yet this vision, if I could win it, would constitute an event where-in your will to be interpreted would also be fulfilled. For if you are indeed ready to accept my service as interpreter, you even now pos-sess this will to be interpreted. And if there exists the one to whom I can interpret you, that other also wills that you should be interpreted to him, and that I should be the interpreter.

If, then, I am worthy to be an interpreter at all, we three,—you, my neighbor, whose mind I would fain interpret,—you, my kindly listener, to whom I am to address my interpretation,—we three constitute a Community. Let us give to this sort of community a technical name. Let us call it a Community of Interpretation.

The form of such a community is determinate.

One goal lies before us all, one event towards which we all direct our efforts when we take part in this interpretation. This ideal event is a goal, unattainable under human social conditions, but definable, as an ideal, in terms of the perfectly familiar experience which every successful comparison of ideas involves. It is a goal towards which we all may work together: you, when you give me the signs that I am to interpret; our neighbor, when he listens to my interpretation; I, when I devote myself to the task.

This goal:—Our individual experience of our successful compar-isons of our own ideas shows us wherein it consists, and that it is no goal which an abstract conception can define in terms of credit-values, and that it is also no goal which a possible perception can ren-der to me in the cash of any set of sensory data. Yet it is a goal which each of us can accept as his own. I can at present aim to approach that goal through plans, through hypotheses regarding you which can be inductively tested. I can view that goal as a common future event. We can agree upon that goal. And herewith I interpret not only you as the being whom I am to interpret, but also myself as in ideal the interpreter who aims to approach the vision of the unity of precisely this community. And you, and my other neighbor to whom I address my interpretation, can also interpret yourselves accordingly.

The conditions of the definition of our community will thus be perfectly satisfied. We shall be many selves with a common ideal future event at which we aim. Without essentially altering the nature of our community, our respective offices can be, at our pleasure, interchanged. You, or my other neighbor, can at any moment assume the function of interpreter; while I can pass to a new position in the new community. And yet, we three shall constitute as clearly as before a Community of Interpretation. The new community will be in a perfectly definite relation to the former one; and may grow out of it by a process as definite as is every form of conscious interpretation.

Thus there can arise, in our community, no problem regarding the one and the many, the quest and the goal, the individual who approaches the goal by one path or by another,—no question to which the definition of the community of interpretation will not at once furnish a perfectly precise answer.

Such an answer will be based upon the perfectly fundamental triadic relation which is essential to every process of interpretation, whether such process takes place within the inner life of an individual human being, or goes on in the world of ordinary social intercourse.

XI

Thus, then, if I assume for the moment the rôle of an interpreter, I can define my office, my Community of Interpretation, and my place in that community.

It will be observed that the sort of truth which, as interpreter, I seek, cannot be stated in terms as simple as those with which the current pragmatism is satisfied. My interpretation, if I offer to our common neighbor any interpretation of your mind, will of course be an idea of my own,—namely, precisely that "third" idea which I contribute to our community as my interpretation of you. And no doubt I shall desire to make as sure as I can that this idea of mine "works." But no data of my individual perception can ever present to me the "workings" which I seek.

For I want my interpretation of you to our neighbor to be such as you would accept and also such as our neighbor would comprehend, were each of us already in the position of the ideal observer from above, whose vision of the luminous unity of my interpretation and its goal I am trying to imitate whenever I try to interpret your mind.

Thus, from the outset, the idea which I offer as my interpretation of your mind, is offered not for the sake of, or in the pursuit of, any individual or private perception of my own, either present or expected or possible. I am not looking for workings that could conceivably be rendered in my perceptual terms. I am ideally aiming at an ideal event,—the spiritual unity of our community. I can define that unity in perfectly empirical terms; because I have compared pairs of ideas which were my own, and have discovered their mediating third idea. But I do not expect to perceive that unity as any occurrence in my own individual life, or as any working of one of my own personal ideas. In brief, I have to define the truth of my interpretation of you in terms of what the ideal observer of all of us would view as the unity which he observed. This truth cannot be defined in merely pragmatic terms.

In a community thus defined, the interpreter obviously assumes, in a highly significant sense, the chief place. For the community is one of interpretation. Its goal is the ideal unity of insight which the interpreter would possess were these who are now his neighbors transformed into ideas of his own which he compared; that is, were they ideas between which his own interpretation successfully mediated. The interpreter appears, then, as the one of the three who is most of all the spirit of the community, dominating the ideal relations of all three members.

But the one who is, in ideal, this chief, is so because he is first of all servant. His office it is to conform to the mind which he interprets, and to the comprehension of the mind to which he addresses his interpretation. And his own ideas can "work" only if his self-surrender, and his conformity to ideas which are not his own, is actually a successful conformity; and only if his approach to a goal which, as member of a human community of interpretation, he can never reach, is a real approach.

XII

Such are the relationships which constitute a Community of Interpretation. I beg you to observe, as we close, the ethical and religious significance which the structure of such a community makes possible. In case our interpretations actually approach success, a community of interpretation possesses such ethical and religious significance, with increasing definiteness and beauty as the evolution of such a community passes from simpler to higher stages.

Upon interpretation, as we have already seen, every ideal good that we mortals win together, under our human social conditions, depends. Whatever else men need, they need their communities of interpretation.

It is indeed true that such communities can exist, at any time, in the most various grades of development, of self-consciousness, and of ideality. The communities of interpretation which exist in the market-places of the present social world, or that lie at the basis of the diplomatic intercourse of modern nations, are communities whose ideal goal is seldom present to the minds of their members; and it is not love which often seems to be their consciously ruling motive.

Yet, on the whole, it is not perception, and it is not conception; while it certainly is interpretation which is the great humanizing factor in our cognitive processes and which makes the purest forms of love for communities possible. Loyalty to a community of interpretation enters into all the other forms of true loyalty. No one who loves mankind can find a worthier and more significant way to express his love than by increasing and expressing among men the Will to Interpret. This will inspires every student of the humanities; and is present wherever charity enters into life. When Christianity teaches us to hope for the community of all mankind, we can readily see that the Beloved Community, whatever else it is, will be, when it comes, a Community of Interpretation. When we consider the ideal form and the goal of such a community, we see that in no other form, and with no other ideal, can we better express the constitution of the ideal Church, be that conceived as the Church on earth, or as the Church triumphant in some ideal realm of superhuman and all seeing insight, where I shall know even as I am known.

And, if, in ideal, we aim to conceive the divine nature, how better can we conceive it than in the form of the Community of Interpretation, and above all in the form of the Interpreter, who interprets all to all, and each individual to the world, and the world of spirits to each individual.

In such an interpreter, and in his community, the problem of the One and the Many would find its ideally complete expression and solution. The abstract conceptions and the mystical intuitions would be at once transcended, and illumined, and yet retained and kept clear and distinct, in and through the life of one who, as interpreter, was at once servant to all and chief among all, expressing his will through all, yet, in his interpretations, regarding and loving the will of the least of these his brethren. In him the Community, the Individual, and the Absolute would be completely expressed, reconciled, and distinguished.

This, to be sure, is, at this point of our discussion, still merely the expression of an ideal, and not the assertion of a metaphysical proposition. But in the Will to Interpret, the divine and the human seem to be in closest touch with each other.

The mere form of interpretation may be indeed momentarily misused for whatever purpose of passing human folly you will. But if the ideal of interpretation is first grasped; and if then the Community of Interpretation is conceived as inclusive of all individuals; and as unified by the common hope of the far-off event of complete mutual understanding; and, finally, if love for this community is awakened, — then indeed this love is able to grasp, in ideal, the meaning of the Church Universal, of the Communion of Saints, and of God the Interpreter.

Merely to define such ideals is not to solve the problems of metaphysics. But it is to remove many obstacles from the path that leads towards insight.

These ideals, however, are grasped and loved whenever one first learns fully to comprehend what Paul meant when he said: "Wherefore let him that speaketh with tongues pray that he may interpret." This word is but a small part of Paul's advice. But in germ it contains the whole meaning of the office, both of philosophy and of religion.

XIII

The World of

Interpretation

In the closing lecture of a course delivered a few years since, on the "Problem of Age, Growth, and Death," Professor Charles S. Minot, of Harvard University, in summarizing the results of his studies, used these words: "I do not wish to close without a few words of warning explanation. For the views which I have presented before you in this series of lectures, I personally am chiefly responsible. Science consists in the discoveries made by individuals, afterwards confirmed and correlated by others, so that they lose their personal character. You ought to know that the interpretations which I have offered you are still largely in the personal stage. Whether my colleagues will think that the body of conceptions which I have presented are fully justified or not, I cannot venture to say."

This was the word of a distinguished leader of research in Comparative Anatomy. It expressed, in passing, a view about the general character of scientific method which the same author, not very long afterwards, set forth at much greater length in a lecture before his own section at a meeting of the American Association for the Advancement of Science. In that lecture "On the Method of Science" Professor Minot carefully expounded, and very extensively illustrated, the thesis that, while natural science is dependent upon the experiences of individuals for every one of its advances in the knowledge of the facts of nature, no experience of any individual man can count as a scientific discovery until it has been sufficiently confirmed by other and by independent observers. Professor Minot speaks of this confirmation by fellow workers as constituting a sort of "depersonalizing" of the discoveries of each individual observer.

The thesis here in question is familiar. I cite Professor Minot's words, not as if he himself thought them at all novel, but merely in order to bring at the moment as directly as possible to your minds what we all know to be an essential feature of the methods of natural science.

I

For my own part, I should not say, as Dr. Minot does, that the discoveries of the individual worker in a natural science "lose their personal character" by receiving the confirmation which makes them possessions of science. I think that I understand what my colleague means by calling this process a "depersonalizing" of the individual's contributions to scientific work. But I should myself prefer to express this well-known maxim of method by saying that the individual observer's discoveries have first to be interpreted to the scientific community, and then substantiated by the further experience of that community, before they belong to the science. In still other words, the work of science is what, in the athletic phrase, is called team-work. The spirit of science is one of loyalty to a Community of Interpretation. The term Community of Interpretation I here use in the technical sense defined in the foregoing lecture.

But however you choose to formulate the rule, the lesson of which it reminds us is one which concerns philosophers quite as much as it does the students of nature. Let us attempt to read this lesson, and to generalize it. We shall find it to be a lesson in metaphysics.

Our knowledge of nature depends upon experience. An experience, in order to be useful for the purposes of physical science, must involve the testing, or at all events the present success, of an idea. In this experience percepts and concepts must be brought into synthesis. Some idea about nature, as the pragmatists tell us, must be found to "work," at least in the one case which is first in question when a new natural fact is found. A scientific discovery consists in the observation of such a "working." And so far all who have learned how the study of the physical world is carried on, will agree regarding the bases of scientific knowledge.

II

Discoveries, however, are made by individuals. The individual discoverer, then, must be the one who first finds that, at a certain moment, and for him personally, concepts and percepts meet thus and thus. Some question of his is answered, and, in general, some hypothesis of his is for the moment verified. The individual observer finds that "cash" is rendered to correspond to certain "credit-values" which he has previously possessed only in conceptual form. Some interest of his in the search for percepts is, at least momentarily, fulfilled. Unless at least so much takes place in the life of somebody, science is not enriched by a new discovery.

Such, then, are the necessary conditions which must be met if a scientific advance is to take place. But are these conditions sufficient? Does every case wherein the individual finds novel "cash payment" rendered for some of his own "credit-values," and new perceptual answers given to his conceptual questions, and "workings" crowning with at least momentary success an idea of his own about nature,—an idea which has heretofore "worked" for no other man,—does every such case involve a genuine scientific discovery? Can the individual simply turn over to his science the "cash" which his percepts have now rendered? Can he address all who are concerned thus?—"Lo, I have indeed found a new scientific fact. Scientific facts are facts of experience. I have had an experience. True ideas are ideas which 'work.' Here is an idea of mine; and this time it 'works,' for I have seen its 'working.' You want in science, not mere concepts, but percepts. I have a percept. You want, not mere credit, but cash. I have the cash; and here it is."

Is this the sole way in which the individual wins access to new scientific facts? And is this the spirit in which the trained scientific observer—for instance, the colleague whom I have just cited—reports his discoveries?

No, these conditions of a scientific discovery are necessary, but not sufficient. The individual has made his discovery; but it is a scientific discovery only in case it can become, through further confirmation, the property and the experience of the community of scientific observers. The process whereby the transition is made from the individual observation to the needed confirmation is one whose technical details, as they appear in the life of any one special science, interest us here not at all. But what does interest us, first of all, is the fact that this confirmation always involves a typical instance, or a series of instances, of Peirce's cognitive process called interpretation. What further concerns us is that this interpretation is guided by principles which are, in their bearings, both very general and highly metaphysical. One needs no other principles than these for dealing with all the central problems of philosophy.

I am far from accusing my colleague, Professor Minot, of any conscious intention to express an opinion about a problem of metaphysics when he uttered his loyal word of warning regarding his own scientific discoveries. But none the less, this appeal to the scientific community implies a belief that there is such a community. This belief is due not to perception or to conception alone. This belief in the reality of the scientific community is itself no belief in a fact which is open to the scientific observations of any individual. No observer of nature has ever discovered, by the methods used in his or in any natural science, that there exists any such community. The existence of the community of scientific observers is known through interpretation. This interpretation expresses essentially social motives, as well as profoundly ethical motives. And this interpretation is also of a type which we are obliged to use in dealing with the whole universe.

III

Let me illustrate the thesis which I have just expressed. Let us first consider why the individual observer must await the confirmation of others before his discovery can get its place as a contribution to a physical science. Let us use our foregoing study of the cognitive process of interpretation as a further aid towards the understanding of the relations between an individual scientific man and the work of the natural science to which he may contribute.

There is a well-known maxim of common sense which tells us that no man should be judge in his own case. The patient does ill who attempts to be his own physician. The litigant, even if he happens to be a lawyer, needs somebody besides himself as his counsel. The judge on the bench may not undertake to try a suit in which he is plaintiff or defendant. Even a great statesman needs aid when his own fitness for office is in question. The artist, however original, may be an untrustworthy critic of his own genius.

This maxim of common sense, at least in its application to patients, to litigants, to office seekers, or to artists, seems to be somewhat remote from the maxim of scientific method which Professor Minot formulated. And yet, in both maxims, essentially the same principle is in question. Why is a man in so many cases so poor a judge of his own case? Why ought not the most expert of judges to undertake to decide a case in which he is plaintiff or defendant? Why is it, in general, true, as they say, that the man who is his own lawyer has a fool for a client? Why is every one of us disqualified from self-estimate in respect of some of the matters which personally concern us most of all?

IV

The general answers to these questions are easy. A man's own case is usually not *merely* his own. It also concerns some social order to which he belongs. The litigant stands in presence, not merely of his own rights and wrongs, but of the whole social will. The decision of his case will affect many besides himself, and sometimes might save or wreck a nation. The patient's illness is not merely a medical phenomenon, and not merely an individual misfortune, but also is an event of social moment. His family, and perhaps his country, may be affected by what is done with this single case. Napoleon's state of health, during the later years of his power, probably influenced the course of all future European history. And the obscurest victim of the plague may prove to be a centre of infection for a whole continent. Hence, when anybody is ill, his case is not merely his own.

When a man's affairs deeply concern other people besides himself, the only way to deal justly with the case is to interpret this man's own individual views and interests to some fitting representative of the social will, in order that the matter may be arbitrated, or in order that the wills of all concerned may be, as far as possible, both harmonized and expressed. A Community of Interpretation must exist or must be formed.

The sufferer who is ill, or the man who is haled into court, needs, then, not only to be an object of perception or of conception. It is not enough to wait in order to see whether his ideas "work" or not. What is needed is the triadic process of mediating between his mind and some other mind, between his ideas and other men's ideas.

And no interpreter who merely blended with the mind and the ideas of the one whom he is to interpret, or with the interests of those whom he is to address, could do the work. The distinction of the persons, or of the personal functions involved, is as essential to a Community of Interpretation as is the common task in which these three persons engage, or in which these three distinct ideas or personal functions coöperate.

Now it is indeed perfectly possible for a man to undertake the task of interpreting his own case. There are instances in which we all of us wisely attempt some form of self-interpretation. There are callings, such as those of the trained administrators and of the sea-captains, in which it becomes a regular part of a man's duty, even at moments when great and novel emergencies arise, to interpret his own duty to himself.

In a previous lecture, we have seen how such enterprises of self-interpretation are actually carried out. At some present moment, a man may interpret his past plans, his habits, his resolutions, his ideals, his obligations, to his future self, and thereupon may give commands to himself.

The psychology of such processes is simply that of comparison, when comparison is taken in Peirce's sense, as a triadic mode of cognition. In such instances a man discovers a third or mediating idea, whereby two of his own distinct ideas are, within the limits of his individual consciousness, woven into a threefold unity. Now that this can sometimes be accomplished with success, the sea-captain — who, while on the bridge, faces a great emergency and consults no other man, yet gives fitting orders and succeeds — well illustrates. The captain's task, of course, concerns the interests of a social order. But his training has prepared him to unite in his own person certain functions of a community.

From one essential feature of his self-imposed task, however, the man who acts as his own adviser in any socially significant situation, cannot be relieved. He attempts, at such a moment, to do the work of three men at once. The three personal functions which must be brought into unity if the work is to be successfully done, remain distinct. They must not blend. If they actually blend, the whole affair becomes a blind product of instinct or of routine, and not any genuine self-direction whatever. As a fact, there are some callings which train a man for such a threefold task. There are some situations in life wherein any mature man who knows his own business has to act as his own adviser. But the task has its difficulty determined by its form. An individual has, in all such instances, to do the work of a community.

Now in case of illness, of legal peril, or of the personal estimate to which the artist or the statesman is subjected by the social will, experience shows that a man is seldom, and, in sufficiently great emergencies, is never able to act with success as his own adviser. The reasons for this sort of defect are two: First, the question at issue concerns the interests of at least two distinct individuals; and hence, whether the patient or the litigant, or other man in question endeavors to be his own director or not, the task is essentially such that it can be accomplished only by the aid of an interpreter. For just because more than one individual must be rightly treated, there exists some social boundary which must be crossed. Therefore neither the "cash-values" nor the "credit-values" of individual ideas are mainly in question. The "exchange-values" of two distinct forms of ideal coinage are to be considered. And so the adjustment required has to be triadic in its inmost form. But secondly, while this process of interpretation, this crossing of our ideal boundary, can indeed be undertaken within the limits of an individual man's consciousness, as it is undertaken whenever we compare two distinct ideas of our own,—experience shows that the effort to fill at once the functions of three distinct persons does not succeed with the patients and with the litigants, although analogous threefold functions may succeed in case of the sea-captains and the great administrators.

V

Let us return to the case of the scientific observer,—not because the maxim defined by my colleague is either obscure or doubtful, but because the underlying principle needs to be brought clearly to our consciousness.

Common sense regards the physical world as a realm whose objects can be experienced in common by many observers. We have not here to inquire into the origin of this special belief. But the belief can be readily illustrated by the way in which two men who row in the same boat regard the boat and the oars which they see and touch, and the water over which they fly.

Each man views the boat and the oars and the water as objects which he experiences for himself. At the same time, each of the two men believes that both of them are experiencing, while they row together, the *same* external facts,—the *same* boat, the *same* oars, the *same* water.

It is important for our purposes to notice that, while each individual, as he pulls his oar, verifies some of his own ideas, and finds them "working" in his own individual experience, neither of them individually verifies the "workings" of the other man's ideas. Consequently, when each man believes that the boat in which he observes himself to be rowing is the same boat as the one which the other man also finds as an object in his own experience,—this belief, as each of the men possesses it, is *not* a perception and is not verified by the individual "workings" of the ideas of either of the men.

This belief in the common object is, for each of the men, an interpretation, which he may address to the other man, or may regard the other as in turn addressing to him.

The cognitive process involved is through and through triadic.

The boat which each man finds, sees, touches, and feels himself pull, appears to him as verifying his own ideas. The common boat, the boat which each man regards as an object not only for his own, but also for his neighbor's experience, is essentially an object of interpretation.

The real boat may indeed actually be what each of the two men takes it to be; and it may be the same boat as that boat which each man verifies in his own experience. But if this is the case, and if the boat is really a common object of experience for both the oarsmen, then the community of interpretation into which the two men enter whenever they talk about their boat or about their rowing, is a community which even now views both itself and its boat as it would view both of them in case its goal were actually attained, and in case the interpretation had been transformed to a perfectly clear vision of a comparison of ideas.

In any case, however, it is useless to attempt to express the community of experience which the two oarsmen possess in terms of the separate "workings" of the ideas of either of them or of both, taken as mutually detached individuals.

Each rower verifies his own idea of the boat. Neither of them, as an individual, verifies the other's idea of this boat. Each of them, as interpreter, either of himself or of the other man, believes that their two individual experiences have a common object. Neither can (merely as this individual) verify this idea. Neither could, as an individual, ever verify his belief in the interpretation, even although they two should row in the same boat together until doomsday.

If the common interpretation is true, then the two oarsmen actually form a community of interpretation, and are even now believing what would be seen to be true if, and only if, this community of interpretation were actually to reach its goal.

Pragmatism, whose ideas, like those of the bewitched Galatians, are fain to be saved solely by their own "works," is, as I believe, quite unable to define in its own dyadic terms, the essentially spiritual sense in which any interpretation can be true, and the sense in which any community of interpretation could reach its goal. Nothing, however, is better known to us, or is more simply empirical, than is the reaching of such a limited but determinate goal of interpretation, whenever we ourselves compare two distinct ideas of our own, and survey with clearness the union of the mediating or third idea with those whose contrasts it interprets. The oarsmen who not only row in the same boat, but who are able to talk over together their boat and their rowing, interpret their united life and work as such a real community of interpretation.

They constantly interpret themselves as the members, and their boat as the empirical object of such a community. And they constantly define what could be actually verified only if the goal of the community were reached. By merely rowing they will indeed never reach it. But does the real world anywhere or anyhow contain the actual winning of the goal by the community? If not, then the ideas of the interpreters are actually and always quite unverifiable. Yet their community, by hypothesis, is real. But if the real world contains the actual winning of the goal by the community, then the verifying experience is not definable in in the terms which pragmatism uses.

For such a goal is essentially the experience of a community; and the success, — the salvation, — the final truth of each idea, or of each individual person, that enters into this community, is due (when the goal is reached) neither to its "works" nor to its workings, but to its essentially spiritual unity in and with the community.

VI

The case of the two men rowing together in the same boat is a case in which common sense raises no question regarding the physical reality of the boat. Such a question is, for common sense, unnecessary, simply because the interpretation of the boat as the common object of the experience of both the rowers is already made obvious by the essentially social nature and training of all of us. Our social consciousness is, psychologically speaking, the most deeply rooted foundation of our whole view of ourselves and of the world; and we therefore tend from the outset to make interpretation, rather than perception or conception, our ruling cognitive process whenever explicitly social relations are concerned. And so, for common sense, the physical objects, especially when they appear to us in the field of our experience of sight and of touch, are regarded as essentially common objects, — the same for all men. For do we not appear to see men dealing together with these common objects?

This is an interpretation; but it is an early and a natural interpretation. So long as we are untrained to reflection, we remain indeed unaware of the principles which lie at the basis of such common-sense opinions about natural facts.

These principles come to a clearer consciousness only when scientific methods, or similarly critical undertakings, have made us sceptical in our scrutiny of experience.

Professor Minot's maxim expresses one result of such criticism. This maxim simply generalizes the view which the two men rowing in the boat naturally take.

VII

If physical objects are especially to be viewed as objects which are or which can become objects of experience for various men, then whoever says, "I have discovered a physical fact," is not merely reporting the workings of his own individual ideas. He is interpreting. He is therefore appealing to a community of interpretation.

If he has found a really novel object in his own individual experience, then this object has not already won its place, as the boat and the oars and the water have long since done, among the recognized objects of common experience. If hereupon the discoverer persists, as an individual, in interpreting his own experience; if he says, with direct confidence, "Since my ideas here work in this novel way, I have found a new physical fact," — then the discoverer is attempting to be judge in his own cause. His perils are, therefore, quite analogous to those which the patient faces who attempts to be his own physician, or to the dangers which the man encounters who enters court as his own counsel.

The source and the limitations of these perils we now know. The observer of a new fact may justly be, at least for the time, his own interpreter, in case his training has rightly prepared him for the scientific emergency of a notable discovery made by him while he is working alone. For in such a case the discoverer has already become expert in the arts of his community. Yet always the scientific discoverer is, in principle, subject to Professor Minot's maxim. Isolated observations of individuals, even when these individuals are of the highest grade of expertness, are always unsatisfactory. And the acknowledged facts of a natural science are the possessions of the community.

That the scientific community itself exists, is therefore one of the most important principles used in the natural sciences. Often this principle is more or less subconscious. It is seldom adequately analyzed.

VIII

Our previous study has prepared us to understand the constitution of the scientific community of interpretation more precisely than would be possible without such a basis as we now possess. The scientific community consists, at the least, of the original discoverer, of his interpreter, and of the critical worker who tests or controls the discoverer's observations by means of new experiences devised for that purpose.

Usually, of course, in case the discovery has attracted much attention, the critic whose control is in question is no one individual man. For then the work of testing the discovery is done by a large body of individual workers.

In many cases, in the routine work of the highly developed sciences, the interpreter's task takes, in large part, the form of simply reporting and recording the discoverer's observations.

But Professor Minot calls attention to another and a very important part of the office of mediating between the discoverer and his community. Professor Minot speaks of the way in which scientific discoveries are "correlated" by others than those who made them. This process of correlation involves, upon its higher levels, elaborate comparisons. How complex and how significant, for the advance of science, this aspect of the process of interpretation may be, the historical instance of Clerk Maxwell's theoretical interpretation of Faraday's discoveries in Electricity and Magnetism will suggest sufficiently for our present purpose.

As for the work of criticism and of control to which the interpretation leads, it is not only capable of infinite complexity, but involves various reversals in the direction of the process of interpretation. Criticism and control often come from those who, as in the
typical case of the discoveries of Darwin, address the discoverer,
and arouse him to make new discoveries.

But however complex the processes which arise in the course of
such undertakings, the essential structure of the community of scientific interpretation remains definitely the same. The existence of this
community is presupposed as a basis of every scientific inquiry into
natural facts. And the type of truth which is sought by scientific
investigators is one which indeed includes, but which simply cannot
be reduced to, the dyadic type to which pragmatism devotes its exclusive attention. For everybody concerned, while he indeed aims
to have his own ideas "work," is also concerned with the truth of his
interpretations, and of those which are addressed to him. And such
truth can be fully tested, under our human conditions, only in the
cases wherein, for the interpretation of another human individual's
mind, the comparison of distinct ideas is substituted, while these
ideas fall within the range of our individual insight.

In all other cases, just as in our ordinary social dealings with one
another, we aim towards the goal of the community of interpretation.
Our will is the "will to interpret." We do not reach the goal in any
one moment, so long as we are dealing with other human beings. Yet
we interpret the goal. For the goal of the community is always precisely that luminous knowledge which we do, in a limited but in a
perfectly definite form, possess, within the range of our own individual life whenever our comparisons of distinct ideas are made with
clearness.

We define the facts of the common social experience in terms of
this perfectly concrete and empirical goal of the scientific community of interpretation. This goal is a certain type of spiritual unity.
All scientific research depends upon loyalty to the cause of the
scientific community of interpretation.

IX

But how — so one may still insist — should we know that any community of interpretation exists?

This question brings us indeed to the very centre of metaphysics.
From this point outwards we can survey all the principal problems

about reality. The will to interpret, in all of its forms, scientific or philosophical or religious, presupposes that somehow, at some time, in some fitting embodiment, a community of interpretation exists, and is in process of aiming towards its goal. Any conversation with other men, any process of that inner conversation whereof, as we have seen, our individual self-consciousness consists, any scientific investigation, is carried on under the influence of the generally subconscious belief that we all are members of a community of interpretation. When such enterprises are at once serious and reasonable and truth-loving, the general form of any such community, as we have already observed, is that of the ideal Pauline Church. For there is the member whose office it is to edify. There is the brother who is to be edified. And there is the spirit of the community, who is in one aspect the interpreter, and in another aspect the being who is interpreted. Now what is the warrant for believing in the reality of such a community?

For a general answer to this question let us hereupon consult the philosophers. The philosophers differ sadly amongst themselves. They do not at present form a literal human community of mutual enlightenment and of growth in knowledge, to any such extent as do the workers in the field of any one of natural sciences. The philosophers are thus far individuals rather than consciously members one of another. The charity of mutual interpretation is ill developed amongst them. They frequently speak with tongues and do not edify. And they are especially disposed to contend regarding their spiritual gifts. We cannot expect them, then, at present to agree regarding any one philosophical opinion. Nevertheless, if we consider them in a historical way, there is one feature about their work to which, at this point, I need to call especial attention.

I have already more than once asserted that the principal task of the philosopher is one, not of perception, not of conception, but of interpretation. This remark refers in the first place to the office which the philosophers have filled in the history of culture.

X

Common opinion classes philosophy among the humanities. It ought so to be classed. Philosophers have actually devoted themselves, in the main, neither to perceiving the world, nor to spinning webs of conceptual theory, but to interpreting the meaning of the civilizations which they have represented, and to attempting the interpretation of whatever minds in the universe, human or divine, they believed to be real. That the philosophers are neither the only interpreters, nor the chiefs among those who interpret, we now well know. The artists, the leaders of men, and all the students of the humanities, make interpretation their business; and the triadic cognitive function, as the last lecture showed, has its applications in all the realms of knowledge. But in any case the philosopher's ideals are those of an interpreter. He addresses one mind and interprets another. The unity which he seeks is that which is characteristic of a community of interpretation.

The historical proofs of this thesis are manifold. A correct summary of their meaning appears in the common opinion which classes philosophy amongst the humanities. This classification is a perfectly just one. The humanities are busied with interpretations. Individual illustrations of the historical office of philosophy could be furnished by considering with especial care precisely those historical instances which the philosophers furnish who, like Plato or like Bergson, have most of all devoted their efforts to emphasizing as much as possible one of the other cognitive processes, instead of interpretation. For the more exclusively such a philosopher lays stress upon perception alone, or conception alone, the better does he illustrate our historical thesis.

Plato lays stress upon conception as furnishing our principal access to reality. Bergson has eloquently maintained the thesis that pure perception brings us in contact with the real. Yet each of these philosophers actually offers us an interpretation of the universe. That is, each of them begins by taking account of certain mental processes which play a part in human life. Each asks us to win some sort of touch with a higher type of consciousness than belongs to our natural human existence. Each declares that, through such a transformation of our ordinary consciousness, either through a flight from the vain show of sense into the realm of pure thought, or else through an abandonment of the merely practical labors of that user of tools, the intellect, we shall find the pathway to reality. Each in his own way interprets our natural mode of dealing with reality to some nobler form of insight which he believes to be corrective of our natural errors, or else, in turn, interprets the supposed counsels of a more divine type of knowledge to the blindness or to the barrenness or to the merely practical narrowness of our ordinary existence.

Each of these philosophers mediates, in his own way, between the spiritual existence of those who sit in the darkness of the cave of sense, or who, on the other hand, wander in the wilderness of evolutionary processes and of intellectual theories; — he mediates, I say, between these victims of error on the one hand, and that better, that richer, spiritual life and the truer insight, on the other hand, of those who, in this philosopher's opinion, find the homeland — be that land the Platonic realm of the eternal forms of being, or the dwelling-place which Bergson loves, — where the artists see their beautiful visions of endless change.

In brief, there is no philosophy of pure conception, and there is no philosophy of pure perception. Plato was a leader of the souls of those men to whom he showed the way out of the cave, and in whom he inspired the love of the eternal. Bergson winningly devotes himself to saying, as any artist says, "Come and intuitively see what I have intuitively seen."

Such speech, however, is the speech neither of the one who trusts to mere conception, nor of one who finds the real merely in perception. It is the speech of an interpreter, who, addressing himself to one form of personality or of life, interprets what he takes to be the meaning of some other form of life.

This thesis, that the philosopher is an interpreter, simply directs our attention to the way in which he is required to define his problems. And the universality of these problems makes this purely elementary task of their proper definition at once momentous and difficult. We shall not lose by any consideration which rightly fixes our attention upon an essential aspect of the process of knowledge which the philosopher seeks to control. For the philosopher is attempting to deal with the world as a whole, with reality in general.

Why is it that the philosopher has to be an interpreter even when, like Bergson or like Plato, he tries to subordinate interpretation either to conception alone or to perception alone? Why is it that when, in his loftiest speculative flights, he attempts to seize upon some intuition of reason, or upon some form of direct perception, which shall reveal to him the inmost essence of reality, he nevertheless acts as interpreter?

The answer to this question is simple.

XI

If, as a fact, we could, at least in ideal, and as a sort of speculative experiment, weld all our various ideas, our practical ideas as well as our theoretical ideas, together into some single idea, whose "leading" we could follow wherever it led, from concept to percept, or from percept to concept; and if we could reduce our problem of reality simply to the question, Is this one idea expressive of the nature of reality? — then indeed some such philosophy as that of Bergson, or as that of Plato, might be formulated in terms either of pure perception or of pure conception. Then the philosopher who thus welded his ideas into one idea, and who then assured himself of the success of that one idea, would no longer be an interpreter.

Thus, let us imagine that we could, with Spinoza, weld together into the one idea of Substance, the totality of ideas, that is of pragmatic leadings, which all men, at all times, are endeavoring to follow through their experience, or to express through their will. Suppose that this one idea could be shown to be successful. Then our philosophy could assume the well-known form which Spinoza gave to his own: —

By substance, Spinoza means that which is "in itself" and which needs no other to sustain or in any ideal fashion to contain it. Hereupon the philosopher finds it easy to assert that whatever is in any sense real must indeed be either "in itself" or "in another." No other idea need be used in estimating realities except the idea thus defined. The only question as to any object is: Is this a substance or not? A very brief and simple process of conceptual development, then, brings us to Spinoza's result that whatever is "in another" is not in the highest sense real at all. Therefore there remains in our world only that which is real "in itself." The one idea can be realized only in a world which is, once for all, the Substance. The tracks of all finite creatures that are observed near the edge of the cave of this Substance lead (as was long ago said of Spinoza's substance) only inwards. The world is defined in terms of the single idea, all other human ideas or possible ideas being but special cases of the one idea. The real world is purely conceptual, and is also monistic.

Suppose, on the other hand, that we indeed recognize with Bergson, and with the pragmatists, an endless and empirical wealth of ideas which, in practical life, lead or do not lead from concepts to percepts, as experience may determine. Suppose, however, that, with Bergson, we first notice that all these ideal leadings of the intellect constitute, at best, but an endlessly varied using of tools. Suppose that hereupon, with Bergson and with the mystics, we come to regard all this life of the varied ideas, this mechanical using of mere tools, this mere pragmatism, as an essentially poorer sort of life from which nature has long since delivered the nobler of the insects, from which the artists can and do escape, and from which it is the loftiest ideal of philosophy to liberate those who are indeed to know reality.

Then indeed, though not at all in Spinoza's way, all the ideal leadings which the philosopher has henceforth to regard as essentially illuminating, will simply blend into a single idea. This idea will be the one idea of winning a pure intuition. We shall define reality in terms of this pure intuition. And hereupon a purely perceptual view of reality will result.

If, then, all the ideas of men, if all ideas of reality, could collapse or could blend or could otherwise be ideally welded into a single idea, then this idea could be used to define reality, just as pragmatism has come to define all the endless variety of forms of "truth" in terms of the single idea which gets the name "success" or "working" or "expediency" or "cash-value," according to the taste of the individual pragmatist.

XII

As a fact, however, the genuine problem, whether of reality, or of truth, cannot be faced by means of any such blending of all ideal leadings into a single ideal leading.

We all of us believe that there is any real world at all, simply because we find ourselves in a situation in which, because of the fragmentary and dissatisfying conflicts, antitheses, and problems of our present ideas, an interpretation of this situation is needed, but is not now known to us. *By the "real world" we mean simply the "true interpretation" of this our problematic situation.* No other reason can be given than this for believing that there is any real world at all. From this one consideration, vast consequences follow. Let us now sketch some of these consequences.

Whoever stands in presence of the problem of reality has, at the very least, to compare two essential ideas. These ideas are, respectively, the idea of present experience and the idea of the goal of experience. The contrast in question has countless and infinitley various forms. In its ethical form the contrast appears as that between our actual life and our ideal life. It also appears as the Pauline contrast between the flesh and the spirit; or as the Stoic contrast between the life of the wise and the life of the fools. It is also known to common sense as the contrast between our youthful hopes and our mature sense of our limitations. The contrast between our future life, which we propose to control, and our irrevocable past life which we can never recall, presents the same general antithesis. In the future, as we hopefully view it, the goal is naturally supposed to lie. But the past, dead as it is often said to be, determines our present need, and sets for us our ideal task.

In the world of theory the same contrast appears as that between our ignorance and our possible enlightenment, between our endlessly numerous problems and their solutions, between our innumerable uncertainties and those attainments of certainty at which our sciences and our arts aim. For our religious consciousness the contrasts between nature and grace, between good and evil, between our present state and our salvation, between God and the world, merely illustrate the antithesis.

One can also state this antithesis as that between our Will (which, as Schopenhauer and the Buddhists said, is endlessly longing) and the Fulfilment of our will. Plato, on the one hand, and the mystics on the other, attempt to conceive or to perceive some such fulfilment, according as Plato, or as some mystic, emphasizes one or the other of the two cognitive processes to which the philosophers have usually confined their attention.

This antithesis between two fundamental ideas presents to each of us the problem of the universe, and dominates that problem. For by the "real world" we mean the true interpretation of the problematic situation which this antithesis presents to us in so far as we compare what is our ideal with what is so far given to us. Whatever the real world is its nature has to be expressed in terms of this antithesis of ideas.

Two such ideas, then, stand in contrast when we face our problem of reality. They stand as do plaintiff and defendant in court, or as do the ideas of the suffering patient and his hopes of recovery, or as do the wrongs which the litigant feels and the rights or the doom which the law allows him. The empirical shapes which the antithesis takes are simply endless in their wealth. They furnish to us the special topics which science and common sense study. But the general problem which the antithesis presents is the world-problem. *The question about what the real world is, is simply the question as to what this contrast is and means.* Neither of the two ideas can solve its own problem or be judge in its own case. Each needs a counsel, a mediator, an interpreter, to represent its cause to the other idea.

In the well-known metaphysical expression, this contrast may be called that between appearance and reality. The antithesis itself is in one sense the appearance, the phenomenon, the world-problem. The question about the real world is that furnished to us by our experience of this appearance. When we ask what the real world is, we simply ask what this appearance, this antithesis, this problem of the two contrasting ideas both is and means. So to ask, is to ask for the solution of the problem which the antithesis presents. That is, we ask: "What is the interpretation of this problem, of this antithesis?" The real world is that solution. Every special definition of reality takes the form of offering such a solution. Whether a philosopher calls himself realist or idealist, monist or pluralist, theist or materialist, empiricist or rationalist, his philosophy, wherever he states it, takes the form of saying: "The true, the genuine interpretation of the antithesis is such and such."

If you say that perhaps there is no solution of the problem, that hypothesis, if true, could be verified only by an experience that in itself would constitute a full insight into the meaning of the real contrast, and so would in fact furnish a solution. In any case, the real world is precisely that whose nature is expressed by whatever mediating idea is such that, when viewed in unity with the two antithetical ideas, it fully compares them, and makes clear the meaning of the contrast. *But an interpretation is real only if the appropriate community is real, and is true only if that community reaches its goal.*

In brief, then, the real world is the Community of Interpretation which is constituted by the two antithetic ideas, and their mediator or interpreter, whatever or whoever that interpreter may be. If the interpretation is a reality, and if it truly interprets the whole of reality, then the community reaches its goal, and the real world includes its own interpreter. *Unless both the interpreter and the community are real, there is no real world.*

XIII

After the foregoing discussion of the nature and the processes of interpretation, we are now secure from any accusation that, from this point of view, the real world is anything merely static, or is a mere idea within the mind of a finite self, or is an Absolute that is divorced from its appearances, or is any merely conceptual reality, or is "out of time," or is a "block universe," or is an object of a merely mystical intuition.

Interpretation, as we have seen in our general discussion of the cognitive process in question, demands that at least an infinite series of distinct individual acts of interpretation shall take place, unless the interpretation which is in question is arbitrarily interrupted. If, then, the real world contains the Community of Interpretation just characterized, this community of interpretation expresses its life in an infinite series of individual interpretation, each of which occupies its own place in a perfectly real order of time.

If, however, this community of interpretation reaches its goal, this whole time-process is in some fashion spanned by one insight which surveys the unity of its meaning. Such a viewing of the whole time-process by a single synopsis will certainly not be anything "timeless." It will not occur, on the other hand, at any one moment of time. But its nature is the one empirically known to us at any one moment when we clearly contrast two of our own ideas and find their mediator.

XIV

Nothing is more concretely known to us than are the nature, the value, and the goal of a community of interpretation. The most ideal as well as the most scientifically exact interests of mankind are bound up with the existence, with the purposes, with the fortunes, and with the unity of such communities.

The metaphysical doctrine just set forth in outline can be summed up thus: The problem of reality is furnished to us by a certain universal antithesis of two Ideas, or, if one prefers the word, by the antithesis of two Selves. The first thesis of this doctrine is that Reality — the solution of this problem — is the interpretation of this antithesis, the process of mediating between these two selves and of interpreting each of them to the other. Such a process of interpretation involves, of necessity, as infinite sequence of acts of interpretation. It also admits of an endless variety within all the selves which are thus mutually interpreted. These selves, in all their variety, constitute the life of a single Community of Interpretation, whose central member is that spirit of the community whose essential function we now know. In the concrete, then, the universe is a community of interpretation whose life comprises and unifies all the social varieties and all the social communities which, for any reason, we know to be real in the empirical world which our social and our historical sciences study. The history of the universe, the whole order of time, is the history and the order and the expression of this Universal Community.

XV

The method by which this doctrine has been reached may also be summarily stated thus: We began with a sketch of the essentially social character which belongs to our human knowledge of the physical world. Here one of our guides was the way in which common sense interprets the being of material objects. Our other guide was the maxim of scientific method which Professor Minot, wholly without any technically metaphysical purpose, has stated. The result of regarding our human experience of nature from these two points of view was that we found our belief in the reality of the physical world to be inseparable from our belief in the reality of a community of interpretation. The rest of our discussion has been a metaphysical generalization of this first result.

Turning from these special instances to the general philosophical problem of reality, we next noticed the historical fact that philosophers have never been able to define a theory of the universe in purely conceptual terms, and have been equally unable to state their doctrines about the world in purely perceptual terms. The philosophers have always been interpreters, in our technical sense of that term.

Is this limitation of the philosophers (if you call it a limitation) due to the fact that they have been, themselves, human beings, busied with interpreting life to their fellow-men, and unable therefore to dwell exclusively either upon perception or upon conception?

To this question we have answered that the philosopher's office as interpreter is not forced upon him merely by the fact that he is appealing, as man, to other men. The source of his task as interpreter lies deeper. Reality cannot be expressed exclusively either in perceptual or in conceptual form. Nor can its nature be described in terms of the "leadings" which any one idea can express. However you attempt to weld all ideas into one idea (such as Spinoza's idea of substance), and then to hold that reality is the expression of this one idea, you stand in presence of a contrast, an antithesis of at least two ideas, "Appearance and Reality," "Actual and Possible," "Real and Ideal," or some other such pair. If you succeed in reducing this antithesis to its simplest statement, the world-problem then becomes the problem of defining the mediating idea in terms of which this contrast or antithesis can be and is interpreted. If you define, however tentatively, such a mediating idea, and then offer the resulting interpretation as an account of what the real world is, your philosophy becomes an assertion that the universe itself has the form and the real character of a community of interpretation. You have no reason for believing that there is any world whatever, except a reason which implies that some interpretation of the antithesis both exists and is true. A real and a true interpretation occur only in case the corresponding community exists and wins its goal.

In brief, if any single idea endeavors to define in terms of its own "leadings" the whole nature of things, that idea is in the position of the man who undertakes to be judge of his own cause. For it belongs to the nature of things to involve an interpretation of its own contrasts, and a mediation of its own antitheses. To the world, then, belongs an Interpreter of its own life. In this sense, then, the world is the process and the life of the Spirit and of the Community.

XIV

The Doctrine
of Signs

The Christian doctrine of life is dominated by the ideal of the Universal Community. Such was the thesis defended in the first part of this series of lectures. The real world itself is, in its wholeness, a Community. This is the metaphysical result in which our study of the World of Interpretation, at the last time, culminated.

I

Herewith the two assertions to which our study of the Problem of Christianity leads, are before you. Our concluding lectures must make explicit the relations between these two assertions. Hereby each of them will be interpreted in the light of the other.

Metaphysical theory and religious experience are always contrasting realms of inquiry and of insight. Therefore the task of our three concluding lectures constitutes a typical exercise in the process of interpretation. We have to compare results which have been reached by widely different methods. We have to mediate between them. The method of interpretation is always the comparative method. To compare and to interpret are two names for the same fundamental cognitive process.

The fitting order for such an enterprise is determined by the subject-matter. Since the metaphysical thesis with which our last lecture closed is very general, it will prove to be, indeed, a worthless abstraction, unless we illustrate its application to various special problems of life as well as of philosophy. What I can hope, within the limits of our brief remaining time, to make clearer, is what I may call the ground plan of the World of Interpretation.

The universe, if my thesis is right, is a realm which is through and through dominated by social categories. Time, for instance, expresses a system of essentially social relations. The present interprets the past to the future. At each moment of time the results of the whole world's history up to that moment are, so to speak, summed up and passed over to the future for its new deeds of creation and of interpretation. I state this principle here in a simply dogmatic form, and merely as an example of what I have in mind when I say that the system of metaphysics which is needed to define the constitution of this world of interpretation must be the generalized theory of an ideal society. Not the Self, not the Logos, not the One, and not the Many, but the Community will be the ruling category of such a philosophy.

I must attempt, then, within our brief remaining time, to make this general metaphysical theory less abstract and more articulate. I must contrast our theory with others. I must make more explicit its relation to the Christian ideas. And then I must, in conclusion, survey what we have won, and summarize the outcome.

II

Let me begin by a few purely technical formulations. Charles Peirce, in the discussions which we have now so freely used, introduced into logic the term "Sign." He used that term as the name for an object to which somebody gives or should give an interpretation. I have not here to deal, at any length, with Peirce's development of his theory of Signs. His doctrine was, as you will recall, not at first stated as the basis for a metaphysical system, but simply as a part of a logical theory of the categories. My own metaphysical use of Peirce's doctrine of signs, in my account of the World of Interpretation at the last time, is largely independent of Peirce's philosophy. For the moment it is enough to say that, according to Peirce, just as percepts have, for their appropriate objects, individually existent Things; and just as concepts possess, for their sole objects, Universals—so interpretations have, as the objects which they interpret, Signs. In its most abstract definition, therefore, a Sign, according to Peirce, is something that determines an interpretation. A sign may also be called an expression of a mind; and, in our ordinary social intercourse, it actually is such an expression. Or again, one may say that a sign is, in its essence, either a mind or a quasi-mind,—an object that fulfils the functions of a mind.

Thus, a word, a clock-face, a weather-vane, or a gesture, is a sign. Our reason for calling it such is twofold. It expresses a mind, and it calls for an interpretation through some other mind, which shall act as mediator between the sign, or between the maker of the sign, and some one to whom the sign is to be read.

Since an interpretation of a sign is, in its turn, the expression of the interpreter's mind, it constitutes a new sign, which again calls for interpretation; and so on without end; unless the process is arbitrarily interrupted. So much can be asserted as a purely logical thesis, quite apart from metaphysics. A sign, then, is an object whose being consists in the fact that the sign calls for an interpretation.

The process of interpretation, as it occurs in our ordinary social life, sufficiently illustrates the meaning of Peirce's new term. Peirce insists that the signs, viewed simply from a logical point of view, constitute a new and fundamentally important category. He sets this category as a "third," side by side with the classic categories of the "universals" which form the "first" category, and the "individuals," which, in Peirce's logic, form the "second" category.

Peirce, as I have said, is not responsible for the metaphysical theory about the world of interpretation with which our last lecture closed. But his terminology enables us to summarize that theory by stating our own metaphysical thesis thus: "The universe consist of real Signs and of their interpretation."

In the order of real time the events of the world are signs. They are followed by interpreters, or by acts of interpretation which our own experience constantly exemplifies. For we live, as selves, by interpreting the events and the meaning of our experience. History consists of such interpretations.

These acts of interpretation are, in their turn, expressed, in the order of time, by new signs. The sequence of these signs and interpretations constitutes the history of the universe. Whatever our experience exemplifies, our metaphysical doctrine of signs generalizes, and applies to the world at large.

The world's experience is, from this point of view, not merely a flux. For, as Bergson rightly asserts, the world of any present moment of time is a summary of the results of all past experience. This view of Bergson's, however, is no mere intuition, but is itself an interpretation. Our own metaphysical thesis states in terms of interpretation what Bergson states as if it were a result of simple intuition.

Since any idea, and especially any antithesis or contrast of ideas, is, according to our metaphysical thesis, a sign which in the world finds its real interpretation, our metaphysical theory may be called a "doctrine of signs."

The title which I have given to this lecture serves to direct attention, through the use of a purely technical term, to the main issue. This issue is the one presented by the thesis that the very being of the universe consists in a process whereby the world is interpreted, —not indeed in its wholeness, at any one moment of time, but in and through an infinite series of acts of interpretation. This infinite series constitutes the temporal order of the world with all its complexities. The temporal order is an order of purposes and of deeds, simply because it is of the essence of every rational deed to be an effort to interpret a past life to a future life; while every act of interpretation aims to introduce unity into life, by mediating between mutually contrasting or estranged ideas, minds, and purposes. If we consider the temporal world in its wholeness, it constitutes in itself an infinitely complex Sign. This sign is, as a whole, interpreted to an experience which itself includes a synoptic survey of the whole of time. Such is a mere sketch of our doctrine of the world of interpretation.

I may aid towards a further understanding of our metaphysical thesis by using, at this point, an illustration.

When you observe, at a crossing of roads, a sign-post, you will never discover what the real sign-post is, either by continuing to perceive it, or by merely conceiving its structure or its relations to any perceived objects, or to any merely abstract laws in heaven or in earth. Nor can you learn what the sign-post is by any process of watching in the course of your individual experience the "workings" of any ideas that it suggests to you as this individual man. You can understand what the sign-post is only if you learn to read it. For its very being as a sign-post consists in its nature as a guide, needing interpretation, and pointing the way. To know the real sign-post, you must then learn to interpret it to a possible hearer to whom you address your interpretation. This being to whom you address your interpretation must be a self distinct from your individual self. If, then, the sign-post is a sign-post at all, there are beings in the world that are neither individual objects of perception nor yet beings such that they are mere universals,—the proper objects for conception.

If the sign-post is a real sign-post, there is in the world a community constituted of at least three distinct minds. There is, first, the mind whose intention to point out the way is expressed in the construction of this sign-post. There is the mind to which the sign-post actually points out the way. But the sign-post does not effectively point out the way to anybody unless, either by the aid of his own individual memory, or of somebody who helps him to read the sign, he learns what the sign means. There must then be a third mind which interprets the sign-post to the inquiring wayfarer. The wayfarer, if he knows how to read, may be his own interpreter. But there remain the three distinct mental functions. There is the function of the mind whose purpose the sign expresses; there is the mind which is guided by the interpretation of the sign; and there is the function of the interpreter to whom the reading of the sign is due. All these minds or functions must be real and distinct and must form one real community, if indeed the sign-post is a real sign-post at all.

This illustration may help us to grasp what the first thesis of our metaphysical doctrine means. Our experience, as it comes to us, is a realm of Signs. That is, the facts of experience resemble sign-posts. You can never exhaustively find out what they are by resorting either to perception or to conception. Nor can you define experience merely in terms of the sort of knowledge which pragmatism emphasizes. No "working" of any single idea can show what a real fact of experience is. For a fact of experience, as you actually view that fact, is first an event belonging to an order of time,—an event preceded by an infinite series of facts whose meaning it summarizes, and leading to an infinite series of coming events, into whose meaning it is yet to enter. But the past and future of our real experience are objects neither of pure perception nor of pure conception. Nor can you, at any present moment, verify any present idea of yours about any past event. Nor can you define past and future in terms of the present workings of any ideas. Past time and future time are known solely through interpretations. Past time we regard as real, because we view our memories as signs which need and possess their interpretations. Our expectations are interpreted to our future selves by our present deeds. Therefore we regard our expectations as signs of a future.

Therefore, to a being who merely perceived and conceived, or who lived wholly in the present workings of his ideas, past time and future time would be as meaningless as the sign-post would be to the wayfarer who could not read, and who found nobody to interpret to him its meaning. If the past and future are realities, then they constitute a life which belongs to some real community, whose ideas of past and of future are really interpreted.

Now our doctrine of the world of interpretation extends to all reality the presuppositions which we use in all our dealings with past and future time. Our memories are signs of the past; our expectations are signs of the future. Past and future are real in so far as these signs have their real interpretation. Our metaphysical thesis generalizes the rules which constantly guide our daily interpretations of life. All contrasts of ideas, all varieties of experience, all the problems which finite experience possesses, are signs. The real world contains (so our thesis asserts) the interpreter of these signs, and the very being of the world consists in the truth of the interpretation which, in the whole realm of experience, these signs obtain.

Let us turn back from these technical formulations and from these illustrations, and come again closer to the real life for which they are intended to stand.

IV

Despite my frequent mention of differences, there is one respect in which I am in full agreement with the spirit of pragmatism, as James defined it. Any metaphysical thesis, if it has a meaning at all, is the expression of an attitude of the will of the one who asserts this thesis.

In a remarkable recent book, entitled: "Die Philosophie des Als Ob," Vaihinger has given his own formulation to a view which he originally reached independently of the influence of pragmatism. It is the view that a philosophy is, in its essence, a resolution to treat the real world as if that world possessed certain characters, and as if our experience enabled us to verify these characters. This resolution is, in its essence, an active attitude of the will. Therefore Voluntarism must form an essential part of every philosophy which justly interprets our metaphysical interests. For our metaphysical interests are indeed interests in directing our will, in defining our attitude towards the universe, in making articulate and practical our ideals and our resolutions. So far, I say, Vaihinger and the pragmatists are right.

I do not believe, however, that our voluntarism must remain a *mere* pragmatism. I have long defended a philosophy, both of human life and of the universe, which I have preferred to call an "Absolute Voluntarism." I developed such a philosophy, partly under the influence of James, but long before recent pragmatism was in question. In its most general form, this philosophy to which I myself adhere, asserts that, while every metaphysical theory is the expression of an attitude of the will, there is one, and but one, general and decisive attitude of the will which is the right attitude, when we stand in presence of the universe, and when we undertake to choose how we propose to bear ourselves towards the world. Any philosophy is inevitably a doctrine which counsels us to bear ourselves towards our world *as if* our experience were such and such. But I do not believe that the "Philosophy of the 'As if'" is, as Vaihinger asserts, merely a system of more or less convenient fictions. For if there are absolute standards for the will (and, in my own opinion, there are such standards), then the world of the will is no world of fictions. If there is one, and but one, right attitude of the will towards the universe, this attitude, when once assumed, is essentially creative of its own realm of deeds. Its so-called fictions are, therefore, not mere fictions, for they constitute a real life. Its so-called successes are no merely transient successes. For if there is any true success at all, every such success, however petty it seems, has a world-wide meaning. The realm of true success is not merely a world of change. For deeds once done are irrevocable; and every deed echoes throughout the universe. The past is unchanging. The expression of the will constitutes itself an actual life. The creative activity of the will is therefore no mere play with figments. It has the reality of a realm of deeds. And every deed has a value that extends throughout the world of the will. Each act is to be judged in the light of the principle: "Inasmuch as ye have done it unto the least of these."

I do not wish here to dwell upon the general features which I have repeatedly ascribed to this world of the will, where every fact is the expression of an individual decision, and is therefore an absolute fact. I do not intend to repeat even the outlines of my former statements, both of this absolute voluntarism and of my own type of idealism. I have too often told that tale. So far as possible, I wish, in the present exposition, to speak as if all my former words were unspoken.

As a fact, I still hold by all the essential features of these former attempts to state the case for idealism. But at present I am dealing with the World of Interpretation, and with the metaphysics of the Community. This I believe to be simply a new mode of approach to the very problems which I have formerly discussed.

My present interest lies in applying the spirit of my absolute voluntarism to the new problems which our empirical study of the Christian ideas, and our metaphysical theory of interpretation, have presented for our scrutiny.

With this, then, as the end now in view, let me try to tell you what attitude of will, what practical bearing towards the universe, what resolution, what plan of life, should characterize, in my opinion, any one who undertakes to view the world in the light of that doctrine concerning the nature and the business of interpretation, which, at the last time, I sketched.

This essentially social universe, this community which we have now declared to be real, and to be, in fact, the sole and supreme reality,—the Absolute,—what does it call upon a reasonable being to do? What kind of salvation does it offer to him? What interest does it possess for his will? If he accepts such a view of things, how should he bear himself towards the problem of life? To what ideas of his own does such a view offer success? How can he bring such a view into closer relations with ordinary human experience?

V

James declared that the typical pragmatist is a man of an essentially dramatic temper of mind. I now have to point out that the believer in our world of interpretation also centres his interests about a genuinely dramatic undertaking.

I have already said that the world of interpretation includes an infinite series of acts of interpretation. I have shown, in an earlier lecture, that every act of interpretation involves novelty. The believer in this doctrine of signs, the one to whom every problem, every antithesis, every expression of mind, every tragedy of life, is a sign calling for interpretation, and in whose belief the world contains its own interpreter, both contemplates and shares in a world drama. But the attitude of will which befits one who holds this doctrine of signs can only be rightly understood in case we first distinguish three very general attitudes of the will with which, in certain of their special forms, we have now become well acquainted. Our will is always dramatic in its expressions. It passes from deed to deed. Its world is a world of sequences and of enterprises. But when it surveys this world, and when it summarizes the spirit of its undertakings, the will may assume any one of three distinct modes of appreciating both itself and its realm of actual or of possible deeds.

VI

The first of these modes, the first of the attitudes of the will to which I here direct your attention, is that to which Schopenhauer gave the name, "The Affirmation of the Will to live." This phrase of Schopenhauer is intended by its author to be extremely general, and to apply to active dispositions which are exemplified by all sorts and conditions of men. Whatever the natural man seeks, he intends, says Schopenhauer, to live if he can. And when the natural man affirms this will to live, he may have in mind any one of countless different, or even conflicting, motives and purposes.

He may be seeking pleasure, wealth, power, praise, material possessions, or manifold spiritual goods. He may call it righteousness or food, that he desires. It may be the destruction of his enemies or the prosperity of his friends that he has in mind when he sets out towards his goal. He may be of any calling that you please. He may be a worldling or a recluse; a beggar or a king; an outcast or the centre of an admiring company. In brief, his special purposes may vary as you will. The ideas, the "leadings," which, in the pragmatic sense, he desires to have succeed, may vary from man to man and from life to life, throughout the whole range of our social and individual objects of desire.

But, in any case, if, in Schopenhauer's sense, such a man affirms the will to live, he essentially desires to be himself, whoever he may be, and to win his aims, whatever the special aims be to which he commits himself. This desire for self-assertion, then, is present in all the Protean shapes of the affirmation of the will to live, and vivifies them.

While one affirms the will to live, he therefore gives himself over to the great game of life. As an individual man he has his friends and his enemies; his triumphs and defeats; his joys and his sorrows of pain and grief. But what happens to him does not, in so far, touch the heart and core of his will. He may shout with triumph, or cry aloud in his woe; he may pray to his gods for help, or may curse his fate in what he calls his despair; but withal, he means to continue his pursuit of the objects of desire. He may repent of his sins; but not of being himself. He may, in his hatred of ill-fortune, resort even to suicide. But such suicide is merely a revolt against disaster. It only affirms in its own passionate way the longing for some life which is not indeed the present life of the rebel who seeks suicide, but which, in all his condemnation of his own deeds or of his own misadventures, he still longs to live, if only death and the universe will yet permit him to express himself.

VII

Schopenhauer usually emphasizes the essentially selfish nature of this will to live, as it inspires the individual man. Yet Schopenhauer fully recognizes that we are all social beings, and that the will to live can keep us eagerly busy in and with the world of our fellows. Only, as Schopenhauer rightly interprets this affirmation of the will to live, the recognition of his fellow-men which the victim of this will to live constantly makes, is based, so to speak, upon the natural solipsism of the individual will.

And here we come to the very root, the inmost meaning, of this first of the three attitudes of the will which we are here considering.

One who thus, in Schopenhauer's sense, affirms the will to live, may cheerfully and sincerely acknowledge that other men exist, and he may be a good member of society. But he tends to found this acknowledgment of his fellow-man, and of the social will, upon what most philosophers regard as an argument from analogy. A man may, by reason of such analogy, extend the realm to which his will to live applies its interests. The early and purely natural forms of family loyalty and of clan loyalty depend upon such practical expansions of the self. But, as we saw when we studied the Pauline doctrine of original sin, the will to live constantly meets its opponent in the wills of other individuals. And then its primal solipsism revives; and it hates its fellows. And even when such a will recognizes that an organized social will is in some sense a reality, it finds this social will either as a foreign fact, or as a mystery.

In brief, all the social facts seem to a man in whom Schopenhauer's will to live finds its natural affirmation, external and in general problematic, — known only through analogy and doubtfully. I will my own life; and observe my own life. My dealings with you seem, from this point of view, to be due to motives external to this will of mine.

"Why," says Professor James, addressing a supposed fellow-man in one of his essays on Radical Empiricism, "Why do I postulate your mind? Because I see your body acting in a certain way. Its gestures, facial movements, words, and conduct generally are 'expressive,' so I deem it actuated, as my own is, by an inner life like mine. This argument from analogy is my *reason*, whether an instinctive belief runs before it or not. But what is 'your body' here but a percept in *my* field? It is only as animating *that* object, *my* object, that I have any occasion to think of you at all."

In the form of this familiar argument from analogy, — an argument which many philosophers indeed regard as expressing our principal reason for believing that our neighbors' minds are realities, — James also puts into words an equally familiar aspect of the metaphysical view which naturally accompanies this affirmation of the will to live. I perceive my own inner life, or, at all events, my own facts of perception. By analogy I extend the world thus primarily known to me. Other men are, in this way, hypothetical extensions of myself. For the rest, I believe in them because, unless I take due account of them, they snub or thwart my own will to live. My ideas are my own, and it is of the essence of my life as this individual that I want my own ideas to "work." Upon this affirmation of my will to live depends all the truth that I shall ever come to know.

Pragmatism, in its recent forms, is indeed one of the most effective philosophical expressions which Schopenhauer's "Will to live" has ever received. Pragmatism is fond of insisting upon its cordial and unquestionably sincere recognition both of the social world and of the real existence of many selves, and of countless distinct ideas.

But as a fact, this recognition of the many selves, of the real world, and of the infinite variety of ways in which different ideas obtain now one and now another "working," — this entire view of truth and of reality, — when pragmatism deals with such matters, is founded upon the view that (as James loved to say) all "workings" are "particular." Each idea aims at accomplishing the event which, if reached, then and there constitutes the truth of that particular idea. Each idea therefore expresses and, as far as it can, affirms its own will to live. Each idea aims at its own success. Ideas, like all the other facts of James's world, hang together, as James was accustomed to say, "by the edges," if indeed they hang together at all. Their unities are temporary, accidental, and nonessential. The world of truth is thus indeed a dramatic world where each idea asserts itself while it can.

The life of truth is a drama wherein each pragmatic "leading," each individual expression of the will to succeed, "struts and frets its hour upon the stage, and then is heard no more."

Such is the philosophy wherein Schopenhauer's affirmation of the will to live finds its most recent, and, on the whole, as I suppose, its most effective expression.

VIII

In strong contrast to the affirmation of the will to live, Schopenhauer placed that attitude which he defined as the resignation, — the denial of the will to live. Here we have to deal with a tendency too well known to all students of the history of the spiritual life to need, in this place, extended portrayal, and too simple in its fascinating contrast with our natural life to require minute analysis. This is the attitude of the will which Southern Buddhism taught as the sole and sufficient way of salvation. In the form of saintly resignation the same ideal has received countless Christian expressions. Repeatedly this form of self-denial has been supposed to constitute the essence of Christianity. Repeatedly the expounders and defenders of the Christian doctrine of life have been obliged to insist that the Christian form of salvation does *not* consist in this simple abandonment of the will to live. I will not here repeat the tale which the greatest work of Christianity throughout the ages has so freely illustrated. Resignation alone does not save. To abandon his will to live does not by itself enable the individual to win the true goal of life. Let us, for the moment, simply accept this fact.

But since we are here interested in the metaphysical relations of these attitudes of the will, let us mention, in passing, that the resignation of the will to live is an attitude to which there correspond appropriate forms of metaphysical opinion. Here, again, the connections are well known, and need not here be dwelt upon. It is enough to say that whoever abandons the will to live, ceases, of course, to be interested in those "workings" of ideas which pragmatism regards as bringing us into empirical and momentary touch with the real. To such a resigned will, there remain only the cognitive processes of pure conception and of pure perception to consider. On the whole, in the history of thought those for whom salvation consists in the denial of the will to live have resorted to the metaphysics of pure perception, and have been mystics.

As has now been repeatedly pointed out by his critics, Bergson's philosophy consists of two parts,—a pragmatism which he regards as always incomplete and unsatisfactory, and a mysticism which, as he more fully expresses himself, he tends to make more prominent. The corresponding attitudes of the will also play their part, both in Bergson's cosmology and in his metaphysics. On the whole, Bergson thus far emphasizes the joyous aspect of his own philosophy of life. But plainly, in his view, the evolutionary process has been dominated by the will to live. And the inevitable outcome of such a domination, so long as the will to live takes the form which Schopenhauer and Bergson ascribe to it, is the discovery that such a realm of mere vital impulse is vanity, and vexation of spirit. Whenever the mysticism of Bergson is fully developed, by himself or by his followers, there will come to be expressed the corresponding attitude of the will. The vital impulse will be transformed into resignation; as Bergson's insistence upon free activity has already been subordinated to his counsel that we should give ourselves over to mere perception. When he tells us that the true artist perceives "for the sake of nothing, for the mere pleasure of perceiving," we remember Schopenhauer's saint, for whom "This our so real world, with all its suns and its milky ways," became "Nothing." Such, in fact, is the end of the mystic.

IX

But there is indeed a third attitude of the will. It is not Schopenhauer's attitude of the affirmation of the will to live. It is also not the other attitude which Schopenhauer believed to be the sole and sufficient salvation of the will. And this third attitude of the will possesses its appropriate metaphysics.

As for what this attitude of the will is,—when we consider, not its doctrine of the universe, but its doctrine of life,—we are already well acquainted with it, because our entire discussion of the Christian ideas was devoted to making us familiar with its moral and its religious meaning. In returning, at this point, to the mention of this attitude of the will, I do so because we now are ready to understand the relation between this type of will, and the metaphysical doctrine of which I believe it to be the fitting accompaniment. Whoever has learned to understand the meaning of this third way in which the will can bear itself towards its world, will therefore be better prepared to grasp the foundations upon which the metaphysics of interpretation rests. The human value of this practical attitude does not by itself fully reveal the grounds of the technical theory which is here in question. But the intimate relations between theory and life are nowhere more pronounced than in this case, where reason and sentiment, action and expression, throw light, each upon the other, as is hardly anywhere else the case.

The attitude of the will which Paul found to be saving in its power, just as, to his mind, it was also divine in its origin, was the attitude of Loyalty. Now loyalty, when considered from within, and with respect to its deepest spirit, is not the affirmation of the will to live of which Schopenhauer spoke. And loyalty is also not the denial of the will to live. It is a positive devotion of the Self to its cause, — a devotion as vigorous, as self-asserting, as articulate, as strenuous, as Paul's life and counsels always remained. The apostle himself was no resigned person. His sacrifices for his cause were constant, and were eloquently portrayed in his own burning words. They included the giving of whatever he possessed. But they never included the negation of the will, the plucking out of the root of all desire, in which Gotama Buddha found salvation. Paul died at his conversion; but only in order that henceforth the life of the spirit should live in him and through him.

X

Now this third attitude of the will, as we found in dealing with the whole Christian doctrine of life, has in any case its disposition to imagine, and also practically to acknowledge as real, a spiritual realm, —an universal and divine community. Christian theology, in its traditional forms, was a natural outcome of the effort to define the world wherein the loyal will can find both its expression and its opportunity. We have not now to consider the religious aspect of this third attitude of the will. But we are now fully prepared to state its relation to the metaphysical problems. All the threads are in our hands. We have only to weave them into a single knot.

As a reasonable being, when once I have come to realize the meaning of my dealings both with life and with the world, the first practical principle, as well as the first theoretical presupposition of my philosophy must be this: Whatever my purposes or my ideas, — whatever will to live incites me to create and to believe, whatever reverses of fortune drive me back upon my own poor powers, whatever problems baffle me, through their complexity and my ignorance, one truth stands out clear: Practically I cannot be saved alone; theoretically speaking, I cannot find or even define the truth in terms of my individual experience, without taking account of my relation to the community of those who know. This community, then, is real whatever is real. And in that community my life is interpreted. When viewed as if I were alone, I, the individual, am not only doomed to failure, but I am lost in folly. The "workings" of my ideas are events whose significance I cannot even remotely estimate in terms of their momentary existence, or in terms of my individual successes. My life means nothing, either theoretically or practically, unless I am a member of a community. I win no success worth having, unless it is also the success of the community to which I essentially and by virtue of my real relations to the whole universe, belong. My deeds are not done at all, unless they are indeed done for all time, and are irrevocable. The particular fortunes upon which James lays so much stress are not even particular, unless they consist of individual events which either occur or do not occur. Each of these real events has therefore a being which lasts to the end of time, and a value which concerns the whole universe.

Such, I say, is the principle, at once theoretical and practical, upon which my philosophy must depend. This principle does not itself depend upon the momentary success of any individual idea. For it is a principle in terms of which we are able to define whatever real life there is, while, unless this principle itself holds true, there is no real life or real world in which we can find success.

XI

Now this principle is one which, with various dialectical explanations, I have, in other essays of my own, repeatedly defended. And, as I have said, I have no wish whatever to repeat, in this context, my own previous discussions. The relation of this essentially social attitude of the decisive will to the doctrine of the community, leads me to show what this general and underlying attitude of the social will is, by mentioning, as I pass, and by way of illustration, that most familiar and most profoundly metaphysical of the problems of common sense, the problem: What reason can any one of us give for holding that the mind of his neighbor is real at all? For the attitude of will, the postulate, the resolution which any one of us takes when he says to his fellow, "You are a real being," is precisely that attitude which our metaphysical thesis advises us to take towards the whole world when it tells us to say to the world: "I know that you are real, because my life needs and finds its interpreter. You, O World, are the interpretation of my existence."

At all events, the case of the bases of our ordinary social knowledge is a test case deciding the whole attitude towards life and towards truth and towards the universe.

XII

For James, as you have already seen, my only and, to his mind, my sufficient ground for believing in my fellow's existence, for "postulating your mind," is an argument from analogy,—an extension of the inner life of my already known self, with its feelings, with its will, and with the workings of its ideas, into the perceived body of my neighbor, whose movements and expressions resemble mine.

Now, as a fact, the most important part of my knowledge about myself is based upon knowledge that I have derived from the community to which I belong. In particular, my knowledge about the socially expressive movements of my own organism is largely derived from what I learn through the testimony of my fellow-men. Therefore I cannot use the analogy of our externally expressive movements as my principal reason for believing in the reality of the inner life of my fellow-man, because I am very largely unable to perceive my own expressive movements in as direct a way as is that in which I perceive the organism and the movements of my fellow-man.

For instance, the appearance of my fellow's countenance is to me a sign of his mind. And signs of this type stand in the front rank of those facts of perception upon which my customary interpretation of his mind depends whenever he and I are in each other's presence.

But is my main argument for the thesis that my fellow's face expresses his mind,—and that his facial expressions are evidences of the existence of his mind, — an argument from analogy? Do I reason thus: "When my face looks thus, I feel so and so; therefore, since my neighbor's face looks thus, it is fair to reason by analogy that he feels so and so?" How utterly foreign to our social common sense would be this particular argument from analogy!

For, as a fact, I know very little about my own facial expressions, except what I learn, if indeed I learn it at all, through accepting as true certain reports of my neighbors regarding these facial expressions. I can indeed indirectly perceive my own face by looking in the mirror. But I thus learn hardly anything of importance to me about what my own changes of facial expression are. I have spent years of my life interpreting the signs which I read as I look at the countenances of other men. But when have I said to my neighbor: "Come, let us look in the glass together, so that, observing how my facial expression varies with my state of mind, I can learn to judge by the analogy of my own countenance what your changes of countenance probably mean?" To "postulate your mind" upon such a basis would be a form of solemn fooling.

The case is trivial, but typical for the way in which we interpret the usual signs of his mind which our neighbor gives to us. In large part, since I never normally view my own organism in a perspective which is closely analogous to the perspective in which I constantly perceive the body and the movements of my fellow-man. My most important knowledge about my own expressive movements comes to me at second hand. I learn how my own movements appear through the report of others.

Thus, then, I first believe that my fellow has a mind. As part or as consequence of this belief, I accept his testimony about how the movements of my organism seem when they are perceived by another man. As a result, I learn indirectly, and by the circuitous route that, so to speak, passes through my neighbor's mind, precisely the most significant of the analogies between my neighbor's expressive movements and my own. Yet these analogies are supposed, by James, and by the prevalent theory, to constitute my main evidence that my neighbor has a mind at all!

It would be hard to mention an instance of a more artificial doctrine than this prevailing opinion of philosophers regarding the bases of our social consciousness. Yet this is the very doctrine which James advances as a typical illustration of his own radical empiricism. What I, as an individual, never experience at all, — namely, precisely those analogies between my own doings and my neighbor's outward behavior which are socially most important, are named by James as furnishing my sole reason for "postulating your mind."

XIII

Why, then, do I indeed postulate your mind?

I postulate your mind, first, because, when you address me, by word or by gesture, you arouse in me ideas which, by virtue of their contrast with my ideas, and by virtue of their novelty and their unexpectedness, I know to be not any ideas of my own.

Hereupon I first try, however I can, to interpret these ideas which are not mine. In case you are in fact the source of these new ideas of mine, I fail to find any success in my efforts to interpret these ideas as past ideas of my own which I had forgotten, or as inventions of my own, or as otherwise belonging to the internal realm which I have already learned to interpret as the realm of the self.

Hereupon I make one hypothesis. It is, in its substance, the fundamental hypothesis of all our social life. It is the hypothesis that these new ideas which your words and deeds have suggested to me actually possess an interpretation. They have an interpreter. They are interpreted. This hypothesis simply means that there exists some idea or train of ideas, which, if it were now present within my own train of consciousness, would interpret what I now cannot interpret. This interpreter would mediate between the new ideas which your deeds have suggested to me, and the trains of ideas which I already call my own. That is, this interpreter, if he fully did his work, would compare all these ideas, and would both observe and express wherein lay their contrast and its meaning. My hypothesis is that such an interpreter of the novel ideas which your expressive acts have aroused in me, actually exists.

Now such an interpreter, mediating between two contrasting ideas or sets of ideas, and making clear their contrasts, their meaning, and their mutual relations, would be, by hypothesis, a mind. It would not be my own present mind; for by myself alone I actually fail to interpret the ideas which your deeds have aroused in me. And these ideas which your doings have aroused in me are simply not my own. Now this hypothetical interpreter is what I mean by your self, precisely in so far as I suppose you to be now communicating your own ideas to me. You are the real interpreter of the ideas which your deeds suggest to me. That is what I mean by your existence as an "eject."

The reason, then, for "postulating your mind" is that the ideas which your words and movements have aroused within me are not my own ideas, and cannot be interpreted in terms of my own ideas, while I actually hold, as the fundamental hypothesis of my social consciousness, that all contrasts of ideas have a real interpretation and are interpreted.

XIV

Our illustration has carried us at once into the mazes of our problematic social life together. But the case is a typical case. We have but to view it in its principle, and it shows what attitude of the will is the only decisive one in dealing with the interpretation of experience.

You are not a mere extension by analogy of my own will to live. I do not, for the sake merely of such analogy, vivify your perceived organism. *You are an example of the principle whose active recognition lies at the basis of my only reasonable view of the universe. As I treat you, so ought I to deal with the universe. As I interpret the universe, so, too, in principle, should I interpret you.*

We have no ground whatever for believing that there is any real world except the ground furnished by our experience, and by the fact that, in addition to our perceptions and our conceptions, we have problems upon our hands which need interpretation. Our fundamental postulate is: *The world is the interpretation of the problem which it presents.* If you deny this principle, you do so only by presenting, as Bergson does, some other interpretation as the true one. But thus you simply reaffirm the principle that the world has an interpreter.

Using this principle, in your ordinary social life, you postulate your fellow-man as the interpreter of the ideas which he awakens in your mind, and which are not your own ideas. The same principle, applied to our social experience of the physical world, determines our ordinary interpretations of nature and guides our natural science. For, as we have seen, the physical world is an object known to the community, and through interpretation. The same principle, applied to our memories and to our expectations, gives us our view of the world of time, with all its infinite wealth of successive acts of interpretation.

In all these special instances, the application of this principle defines for us some form or grade of community, and teaches us wherein lies the true nature, the form, the real unity, and the essential life of this community.

Our Doctrine of Signs extends to the whole world the same fundamental principle. The World is the Community. The world contains its own interpreter. Its processes are infinite in their temporal varieties. But their interpreter, the spirit of this universal community,—never absorbing varieties or permitting them to blend,—compares and, through a real life, interprets them all.

The attitude of will which this principle expresses, is neither that of the affirmation nor that of the denial of what Schopenhauer meant by the will to live. It is the attitude which first expresses itself by saying "Alone I am lost, and am worse than nothing. I need a counsellor, I need my community. Interpret me. Let me join in this interpretation. Let there be the community. This alone is life. This alone is salvation. This alone is real." This is at once an attitude of the will and an assertion whose denial refutes itself. For if there is no interpreter, there is no interpretation. And if there is no interpretation, there is no world whatever.

In its daily form as the principle of our social common sense, this attitude of the will inspires whatever is reasonable about our worldly business and our scientific inquiry. For all such business and inquiry are in and for and of the community, or else are vanity.

In its highest form, this attitude of the will was the one which Paul knew as Charity, and as the life in and through the spirit of the Community.

Such, then, is the relation of the Christian will to the real world.

The Historical
and the
Essential

In the fourth lecture of his book on "Christologies, Ancient and Modern," Professor Sanday says, of the development which was introduced into theology by Ritschl: "There is a great deal that is very wholesome in the movement out of which this development has sprung. It arose from, and has been sustained by, a great desire to look at the reality of things, to put aside conventions and to get into close and living contact with things as they are. It came to be seen that . . . as a complete philosophy of religion Hegelianism was too purely intellectual. It did not correspond to the true nature of religion, in which the emotions and the will are involved quite as much as the intellect."

I

The criticism of the religious philosophy of Hegel which these words summarily indicate, is further expressed by what Professor

Sanday says about the famous words in which David Frederic Strauss stated his own version of the Hegelian position regarding the person and work of Christ.

Strauss, as you remember, said: "As conceived of in an individual, a God-man, the attributes and functions which the Church doctrine ascribes to Christ contradict each other; in the idea of the Race they agree together. Humanity is the union of the two natures, God become man, the Infinite Spirit externalized as finite, and the finite spirit remembering its infinitude."

Professor Sanday makes the comment: "Strauss was driven to this substitution of the idea for the Person by his assumption that the idea never reaches its full expression in the individual, but only in the race. It is, however, not at all surprising that, after reducing Christianity to this shadowy semblance of itself, he should end by throwing it over altogether."

The criticism of Hegel's version of Christianity which Professor H. R. Mackintosh, of Edinburgh, expresses in the course of the historical section of his recent book on "The Doctrine of the Person of Jesus Christ," is longer and is also more explicitly hostile to Hegel's whole religious philosophy than are the few words which I have just cited from Professor Sanday. Professor Sanday — I ought to add — does not intend his own remark as any complete characterization of the position either of Hegel of Strauss.

Professor Mackintosh says, concerning the Hegelian view: "Christianity receives" (according to Hegel) "absolute rank, but at the cost of its tie with history. For only the world-process as a whole, and no single point or person in it, can be the true manifestation of the Absolute." . . . "Thus, when Hegel has waved his wand, and uttered his dialectical and all-decisive formula, a change comes over the spirit of the believer's dream; everything appears to be as Christian as before, yet instinctively we are aware that nothing specifically Christian is left." . . . "When once the Gospel has been severed from a historic person, and identified with a complex of metaphysical ideas, what it ought to be called is scarcely worth discussion; that it is no longer Christianity, is clear." . . . "Sooner or later, then, some one was bound to speak out, and expose the hollow and precarious alliance which had been proclaimed between the Christian faith and dialectic pantheism. The word which broke the spell came from Strauss."

Professor Mackintosh hereupon quotes from Strauss the further statement: "The Idea loves not to pour all its fulness into one example, in jealousy towards all the rest. Only the race answers to the Idea"; and adds, in a foot-note, "This formula has made a profound impression." And Professor Mackintosh continues: "It ought to be clear, by this time, that the proposed identification of the Christian faith with the ontological theory that God and man are one, — God the essence of man, man the actuality of God, — is an utterly hopeless enterprise, which the scientific historian cannot take seriously. . . ." "The truth is that the very idea of religion as consisting in personal fellowship with God, has faded from Strauss's mind, and with its disappearance went also in large measure the power to sympathize with, or appreciate, essential Christian piety as it existed from the first. . . ." "In general, it may be concluded that Hegelianism tended to commit a grave offence against history by construing Christianity as a system of ideas which is intelligible and effective apart from Jesus Christ."

II

I have quoted these two expressions of opinion, the one from Professor Sanday, and the other from Professor Mackintosh, in order to introduce the issue which in this lecture I have yet to face. I shall try to meet that issue as directly as I can.

We have not, in this discussion, first approached our problem of Christianity from the side of speculation, and then attempted to find a way of identifying a group of abstract ontological conceptions with those religious convictions which have been most prominent in the history of the Christian religion. On the contrary, my sketch of the Christian doctrine of life, and of the ideas which seem to me to be essential to that doctrine, made use of facts which belong to our common ethical and religious experience. We began with these facts. The metaphysical problems were kept in reserve until this more empirical part of the work was completed.

My hearer, if he kindly takes any interest in the present account of our problem, may indeed question whether those Christian ideas which I selected for discussion were rightly chosen. He may well insist that, in emphasizing certain aspects of Christianity, I have either ignored or slighted other aspects to which tradition has assigned the highest prominence. Such a criticism is, in part, obviously warranted. I have deliberately ignored much that tradition regards as the head of the corner. My hearer has a right to ask how my estimate of the essence of Christianity stands related to the historical faith; and he may think, if that seems to him just, that my views have involved "an utterly hopeless enterprise, which the scientific historian cannot take seriously." I cheerfully accept the risk of such a judgment upon my study of our problem of Christianity.

But I do not believe that the foregoing lectures can justly be accused of attempting to "identify the Gospel" with any *mere* "complex of metaphysical ideas."

Such Christian ideas as I have tried to interpret, I certainly did not invent. They found me. I did not devise them. They have led us, indeed, into the presence of the most intricate metaphysical problems; but no metaphysician ever discovered them. Nor are they merely a "complex of metaphysical ideas." They come to us from human life, from the life both of the Christian Church itself, and of those communities, secular or religious, which the noblest forms of loyalty have informed, and have redeemed, precisely in so far as men have yet learned to live the life of the universal brotherhood. For us the metaphysical meaning of these ideas has occupied, in our discussion, the second place.

Now I am indeed far from supposing that my fragmentary arguments and illustrations have exhausted the meaning of those Christian ideas which I have selected for discussion. I have been trying to tell what I see, and no more. Whoever finds in the Christian gospel meanings which tradition has emphasized, and which I have ignored, is welcome to put me in my place by whatever authority or reason he is able to employ. And since I am neither apologist, nor assailant, but am only, with the aid of my "broken light," an interpreter, I can feel no disappointment with my critic, and can find no painful defeat in the exposure of my inadequacy as an expounder of historical Christianity.

III

Scholarly opinion has, in recent decades, undergone many disappointing changes relating to the history of Christian origins. The goal of scientific agreement, both regarding the founder of Christianity, and regarding the life and history of the Christian Church in the apostolic age, is very remote. And I have no right to an opinion about problems of historical criticism.

Hence I have constantly tried, in these discussions, to avoid hazarding any personal impressions of mine about what actually took place on earth at the moment when the Christian religion originated. That there were the visions of the risen Lord, we know. I have no theory regarding how they originated. I do not know to what they were due. We are sure that what was called the presence of the Spirit in the Church displayed itself in the ways which Paul describes; for the writer of the greatest of the words in the Pauline epistles spoke to those to whom these experiences were present facts. The picture of the typical Pauline Church, and its faith, as the epistles present this picture, bears witness to its own essential human meaning. Furthermore, we possess that body of sayings and of parables which early tradition attributed to the founder. I am disposed to read these sayings as simple-mindedly as I can. They do not appear to me to constitute an expression of the whole Christian doctrine of life. They seem not to be intended as such a complete expression. I have tried to indicate some few ways in which these teachings, attributed to the founder, are most obviously related to the subsequent development of the main Christian ideas. The founder's life I must leave those to portray who have a right to judge the documents.

It will be remembered that I in no wise imagine, and have nowhere suggested, that Paul, in any just sense, was the real founder of Christianity. The Christian community into which Paul entered, and whose life he, as convert, so vastly furthered, this — I have said — this, together with its spirit, is the true founder of Christianity.

Such is the meagre foundation of historical fact by means of which I have ventured to justify the view regarding the Christian ideas which I have now laid before you. It is only my comment upon these ideas which has brought us into the region where, as a student of philosophy, I have some right to form and to express an opinion. In stating this opinion, I have of course been obliged to interpret some of those larger historical connections which even the layman in all matters of historical scholarship has a right, I believe, to regard as topics of general knowledge.

The thesis that the religious experience of the earliest Christian community, and in particular of the Pauline churches, lies, as a deeper motive, at the basis of the whole development and dogmatic formulation of the doctrine of the person of Christ, is not a new thesis. But in the form in which I have stated it, this assertion gets its most important meaning, in my own mind, through an interpretation of the nature of communities. This interpretation, as you now know, has an aspect which I have formulated in terms of human experience. It has also its technically metaphysical aspect. To insist upon this view of the nature of the community, and to develop the consequences that follow upon such a view, these enterprises have constituted the novelty, if there be any novelty, in my study of the essence of Christianity. These matters, as I believe, have not always been seen in the right perspective. I have done what I could to make them plain.

Now that my case has been stated, any one who holds opinions analogous to those of Professor H. R. Mackintosh might still urge upon me this question: "Is the fragment of traditional Christian doctrine which, in your own way, you interpret and defend, worthy to be called a religion at all? And if it is a religion, is this religion Christian?"

A plain question needs a plain answer. I feel a great indifference to the use of names in such regions. I am anxious to see the relations of the things that are named. So long as only technical theological formulas are in question, I do not in the least care whether this or that theologian calls me a Christian or not. But let me attempt one more mode of making clear the historical rights of my whole account of the essence of Christianity.

IV

One of the best ways of understanding our own religious ideas is to compare them, when we can, with those of some representative and highly trained Oriental mind. When intimate and practical religious interests are in question, such comparison is most effectively made through conversation with an Oriental friend, face to face. For a man speaks better than a book. Many of us will recall opportunities for personal meetings with men trained in civilizations remote from our own, as amongst the most instructive of our glimpses of what our own religion means to ourselves. The faith of our childhood, the religion of our social order, becomes for the first time clear to our consciousness when we try, at a moment of chance intimacy, to convey its deeper import to a mind that has been a total stranger to our own.

Now just as mutual remoteness of our present lives, when we are contemporaries one of another, sometimes helps an Oriental companion and myself to understand each his own faith better when we take counsel together, — even so the attainment of a new understanding of my faith might be accomplished for me, as one may imagine, if I were permitted to converse with fellow-men belonging, not only to a distant civilization, but also to a distant century. How precious for our appreciation, not only of antiquity but of ourselves, it would be if, escaping from the flood of time, we could talk over the essence of Christianity with an earnest and thoughtful Christian of the apostolic age,—not with an apostle, but simply with a convert whose personal experience was deep and genuine.

For my present purpose, the fiction—the arbitrary fancy, that such converse across the centuries might take place—has one very special and limited interest.

I have stated a thesis concerning the essence of Christianity. I should understand that thesis, no doubt, better, if indeed I were able to converse, in some fictitious realm, with a Pauline Christian,—a member of one of the apostolic churches. Let me try, in a few words, to make such a fiction momentarily intelligible to you.

It is easy to do this, I think, without trespassing upon any of the sacred places or memories of early Christian history. My sole intent is to furnish a test of the degree to which the account of the Christian ideas upon which I have insisted does furnish a just view of the essence of Christianity.

We have to compare what I take to be essential with what was, at all events in the Pauline churches and, for a time, historical Christianity. It would be useless, even were it possible, for me to make this comparison by means of any analysis of the Pauline Christology. And I could gain nothing by any poor effort of mine to amplify the picture which the best known of the epistles have left in the minds of all of us. Besides, I desire to bring the essential and the historical together in our minds, at this point, only for the sake of indicating a few very general relations of both of them to our modern problems.

My fiction must therefore illustrate large and abstract principles. It must also suggest the significance of certain very concrete religious experiences. Yet it must do this without leading us into any maze of historical details. And it must aid me to state my own case, and to show you what I suppose to be the situation which the modern mind has to face when we estimate the Christian ideas, not only in the light of human nature and of history, but also in their relation to the most abstruse problems of metaphysics. You will premit me the freedom of construction which is needed for just such a purpose.

V

Let us suppose, then, that some highly trained Greek,—as learned in philosophy as an extended sojourn in Athens, and as the training of any of the schools of his time, could make him, had been converted by Paul, had then for some years been a member of whatever Pauline church you please. I have in mind no man whose name the Acts, or the Epistles, or the legends of later days, have preserved to us. I am thinking of no famous saint, and of no one whose earlier life as a philosopher, or whose later devotion as a Christian, became a matter of record. As I now shall feign, my Greek of the first century was one to whom the ancient cultivation had made the highest appeal which it could make to the deeply religious mind of an ingenious child of his age.

Later, at the time of his conversion, my hero heard the message that Paul brought to the Galatians, to the Corinthians, — to the other best-known Pauline churches. Thereafter, quickened, made a new creature, our convert entered into the life of his own Christian community with all the fervor, the love, the patience, and the hope which the apostle had taught him to know. With the saints that were of his company, he rejoiced in the gifts of the spirit; he awaited longingly the last great change, and the return of the heavenly man whose death had saved him. Our hero treasured up and pondered long the apostle's words as various epistles, eagerly copied and transmitted from hand to hand and from church to church, brought them to his knowledge. And all this faith of the Church he interpreted with the clearness that his previous philosophical training had made possible.

And then, after years enough had passed to fill his soul completely with the full vision of the salvation of the whole world, — suddenly, in the fulness of grace, at the height of his own powers of mind, in the midst of his life of service, — he fell asleep, — whether at some moment of local persecution and of martyrdom, in blessed fulfilment of his dearest earthly desires, I know not.

So much my fiction first in outline sketches. But hereupon I shall imagine a great change. This is not the change which Christian hope, in the mind of a member of a Pauline church, contemplated. The fictitious change shall be this: From centuries of dreamless slumber, our Pauline Christian awakes in this modern world of ours. He retains, or soon again resumes, a perfect memory of all his former life, with its hopes, its religion, its faith, and its opinions regarding things on earth and in heaven. He awakes with the full consciousness of a mature and earnest Pauline Christian, but with no faintest ray of knowledge, at the moment when he returns to life, concerning the entire intervening history of mankind. He awakes, moreover, with the full intellectual equipment, with the ingenuity, and the thoughtfulness which his early training as a Greek philosopher had bred in him before his conversion.

And the task which some higher power sets him in our own day is the task of entering our world under conditions which are first to train him in the lore of our modern, of our secular, of our scientific, of our political, life, before his new education shall be allowed to bring him into contact with any form, or opinion, or tradition of the modern Christian Church.

He is to learn about what Christianity now means only after he has first been permitted, and stimulated, to become a highly trained product of the worldly cultivation of our age. In ancient times, before Paul's message told him of the power of grace, he was a philosopher. And even so, in the modern world, he has every opportunity which scientific study and which all forms of secular learning can furnish to him, within the time allowed for his new career. The result is to reawaken and train his philosophical interest; and to prepare him to master our problems,—except for one great limitation. Namely, until this new course of preliminary training has been duly completed by the powers who have his new life in their control, he is allowed to learn nothing of our problem of Christianity, nothing of what dogmas the Councils of the Church ever defined, nothing of the past relations between Christianity and the philosophers,—in brief, nothing that lets him know what any form of Christianity has been, except the one Christian faith under whose spell he lived of old, before the long sleep overtook him.

We are feigning indeed an artificial course for the new education to which our reawakened Christian is to be subject. Yet, if you choose to aid my halting imagination a little, I believe that you can even picture, yes, if you choose, can name, the places in our modern world where the ingenious and potent teachers, to whom charge over our hero has been committed, are able to keep their scholar long secluded from all knowledge of the Christian religion as it now exists, and of Christian history as it has run its course since the first century passed away. And yet, in such places (I leave you to name them),—these guides of our returned Greek, through due censorship of what he is permitted to read, and through a control of the things and of the people that he is permitted to see, allow him to gratify a vast range of modern curiosity; yet keep him, during his period of preparation, unaware of the very existence of a post-Pauline Christianity, and of our present religious situation. He studies long and deeply in the various realms of our science and of our art. When he meets in the course of these studies with allusions to religion, nobody, for a long time, tells him what they mean. He becomes absorbed in many of the problems of our social order. Nobody explains to him that this is a Christian social order. For in our day, as we all know, secular learning and religious lore live so much apart that he long fails to observe that they have any connections.

But I care not further to elaborate my fiction. Its purpose appears when I add that, by the will of the higher powers concerned, all this preliminary training of our hero is intended to lead to the moment when, still clear in his memory both of the Greco-Roman world as it was, and of Christianity as the apostolic churches had experienced its meaning, but now brought into close touch with the spirit of our own age, and acquainted with important results of our own science and art, our visitor from a former world is ready for the great issue. One more change comes.

At last, then, he is led face to face with Christianity as it is; and he is acquainted with the outlines of its history from his day to our own. Hereupon, indeed, his problem of Christianity and our problem stand together before him.

What has he now to say? And,—since I am here venturing to feign all this only as a means for making clearer my own case,—what, in reply to his imagined words, should I, if I were permitted to speak to him, have to offer to him as an answer to his problem?

VI

Our stranger from the past finds that many of the religious ideas which once were to him, as a Pauline Christian, very dear and—as he had supposed—quite essential, now are tragically at variance with what he has learned since he was awakened. The ascertained results of our science, the course of history, yes, some of the very ideas which he now finds to be most emphasized by the official traditions of the existing historical Church,—all these seem to be at war with the spirit which of old promised to guide the faithful into all truth. Our hero has awakened to a sad new world. If I have ventured thus tragically to disturb his slumbers, my only justification for the seemingly wanton intrusion upon his peace lies in the fact that his imaginary case is an allegorical picture of our own real case. As he wonders over the strange vicissitudes of faith, so ought we to wonder. Let us learn some of the lessons which he has to learn about the contrast between what is historical and what is essential in Christian faith.

Before any of his other instruction came to him, our guest from the apostolic age began his new life by finding, with deep disappointment, that the hope of which all the apostles, as far as he knew the apostles, made so much, has never been fulfilled. The end has never come. The Lord has not returned. The saints have not triumphed. The bride who waits in vain for the bridegroom. When Paul said, "Behold, brethren, I show you a mystery; we shall not all sleep; but we shall all be changed," the words seemed to our Pauline Christian an expression of an essential part of the faith. Both the resurrection of the dead and its early occurrence; both the meaning of the resurrection of Christ, and the certainty of the nearness of the Lord's return; both the hope of immortality and the assurance that the Kingdom must quickly come,—these matters together had seemed, to the apostolic converts, equally of the very essence of the faith. Paul had not divided these various teachings one from another. If some one of old had said to the believers: "The return of Christ is *not* near. The world is to undergo centuries of torment and of division; the Church itself is to be corrupted with power and distracted with earthly cares; the gifts of the spirit are to be for ages withdrawn; and no sign of heavenly salvation is for all those years to appear in the clouds";— then the faithful of the former time would have answered such a scoffer according to his faithlessness. They would have said of his words what Professor Mackintosh says of Hegel's waving of the dialectual wand; namely, that what the scoffer taught was possibly not worthy of any religious name; but was very certainly not Christianity.

Yet the very first discovery of our Greek, upon awakening, has been that every dearest hope of the early Church concerning the near deliverance of the suffering world was a delusion; and that certain of the apostle Paul's most burning and seemingly inspired words were a statement of literally and historically false predictions.

Since he became aware of what the Christian Church has become since the apostolic age, our Greek has had many reasons to reflect that if he, at least, is to remain a modern Christian, he must remember that he is a philosopher, and must begin in a new form the ancient task of distinguishing between symbol and truth, between figure and literally accurate statement, between parable and interpretation. So far as the end of the world is concerned, he has now learned that the Church itself, not long after the apostolic age, began a course in which all but certain transient and enthusiastic sects have persisted until this day. The Church learned, namely, to defend what it viewed as the essential faith of the apostles concerning the end of the world, only by declaring henceforth that the apostles either were not permitted truthfully to grasp this essential faith concerning last things, or else did not mean what they said, but used figures of speech.

This has constituted the first lesson concerning the relations between the historical and the essential which our early Christian saint, now transformed into a latter-day philosopher, has been forced to learn.

VII

Unquestionably, certain teachings about the person and work of Christ seemed of old, and still seem, to our reawakened Pauline Christian essential to the religion which Paul taught to him.

I will not attempt to restate what constitutes so much of the essence of Christianity: "I make known unto you, brethren, the gospel which I preached unto you, which also ye received, wherein also ye stand, by which also ye are saved, . . . in what words I preached unto you, if ye hold it fast, except ye believed in vain." This gospel, our Pauline Christian fully remembers. The cross, the death, the resurrection, the appearance of the risen Lord to the brethren,—these he knew to be matters which of old he fully accepted, so far as he then understood them. These he believed to be both essential and historical truths. His present problem is: How far, and in what form, is this heart of the Pauline doctrine something which for him to-day in the light of what the modern world has learned, and in view of what it has forgotten, he can still hold to be both true, and unchangeable, and adequate? When he reviews the transformations which time has wrought, is he still able to say, "Christianity is to remain for me what Paul said that it was"? "In this I stand; by this I am saved":—can he persist in using these words?

When he tries to answer this question, our guest has to remember that this modern world differs from the world in whose perspective Paul saw this picture of salvation; and differs too in many other respects besides those which now make Paul's language about the early return of the Lord appear to be a figure of speech whereby the early saints were actually misled.

In all those features which used most to appeal to his imagination, in the days of his apostolic discipleship, our returned Greek knows that the Pauline world has been, both for Christian believers in particular and for all typical modern men in general, simply transformed. Its heavens have passed away. Its very earth has become almost unrecognizable. All the most vividly interesting of those orders of spiritual beings whom Paul imagined as the background of his picture of salvation, have changed, or have entirely lost their meaning, for most of us. The Pauline angels were by no means similar even to those incorporeal spiritual beings of whom a later orthodox theology discoursed; and whom the scholastic angelology made a topic of learned speculation. Whatever non-human spiritual beings there are, nobody, whether orthodox mediæval Christian or modern man of science, conceives them as Paul imagined his angels. The Pauline demonology, too, has no meaning at all closely resembling its apostolic form, when even the most conservative scholastic theologian deals to-day with the beings still called by the same name.

Paul's whole picture of nature is remote from ours. Our re-awakened Greek knows that all the references to warfare with principalities and powers, that all the words of Paul regarding the mystery cults as involving a partaking of the cup of demons, must be interpreted in a profoundly symbolic fashion before they can now be understood or accepted. In fact, whatever the apostle told the churches of old can be retained only in case a large use of symbols is made.

When our Pauline Christian turns to the dogmas which the later Church has defined, and looks to them as his guides for interpreting the gospel wherein he once stood, and by which he was to be saved, he finds, in these later formulations, very much that seems to him almost as strange as Paul himself would have seemed if the apostle had been present to take part in a scholastic disputation during the Middle Ages.

And as to the central doctrine of the person of Christ, it was inseparable, in the mind of the Pauline Christian, from the doctrine of the living divine spirit present in the Church. And that, after all, was what the whole story of the life, the death, and the exaltation of Christ most meant to the Pauline believer. Moreover, as such a believer, our guest had known very little about the person of the historical Jesus, except what the story of the Divine death, of the resurrection, of the reappearance, of the exaltation, and of the indwelling of Christ, both in the Church, and in the believer's heart, had made for our guest himself, and for his brethren, in the old days, a matter of common social religious experience, and not of mere narrative. If the Pauline doctrine of the person of Christ was, then, indeed essential to the Pauline faith, this, its very essence, consisted in its character as a doctrine of the nature and life of the Church. For the exalted and divine Christ was explicitly known and interpreted by Paul as the very life of the Church itself. And his appearance on earth had its redemptive meaning through its power as the work of the founder of the beloved community.

Our returned saint stands, then, in presence of a great problem. If all this old faith is to mean anything to him to-day, *some* vast range of Pauline religious ideas must be regarded henceforth as symbols, as parables, as shadows cast by the things of some higher world, when they pass between the entrance of our cave and the realm of unapproachable light beyond. Our Pauline Christian of the twentieth century may well remember the vision of the divine which once was his. He may fully believe still in its essential truth. He may believe that this truth had its historical basis. But now that he has returned to our world, he must no longer trust indiscriminately all the shadowy appearances. He must distinguish between those which reveal the things of the spiritual world as they are, and those which essentially belong to the eyes of us who dwell in the cave. Our guest can remain, in spirit, a Pauline Christian, only in case he also learns, while justly recognizing the known world of to-day, how *not* to confer henceforth with flesh and blood, and how to discern spiritually the things of the spirit, despite the complexities of our modern realm.

What way will he find to escape from his problems, — to be just to the countless novelties of our present century, and yet not to lose the essence of the gospel which Paul preached unto him, which he also received, wherein also he stood, by which also he was to be saved?

VII

I have no right to mention any one answer which our guest must necessarily give to all the questions thus forced upon him. He may, for all that I know, either at this moment accept, or hereafter come to accept, any one of our current doctrines of the person of Christ, orthodox or liberal, dogmatic or speculative. But of this I am sure.

If he can, despite all the changes and the disillusionments to which he has already been subjected, and also despite all the further changes which he has yet to undergo; and in all the new light upon the essence of Christianity which coming centuries will bring to him, —if, I say, he can through all this remain true to the deepest spirit of his Pauline Christianity, despite the vast masses of ancient imagery and of legend which he must learn to view as mere symbols of deeper truth,—then the one thing by which he must hold fast is the Pauline doctrine of the presence of the redeeming divine spirit in the living Church. This doctrine, in some form, he must retain. If he can retain it, he will be in spirit a Pauline Christian, however he otherwise interprets the person of Christ.

So long as he is able somehow to hold fast to the principle of this doctrine,—then, no matter what he has already learned or hereafter learns to sacrifice, both of legend and of miracle; both of narrative and of abstractly formulated dogma; both of the literally interpreted words of the apostle concerning angels and concerning demons and concerning the coming end of the world; and no matter what, in due time, he has to sacrifice of the literally interpreted records of the gospel history,—through all this he will remain true,—not necessarily to all that, as Pauline Christian, he once held, or even thus far holds, to be essential. He will, however, remain true to what, as a fact, was the very heart of all the hearts of the faithful, both in the Pauline churches and in all the subsequent ages of Christian development.

The one condition of such holding fast by the deepest spirit of all the Christian ages is, I repeat, that he should still be able to say: The redeeming divine spirit that saves man dwells in the Church. So much our guest said when he was a saint of old. His problem of Christianity is now simply the problem whether he can say this to-day. His problem for the future is the problem whether he can continue to say this.

If, in order to be able to say this, he has to learn now, or in the future, to view as symbol, as legend, as myth, any accepted narrative that you may mention concerning the person of Christ, he will be in genuine touch both with the perfectly historical Christianity of Paul, and with the deepest meaning of the whole of Christian history, so long as he able to say, The divine spirit dwells in the Church, and thereby redeems mankind. So long as, for him, the Christ whom Paul preached is known, as he was to Paul, not mainly after the flesh, but after the Spirit, our returned Pauline Christian will deal with literal truth, precisely in so far as the divine spirit does dwell in the Church. And our guest will never lose touch with genuine historical Christianity, precisely so long as he, who learned this teaching, as Paul learned it, from the Church itself, holds it as the doctrine wherein is expressed whatever is most vital in Christianity, and whatever has always been most at the heart of the influence of Christianity upon civilization.

IX

Hereupon you may ask: "But what church shall our Pauline Christian accept as the true Christian Church?" The answer is simple. I have indicated that answer in the first part of our lectures.

Our guest will certainly *not* take a very profound interest in whatever has divided the later Christian world into great or into little mutually exclusive partitions. The official aspects of the post-Pauline church will *not* attract his most eager interest. Still less will he feel much concerned with the endless ebb and flow of the more petty sectarian strifes. His church, then, will be neither the official church nor the sect. Those efforts which ignore the larger human hopes and the universal mission of the apostolic Church, — those efforts which exhaust themselves in barren imitations of the enthusiastic accidents of the early communities, will not seem to our Pauline Christian to represent the Church which he knew.

He will therefore care not at all for the founding of still other and new sects. The great Church organizations he will value for whatever life of the spirit they have fostered. Their wars with one another or with the heretics he will regard as due to blindness, — to the original sin of man the social animal.

Least of all will he accept an interpretation of Christianity, if such there be, which, centering all its interests in an effort to perfect its picture of the human personality of the founder, believes the Church itself to be a relatively accessory or accidental feature of Christianity, — least of all will our Pauline Christian accept, I say, this interpretation (amongst all the serious attempts to deal with his problem) as the true expression of the essence of Christianity.

No, if our Pauline Christian is to remain true to the spirit of his original faith, the one essential article of his creed must be: The divine spirit dwelling in the living Church redeems mankind. Therefore, his test of the Church will simply be this, that, in so far as it is indeed the Church, it actually unifies all mankind and makes them one in the divine spirit. All else in Paul's teaching our guest may come to regard as symbol, or as legend. This he must hold to be literally true, or else he must lose the essence of his faith. The Church, however, must mean the company of all mankind, in so far as mankind actually win the genuine and redeeming life in brotherhood, in loyalty, and in the beloved community.

Our guest from the far-off first century has learned that the very power of the early Church was inseparable from its erroneous belief that the world was about to end. For only through this belief was it able to become sure that, through God's power, its intimate little companies, when they loved so well their life of the spirit, were witnessing, or were about to witness, the salvation of all mankind.

Now just as the Pauline churches were able to win truth even through the heart of their error,—even so, for our Pauline Christian, whatever errors have still to be abandoned, and whatever symbols have to be translated into new speech, the true Church is represented on earth by whatever body of men are most faithful, according to their lights, to the cause of the unity of all mankind. Therefore no sect, no detached individual, and no official organization can constitute the true Church, except in so far as such body or individual shall be found full of the spirit and actually furthering the advent of the universal community. Yet, for our Pauline Christian, if he can indeed hold fast his early faith, the Church will be a reality, just as, to his mind, it was already real in the little Pauline communities, and just as it is now real wherever two or three are gathered together in the name of the genuinely divine spirit.

All this, I say, our Pauline Christian can regard as in essence the faith of the apostles. If despite all changes he still can hold that so much of their faith was literally true, then nobody need dictate to him what he shall further hold regarding the person or regarding the work of Christ. Christ was for Paul the indwelling Spirit of the community, whose personal history was, for him, an historical reality, spiritually interpreted, just as the coming judgment was a near future historical event, and was also to be historically interpreted. Our reawakened Pauline Christian will remain true to his original faith so long as he can retain its spiritual interpretation. He will also remain true to a genuinely historical Christianity, so long as he holds fast by his Pauline faith. And this essential faith in the divine presence of the spirit in the Church he can retain, whatever be his view as to the literal correctness of the reports of the coming judgment, and whatever he comes to hold, as to the correctness of this or of that account of the person of Christ.

X

Herewith I come to the one word which I should wish to offer to our guest were I permitted to present to him the doctrine of the community which, in this second portion of our discussion, I have attempted in outline to expound and to defend.

The final task of interpretation which I thus assume is determined, for me, both by the general plan of our whole inquiry, and by the feigned situation of our Pauline Christian. His case, as I have stated it, is a dream of my own. But in the truth his fancied case is our real case. He is our genuine modern man. He is the child of the whole historical process of humanity. His is the education of the human race. Modern civilization, with all its problems and its tragedies, is, in the very loftiest of its hopes, in the most precious of its spiritual possessions, in the heart of its deepest faith, a product, — yes, if you will, despite its endless crimes, — a disciple and a convert of the divine spirit that for a while manifested itself in the Pauline churches.

I say this in no partisan spirit, and not in the defence or in the praise of any sect, or of any one Christian church, nor even for the sake of extolling the work which the whole Christian labor of the centuries has accomplished. The Christian churches and nations of mankind have done as yet but the very least fragment of what it was their task to accomplish; namely, to bring the Beloved Community into existence, or to bring the Kingdom of Heaven to earth. But, in all their weakness, their blindness, their strifes, the Christian churches and nations have had this to their spiritual profit; namely, that to them has been committed the greatest task of the ages; and they have been more or less clearly aware of the fact. So far as they have been thus aware, they have gradually grown in the practice and in the love of the art of brotherhood. They have also tended towards the organization, still so remote, in which the ideal of the Church is yet to find its expression, if indeed humanity ever succeeds in its task at any time. Hence, indeed, our Christian civilization, precisely in so far as it has thus succeeded, has expressed the power of precisely that spirit which manifested itself in the Pauline churches. And if, hereafter, what we now call Christian civilization passes away, and if what we now know as a civilization alien or hostile to Christianity comes to undertake this task of unifying mankind, and succeeds therein, — then that strange new civilization will never be more remote, we may be sure, from the life of the Pauline churches, and from the spirit which dwelt in them, than we now are. Even now, the name Christian is a very small thing in comparison with the right to use that name which any company of men, of any faith under heaven, possess, if indeed the Pauline charity pervades their life, unifies their own community, and thus brings nearer the brotherhood of all mankind, and the triumph of the true and only church universal.

Our guest, then, has the same problem with ourselves. If he is true to his faith, and if we know what true loyalty is, he and we acknowledge one Lord and one faith. What we both desire to know is whether this faith has a literal foundation in the deepest nature of things. Is the whole real world the expression of one divine process? And is this process the process of the Spirit?

XI

Our guest is a philosopher. As such I address him. In his case there is no fear lest I should arouse false hopes of merely verbal agreements. He has been too much and too often disillusioned to be likely to mistake my own use of symbols for a careless or an unjust desire to arouse false hopes. He knows that I have no legends to defend from critical attacks. He knows that the world of which I speak is one to which only one perfectly determinate portion of the Pauline phraseology applies. I have already said what that portion is. I now have only to summarize that word.

Addressing our guest, I should sum up the result of our metaphysical inquiry thus: The world is the process of the spirit. An endless time-sequence of events is controlled, according to this account, by motives which, endless in their whole course, interpret the past to the future. These motives express themselves in an evolution wherein to every problem corresponds, in the course of the endless ages, its solution, to every antithesis its resolution, to every estrangement its reconciliation, to every tragedy the atoning triumph which interprets its evil. That this, on the whole, is the character of the world-process, our argument has insisted. But how this reconciliation takes place, we have not attempted to know. Concerning the details of the world of time, we can learn only by historical experience.

But, this,—such is my thesis,—this is the world of interpretation whose outlines, in the foregoing, I have been attempting, very dimly, to portray. This world is throughout essentially social, as is also our own human world. It is essentially historical, as is any world involving a time-process. It is essentially teleological as is every world wherein we can speak, as, according to our philosophy of interpretation, we can justly speak, of a process involving true development.

Now of this world as a whole, our sketch has indeed attempted to suggest the barest outlines. The principal feature which, in these lectures, I have been able to portray, is that this world has the structure of a community.

But hereupon there remains one further and centrally important feature upon which to insist. This endless order of time stands in contrast to an ideal goal, which the world endlessly pursues with its sequence of events, but never reaches at any one moment of the time sequence. The pursuit, the search for the goal, the new interpretation which every new event requires,—this endless sequence of new acts of interpretation,—this constitutes the world. This *is* the order of time. This pursuit of the goal, this bondage of the whole creation to the pursuit of that which it never reaches,—this naturally tragic estrangement of this world from its goal,—this constitutes the problem of the universe.

"Such," so I should say, addressing our guest: "Such was your Pauline world. Lost it was; because through no earthly power could it ever reach its goal. It was groaning and travailing in pain until now. It needed a deliverer. It hoped for such a deliverer. The Christian Church believed that, through the might of the spirit, the world had, at last, found its deliverer. The divine spirit had appeared on earth, and now dwelt in the community of the faithful."

"Paul's symbols," so I should continue (still addressing our guest), "were but images of the truth when he spoke of the coming end of the world. So were his symbols but allegorical when he told of the way in which the world was redeemed. But concerning the redemption of the world he knew two absolute truths. Both of them he expressed in figures. Let me express both of them in terms of our doctrine of the real community.

"The salvation of the world occurs progressively, endlessly, in constant contest with evil, as a process that is never ended. The deeds which we know as genuinely interpreting the past to the future, as the reconciling deeds, as the deeds which accomplish what is possible towards making the world seem to us a divine process, are deeds of charity and of atonement. These can exist in their true form only in the community. In the human world you of the Pauline churches knew them as the deeds through which the divine spirit was manifested. These deeds, as you asserted, not the power of flesh and blood, but the spirit who founded the Church, and who dwelt in it, accomplished.

"Our doctrine of the world as a community, of the social life of the universe endlessly revealing the divine,—never wholly at any one time, but in the world's process, expresses in the form of the metaphysics of the community what you grasped through an intuition of faith.

"But the salvation of the whole world, the consciousness that in its wholeness the world is and expresses and fulfils the divine plan, and is wholly interpreted and reconciled,—this is something which is never completed at any point of time. Yet this unity of the spirit, this consciousness of reconciliation, this triumph over the universal death whereof every event in time furnishes an illustration, this occurs, in our world of interpretation, not at any one moment of time, but through an insight into the meaning of all that occurs in time. We do not declare, in our metaphysical doctrine, that the divine consciousness is timeless. We declare that the whole order of time, the process of the spirit, is interpreted, and so interpreted that, when viewed in the light of its goal, the whole world is reconciled to its own purposes. The endless tragedies of its sequence are not only interpreted step by step through deeds of charity and of atonement, but, as it were (I speak now wholly in a figure), 'in a moment, in the twinkling of an eye,' the whole of time, with all its tragedies, is, by the interpreter of the universe, reconciled to its own ideal. And in this final union of temporal sequence, of the goal that is never attained in time, and of the divine spirit through whom the world is reconciled to itself and to its own purpose, the real community, the true interpretation, the divine interpreter, the plan of salvation,— these are expressed."

"This," I should say to our guest, "is indeed not religion, but metaphysics. You as philosopher, and as Pauline Christian, well know the distinction. But you at least know what is vital in Christianity. You know your own problem and ours. You then can judge, you who are the true heir of all the ages,—the true modern man,—whether we have, in all this, duly distinguished between the essential and the historical, and shown their unity."

"At all events," so I should finally say, "we know that whether the modern man calls himself a Christian or not, is a matter of names. We know, however, what it is to believe in the presence of the spirit in the Church. We know that whoever can see his way to define and to justify such a belief, may indeed not be called a Christian, but has solved what is indeed essential about the problem of Christianity."

XVI

Summary and Conclusion

In beginning these lectures I said that I should undertake the task neither of the apologist nor of the hostile critic of Christianity.

I

Some of my hearers may have thought this statement to be modelled after the word of "jesting Pilate," who asked, "What is truth?" but "stayed not for an answer." When I added, at the same time, that I should also avoid the position, not only of the hostile, but of the indifferent critic of Christianity, the paradox of this initial definition of our undertaking may have appeared to become hopeless. "What?" —so my hearer may have inwardly exclaimed,—"neither apologist, nor hostile critic, nor yet indifferent? What manner of philosophy of the Christian religion can such a student propound? A Pilate,—but a Pilate who adds that he is not even indifferent,—who shall assume and maintain this character?"

I was willing, at the outset of our course, to accept the risk of such a judgment. I then justified my position merely in so far as the emphasis upon our title: "The Problem of Christianity," enabled me to remind you from the outset that problems ought to be considered, if possible, with an open mind. Yet you will also have felt that whoever discusses a problem hopes to reach some result; and that whoever invites others to take part with them in such a discussion is responsible for showing in the end, to those who listen, some outcome which will make the quest seem to them worth while. And if indeed we are to get any result from the study of the problem of Christianity, must not such a result take the form either of a defence or of an attack, or of a counsel to regard the whole topic with indifference? With such obvious objections in mind some of you may have listened to our first lecture.

But now that our inquiry is completed, and now that we come to summarize its results, are we not prepared to return to our initial statement, and to see why, despite its paradox, it was justified, and has not proved fruitless? Nothing is farther from my wish than to magnify unduly the extremely modest office of the philosophical inquirer. But when I now ask, not: "What have I, in all my weakness as a student of philosophy, accomplished in the course of these few lectures?" but "What word would an ideally trustworthy teacher, if such were accessible to us, address to the modern man concerning the problem of Christianity?" I have to remember that not merely Pontius Pilate, but quite another man, is reported to have said something that bears upon this very problem. Let my words, so far as they are mine, be forgotten. But let us remember that John the Baptist, according to the gospel story, was no apologist for the teaching of the Kingdom of Heaven, and was still less its hostile critic, and was least of all an indifferent critic. What the burden of his preaching was, we all know: "The axe is laid at the root of the tree. The Kingdom of Heaven is at hand." John did not create a new sect. He did not preach a new creed. He did not himself undertake to found a new religion. He did not defend; he did not assail the Kingdom of Heaven. He announced that a religion, long needed, was yet to come. His references to the early end of all things, and to the imminence of the final transformation of human affairs, may well have been, like all other Apocalyptic announcements of those days, only symbols. But the deeper meaning that lay beneath his teaching was none the less true. I hold that this deeper meaning is still true. The

Kingdom of Heaven is still at hand in precisely the sense in which every temporal happening is, in its own way, and, according to its special significance, a prophecy of the triumph of the spirit, and a revelation of the everlasting nearness of the insight which interprets, and of the victory which overcomes the world.

II

The essential message of Christianity has been the word that the sense of life, the very being of the time process itself, consists in the progressive realization of the Universal Community in and through the longings, the vicissitudes, the tragedies, and the triumphs of this process of the temporal world. Now this message has been historically expressed through the symbols, through the traditions, and through the concrete life of whatever human communities have most fully embodied the essential spirit of Christianity. We know not in what non-human forms the spiritual life may now or hereafter find its temporal embodiment. Our metaphysical doctrine, dealing, as it does, with universal issues, is quite unable to extend our vision to any heavenly realm of angelic powers. We have undertaken merely to defend a thesis regarding the form in which the life of the community, whether human or non-human, finds its conscious expression.

On earth, as we have seen, the universal community is nowhere visibly realized. But in the whole world, the divine life is expressed in the form of a community. Herewith, in teaching us this general but intensely practical truth, the "kindly light" seems also to show us not, in its temporal details, "the distant scene," but the "step" which we most need to see "amid the encircling gloom." And our little task it has been to learn whether, for our special purpose, that step is not, in just our present sense, "enough."

III

This is why we have been right to take, not Pilate indeed, but John the Baptist, for our guide. The Kingdom of Heaven is "at hand." For, in the true unity of the spirit, we always stand in the presence of the divine interpretation of the whole temporal process, and are members, if we choose, of the truly universal community. Yet, since only the whole of time can express the whole of the ideal, and can exhaust the meaning of the process of the spirit, no one event constitutes "the coming of the end," and the true church never yet has become visible to men. And that is true simply because the meaning of the whole of time can never become adequately visible at any one moment of time. Whoever preaches the Kingdom must accept this limitation of every finite and temporal being. He must not say: Lo here! and Lo there! Signs and wonders will not be vouch-safed to him, or to his hearers, as sufficient to present any immediate vision of the divine presence. The truth of the word: "Lo, I am with you alway, even unto the end of the world," will never be merely perceived; just as this same truth will never be expressible in terms of the abstract conceptions which James found to be so "sterile." This truth is simply the truth of an interpretation. What it means is that, for every estrangement that appears in the order of time, there somewhere is to be found, and will be found, the reconciling spiritual event; that for every wrong there will somewhere appear the corresponding remedy; and that for every tragedy and distraction of individual existence the universal community will find the way — how and when we know not — to provide the corresponding unity, the appropriate triumph. We are saved through and in the community. There is the victory which overcomes the world. There is the interpretation which reconciles. There is the doctrine which we teach. This, so far as we have had time, in these brief lectures, to state our case, is our philosophy, and this doctrine, as we assert, is in agreement with what is vital in Christianity.

The apologists for Christian tradition generally fail to express such a doctrine, because they misread the symbols which tradition has so richly furnished. The assailants of Christianity are generally ignorant of the meaning of the ideal of the universal and beloved community. Those who are indifferent to Christianity are generally unaware of what salvation through loyalty signifies. Hence it has been necessary for us to refuse to take part with any of the parties to the traditional controversies. Hereby we have been able to interpret, however, what the apologists and the critics of Christianity equally need to recognize. Therefore I submit that our quest has not been fruitless.

IV

Our last words must include two final attempts to set our case before you for your judgment. The first of these attempts will be an effort to furnish one more illustration of our philosophy. The second attempt will endeavor to point out a practical application of our foregoing teaching.

Let me briefly indicate what each of these closing considerations will be. First, let me speak of the illustration of our philosophy which I here propose to offer.

I have already said that we cannot, like the founders of new religious faiths, point to any sign or wonder as the evidence that we have rightly interpreted the divine process of which the world is the expression. Yet, as I leave our argument, in its incomplete statement, to produce, if possible, some effect upon your future thoughts about these matters, I wish to call your attention,—not to a further technical proof of our philosophy of interpretation, but to a closing exemplification of its main doctrine. This example may serve to bring our philosophy, which many of you will have found too recondite and too speculative, into closer touch with certain thoughtful interests which not only our own age, but many future ages of human inquiry, are certain to cherish.

I wish, namely, to indicate that our main thesis concerning the World of Interpretation is not only in harmony with the spirit which guides the researches of the empirical natural sciences, but is, in a very striking way, suggested to us afresh when we ponder the meaning which the very existence and the successes of the empirical sciences seem to imply. In other words, I wish to show you that our theory of the World of Interpretation, and our doctrine that the whole process of the temporal order is the progressive expression of a single spiritual meaning, is—not indeed proved—but lighted up, when we reconsider for a moment the question: "What manner of natural world is this in which the actual successes of our inductive sciences are possible?"

You will understand that what I say in this connection is a mere hint, and is not intended as a demonstrative argument. Our philosophy of interpretation teaches that the whole of time is a manifestation of a world-order which contains its own interpreter. But the illustration to which I shall call your attention shows us a connection between philosophical idealism and natural science such as few have ever recognized. Once more I have here to express my indebtedness to Charles Peirce. For it is he who has repeatedly pointed out that this matter to which I shall call your attention has a deep meaning, and tends to make probable a thesis about the nature of things which we shall find to be in close harmony with our doctrine of the world as a progressively realized Community of Interpretation.

So much for a hint of the first of the two matters which these closing words will call to your notice. The second matter will concern the practical outcome of our quest. I have no new faith to preach, and no ambition to found either a sect or a party. But it is fair to ask yet one question as the last issue which we have time to face. If our account of the Problem of Christianity is true, what ought we to do for the furtherance of our common religious interests? With a summary formulation of that question, and with a very little counsel regarding its answer, my lecture, and this course, will end.

V

Next, then, let me sketch my closing illustration of our philosophy of interpretation. Let me show you that there is a harmony, unexpected and interesting, between the view of the universe which the general philosophy of these lectures defends, and the result to which we are led when we ponder, as Charles Peirce has taught us to ponder, upon the conditions which make the actual successes of our natural sciences possible.[1]

Every one knows that the natural sciences depend, for their existence, upon inductive inquiries. And all of us are aware, in a general way, of what is meant by induction. When one collects facts of experience and then infers, with greater or less probability, that some proposition relating to facts not yet observed, or relating to the laws of nature, is a true proposition, the thinking process which one uses is called inductive reasoning. The conditions which make a process of reasoning inductive are thus twofold. First, inductive reasoning is based upon an experience of particular facts. That is, inductions depend upon observations or experiments. Secondly, what one concludes or infers, from the observations or experiments in question, follows from these facts not necessarily, but with some more or less precisely estimable degree of probability. The terms "inductive inference" and "probable inference" are almost precisely equivalent terms.[2] If you draw from given premises or presuppositions a conclusion such that, *in case* the premise is true, the conclusion *must* be

[1]Charles Peirce has repeatedly given expression to the thoughts about the nature and conditions of the inductive sciences to which I here, in passing, shall refer. A notable expression of opinion upon the subject occurs in a brief passage contained in his extremely interesting essay entitled "A Neglected Argument for the Being of God," published in the *Hibbert Journal* during 1908.

[2]Objections to an assertion of the *precise* equivalence of the terms "inductive inference" and "probable inference" exist, but need not be discussed in the present

true, the process of reasoning which is in question is called "necessary inference" or "deductive inference" (these two terms being, for our present purposes, equivalent). But if, upon assuming certain premises to be true, you find that they merely make a given conclusion *probable*, the inference which guides you to the conclusion is an inductive inference.

Examples of such inference may easily be mentioned. Thus a life insurance company, in assuming new risks, and in computing premiums, is guided by mortality tables. Such tables summarize, in a statistical fashion, facts which previous experience has furnished regarding the ages at which men have died. The insurance actuaries compute, upon the basis of the tables, the mortalities of men who are yet to be insured. The results of the tables and of the computations are probable inferences to the effect that of a certain number of men, who are now in normal condition and who are of a given age, a certain proportion will die within a year, or within ten years, or within some other chosen interval of time. Such probable inferences are used, by the insurance company, in determining the rate at which it is safe to insure a given applicant who appears to be, upon examination, a "good risk" for his age. Nobody can know when any one individual man will die; and the insurance company draws as few inferences as possible regarding the case of any one individual man. But the premium charged to the individual man who wishes to insure his life is determined by the fact that the company is insuring, not this man alone, but a large number of men at about the same time; and inferences about the proportion of some large number of men who will die within a year, or within ten years, can be rendered, through the use of good methods, very highly probable. Now the insurance company's processes of inference include some numerical computations which, within certain limits, remain mainly deductive. For the outcome of a correct numerical computation is, when considered in itself, a necessary inference. But the principal and decisive basis of the insurance company's inferences is such that the inferences drawn are inductive and not deductive. That is, the reasoning of the insurance company is based upon particular observed facts, and the conclusions drawn are merely probable conclusions. If the mortality tables are correct, these conclusions, when applied to

connection, since they are irrelevant to the matter which Charles Peirce's comment here calls to our notice.

large numbers of insured persons, are highly probable. They are never certain.

What the insurance companies do when they reason about taking new risks is an example of a method widely used in the natural sciences. A collection of facts of observation, a statistical study of these facts, and a probable inference based upon such statistics,— these, in many cases, make up a great part of the work of an inductive science.

VI

But the statistical methods used by the insurance companies are not the only methods known to natural science. Another sort of probable inference is also known, and is, in many cases, of much more importance for natural science than is the more directly statistical method which the insurance companies use. This other method is known to you all. It is the method of forming hypotheses and of testing these hypotheses by comparing their results with experience. Let me mention a well-known instance of this method. We can then see how it contrasts with the methods most frequently used by the insurance companies, and why it is a valuable method.

An enthusiastic student of antiquity, the now celebrated Schliemann, was deeply influenced, a half century ago, by the hypothesis that the story of the Trojan war, as told in the "Iliad," had a substantial basis in historical fact. This hypothesis was not new; but just at that time it was in disfavor when judged in the light of the prevailing opinions of the classical historians. Schliemann gave to this hypothesis a new vividness; for he was an imaginative man. But in making the hypothesis vivid, he made it more and more improbable by adding to it the further hypothesis that the ancient tradition as to the site of Troy was also historically well founded. Having formed his hypothesis, he reasoned in a way that, for our momentary purpose, we may roughly summarize thus: "If the Homeric story of the Trojan war was historically well founded, and if the ancient traditions about the site of the real Troy were also true, and if nothing has since occurred to render unrecognizable the ruins which were left when Troy was burned,—then, in case I dig in just that mound, yonder, I shall find the ruins of a large city, which once contained palaces and treasures, and which will show signs of having been burned."

Now this hypothesis of Schliemann about Troy was, when he

formed or reformed his conjectures upon the topic, a seemingly very unlikely hypothesis. But Schliemann dug, and the now well-known ruins came to light.

Hereupon you will all agree that, from the facts of experience which were thus presented for further judgment, no important conclusion could be said to follow deductively and as a necessary condition. And as a fact Schliemann is known to have overestimated both the probability and the importance of the conclusions which he himself drew from his discoveries. Later research corrected his conclusions in many respects. But all of us will agree that in one respect Schliemann's success when his excavations were made very greatly changed the probability of his own assertion that the Homeric story of the Trojan war had some basis in historical facts. What he said was: "If this old story is true, and if I dig in yonder mound, such and such things will come to light." The success of his excavations, the fact that such things as he had predicted actually came to light when he dug, — all this did not demonstrate, but did make probable, the assertion: "This old story has a real basis in historical truth." The very fact that, before the excavation was tried, Schliemann's hypothesis about the truth of the old story of the sack of Troy seemed improbable, and that his expectations of success in digging for the ruins appeared extravagant and unwarranted, — this very fact made his actual success all the more significant. Common sense at once commented: What could lead to such an antecedently unlikely success as that of Schliemann, unless the idea which guided Schliemann's excavations had some basis in fact? Nothing was demonstrated by Schliemann's first discoveries. But a new probability had henceforth to be assigned to the hypothesis which had led to Schliemann's predictions and discoveries, — namely, that some historical foundation existed for the story of the Trojan war.

VII

Schliemann's triumph, such as it was, is familiar. It furnishes a typical instance of the second of the two leading processes of inductive reasoning. This second method is that of hypothesis and test. Suppose that we make some hypothesis A. Hereupon suppose that we are able to reason, in advance of further experience, that if A is true, some fact, let us say E, will be observed, in case we meet certain conditions of observation or of experiment. Then, the more unlikely it is, in the light of previous knowledge, that the fact E should be observable under the mentioned conditions, the more does our actual success in finding the fact of experience, E, at the place and time where the hypothesis had led us to look for it, render probable the assertion that there is at least some measure of truth about the hypothesis A.

The method used by the insurance companies, when they apply facts which are summarized in the mortality tables as a guide for future insurance transactions, depends upon reasoning from experiences which we have already collected, to the probability of assertions about facts which are as yet unobserved. The other method of induction,—the method which, in his own way, Schliemann exemplified, follows an order which is, in part, the reverse of the order of the reasoning process which the insurance companies emphasize. This second method of induction consists of first inventing some hypothesis A, which is adapted to the purpose of the investigator. Then the user of this method discovers, usually by some process of deductive reasoning, that, if the hypothesis A is true, some determinate fact of experience E will be found under certain conditions. The investigator hereupon looks for this predicted fact E. If he fails to find it, his hypothesis is refuted, and he must look for another. But if he finds E where his hypothesis had bidden him to look for E, then the hypothesis A begins to be rendered probable. And the more frequently A is verified, and the more unexpected and antecedently improbable are these verifications, the more probable does the hypothesis A become.

The most important and exact results of the inductive sciences are reached by methods in which the verification of hypotheses plays a very large part. Galileo used hypotheses, computed what the results would be in case the hypotheses were true, and then by further experience verified the hypotheses. So did Newton; so in a very different age, and in a very different field, did Darwin. Upon the process of inventing hypotheses, of computing their consequences, and of then appealing to experience to confirm or refute the hypotheses, the greatest single advances in physical science rest.

And the principle used in this branch of induction may be stated thus: —

When without any antecedent knowledge that the consequences of a given hypothesis are true, we find, upon a fair examination of the facts, that these consequences are unexpectedly verified, then the hypothesis in question becomes, not certainly true, but more and more probable.

VIII

These general remarks about the inductive methods used in science may seem to some of you to be mere commonplaces. But they have been needed to bring us to the point where Charles Peirce's remark about the significance of the actual successes of scientific method can at length be appreciated.

If the only methods followed by the natural sciences were the statistical methods of the insurance companies; if all the work of scientific induction were done, first by making collections of facts, such as mortality tables exemplify, and secondly by making probable predictions about the future based mainly upon the already observed facts, as the insurance companies issue new policies on the basis of the already existing tables, then indeed the work of the inductive sciences would be progressive, but it would not be nearly as creative as it actually is.

In fact, however, the inductive sciences owe their greatest advances to their greatest inventors of hypotheses, — to men such as Galileo or as Darwin. To be sure, when the inventors of scientific hypotheses are in question, these inventors must also be not only inventors, but also verifiers, and must be willing readily to abandon any hypothesis whose consequences conflict with experience. But since it is the actually successful, while far-reaching, hypothesis which adds the most new probabilities to science, the art of making great advances, especially in the most exact branches of physical science, must especially depend upon the power to invent fitting hypotheses.

Now a very good hypothesis depends, in general, for its high value, first upon its novelty; secondly, upon the fact that, when duly tested, it is verified. If it is not novel, the verification of its consequences will make comparatively little difference to the science in question. If it cannot be verified, and especially if experience refutes it, it does not directly contribute to the progress of science. But the more novel an hypothesis is, the more in advance of verification must it appear improbable; and the greater are the risks which its inventor seems to run when he first proposes it.

IX

Now in what way shall a good inventor of hypotheses be guided to his invention? Shall he confine himself only to the hypotheses which, when first he proposes them, seem antecedently probable? If he does this, he condemns himself to relative infertility. For the antecedently probable hypothesis is precisely the hypothesis which lacks any very notable novelty. Even if such an hypothesis bears the test of experience, it therefore adds little to knowledge. Worthless for the purposes of any more exact natural science until it has been duly verified, the hypothesis which is to win, in the advancement of science, a really great place, must often be, at the moment of its first invention, an apparently unlikely hypothesis, — a poetical creation, warranted as yet by none of the facts thus far known, and subject to all the risks which attend great human enterprises in any field. In such a position was Darwin's hypothesis regarding the origin of species through natural selection, when first he began to seek for its verification.

This, however, is not all. A highly significant scientific hypothesis must not only be a sort of poetic creation. There is another consideration to be borne in mind. The number of possible new hypotheses, in any large field of scientific inquiry, is, like the number of possible new poems, often very great. The labor of testing each one of a number of such hypotheses, sufficiently to know whether the hypothesis tested is or is not probably true, is frequently long. And the poetic skill with which the hypotheses are invented, as well as their intrinsic beauty, gives, in advance of the test, no assurance that they will succeed in agreeing with experience. The makers of great scientific hypotheses, — the Galileos, the Darwins, — are, so to speak, poets whose inventions must be submitted to a very stern critic, namely, to the sort of experience which their sciences use. And no one can know in advance what this critic's verdict will be. Therefore, if it were left to mere chance to determine what hypotheses should be invented and tested, scientific progress would be very slow. For each new hypothesis would involve new risks, would require lengthy new tests, and would often fail.

As a fact, however, the progress of natural science, since Galileo began his work, and since the new inductive methods were first applied, has been (so Charles Peirce asserts) prodigiously faster than it could have been had mere chance guided the inventive processes of the greater scientific thinkers. In view of these facts, Charles

Peirce reasons that the actual progress of science, from the sixteenth century until now, could not have been what it is, had not the human mind been, as he says, in some deep way attuned to the nature of things. The mind of man must be peculiarly fitted to invent new hypotheses such that, when tested by experience, they bear the test, and turn out to be probably true. The question hereupon arises, "To what is this aptness of the human mind for the invention of important and successful scientific hypotheses due?"

X

This question is not easy to answer. Were new hypotheses in science framed simply by processes analogous to those which the insurance companies employ when they take new risks, the matter would be different. For the insurance companies adapt the existing tables of mortality to their new undertakings, or else obtain modified tables gradually, by a mere process of collection and arrangement. And all the statistical sciences make use of this method; and there is, of course, no doubt that this method of gradual advance, through patient collection of facts, is one of the two great sources of scientific progress.

But the other method, the method of inventing new hypotheses which go beyond all results thus far obtained,—the method which first proposes and then tests these hypotheses,—involves at every stage a venture into an unknown sea. Unless some deep-lying motive guides the inventor, he will go uselessly astray, and will waste his efforts upon inventions which prove to be failures.

In many branches of science such fortunes have in fact long barred the way. Consider, for instance, the fortunes of modern pathological research, up to the present moment, in dealing with the problem furnished by the existence of cancer. The most patient devotion to details, the most skilful invention of hypotheses, has so far led only to defeat regarding some of the most central problems of the pathology of cancer. These problems may be solved at any moment in the near future. But up to this time it seems—according to what the leading pathologists tell us—as if the human mind had not been attuned to the invention of fitting hypotheses regarding the most fundamental problems of the "cancer-research."

How different, on the other hand, were the fortunes of mechanics from Galileo's time to that of Newton. What wonderful scientific inventiveness guided the early stages of electrical science. How rapidly some portions of pathological research have advanced. And, according to Charles Peirce, in all these most successful instances it is the happy instinct for inventing the hypotheses which has shortened a task that, if left to chance and to patience, would have proved hopelessly slow. If science had advanced mainly by the successive testing of all the possible hypotheses in any given field, the cancer-research, in its period of tedious trials and errors, and not the physical science of Galileo, with its dramatic swiftness of progress, nor yet the revolutionary changes due to the influence of Darwin, would exemplify the ruling type of scientific research. But as a fact, the great scientific advances have been due to a wonderful skill in the art of Galileo, and of the other leading inventors of new scientific ideas.

The present existence, then, and the rapid progress of the inductive sciences, have been rendered possible by an instinctive aptitude of the human mind to shorten the labors of testing hypothesis through some sort of native skill in the invention of hypotheses such as are capable of bearing the test of experience.

XI

Now one cannot explain the existence of such an aptitude for inventing good hypotheses by pointing out that the processes of science are simply a further development of that gradual adaptation of man to his environment which has enabled our race to survive, and which has moulded us to our natural conformity to the order of nature. For the aptitude to invent scientific hypotheses is not like our power to find our way in the woods, or to get our food, or even to create and to perpetuate our ordinary social orders. Each new scientific hypothesis of high rank is a new creation which is no mere readapting of habits slowly acquired. The conditions which enable the creator of the hypothesis to invent it never existed before his time. Human beings could have continued to exist indefinitely had Galileo never appeared. Science gets what may be called its "survival value" only after its hypotheses have been invented and tested. Without science, the race could have found its food, and been moulded to its environment, for indefinitely numerous future ages. Natural selection could never, by itself, have produced, through merely favoring the survival of skilful warriors or of industrious artisans, the genius which was so attuned to the whole nature of things as to invent the atomic hypothesis, or to discover spectrum-analysis, or to create electrical science. Our science invents hypotheses about phenomena which are, in appearance, utterly remote from our practical life. Only after a new science, such as that of electricity, has grown out of this mysterious attuning of man's creative powers to the whole nature of the physical universe, then, and only then, does this science prove, in its applications, to be useful.

We can therefore here sum up the matter by saying that the natural world has somehow created, in man, a being who is apt for the task of interpreting nature. Man's interpretation is halting and fallible; but it has shown itself, since Galileo's time, too rapidly progressive in its invention of successful hypotheses to permit us to regard this aptitude as the work of chance. Man's gradual adjustment to his natural environment may well explain his skill as artisan, or as mere collector and arranger of natural facts, but cannot explain the origin of his power to invent, as often and as wonderfully as he has invented, scientific hypotheses about nature which bear the test of experience.

XII

If, then, you seek for a sign that the universe contains its own interpreter, let the very existence of the sciences, let the existence of the happy inventive power which has made their progress possible, furnish you such a sign. A being whom nature seems to have intended, in the first place, simply to be more crafty than the other animals, more skilful in war and in hunting, and in the arts of living in tribal unities, turns out to be so attuned to the whole of nature that, when he once gets the idea of scientific research, his discoveries soon relate to physical matters as remote from his practical needs as is the chemical constitution of the nebulæ, or as is the origin and destiny of this earth, or as is the state of the natural universe countless ages ago in the past. In brief, man is not what he seems, a creature of a day, but is known to be an interpreter of nature. He is full of aptitudes to sound the depths of time and of space, and to invent hypotheses which it will take ages to verify, but which will, in a vast number of cases, be verified. Full of wonders is nature. But the most wonderful of all is man the interpreter,—a part and a member (if our philosophy is right) of the world's infinite Community of Interpretation.

The very existence of natural science, then, is an illustration of our thesis that the universe is endlessly engaged in the spiritual task of interpreting its own life.

XIII

The older forms of teleology, often used by the theologians of the past, frequently missed the place where the empirical illustrations of the workings of intelligence, in the universe, and where the signs of the life of the divine spirit are most to be sought. The teleology of the future will look for illustrations of the divine, and of design, neither in miracles nor in the workings of any continuously striving "will" or "vital impulse" which from moment to moment moulds things so as to meet present needs, or to guide present evolution.

Man, as we have seen, has an aptitude to invent hypotheses that, when once duly tested, throw light on things as remote in space as are the nebulæ, as distant in time as is the origin of our whole stellar system. This aptitude lies deep in human nature. Its existence is indeed no miraculous event of to-day. Man's power to interpret his world has somehow evolved with man. The whole natural world of the past has been needed to produce man the interpreter. On the other hand, this power of man cannot have been the result of any "vital impulse" "canalizing" matter or otherwise blindly striving continuously and tentatively for light. For this scientific aptitude of man links him even now with the whole time-order. He is so attuned by nature that, imperfect as he now is, he is adapted to be or to become, in his own halting way, but not in totally blind fashion, an interpreter of the meaning of the whole of time. Now such a teleological process as this which man's scientific successes express, illustrates the teleology of a spiritual process which does not merely, from moment to moment, adapt itself to a preëxistent world. Nor does this process appear as merely one whereby an unconscious impulse squirms its way through the "canals" which it makes in matter. No, this teleology appears to illustrate a spiritual process which, in its wholeness, interprets at once the endless whole of time.[3]

[3] While I write these words, a colleague of mine, Professor L. J. Henderson, is publishing a book, entitled "The Fitness of the Environment," wherein he points out that however we may interpret the facts, there exists, in the natural world, an instance of apparent adaptation which has never before been clearly apprehended and described. This instance, viewed by itself, furnishes no proof of our present philosophy, and no proof of any other philosophy; but it furnishes an illustration of the sort of evidence for teleology which, as I believe, the teleologically disposed philosophers of the future will ponder, and will interpret.

What Professor Henderson points out is that the physico-chemical constitution of

XIV

I have spent most of our brief time, in our closing lecture, in illustrations of our metaphysical doctrine. For it is needful to leave this doctrine in your minds as one which calls attention to an essentially new aspect of philosophical idealism, as well as to a doctrine of Life.

Time, Interpretation, and the Community, and finally, The World as a Community,—these have been the central ideas of the metaphysical portion of our course. We have everywhere pointed out, as we went, the connection between these ideas and the ethical and religious interests which we have also expounded and defended. Our last words of all must relate to the practical consequences which follow for us, and for our present age, if our view of the historical mission of Christianity is true, and if the form of idealism, which we have here expounded, rightly states the relation of the Christian ideas to the real world. Let me sum up these practical consequences as briefly as I can. In sum, they amount to two maxims.

the whole natural world, so far as that world is accessible to scientific study, is "preadapted," is "fitted" to be an environment for living beings. This "fitness" is of a nature which cannot have resulted from the processes whereby life has been evolved. The same fitness involves an union of many different physico-chemical properties of the environment of living beings,—an union so complicated that one cannot suppose it due to chance. And finally the origin of this fitness must have preceded by countless ages any physical event of which we now have any probable knowledge. If life itself ever had an origin, the physical world was thus, in a manner which is new to us, inexplicably preadapted to the coming life for an indefinitely vast period before the life appeared. If life had (as Arrhenius has supposed) no origin whatever, the fitness of the environment which is here in question, being due neither to life nor to chance, remains a problem requiring scientific study, but at present promising no scientific solution.

As Professor Henderson points out, the "fitness of the environment" which he has thus discovered is so vast and pervasive, and so incapable of explanation in "vitalistic" terms as to render all forms of vitalism (including that of Bergson) superfluous as explanations of the true mutual fitness of organism and environment. In a natural world which is once for all, as Professor Henderson points out, "biocentric," why seek any longer after special vitalistic explanations for special instances of adaptation?

My own view of the relation of Professor Henderson's discovery to the sort of philosophy which these lectures have defended, is that here we have just that sort of preadaptation of earlier stages of the time-process to later stages which of course does not prove, but does illustrate, our own view of the time-process. Professor Henderson's "fitness of the environment" is analogous to Charles Peirce's "attuning" of the human mind to the universe which our sciences progressively interpret. Whatever else life is, it contains the natural conditions for an interpretation of the world. What Professor Henderson's facts, and Charles Peirce's facts, do not prove, but illustrate, is our philosophical thesis that the time-world viewed as a whole, or in very long stretches, is a process which possesses, and includes, not mere miracles and efforts and vital impulses, but a total meaning and a coherent interpretation.

In the past, the teaching of Christian doctrine has generally depended upon some form of Christology. In recent times the traditional problems of Christology have become, in the light of our whole view of the world, of mankind, and of history, increasingly difficult and perplexing. Whoever asserts that, at one moment of human history, and only at that one moment, an unique being, at once an individual man, and at the same time also God, appeared, and performed the work which saved mankind, — whoever, I say, asserts this traditional thesis, involves himself in historical, in metaphysical, in technically theological, and in elementally religious problems, which all advances in our modern sciences and in our humanities, in our spiritual life and in our breadth of outlook upon the universe, have only made, for the followers of tradition, constantly harder to face and to solve. The first of our practical maxims is: *Simplify your traditional Christology, in order thereby to enrich its spirit. The religion of loyalty has shown us the way to this end.*

Henceforth our religion must more and more learn to look upon the natural world as infinite both in space and in time, and upon the salvation of man as something bound up with the interpretation of an infinitely rich realm of spiritual life, — a realm whose character the legends of early Christian tradition did not portray with literal truth. Therefore, if religious insight is indeed to advance, and if the spirit of Christianity is to keep in touch with the growing knowledge of mankind, *the Christology of the future cannot permanently retain the traditional forms which have heretofore dominated the history both of dogma, and of the visible Christian church.*

And yet, if our previous account of the Christian ideas has been sound, the Christology of the past has been due to motives which are perfectly verifiable in human religious experience, and which can be interpreted in terms of a rationally defensible philosophy both of life and of the universe. As a fact, whatever Christology Paul, or any later leader of Christian faith, has taught, and whatever religious experience has been used by the historical church, or by any of its sects or of its visible forms, as giving warrant for the Christological opinions, *the literal and historical fact has always been this, that in some fashion and degree those who have thus believed in the being whom they called Christ, were united in a community of the faithful, were in love with that community, were hopefully and practically devoted to the cause of the still invisible, but perfectly real and divine Universal*

Community, and were saved by the faith and by the life which they thus expressed.

Now in general, whatever else they held to be true, all the communities of Christian believers have viewed their Christ as the being whose life was a present fact in their community, inspiring its doings, uniting its members, and pointing beyond the little company of the present believers to the ideal communion of all the saints, and to the triumph of the Spirit.

Now if my account of the matter is well founded, the fact that believers have expressed their views about Christ in terms which involved symbols, legends, doubtful dogmas, and endlessly perplexing theological problems need not obscure from us any longer a truth which is verifiable, is literal, and is saving. This is the one truth which has been grasped, in a concrete and practical form, whenever the religion of loyalty has found on earth its own. *The name of Christ has always been, for the Christian believers, the symbol for the Spirit in whom the faithful—that is to say the loyal—always are and have been one.*

Now the first practical result of recognizing that in this faith lies the genuine meaning which has lain beneath all the various and perplexing Christologies of the past is, otherwise, expressed thus: It is unwise to try to express this genuinely catholic faith of all the loyal by attempting to form one more new sect. I do not wish to see any such new sect, or to hear of one. It is needless to expect that those whom tradition now satisfies will at present first abandon tradition in order to learn the truth which, in their heart of hearts, they know that tradition has always symbolized. If men are loyal, but are in doubt as to traditional theology, it is a waste of time to endeavor to prove the usual theses of dogmatic Christology by any collection of accessible historical evidences. Such historical evidences are once for all insufficient. The existing documents are too fragmentary. The historical hypotheses are too shifting and evanescent. And if it is faith that is to be, in Christological matters, the real substance of things hoped for and the evidence of things not seen, what faith has ever been more Christian in spirit, more human in its verifiability, more universal, more saving, more concrete, than the faith of the Pauline churches? Our practical maxim is: *Hold fast by that faith.*

What is practically necessary is therefore this: Let your Christology be the practical acknowledgment of the Spirit of the Universal and Beloved Community. This is the sufficient and practical faith. Love this faith, use this faith, teach this faith, preach this faith, in whatever words, through whatever symbols, by means of whatever forms of creeds, in accordance with whatever practices best you find to enable you with a sincere intent and a whole heart to symbolize and to realize the presence of the Spirit in the Community. All else about your religion is the accident of your special race or nation or form of worship or training or accidental personal opinion, or devout private mystical experience, — illuminating but capricious. The core, the center of the faith, is not the person of the individual founder, and is not any other individual man. Nor is this core to be found in the sayings of the founder, nor yet in the traditions of Christology. The core of the faith is the Spirit, the Beloved Community, the work of grace, the atoning deed, and the saving power of the loyal life. There is nothing else under heaven whereby men have been saved or can be saved. To say this is to found no new faith, but to send you to the heart of all true faith.

This is no vague humanitarianism, is no worship of the mere natural being called humanity, and is no private mystic experience. This is a creed at once human, divine, and practical, and religious, and universal. Assimilate and apply this creed, and you have grasped the principle of Christian institutional life in the past, and the principle which will develop countless new religious institutions in the future, *and which will survive them.*

The first of my practical concluding maxims may be stated thus: Interpret Christianity and all the problems of its Christology in this spirit, and you will aid towards the one crowning office of all human religion. You will win membership in the one invisible church.

My second maxim is this: *Look forward to the human and visible triumph of no form of the Christian church.* Still less look to any sect, new or old, as the conqueror. Henceforth view the religious ideal as one which, in the future, is to be won, if at all, by methods distinctively analogous to the methods which now prevail in the sciences of nature. It is not my thought that natural science can ever displace religion or do its work. But what I mean is that since the office of religion is to aim towards the creation on earth of the Beloved Community, the future task of religion is the task of inventing and applying the arts which shall win men over to unity, and which shall overcome their original hatefulness by the gracious love, not of mere individuals, but of communities. Now such arts are still to be discovered. Judge every social device, every proposed reform, every national and every local enterprise by the one test: *Does this help towards the coming of the universal community.* If you have a church, judge your own church by this standard; and if your church does not yet fully meet this standard, aid towards reforming your church accordingly. If, like myself, you hold the true church to be invisible, require all whom you can influence to help to render it visible. To do that, however, does not mean that you shall either conform to the church as it is, or found new sects. If the spirit of scientific investigation, or of learned research, shows signs—as it already does—of becoming one of the best of all forms of unifying mankind in free loyalty, then regard science not merely as in possible harmony with religion, but as itself already one of the principal organs of religion. Aid toward the coming of the universal community by helping to make the work of religion not only as catholic as is already the true spirit of loyalty, but as inventive of new social arts, as progressive as is now natural science. So shall you help in making, not merely happy individuals (for no power can render detached individuals permanently happy, or save them from death or from woe). You shall aid towards the unity of spirit of those who shall be at once free and loyal.

We can look forward, then, to no final form, either of Christianity or of any other special religion. But we can look forward to a time when the work and the insight of religion can become as progressive as is now the work of science.

Index